STATE OF THE NATION

STATE OF THE NATION

DEMOCRACY GOVERNANCE AND PARLIAMENT

Subhash C Kashyap

Vitasta
LET KNOWLEDGE SPREAD
www.vitastapublishing.com

Published by
Renu Kaul Verma
Vitasta Publishing Pvt Ltd
2/15, Ansari Road, Daryaganj
New Delhi - 110 002
info@vitastapublishing.com

ISBN 978-93-86473-32-5

First Edition 2018
3rd reprint 2023

MRP ₹995

Editor Veena Batra
Cover and layout by Somesh Kumar Mishra
Printed by Vikas Computer and Printers

Contents

PREFACE

The credit for persuading me to put together in book form my thoughts, analyses and views on various matters of contemporary national concern goes to Vitasta. As a student of Constitutional Law and Parliamentary Political Science, I have been writing for the media and academia now for almost seventy years. Also, a number of addresses have been delivered at universities and other national and international fora in India and abroad in recent years. These constitute the basic material for different chapters of the present work. The book was first published in 2017 under the title *Democracy and Good Governance*. Despite many shortcomings, it was well received. Continuing demand for its copies and subsequent developments on the national scene necessitated a new edition. I am glad to present before the concerned readership this revised, edited and updated edition. In fact, it has turned out to be a new book. The material now added includes chapters on (1) the current debate on simultaneous elections for Lok Sabha and State Assemblies, and (2) the newly emerging concept of glocalisation and federal governance.

An anthology of my papers published earlier in 2010 by Vitasta under the title "Indian Constitution—Conflicts and Controversies" remains separate, self-contained and still relevant. It was also reprinted. The present work consists of 40 chapters under five broad subject-heads. The focus is on the present state of the nation, revisiting the concept and practice of democracy and ensuring good, citizen-friendly, corruption-free governance. Many significant achievements and dismal failures during the last seventy years of our polity have been discussed. In particular, the challenges and opportunities before the present regime and the hopes and despair of the people have been analysed in a non-partisan and objective manner. The urgency of multiple reforms with the highest priority to electoral and party reforms has been flagged. The process of law making, the much talked about decline and the changing contours and character of Parliament, the indecorous behaviour and indiscipline of our representatives and the resultant disorder and disruption in the functioning of the Houses of Parliament with possible remedial action agenda have been underlined. The role, conduct and cost of the Honourable Members as also the terrible disconnect and loss of faith between the people and the politicians have been highlighted. Besides, one part of the contents is devoted to remembering some of the great parliamentarians. Other issues covered under the concluding part 'Miscellany' include the importance of the North-East in national resurgence, state of higher education, role of universities and education in citizenship values.

In a work of this kind, some repetition of facts, arguments and ideas is natural. All efforts, however, have been made to remove avoidable repetition and to lend thematic coherence to presentations. The thread of a basic perspective that runs through all the chapters of the book and the quintessential points that emerge relate to the need to restore the credibility of the institutions of the State—the Executive, the Legislature and the Judiciary—and to reduce the widening gulf between the people and the politicians and between promise and performance. Instead of promising the moon, if our people were taken into confidence and the real state of the nation and the legacy of decades of governance deficit explained to them, they would have surely understood and gladly agreed to suffer and sacrifice for the nation and future generations. The only condition was that the sacrifices should have started from the top functionaries—the politicians and bureaucrats. Ministers and legislators, for example, could set an example by giving up part of their pay, allowances and perks. The overriding message, however, is that much has been done but much more remains to be done. In any case, we must not lose sight of the oases in the glare of the vast desert. In democracy, an effective Opposition is as necessary as a stable and strong Government. Both are expected to be equally devoted to the nation and good governance for the welfare of the people. In the present state of the nation, if democracy has to survive, irrespective of the parties, the Government with a massive mandate from the people must succeed. The alternative threatens to be anarchy and chaos. I hope the book will be welcomed and read widely and generate some debate among thinkers, policy makers and concerned citizens. Critical comments from readers will be most welcome as always.

I would be glad to put on record my special thanks to the publisher Renu Kaul Verma and the editor Veena Batra for the alacrity and competence with which this work has been handled at their end.

New Delhi
March, 2018

Subhash C. Kashyap
(sckashyap@gmail.com)

STATE OF INDIAN DEMOCRACY

The Republic of India

From Independence Pledge to Republic Day

ON THE midnight of 31 December 1929, in an atmosphere of great excitement and enthusiasm, the Lahore Congress adopted the historic resolution on complete independence moved by Mahatma Gandhi. It was decided that the Independence Pledge, also drafted by Gandhiji, be taken all over the country on 26 January 1930, and that it be repeated each year on that day till complete independence was achieved. The pledge was taken by millions of people in all parts of the country, year after year till 1947. In his famous midnight speech in the Constituent Assembly on 14 August 1947, Pandit Nehru referred to this pledge of 26 January as the 'Tryst with Destiny'.

To immortalise this day and to pay homage to all those who fought, suffered and sacrificed for fulfilling the pledge of complete independence, 26 January 1950 was declared as the date of enforcement of the Constitution of independent India and the birth of the sovereign democratic republic of India. Accordingly, since 1950, 26 January is celebrated every year as our Republic Day.

On its very first day, our Constituent Assembly, before it proceeded to frame a Constitution for this ancient land, was reminded of the words of warning uttered by one of the greatest jurists, Joseph Storey. He said that howsoever immaculately built by the founding fathers to last for eternity, a republic may 'perish in an hour by the folly, or corruption, or negligence of its only keepers, the people'. Storey added:

> Republics are created by the virtue, public spirit and intelligence of the citizens. They fail when the wise are banished from the public councils because they dare to be honest, and the profligate are rewarded because they flatter the people, in order to betray them.

The concept of a republic is that of a state in which the people are supreme, there is no privileged class and all public offices are equally open to every citizen without any discrimination. There is no hereditary ruler and the head of the state is elected by the people for a fixed term. At all times, in a republic, the government derives its powers from the people but it is for a limited period of time. At the root of all variants of republican polity is the principle of sovereignty vested in the people, of the citizens being both the rulers and the ruled at the same time, of the people ruling over themselves through their freely elected representatives and having an elected Head of the state, most often called the President. Republics generally go well with a presidential system. In a classic parliamentary model, on the other hand, Parliament is supposed to be sovereign in theory and the Head of the state is usually some hereditary or non-elected dignitary.

For India, a democratic republic was never an alien plant. There is ample historical evidence to show that republican forms of government and democratic self-governing institutions existed in many parts of India from as early as the Vedic Age (circa 3000-1000 BC). In fact, India can be considered to be the birthplace and the first cradle of democracy. The *Rigveda*, believed to be the earliest known literary work of mankind, mentions the word *gana* literally meaning numbers but also used for assembly or for rule by numbers—*ganarajya, sangha* or republic—at forty-six places. There was a time when India was studded with a large number of republics, even though the size of such republics was small like the later city states of Greece or the native tribal republics. Also, where there were monarchies, they were either elected or limited and had to function in accordance with 'Dharma' or what we now call the Rule of Law. Pali texts provide interesting details of how the assemblies of the republics in the post-Vedic period functioned like parliaments and followed highly sophisticated procedures.

When our founding fathers sat down to frame a constitution for independent India, they decided to put it in the unique position of being both a parliamentary democracy and a republic. It is in the widest sense that the Preamble speaks of India being a republic. All citizens are equal in the eyes of law. The Constitution guarantees as fundamental rights; equality before law, equal protection of laws and non-discrimination on grounds of race, caste, religion, sex or place of birth. There is no privileged class and all public offices are open for every citizen without any discrimination. The head of the Union is the President who is elected for a fixed term by an electoral college consisting of the elected representatives of the people. All executive powers of the Union reside in the President and have to be exercised in his name. He is also the Supreme Commander of the armed forces. It has been held, however, that unlike the US President, our President is only a constitutional head and real political power lies with the ministers who are drawn from among members of Parliament and the Council of Ministers remains collectively responsible to the popular house of Parliament, ie. the House of the People.

The journey of 68 years traversed by our republic was most eventful and full of many challenges. There were scores of substantial achievements coupled with some dismal failures. The phenomenon of increasing globalisation and newer and newer advances in technology led to developments at the speed of a hurricane. Centuries got compressed into years and pressures of various sorts made basic changes in Indian polity a categorical imperative.

In the context of the present state of the Republic of India, the reality is that we are far from fulfilling the basic principles of a republic. Our republic is under tremendous strains. Without getting into details, an attempt may be made to analyse to what extent the position on the ground matches the essential requirements of a republican system and whether the precepts have been translated into practice. The following points may need to be flagged.

In a republic, people are supposed to be the supreme masters and all state functionaries are at their service and accountable to them. Unfortunately, following independence and even after the commencement of our Constitution, we continued the colonial model of legislative, judicial and administrative institutions and practices developed on the Indian soil by the British colonial masters to rule over India. Masters changed but the gulf between the rulers and the ruled continued. The people did not graduate from the status of subjects to that of citizens of a free country or masters in a democratic polity. The Ministers, MPs, MLAs, bureaucrats and babus, from constables and messengers to Principal and Cabinet Secretaries constitute the ruling class and consider the ordinary citizens as nothing more than their *riyaya* or subjects. The 'public' component in our 'Republic' is the least remembered except at election time.

In a republic, there is no privileged class and all the citizens are equal and cannot be discriminated. Our daily experience as ordinary citizens is enough to conclusively prove that the present state of our polity is an antithesis of an ideal republic inasmuch as there is a very wide gulf that separates the common men and women from the privileged VIPs across verticals. India has a VIP or VVIP culture which is unparalleled in the world. While ordinary citizens—men, women and children—do not feel secure, millions are spent on providing many variants of security cover to those who prize it more as a status symbol and to flaunt their privileged position. The public perception is that the privileged, moneyed and the powerful are rarely punished by law for wrong doing. Justice, healthcare and education are all too expensive to be within the reach of the poor who still constitute the majority. Equality and non-discrimination between citizens in our republic thus remain pious aspirations.

It is said that in a republic, all public offices are open to citizens equally, without any discrimination on grounds of caste, gender, religion etc. only on merits. While it would be highly improper to make any sweeping generalisation, the fact is that we all feel that there is no equality before law, no equality of opportunity or status and hardly any equal protection of laws. They remain only as constitutional guarantees. There is both positive and negative discrimination between citizens. Besides, there is rampant corruption. Jobs, posts and positions in various fields are freely bought and sold. There are some serious scrambles on who should control the power of appointment.

In principle, there are no hereditary rulers in a Republic. As it is, in our democracy, politics is run by parties and majority of major national and State parties are dominated by a few families with leadership often getting transferred from father to son/daughter. Thus, both at the Union and State levels, barring a few honourable exceptions, for a large part of the last 68 years, Prime Ministerial, Chief Ministerial and Ministerial positions have very largely revolved round a few privileged families.

Ideally, in a democratic republic, people are presumed to rule over themselves through their freely elected representatives. In the highly divisive electoral system that we have developed, overwhelming majority of those elected have more votes cast against each one of them than for them. In many cases, the winners represent even less than five to fifteen per cent of their electorate. How can they be called the representatives of the people? Their representational legitimacy is in doubt. This is systemic and apart from the much talked about role of the power of money and muscle power in elections. Power for its own sake or for personal ends has become the supreme value. It is well known that huge amounts of black money are spent on elections and that people with a criminal background get elected. Besides the natural attraction of power and position, politics has come to be seen as a lucrative whole-time profession. The number of those who take up this profession with a spirit of self-sacrifice and with an aim to serve the nation is fast declining.

Politics has become synonymous with the struggle for power with political parties becoming transmission belts to power. Communal and caste factors, slogans of secularism, mafia leaders, money, winnability etc. have all become essential parts of Vote bank politics. Public interest seems to occupy the back seat. The party or parties losing the electoral battle come to regard it as their bounden duty to oppose the government, and try by all possible means to make all institutions including the houses of Parliament dysfunctional. This is evident from the way session after session of Parliament is washed away without transacting much meaningful business.

Irrespective of which party or parties constitute the opposition, it seems to have become a part of the opposition culture not to allow the houses of Parliament to function. It is, of course, up to the presiding officers not to yield to unruly and obstructionist tactics of any elements. The Presiding Officer has enough powers under the rules to ensure orderly functioning of the House. But, as at present and for the last several years, what the presiding officers have been often seen to do is to adjourn the House again and again.

On the positive side, it may be said that we have had as many as sixteen general elections to the Lok Sabha and a few hundred for various State Assemblies and all these have been acknowledged to be largely free and fair.

As for the shortcomings in the state of our republic, public memory is proverbially short. It is necessary to point out that those who attribute all this only to the immediate present and to the current leadership forget that the ten years before the 16th general elections to Lok Sabha in 2014 were marked by a very sad record of governance deficit and a long succession of corruption scandals. The people at large were fed up and anxious for a change. They pined for a new leadership. An Alliance, a party and a popular leader came to power with a clear majority and a massive popular mandate in May 2014.

During the election campaign, they could have clearly explained to the people the dismal state of affairs and the need for hard and sustained effort for some years to put the rail back on the track and bring about national regeneration. Perhaps, the people of India would have understood and appreciated just as the British had done when Winston Churchill said before the Second World War that he could promise nothing except 'blood, sweat and tears'. As Prime Minister Lal Bahadur Shastri had done, the people could be taken into confidence and asked to make sacrifices for their fellow citizens. The people would have responded positively, provided the sacrifices began from the top and the political class and the senior bureaucracy also agreed to cut their perks and emoluments. Unfortunately, we were promised too much including the moon and hopes were generated for things which could not be considered achievable. As a result, the public perception is that the promised good days have not come, black money stashed in tax havens abroad has not come back, those guilty of looting the public exchequer have not been punished, poverty and hunger have not vanished and corruption in public dealings continues unabated. On the other hand, it cannot be denied that substantial progress has been made on the development front, in external affairs, in transport, defence, communications, railways and several other areas. The speed of change is not what the people expect. Unfortunately, all the three organs of the state are not performing their assigned roles and discharging their responsibilities. At least partly, the reason for not being able to move faster in national interest is that Parliament is not functioning or not being allowed to function as it should. More than three crore cases are said to be pending in courts, many for more than several decades, and instead of attending to clearing the backlog, the Judiciary is busy arrogating to itself executive, law-making and even constituent powers. Often, we shy away from taking difficult decisions and fail to deliver.

The future of our republic is full of challenges and our hopes consist in turning every challenge into an opportunity by ensuring the well-conceived *Sabka Sath Sabka Vikas* and 'less government, more governance' at every level and in every sector. What we need most is people-friendly, citizen-centric, corruption-free, clean, good governance. That requires that the idiom and image of politics and politicians must change. Democracy should be reinvented in such a manner that, howsoever idealistic it may seem, public life should once again be based on the spirit of self-sacrifice and service to the people. Also, unless we, the people, the keepers of the Republic, are vigilant and conscious of our obligations as citizens, there is no hope.

Irrespective of the political parties involved, it is most important for the future of India and for the survival of our republic, freedom, democracy and rule of law that the agenda of all inclusive good governance succeeds. For, the alternative may be chaos and anarchy.

Democracy Today

Desert of Despair and Oases of Hope

The Concept & Dynamics

DEMOCRACY DEFIES precise definition. It has been variously defined. It has meant different things to different people. It has functioned differently in different socio-political climes and times. Also, it has many variants. But, this much can be definitely agreed—that democracy is a system of governance based on popular will. In a democracy, the people are the masters. They are supreme and are supposed to govern themselves through the representatives they elect, under a system they choose. The most oft-quoted definition of democracy attributed to Abraham Lincoln describes it as the government of the people, by the people, for the people. But, Baba Saheb Ambedkar, speaking in the Constituent Assembly once said that a time could come when we may get so fed up with the vagaries

From an address delivered at India International Centre

of democracy that we may only want democracy for the people and may not be bothered whether it was of or by the people.

Winston Churchill said that democracy was the worst form of government except that there was no better known to men. The fact is that democracy is not a finished product. It is a dynamic process. In the history of democracy world over, there never has been a fully developed or perfect democracy. It is always developing, always in the making. On this road, there is no journey's end. In every country, democratic institutions have to rise from its own soil, to suit its own environs and societal needs. Also, the criteria for measuring the success of democracy has to be different and largely country-specific.

Mere outward trappings of a liberal framework of democratic institutions, a charter of fundamental human rights and periodical elections may mean little unless they lead to real participatory role of citizenry in decision-making processes, clean and people-friendly governance and all inclusive growth. Transcending political rhetoric, electoral sloganeering and mountebankery, *Sabka Sath Sabka Vikas* has got to be the essential goal for any really functioning vibrant democracy. Ideally, five indicators can be flagged as a criteria for measuring the state of democracy:

- Level of citizens' participation in the governance process.
- Free and fair elections of representatives on the basis of equality of rights for electors.
- Citizen-centric governance with full transparency, responsiveness and accountability of government functionaries to the people, with Ministers, MPs and government officers functioning as servants of the people and not their masters.
- Active and alert civil society.
- Preservation of the Rule of Law, equality of citizens, dignity of the individual and agenda of all inclusive growth.

The last century closed with what was considered to be a worldwide triumph for democracy. But, what has passed of the 21st century has brought to light a whole new series of challenges calling for a reexamination of the state of democracy, globally.

We, in India, are very fond of bragging about our democracy being the largest, and among the few functioning democracies in the world. We were very fortunate in having, during the freedom struggle and early decades thereafter, leadership of some of the tallest men and women endowed with sagacity of mind, nobility of character and devotion to the nation and democratic norms.

Our founding fathers, in the name of 'We, the people of India' decided to constitute India into a 'Sovereign Democratic Republic' thereby laying down the fundamental principles that all sovereign powers be vested in the people, that the people of India were one indivisible, that all the citizens of India were equal in the eyes of the law; that there was no privileged class and the people were to govern themselves through their elected representatives in Parliament and State Legislatures and the democracy had to above all assure the dignity of the individual and unity of the nation.

Also, democracy conceived in merely political terms meant the right of every citizen to freely vote at periodic elections. The 'one man, one vote' principle applied in all democratic elections emanated from the recognition of equal rights of all men. For our founding fathers, however, democracy did not mean merely political democracy or the people's right to periodically vote to elect their representatives. Right to vote for a hungry and illiterate man without clothing and shelter meant little. Ambedkar said:

> We do not want merely to lay down a mechanism to enable people to come and capture power. The Constitution also wishes to lay down an ideal before those who would be forming the government. That ideal is of economic democracy.

For Ambedkar, social and economic democracy was the real aim and ultimate goal. Parliamentary democracy was meaningless unless it was geared to achieving the real goal of economic democracy.

Jawaharlal Nehru had observed later:

> We have definitely accepted the democratic process. Why have we accepted it? Well, for a variety of reasons. Because we think that in the final analysis it promoted the growth of human beings and of society; because, as we have said in our Constitution, we attach great value to individual freedom; because we want the creative and the adventurous spirit of man to grow.

The end was a good life for the individual which must include a certain satisfaction of the essential economic needs. Only in the measure that democracy succeeds in solving the economic problems, does it succeed even in the political field. If the economic problems are not solved, then the political structure tends to weaken and crack up. Therefore, from political democracy, we must progress to economic democracy which means 'working for a certain measure of well-being for all'.

Achievements

The early decades after independence were the most eventful. The nation faced a succession of grave crises, internal and external threats, natural and man-made calamities and challenges of terrifying magnitude. Some temporary aberrations like the 19 months of internal emergency apart, whatever problems we faced were resolved within the democratic framework of constitutionalism. India had to its credit many achievements. On the political plane, we were able to bring about and maintain the unity and integrity of post-partition India, and to preserve freedom and democracy. Representative institutions thrived and we remained a vibrant democratic polity.

Indian democracy was widely hailed as the most stable in South Asia—the only one where the democratic system and the Constitution stood the test of time, endured and functioned. Despite once being labeled as a 'soft state' or a 'functioning anarchy' by Galbraith and Myrdal, the performance of India's democratic institutions was widely acknowledged as the best in what continued to be called 'the third world'.

There was some effort to give more space, voice, powers and responsibilities to local self-governing institutions through poverty alleviation, rural development and employment generation programmes, more particularly directed toward the underprivileged. Panchayati Raj institutions played a substantial role in several of these programmes. For example, the *Sampoorna Gramin RojgarYojana, Swarnjayanti Gram Swarozgar Yojana, Pradhan Mantri Gram Sadak Yojana, Indira Awaas Yojana, Pradhan Mantri Gramodaya Yojana, Credit Cum Subsidy Scheme, Samagra Awaas Yojana, Innovative Scheme For Housing And Habitat Development And Rural Building Centres, Annapurna Scheme, Watershed Development Programmes, Accelerated Rural Water Supply Programme, Central Rural Sanitation Programme, Swajaldhara Programme* etc. This was undoubtedly an impressive array of programmes to address the interests and needs of the underprivileged common man. On the whole, we can certainly take great pride in asserting that there is enough to showcase the long strides from representative to participatory democracy and to democratic governance with considerable space for the voice and interests of the common man.

Indisputably, the Judiciary remained independent, the press free and civil authority supreme. The 73rd and 74th Amendments gave constitutional status to local self-government institutions of Panchayats and Nagar Palikas, moving closer to making Indian democracy more participatory by providing Gram Sabhas, compulsory periodic elections and representation of women, Scheduled Castes and Scheduled Tribes. It is unique in the history of democratic parliaments anywhere to have 3.6 million elected representatives—more than a million of them women—as active participants in governance.

Every time during the sixteen general elections for Lok Sabha and the few hundred for State Assemblies, people exercised their franchise to elect the legislatures and the governments of their choice and gave ample evidence of their inherent and innate democratic qualities. With every election, the base of democracy widened and nation building and development continued to be attempted through democratic mobilisation. By now, there have been several instances of peaceful, constitutional transfer of power between political parties or alliances and societal classes both at the Union and State levels. It speaks volumes for the strength and resilience of Indian democracy that more than once the mightiest have been overthrown by the people through the power of the ballot, and that we have remained an agile democratic polity pulsating with life and energy. Some classic examples are the post-Emergency rout of Indira Gandhi and her Congress party and more recently the decisive overthrow of the Sonia-Manmohan Singh regime. Indian democracy can be proud of where it has reached. But, there is a flip side to it too.

Failures

It is a myth that we adopted the British system of parliamentary democracy. Actually, we only continued the colonial model as it was developed by the British in India for ruling over us. The result was continuance of the colonial system of administration, colonial laws and the old relationship between the rulers and the ruled. We did not, in effect, become citizens of a sovereign nation or the ultimate masters in a democratic polity. We continued to be treated as subjects. In this context, two lines of Akbar Allahabadi may be apt:

Mujhe nafrat nahin thi Angrez ki surat se
Nafrat thi to uske tarj-e hukumat se.

The poet did not hate the face of the English men, what he hated was the system of their rule. On independence, the masters changed from one set to another but the system remained the same.

Hukmaran badal gaye, tarj-e hukumat vahi raha.

There was a wide gulf between the conceptual and the factual, between the rhetoric and the real. Many of the programmes for the poor were totally meaningless and actually often turned out to be anti-poor. Notwithstanding the lofty norms of democratic governance, the poor and the marginalised did not have the means to assert their legitimate authority against their exploiters and usurpers. Also, how could we ensure that the stigma of being depressed and underprivileged did not become a matter of privileged status sought in perpetuity or a vested interest was not created in permanently remaining maimed and disabled to continue to be entitled to the support of crutches for all times. Ambedkar stood for a classless and casteless society and was opposed to 'reservations in perpetuity' and to the stigma of the depressed, Dalit or Scheduled Caste becoming permanent.

The large number of poverty alleviation programmes and projects eventually consumed a sizeable portion of the national and State budgets but the results on the ground were most disappointing. It was often asked, where had all the money gone? Rajiv Gandhi was often cited for admitting that of every rupee sanctioned for the poor, hardly 15 paisa reached the poor. Most of the money doled out in the name of various schemes for the poor and the large subsidies under different heads ended up enriching the corrupt functionaries, business persons, middlemen, officials and politicians. No wonder, despite all our pro-poor pontifications, India's position in the UNDP human development index remained one of the lowest. The really poor and deprived hardly benefited from relief funds released in their name or from poverty alleviation programmes. Even when some benefit did reach their categories, most of it would be cornered largely by the privileged amongst them or by the middlemen.

The few prospered at the cost of the many. The rich became far richer and the gulf between them and the poor widened. Consumerism and ostentatious display of affluence generated fresh tensions from those deprived of a share in the cake of development. Democracy became subservient to big business and mafia gangs of smugglers and criminals. Money and success at any cost became the supreme values.

The proclaimed ideals of economic democracy, distributive justice and inclusive growth became casualties. The 73rd and 74th Amendment Acts failed to transfer real power to the grassroots in many States with the MPs and MLAs treating the new emerging leadership—particularly from the otherwise marginalised sections like women and SC/STs—as rival centres posing threats to their leadership. More particularly, if we look at the ten year period just preceding the 16th Lok Sabha elections, it would be very difficult to feel proud. For, there was enough to put Indian democracy to shame. Public thinking stood badly battered by the unprecedented spate of scams and scandals of horrendous magnitude and there was almost total governance deficit on all fronts.

One cannot underestimate the negative impact-potential of the scams which overshadowed all the great achievements as also the new challenges confronting Indian politics. Faith of the people in the quality, integrity and efficiency of the rulers was seriously eroded. The disconnect and alienation between the people and the politicians had assumed alarming proportions. There could be no greater challenge to democracy than a situation where the people lost faith in their representatives. Representative parliamentary institutions threatened to become dysfunctional. Functionaries of the state became self-serving and unaccountable. Those expected to be defenders became destroyers. *Rakshak hi bhakshak ho gaye.* There was a steep fall in the standards of conduct in public life and administration. There was a crisis of character and values in politics and public administration. It was a clear case of democracy degenerating into kleptocracy. Disappointment was not only with those in power but also with the system.

Khwab men bhi na socha thaa hamne kabhi
Yeh alam bhi chaman pe guzar jayega
Bagban chheen lenge libase bahar aur
Phulon ka chehra utar jayega.

The nation was passing through a critical phase. The ground edifice of our polity was seriously threatened. There was shameless flouting of most norms of constitutionalism. Governance was in serious disarray. The situation was grim and disturbing. Democratic governance was being manipulated through the use of flawed processes, money and mafia power. The weak, the poor and the underprivileged became pawns in power games and for petty temptations they bartered away their space to the marauders of democratic governance. If that was not so, with a vast majority of Indians being poor and underprivileged, it should have been possible for them to occupy the largest space in democratic polity and to have their government catering primarily to their interests. But that did not happen, and we were constrained to discuss the question of providing them with some real space and voice in democratic governance, somehow.

Among politicians and political parties, it was painful to listen to debates where the reply to charges of corruption or criminalisation was that the other side was also no different. People on the streets freely talked of the all pervasive political and administrative culture of shameless loot. If you travelled around, you heard folks reactions to the naked politics of loot. In a lighter vein, one may refer to a roadside jibe:

Loot machi hai loot, jitna loot sake tu loot

Phir pachhtayega jab kursi jayegi chhoot.

Democracy and Development

While there are multiple linkages between democracy and development, to measure them in quantitative terms is difficult. But, to be meaningful, both democracy and development must marry. Also, development should not be measured merely in economic, GDP/GNP terms and on the anvil of the prosperity of the few. What is important is effective human development, fulfillment of basic civic and social rights and general improvement in the quality of life for all.

Democracy implies giving attention to the development and well-being of the poorest of the poor citizens of the nation. It must provide to the most marginalised and deprived sections of society, equality of opportunity, right to live with dignity and freedom from want and fear. The UN General Assembly had set eight Millennium Development Goals (MDGs) in the year 2000. These included:

- Eradication of extreme poverty and hunger

- Achieving universal primary education
- Promotion of gender equality and empowerment of women
- Reduction in child mortality
- Improvement of maternal health
- Combating HIV/AIDS, Malaria etc.

India was far behind many of the other countries in achieving any of these goals by the stipulated 2015. There was erosion of the rights of farmers and workers, and widespread competitive consumerism with no thought given to the need for sustainable levels of consumption. The truth was that unemployment had increased, droughts and floods continued. While the granaries were full and grains were rotting in the open, the poor continued to die of starvation or committed suicide in increasing numbers.

Nobody talked of land reforms any more. The chief beneficiaries of various subsidies on fertilisers, diesel, seeds etc. were the big landowners. More and more agricultural land was being acquired for setting up industries, building shopping malls, industrial townships, fancy housing complexes and tourist resorts. SEZs displaced farmers by taking away their land which had provided them sustenance for generations. Core areas like energy, water, power, electricity, insurance, banking and even retail trade needed to be attended to but not in a way that made the poor and the deprived suffer.

The assessment made by the National Commission to Review the Working of the Constitution remained valid and relevant. It said:

> We find that justice—social, economic and political—remains an unrealised dream for millions of our fellow citizens. The benefits of our economic growth are yet to reach them. We have one of the world's largest reservoirs of technical personnel, but also the world's largest number of illiterates, the world's largest middle class, but also the largest number of people below poverty line, and the largest number of children suffering from malnutrition. Our giant factories rise out of

> squalor, our satellites shoot up from the midst of the hovels of the poor. Not surprisingly, there is sullen resentment among the masses against their condition erupting often in violent forms in several parts of the country. Tragically, the growth of our economy has not been uniform. It has been accompanied by great regional and social inequalities. Many a social upheaval can be traced to the neglect of the lowest of society, whose discontent moves towards the apathy of violence.

After more than six decades of democratic rule and all the much-bandied-about programmes, we had some 300 million people below poverty line. In absolute terms, we had more poor people than we did at the time of independence. Also, we had the largest number and majority of the poor of the world. The same was true of the illiterates. More than a lakh of villages did not have drinking water. According to UN statistics, over 60 per cent of Indians—men and women—were constrained to defecate in the open as they lacked toilet facilities. Fortunately, this shame attracted the attention of the current Prime Minister, Narendra Modi, and is being attended to with some priority. But, this is not all. It is a sad commentary on the working of all our poverty alleviation programmes that in the 70th year of our independence (in 2017) and thereafter, 67 per cent of our population was officially acknowledged to be so poor as to stand with a begging bowl for subsidised food grains at 1, 2 or 3 rupees per kilo. Lakhs of young children, laws notwithstanding, are still subjected to high levels of insanitary conditions and work or beg in subhuman conditions. In the matter of national integration and unity, we stand more divided than ever before. Emotional divisions—differences and lack of mutual confidence in the hearts and minds of men—are more dangerous than the dividing lines on maps. The policy of reservation had ceased to be a policy for the upliftment of the deprived sections. Instead, it had become a part of Vote bank politics of always keeping people backward and deprived. There was clamour for representation through reservation for newer and newer categories. There was rampant competition in backwardness, each group claiming to be more backward than others.

Decay of Institutions

The most tragic development for democracy was the sharp decline in the strength and credibility of its institutions. The Legislature, the Executive, the Judiciary and even the fourth estate—the media—suffered an image deficit. The Union government always tried to dominate the States, and often failed to enjoy normal regard and esteem from the State governments.

In 2014, the general perception was that the government threatened people with 'action under the law' in criminal cases against them while those in power kept threatening the government with withdrawal of support if they were not protected by the law and if their demands were not met. Thus, there was mutual blackmail. The price of legislators on sale was said to be running into several crores of rupees per person. As folklore would have it:

Samay Samay ki baat hai, Samay Samay ka yog
Karoron me bikne lage, do do kauri ke log.

The compromise with morality and the Rule of Law was defended by those in power on the ground of what was variously described as the 'Coalition Dharma' or constraints or compulsions of coalition politics. Actually, it was dictated by the sole consideration of somehow continuing to hold on to power at any price in terms of principles.

The then Prime Minister represented in the Rajya Sabha the State of Assam where he had never lived and was a nominee of the leader of the Party in the PM's Chair. The Council of Ministers with the Prime Minister at its head was not, in practice, the supreme executive of the country. Real power vested elsewhere. It was believed that the National Advisory Council (NAC), with the party president at its head, was a sort of super cabinet. Decisions of the cabinet could be dubbed as 'complete nonsense' fit to be torn and thrown away.

The conduct of our legislators, ministers and bureaucrats, and the goings-on in the houses of our Legislatures were matters of disgrace for Indian democracy, some honourable exceptions notwithstanding. With majority of members of the Lok Sabha and State Assemblies being elected with a minority of votes cast, the representative credentials of the representatives came to be questioned. On an average, of all legislators, about 70 per cent were elected by minority of votes cast. In the 15th Lok Sabha election it was 83 per cent and in the pre 2017 UP Assembly as much as 93 per cent. When more votes were cast for others, how could the winners be called 'representatives' of the people? As it is, almost all parties and candidates were busy building their vote banks on the basis of caste, communal, linguistic or other such identities. When with 15 per cent or so votes they could hope to win, why should they bother about the other 85 per cent? There existed major advantages in the power game of playing divisive politics and building separate identities.

It was clearly a sign of degradation of the democratic processes if fighting elections became impossible without crores of rupees and private armies of goons. One honourable member in the 15th Lok Sabha privately confided that he had to pay five crores to get the party ticket and spend another seven crores in the campaign. In big cities, slums and illegal migrants were big businesses and solid votebanks for some politicians. Democracy could be said to be seriously flawed if the poor and the underprivileged, who were in clear majority, got manipulated and sidelined by superior money and mafia power, and a few prospered at the cost of many. If democracy was on sale, naturally only the rich and those working for high ROI (Return on Investment) would rush to grab it. The space for the voice of the poor was bound to get substantially reduced.

The situation was no better on the public administration front. Karl Marx had predicted that the state shall wither away. In large parts of India, Marx seemed to have been proved right as the state appeared to have withered away. There was no sign of administration. Mafia gangs terrorised and ruled. An ugly atmosphere of near anarchy prevailed and even the thin dividing line between the politicians, the policemen and criminals had disappeared. Earlier, the criminal sought the protection of the politician, now it was the politician who needed the protection of the *dada* or perhaps the two had become one and the same person. Security of the citizen was the primary responsibility of the State. But, the policeman in India perceived his role as one of assisting the administration to control the people rather than of being a helper, friend and servant of the citizens. A large percentage of civil servants had become servile or developed a nexus with the politicians in corruption and defrauding the people. They refused to learn the simple truth that in a democracy, the people were the masters and all the functionaries of the state were to function as servants of the people.

After disenchantment with the Legislature and the Executive, one looked up to the Judiciary, but even there things were no better. Society runs on reward-punishment principles. It is necessary to make sure that the Rule of Law prevails and in every case punishment is swift and certain. But, the Indian democracy, as it has always operated, has led to and nurtured an unholy alliance between the businessman, the politician, the civil servant, the police and the criminal.

One of the most foundational norms of India's democracy—sovereignty in the hands of the people—stands grievously eroded. In a democratic polity, by definition, people must be participants in processes of governance. Citizens have also to exercise constant vigil over the conduct of those elected to public office. To save democracy, ways and means have to be found. We cannot blame only the politicians for all our miseries; the responsibility to save India's freedom and democracy is that of 'We, the people of India'.

Democracy is a very tender plant which unless tended with care, may wither away quite fast and the republic may perish. Unfortunately, despite 70 years of freedom, the ordinary Indians in city slums, village huts or hamlets have yet to feel the glow of the dawn of freedom on their faces or the transfer of power into their hands. It needs iteration that with the continuance of the colonial model of administration and the colonial mind set of the ruling class, people continue to be treated as the 'subjects' and not as the citizens of a sovereign democratic republic.

Before his assassination, Mahatma Gandhi wrote in his diary in Gujarati:

> We have gained the respect of the people because of the services we have rendered to them. Now (after Independence), if instead of remaining their servants, we try to become their masters, then, whether I am alive or not, I can say so on the basis of my lifelong experience that soon a wave of revolution will sweep the country and the people will catch hold of all the white-capped ones (netas) and finish them on the streets.

One is also tempted to recall what Sant Tulsi Das said in *Ramcharitmanas*:

Jasu raj priya praja dukhari,
so nripa avasi narak adhikari,
jinahin aniti karat dar nahin,
so jaihan, thore din mahin.

The people threw the thoroughly discredited and corruption tainted regime in the dustbin.

Hope and Beginning of Change

The 16th general elections returned a clear and unqualified mandate to one party and one leader. As a result of the most decisive popular verdict, for the first time, in some decades, we got a strong and stable government committed and oriented to providing clean and corruption free, citizen-friendly governance. Prime Minister Modi came on the national scene as a whiff of fresh breeze. He is a great and charming communicator. He talks to his audience, immediately establishes a personal bond and endears himself to one and all. Even his staunch opponents admit that much. Modi is a man with a vision. He is known to be a no-nonsense man, very clean, decisive, hard working and an equally hard task master for his colleagues and the bureaucracy. All that is welcome. The people have full faith in the integrity, ability and commitment of the Prime Minister. For the first time, political will was evidenced by, for example, in matters like demonetisation, GST, Doklam, strategic strike in Pakistan, the action on the Myanmar border and the agreement with Bangladesh on the exchange of enclaves. At a time when the new government had completed nearly four years in office, it could be said that the direction was right and several beginnings had been made. But, much remains to be done in the context of expectations that had been raised too high. The tasks awaiting urgent attention are too many and of stupendous proportions.

Although the air of despondence, gloom and helplessness has been replaced by hope and expectation, not much has changed yet on the ground level. Many micro level schemes in the direction of public welfare, people-friendly governance and development are taking shape. According to the latest growth chart of major economies of the world presented by the World Bank, India's economy is on the path of recovery. Business and investor confidence is improving, leading to capital inflows and hopefully to 7.5 per cent growth, which is said to be more than China's. But, from the angle of building a proper image for the NDA government and for catching the public's imagination, it is essential that some spectacular things with greatest impact potential are implemented in accordance with a fixed timeframe.

Let us not delude ourselves by assuming that the dark clouds have been lifted, the worst is over and *achche din aa gaye hain* (good days are here). Democracy in India continues to face serious challenges. There is a wide gulf between the conceptual and the factual, between the rhetoric and the real, between intention and implementation. Our polity is still under severe strain. Democratic institutions and values are still passing through a critical phase. That there has been a steep fall in the standards of conduct in public life and administration is widely accepted. That there is a crisis of character and values in politics and public administration is stating the obvious. Nothing can conceal the truth that our democratic processes are still largely dependent on caste and communal vote banks and criminals and are run with colossal amounts of black money generated through crime and corruption in India and abroad.

The 2014 general election is believed to have been the costliest ever and the number of persons with charges of criminal offences pending against them, elected to Lok Sabha, has been the largest this time. Also, those elected included more *crorepaties* than ever before. Despite the rhetoric and slogans of 'secularism' and 'development', it cannot be seriously asserted that vote bank calculations, caste considerations and black money had no role to play in the selection of candidates or in the voting behaviour. Still, the candidates for high offices are being recognised by their caste identities or by their belonging to backward, minorities etc. Selling and purchasing of tickets and votes has not ended. On the positive side, the institution of the Prime Minister has been restored to the position of primacy. Modi is in control, taking decisions and being obeyed. The country is now prepared to wait for a reasonably long time, if required, for substantial changes to take shape under his leadership.

The *loot tantra* and *kleptocracy* of the past need to be replaced by a clean, development-oriented, citizen-friendly *loktantra* or democratic governance and a soft state has to be replaced by a stable, strong-willed and decisive state. The hard truth is that every party needs tons of illegitimate money. The *Economist,* in an article, had some time ago made the point that India's national politicians had surrendered power to global markets and supra-national bodies and were therefore unable to keep promises made to voters.

The source of several of our maladies continues to rest in the utter disregard of the interests of the citizens and the absence of good governance, both at the Union and State levels. Good governance is necessarily democratic, participatory, transparent, accountable and citizen-centric. Administration has to become clean and citizen-friendly. Things will not even begin to improve unless the power returns to the people at the grassroots level where it belongs. The real need is to overhaul the political culture, the colonial model, and bring about systematic changes.

The case for revisiting and reforming democracy is unassailable. To save democracy, ways and means have to be found for reasserting the will of the people over the organs and functionaries of the state and restoring power to the citizen. Perhaps democracy, as we know it, is not enough. We have to transcend it and go beyond to get near the real ethos of democracy suited to 21st century India's needs. We have to reinvent and revitalise it to serve the common man. The task calls for a concerted effort to awaken and motivate the people to discharge their responsibilities, be vigilant and become active participants in democracy. We are a free society. It is to be hoped that corrective measures will surely arise from within the system and Indian democracy will emerge stronger from the churning that has now been put to effect.

We have to consider what changes are imperative to solve the main national problems of poverty, illiteracy, corruption, overpopulation, criminalisation of public life, devaluation of values, crisis of character, casteism, communalism, black money etc. We have to ensure our nation's socio-economic development and quality of life for all citizens. *Sabka sath, sabka vikas* has to be translated into visible reality. Since the representatives are supposed to be responsive to public opinion and pressure, quality of governance is dependent upon the quality of citizens. If the citizens are looking for undeserved or illegitimate benefits from the system through favours, good governance can never take shape. This is a stupendous responsibility and calls for education in the values and responsibilities of good governance in a democratic polity.

The most tragic development for democracy during some thirty years preceding the 16th General Election had been the sharp decline in strength and credibility of its institutions. Even the media, with some exceptions, has largely become an extension of business or even clandestine business. The latest entrant, the 5th estate of NGOs and CSOs have lost much of their shine, credibility and potential to emerge as citizens' movements.

The issues that worry us and call for reforms in the working of our democracy are many. Enough has been written on criminalisation of politics and politicisation of crime, all pervasive corruption, role of money, muscle and mafia power and caste and communal Vote bank politics. Other areas of concern include: (1) Union-State relations, demands for further reorganisation of States, decentralisation of powers to grassroots, responsibilities of handling problems of Jihadi terrorism,Naxalism, Maoism etc. in all their internal and external ramifications. (2) Reforming and regulating by law the political parties and electoral system and review of public administration—all with an aim to ensure citizen-centric, clean and corruption free, transparent and accountable government, thereby assuring equality and non-discrimination to all citizens. (3) Population control, (4) Reviewing the success of reservation policies and the question of the rights of tribals, protection of environment and illegal exploitation of mineral resources. (5) Evolving a new farmer-friendly agriculture policy.

While a campaign for reforming democracy will require action on several fronts and involve a wide range of political, administrative, judicial and parliamentary reforms, electoral and political party reforms are the most imperative and deserve the highest priority attention, because these are at the source of most of the maladies that afflict India's democracy. The present system is most divisive. It puts a premium on separate identities and elects people with doubtful representational legitimacy with a majority of those elected having had more votes cast against each one of them. Elections are no more a once-in-five-years business. We have them almost every year, with heavy costs involved, which disrupts normal life and development activities. Our economic development policies cannot succeed unless they are preceded by political and electoral reforms.

Today, public opinion is anxious for urgent change. The present leadership came to power on the agenda of change. It may be too early to expect things to change fundamentally right away, but if we fail this time the consequences may be disastrous for the nation's freedom and democracy. There may be a tremendous backlash and we may drift into chaos and anarchy. The people may once and for all lose all vestige of faith in democracy. It is therefore a categorical imperative that this government succeeds. Failure is not an option.

At the end of March 2018 and completion of nearly four years of the Modi regime, it seems that if democracy has to survive, it will be necessary to convert every challenge into an opportunity to reform and to end the still-continuing disconnect between the people and the politicians. There is an urgent need to restore faith in the quality, integrity and efficiency of democratic institutions and public administration.

Let us not bemoan the desert but celebrate the oases we have. For the first time in many years, we have a government which is not subject to the game of brinkmanship, bluff and blackmail by coalition partners and outside supporters. Now, there can be no *alibi* for inaction and indecision on crucial issues. People may have shown tolerance for the last 70 years but they may not be prepared to wait for more years now. People wish to see the guilty punished and feel signs of the beginning of a systematic change here and now. One wishes that 2018 goes down in history as the year of national resurgence. This is perhaps the last opportunity. It has to be seized in the spirit of 'now or never'.

Parliamentry Polity

Experience of Seventy Years

ON THE midnight of 14-15 August 1947, India is said to have achieved independence from British rule. We celebrated 15 August as the Independence Day even though we were still a British Dominion and remained so for more than two-and-a-half years thereafter. On 26 November 1949, the Constituent Assembly adopted a Constitution for free India. The Constitution came into operation fully and the 'Sovereign, Democratic Republic' of India was born on 26 January 1950. The Constituent Assembly (Legislative) became the provisional Parliament of India. It continued till 1952 when the two Houses of Parliament were duly constituted.

Our founding fathers adopted for us, what may be called, the system of parliamentary democracy. The term 'parliamentary' refers specifically to a democratic polity wherein the supreme power vests in the body of people's representatives called 'Parliament' or known by some similar name. Parliamentary system is one in which the Parliament enjoys a place of primacy and pre-eminence in the governance of the state. In fact, an essential characteristic of parliamentary democracy is that the executive is not separate from the legislature. Government is a part of the Parliament; it comes out of it and remains fully responsible to the directly elected representatives of the people in Lok Sabha.

Nehru favoured parliamentary democracy because, he thought, it was a peaceful method of dealing with problems. It is a method of argument, discussion and decision and of accepting that decision, even though one may not agree with it. The minority in a parliamentary government has a very important role to play. If the majority ignores the minority or treats it as an untouchable, it is not working in the true spirit of democracy. Similarly, those in the opposition are not expected to function as adversaries to those in power.

As we have repeatedly held, it is a myth that we adopted the British system of parliamentary democracy in India. What we actually adopted and are operating is the colonial model that the British developed for their imperialist purposes in India. The system had an organic growth on the Indian soil. Sixty-eight years is not a long period in a nation's history but it is long enough to take stock of the achievements and failures of our parliamentary system.

India can take legitimate pride in that some temporary aberrations like the 19 months of internal emergency apart—whatever problems we faced were resolved within the democratic framework of constitutionalism. Indian parliamentary democracy had to its credit many achievements. On the political plane, by far our greatest achievements were to (i) bring about and maintain the unity and integrity of post-partition India, and (ii) preserve freedom and democracy. Representative institutions thrived and we remained a vibrant, functioning democratic polity. We had in the Government and in the Parliament some of the tallest men and women endowed with sagacity of mind and nobility of character who were devoted to the nation and to democratic ideals. They helped in strengthening the foundations of parliamentary polity.

Parliamentary democracy as it evolved in India and the experience of working it repudiates the belief that democracy can be successful only in relatively more homogenous societies. India has shown that democracy can survive and succeed in a highly pluralist society as well. In fact, the Indian model of diversity may be said to have proved to be the greatest strength for democratic polity.

In India's traditionally multi-religious, multi-racial, multi-lingual plural society united by a common history, civilisational identity and territory, ethnicity may cut across the dividing lines. In fact, the vast majority of its citizens have multiple identities. The same person may belong to different groups depending upon the distinguishing criterion of religion, language, community, etc. Since society thus gets divided both horizontally and vertically, there are hardly any monoliths left. Every religion has its sects, languages and dialects, and castes and sub-castes. Members of almost every religious group would be divided by language, region and caste just as members of every linguistic group may be divided by religion, region, caste, etc. One may be in majority by religion and in minority by language or *vice-versa*. What divides, also unites. Under the special variant of Indian pluralism, the majority-minority syndrome does not apply to ethnic groups either. In states like Nagaland, Arunachal Pradesh, Meghalaya, for instance, the tribal populations are in majority but for that reason, they do not lose their ethnic group status.

Indisputably, in India, the judiciary has remained independent, the press free and civil authority supreme. Right to Information and Right to Education laws have been really the most revolutionary measures after the 73rd and 74th Constitutional Amendments giving constitutional status to local self-government institutions of Panchayats and Nagar Palikas and moving closer to making Indian democracy more participatory.

But, the nation was passing through very difficult and critical times. Parliamentary democracy was under severe strain. Faith of the people in the quality, integrity and efficiency of governmental institutions stood seriously eroded. The disconnect and alienation between the people and the politicians had assumed alarming proportions. Representative parliamentary institutions threatened to become dysfunctional.

One cannot underestimate the negative impact potential of the scams that overshadowed all the great achievements as also the new challenges confronting parliamentary democracy. Nothing could conceal the truth that our democratic processes were still largely dependent on caste and communal vote-banks and criminals and were run with colossal amounts of black money generated through crime and corruption. No wonder, Prime Minister Manmohan Singh was constrained to express sadness and say that he was worried about the future of parliamentary democracy in India. More than half-a-century earlier, the first Prime Minister, Jawaharlal Nehru, had asked whether with the demands of the people and the problems of Government having multiplied manifold, the political structure and procedures of parliamentary democracy had become 'out of date and may have to go' and 'how far can parliamentary democracy be adapted to meet the new burdens and functions of the government satisfactorily, effectively, and in time?' Answering the questions himself, Nehru had concluded that 'our parliamentary system of Government, with all its failings' was better than all the others 'which lead to some measure of authoritarianism'. But, as Nehru said, 'it does not mean that we should close our eyes to the grave problems we often have to face in the country and the disruptive tendencies that raise their heads and challenge the democratic process....'

The founding fathers had hoped that parliamentary democratic polity would build a strong nation, remove poverty and illiteracy and bring prosperity, economic growth and well-being for all. Democracy implies attention to the development and well-being of the poorest of the poor citizens of the nation. It must provide to the most marginalised and deprived sections of society equality of opportunity and right to live with dignity with freedom from want and fear.

In parliamentary democracy, the people govern themselves through the representatives they elect. Elections therefore are the bedrock. Our electoral system unfortunately has proved to be highly divisive of society. It is afflicted by the maladies of 4 Cs—Corruption, Criminalisation, Casteism and Communalism and 3 MPs—Money Power, Muscle Power and Mafia Power. In fact, electoral system and parties are at the root of corruption, criminalisation, casteism and communalism. Increasing cost of elections is leading to corruption, black economy and funding from the crime world. There is almost a complete absence of public's role in selection of candidates.

With majority of members of the Lok Sabha and State Assemblies elected with minority of votes cast, the representative credentials of the representatives themselves have come to be questioned. When more votes are cast for others, how can the winners be called representatives of the people? Almost all parties and candidates are busy building their vote banks on the basis of caste, communal, linguistic or other such identities with 15 per cent or so votes they can hope to win. There is all the advantage in the power game in playing divisive politics and building separate identities.

Hung Houses became a possibility because the electoral system generated communal and caste vote bank politics. We have been suggesting and the suggestion was unanimously endorsed by the Constitution Commission that in case of a hung House, the leader of the House may be elected by the House (like the Speaker) and the leader so elected must be appointed Prime or Chief Minister and he should be removable only by a constructive vote of no confidence.

It would be a step forward if the Electoral College for electing the President is widened to include all elected representatives from Panchayats to Parliament. Also, political parties should be prevented from making Presidential election an in-house affair and whipping the voters to vote under their dictates.

Parliamentary reforms should include restoring the image of Parliament and State legislatures as the supreme representative bodies of the people, codifying parliamentary privileges and not allowing them to become special rights against the people, scrapping MPLADs, better utilisation of time through advance legislative planning and floor management, either repealing the 10th Schedule 'anti-defection' law or outlawing all defections including those on merger plea, votes of defectors to topple or protect a Government being rejected as invalid, rationalising the pay and perks of all legislators, and requiring party leaders to control the conduct of their members. An overview of developments since the first Lok Sabha reveals some very interesting and some disturbing facts. The number of days on which the Houses of Parliament sit each year to transact business has come down in recent years. Even when they do meet, often little gets done. In the face of disturbances and shouting, the Houses have to be adjourned frequently.

There has been quite some thinking and talking about the decline of Parliament, devaluation of parliamentary authority, deterioration in the quality of Members, poor levels of participation and the like. Today, one notices a certain cynicism towards parliamentary institutions and erosion in the respect for normal parliamentary processes and the parliamentarians.

Members, irrespective of their party affiliations, have themselves become a new caste—parts of the establishment and co-sharers in the spoils. Some honourable exceptions apart, politics and membership of Parliament has emerged as a full-time, highly lucrative profession for majority of those involved. Following the changed composition of the Houses, there has been fast devaluation of all the old values and increase in disorders and pandemonia on the floor. There is general apathy among members, Ministers and public at large in the working of the Parliament.

We have an unending debate in regard to the falling standards in the conduct of legislators as evidenced by poor quality of debates, niggardly attendance in the houses of legislatures, unruly behaviour of members, scenes of pandemonia and the like. Legislatures having members with criminal records, sale and purchase of legislators to obtain majority and stay in power or somehow come to power, mortgaging the interests of the nation and of future generations for self-interest in the business of power politics are the most common topics of popular discussion. People are aghast and, and what is worse, they feel helpless.

On 1 September 1997, the 50th Anniversary of India's Independence was being celebrated by holding a special session of the two Houses of Parliament. A solemn resolution unanimously passed by both the Houses set an agenda for:

- electoral reforms
- transparency, probity and accountability in public life
- preserving the authority and dignity of Parliament
- all political parties starting a powerful national campaign for eradication of criminalisation from politics and controlling population.

But, on the ground level nothing changed. If anything, the situation has since worsened. The Houses are not allowed to function. Parliament is often rendered dysfunctional. Important legislation gets stalled on party lines. The ruling side and the opposition blame each other. The nation and the people suffer.

Expenditure on Parliament is estimated to be several crores per day. And, that is in addition to Rs 5 crore placed at the disposal of each Member every year. Parliament and parliamentarians have to justify themselves. The people need good, corruption free, citizen-friendly governance. It has to be a parliamentary, democratic government that can deliver and not a government only for sharing the spoils and loots of power.

The 2014 General Election

Whirlwind of Expectations and Fears

BEFORE MAY 2014, the nation was passing through very difficult times. We seemed to be heading fast to the lowest levels of decline since independence. The situation was grim. Those at the helm of affairs were oblivious to people's sufferings and did little to address their feelings of deep despair and helplessness. There was tremendous disconnect between the people and their own elected representatives. An unprecedented erosion in the people's faith was being witnessed in the quality, integrity and efficiency of governmental institutions. The organs of the state threatened to become dysfunctional. People, as individuals and as a nation, did not feel safe or secure. Widespread corruption with frequent scams were coming to light. Open loot by Pindari politicians, skyrocketing prices, slump in economic growth, rampant unemployment and total absence of governance were putting democracy itself to severe strain and shame. There was a need for a strong and stable government that could be expected to provide clean, citizen-friendly, development-oriented good governance.

The general elections to the 16th Lok Sabha and to a few State Assemblies were most fiercely and bitterly fought. They were also the most capital intensive so far. The ruling parties were badly decimated. Having been reduced to a dismal below-50 tally, the main party in opposition was not even able to have its leader recognised as the Leader of the Opposition. But, at the end of it all, democracy and the people had won most decisively. This signalled a happy ending to the dirty politics of mutual brinkmanship, bluff and blackmail between the shaky ruling alliance and the so-called supporting parties. It was a dawn of hopes and expectations.

A most welcome by-product of these elections was the prospect of the much sought for two major party system emerging. If the rules for recognition of parties were strictly enforced we would have only two national parties and very soon in almost all the States, we would have only two major State parties even if their names varied from State to State and finally all these could lead to two national pre-poll alliances. Hopefully, as a result, with some systemic reforms in the area of political parties and electoral processes, the present sad spectacle of our having over 1,800 registered parties will change for a saner scenario.

There was, however, a negative side to this as well. An effective opposition is as desirable in parliamentary democracy as a stable and strong government. It was expected that with a strength of over 200 members, all the different parties in opposition would behave responsibly and constructively to safeguard national interests and democratic culture. Also, it was hoped that unlike the UPA, the NDA would not treat the main party in opposition as an untouchable.

Another cause of concern was the cost of these elections—estimated to be in lakhs of crores—some white and much black. There was no dent in the twin malady of increasing number of candidates with criminal background getting elected or the ugly phenomenon of Vote bank politics. This resulted in majority of members still getting elected with minority of votes cast, putting their representational legitimacy in doubt. All this called for immediate systemic reforms.

National Agenda for Reforms

The most foundational postulate of the principle of sovereignty in a democracy is that power vests in the people. The basic question is of necessary reforms to ensure that power returns to the people where it belongs.

Enough has been written and spoken about the urgent need for reforms on almost all fronts—economic, administrative, judicial, parliamentary and political including electoral, political and governance.

There may be full justification for giving primacy to economic reforms but the hard truth is that politics is in the driving seat. The power is in the hands of those elected to form the government. Unless, therefore, some political—electoral and political party—reforms come first, no economic reforms are likely to really succeed.

Why should those who come to power through a corrupt system change it ? Running a political party, election campaigns and carrying on any political activity costs tons of money. Where is it to come from? If it comes from the world of crime, illicit traders, smugglers, arms dealers, land mafia and big contractors, how can the beneficiaries strike at the vested interests of their masters? And, how can high-sounding liberal economic reforms get sold to the people at large?

Subject to the above reservation, the economic reforms that need to constitute guiding objectives may revolve around:

- Generating a psychological environment for major economic reforms by first giving evidence of self-discipline, reducing expenditure on administration and all public/political functionaries including bureaucrats, MPs, Ministers etc. curtailing their perks, phony tours and luxurious lifestyles.
- Creating a more congenial climate for foreign and domestic investment.

- Encouraging savings and productive investments through a policy of tax incentives.
- Rationalising or scrapping some of the populist schemes which do not benefit the people as much as they promote corruption and siphoning off of public funds by intermediaries.
- Abolishing the MPLADS that militates against the federal and separation of powers principles.
- Developing skilled manpower for meeting global and domestic needs leading to greater employment of youth and promotion of service sector industries.
- Emphasis on marrying sustainable consumption with sustainable development instead of competitive consumerism.
- Greater emphasis on quality of life than mere GNP, GDP growth etc.

In keeping with the declared policy of 'more governance and less government', the state should progressively withdraw from businesses except in some core sectors or areas of national security etc. and concentrate on its role as an infrastructure builder and facilitator. Lastly it needs to free the people at the individual level from the plethora of clearances, certificates, permissions and licences required to live their simple day to day lives so that they can feel that they are no more subjects of colonial masters but honourable citizens of a free country.

The new Prime Minister (now four years in power), has given enough evidence of superb leadership qualities. During the 2014 election campaign, very many promises were made to the people to severely deal with and punish those guilty of corruption and public loot and to build a new India with all round development of education, health, housing and employment opportunities for all. Hopes were raised sky high. Some of the promises were perhaps unrealistic and not possible to implement at once.

Perhaps it was necessary in 2014 to instill the fear of God and government in the hearts and minds of the corrupt and the guilty. It has been politically unwise to go soft, not to bring to book and punish the illegitimate beneficiaries of the old regime. Also, perhaps it was possible to implement with a big bang some schemes with great public impact potential. Even though much progress and many good beginnings have been made, the need for growth in public perception is more important and that requires something more spectacular. Perhaps, the priorities of the current government need to be reviewed.

The fear is of the media dictating the national agenda, of the people feeling disillusioned. Also fear emanates from those in the party and in the bureaucracy with deep-seated vested interest in the *status quo* resisting change.

It is in the best interests of the nation and the people at large that the present governments succeed in providing good governance. Failure is not an option. For, if a democratic government with such leadership and such a massive mandate fails, it will threaten freedom, democracy and rule of law and may invite only chaos and anarchy.

Simultaneous or Separate Elections

Desirability and Feasibility

IN THE midst of rising turmoil on many issues, several political reform proposals are being made. Of these, one that is said to be 'under active consideration' is that of holding simultaneous elections to Lok Sabha and all the State Assemblies. The recent calls from the President and the Prime Minister have added further fillip to the debate. But, actually there is nothing new in the proposal. The idea of synchronising general elections has been under discussion for some decades now. The 11-member National Commission to Review the Working of the Constitution (NCRWC) headed by Justice Venkatachaliah (2000-2002), after in-depth and careful study, had found that the framers of our Constitution had themselves visualised simultaneous elections for Lok Sabha and State Assemblies. The first four elections during 1951-52 to 1967 were actually held almost simultaneously. Mid-term elections were largely forced only after 1967 as a by-product of large-scale defections and frequent toppling of governments. The Law Commission suggested simultaneous elections in 1999. On completion of half-a-century of the Constitution and the Republic of India, in the year 2000, the Government headed by Shri Atal Bihari Vajpayee decided to organise a nation-wide debate on the theme of reforms for a resurgent India. A National Committee was set up for organising seminars on electoral reforms all over the country. NCRWC was also appointed by the President the same year.

The National Committee organised several seminars and workshops at different regional centres all over the country. The National Commission (NCRWC) inter alia recommended that the costs of elections needed to be reduced drastically by law and that instead of the existing practice of EC preparing electoral rolls of eligible voters for parliamentary and State Assembly constituencies and the State Election Commissions (SECs) preparing separate rolls for local body elections, a single exercise should be enough for preparing common electoral rolls and Voter ID cards. When with universal adult franchise, the electors were the same, why should we undertake the massive exercise twice and have separate rolls prepared. After all, the exercise required large numbers of teachers and others being removed from their normal duties to go round door to door to register the names in the electoral rolls. The Commission (NCRWC) recommended that "with a view to reducing costs and strain on human and other resources, state and parliamentary elections, to the extent possible, should be held at the same time." That was in 2002.

The spirit of the recommendation was that simultaneous elections should be accepted as the goal to be aimed at but that it may not be feasible to bring about the change at one point of time with a hammer. The then Vice-President B S Shekhawat supported the idea of simultaneous elections and the then Deputy Prime Minister L K Advani said the proposal was under consideration. But, finally, after all the national debate and strong arguments in favour of simultaneous elections, nothing happened because no consensus could be reached among all the political parties. It could be legitimately argued that keeping the nation perennially in election mode involved collossal waste of public money and time and that it was highly detrimental to needs of development and good governance. With E C's Code of Conduct being in force so often, there were also natural constraints of electoral politics affecting the quality and speed of decision-making. With elections taking place in one or the other part of the country all the year round, the essential security arrangements required large parts of our security personnel being taken away from their national security responsibilities to perform election duties. Since the present Prime Minister is openly and strongly for simultaneous elections and is known for the political will of taking hard decisions, it should be legitimately possible to achieve the aim by a two-phase approach. Latest by 2024, we can have simultaneous elections to Lok Sabha and all the State Assemblies without any constitutional amendment or new legislation being required. As it is, the Constitution lays down in articles 83(2) and 172(1) that the House of the People (Lok Sabha) and "every Legislative assembly of every State, unless sooner dissolved, shall continue for five years from the date appointed for its first meeting and no longer..." This clearly means that while the maximum term is prescribed, every House can be dissolved at anytime earlier.

Unfortunately, it is not generally known or appreciated that all the 15 Lok Sabhas were dissolved before exactly completing their full term. The last (15th) came very close to completing its five-year term as the first meeting of the House was held on 1 June 2009 and it was dissolved on 18 May 2014 ie. some 13 days earlier. During the Emergency also, the extended term was not completed. Thus, so far as the Constitution is concerned, there is no difficulty in synchronising Lok Sabha and State Assembly elections. The important question is what after once achieving the goal of simultaneous elections? It is suggested that to prevent a return to the chaos of frequent elections and the whole country possibly reverting to being in election mode all the time, it would be certainly necessary not to think of this change in isolation but to make it part of an integrated electoral reforms package which should include :

- The Lok Sabha or the Vidhan Sabha electing, along with the speaker and in like manner, the Leader of the House who should be appointed as the Prime Minister or the Chief Minister.
- Parliament and State Houses adopting the constructive vote of no-confidence as the only way for bringing about change of Government.
- To rid the system of divisive Vote bank politics, making 50 per cent plus 1 vote the minimum for winning an election, holding on the very next day, where necessary, repolling between the two candidates getting the highest number of votes.
- Drastically reducing by law the cost of elections for the Union and State Governments, for political parties and for candidates.
- Making voting at general elections fundamental duty of every citizen and providing certain incentives and disincentives for voting or not voting, in matters like grant of Passport, Driving License, Ration Card, BPL Card, Income Tax Rebate etc.

Some such steps may minimise the possibilities of mid-term dissolutions of our legislative Houses. In the unlikely event of that still happening, the mid-term election may be only for the remaining period of the term so that the mega festival of democracy continues to be held at the same time every five years.

The case for simultaneous elections for Lok Sabha and all the State Assemblies (and may be, in the long run, for local bodies) is entirely unassailable and unexceptionable. Even those who oppose the proposal are constrained to say that it is "desirable but not feasible". Well, if it is desirable, we should find a way to make it feasible. But, we are very fond of bandying the slogan of "unity in diversity" and rejoicing and celebrating our diversity as the greatest virtue. We conveniently forget that while diversity is an existential reality, our goal is "unity and integrity of the nation". The problem is that we have amongst us some people who pay only lip service to "unity and integrity of the nation". They survive and thrive on dividing society on ethnic, linguistic or regional bases and on building their vote-banks on promoting separate identities. Their road to political success is inevitably paved with competitive communalism, casteism and populism. They, by deliberate design, have no pan-Indian perspective or national agenda. Good governance and development are not their priorities. Also, the phenomenon of the entire country always remaining in election mode and frequency and multiplicity of elections brings to some sections of our people boons of pecuniary and other benefits. How can we expect the beneficiaries of the present system and those having a vested interest in keeping the nation divided to strike at their own feet and support the proposal of holding elections to State Assemblies along with the Lok Sabha election thereby subordinating their regional, party and personal interests to a possible wave, national agenda or towering leadership? A wide all-party consensus on the issue, therefore, may not be possible in the foreseeable future. The earlier this "*mrig-marichika*" or pipe-dream of building a consensus through nation-wide debate is given up the better. There have been enough of national debates on the subject. Now the leadership has to decide whether we merely want the debate to continue as in cases like those of Lokpal and Women's Reservation or what is proposed is concrete action for simultaneous elections in national interest.

India Leads: Myth or Reality

Management Perspective

DEFINITIONAL AND conceptual clarity in regard to governance and question of its interface with institutions of democratic polity and people at large remains complex. However, it is becoming increasingly clear that there is no alternative to clean and quality governance as it affects the lives of the people. There are multiple linkages between development and governance but to measure them in quantitative terms is difficult. Looked at from another angle, governance implies some input of management principle and techniques in the business of the government and public administration. There is, therefore, all the justification for flagging the dire need of management in politics with both macro and micro management techniques. In India today, there are any number of institutes and schools for business management, hotel management, hospital management etc. but there is none for political management.

We cannot manage a nation as we manage a trade, business or market. Politics must not be run as a business or industry. There is every need for an academy of political management for imparting professional practical training to those aspiring for a career in politics. Others like senior business executives or business management professionals may also need to have an inside look into the actual processes of decision-making and the various complex and compelling forces working on them.

There is no straight answer to the question whether 'India leads' is a myth or a reality; whether India is shinning and surging ahead to lead the world in radiant glory or descending fast into gloom and doom to be added to the list of many a fallen star.

'India leads' was a reality when India was at the top of the world in science, technology and trade, when we invented the zero and the wheel, revolutionised mathematics and laid the seeds of industrialisation.

'India leads' was a reality when Sanskrit became the source of all the Indo-European group of languages and Sushruta invented cosmetic plastic surgery and many surgical instruments.

The lead became a myth when India succumbed to foreign invasions. Invaders came, conquered and looted us while we kept fighting among ourselves. Things came to such a pass that an invader left the country to a slave to rule over us and establish a slave dynasty of monarchs. 'India leads' again became a myth when a few thousand white men from a small island ruled over us for some 200 years.

Before the British rule, in 1750, India's share in the world's manufacturing output was 24.5% while that of the UK and the USA was 1.9% and 0.1% respectively. After British rule was firmly established, by 1900, India's share had come down to 1.7% of the global economy while that of the UK and USA increased to 62% and 23.6% respectively. But, 'India leads' became a reality again when for the first time in world history, the mightiest empire on earth had to concede independence after a non-violent struggle under Gandhi's leadership.

'India leads' was a reality when at one time more than 100 nations of the world accepted India's philosophy and leadership of the non-aligned movement.

'India leads' was a reality when through the Green Revolution, India solved its food problem and became self-sufficient in food grains despite massive increase in population. 'India leads' was again a reality when with the white revolution, India became the largest producer of milk.

Thanks to the resilience and accommodative spirit of the Indian Constitution, many major conflicts were satisfactorily resolved. Several ethnic demands were conceded, territorial adjustments made, new States created and the political map of India redrawn.

'India leads' became a myth when our thinking and vision were badly battered by the unprecedented spate of scandals , both at the Union and State levels. The distress of the people at the sky-rocketing prices of essential items of daily need and almost total governance-deficit on all fronts was a reality. Faith of the people in the quality, integrity and efficiency of government institutions stood seriously eroded. The disconnect and alienation of the people and the politicians had assumed alarming proportions. Representative parliamentary institutions threatened to become disfunctional. Governance was in disastrous disarray. There was a steep fall in the standards of conduct in public life and a crisis of character and values in politics and public administration Instead of being a government of the people, by the people, for the people, the government appeared to have become a government of the corrupt, by the corrupt, for the corrupt. What we witnessed was naked politics of loot. Not only did the many scams involve alleged swindling of billions of rupees of public money by persons in high places, but these also had the effect of eroding the credibility of all the known institutional pillars of good governance

The primary governing duty of the state is to provide security to its citizens. But, today, ordinary citizens do not feel at all safe or secure while members of the security forces are engaged in providing security to those, a majority of whom should be behind bars under state security.

Despite all our pro-poor pontifications, India's position in the UNDP human development index and Millennium Development Goals (MDGs) is still one of the lowest.

While much could be said in favour of economic reforms, growth measured in terms of GNP, GDP, per capita NNP etc. is not development. Development, to be meaningful, has got to be inclusive. Also, it must transcend economy and lead to human happiness. When *Sabka Sath, Sabka Vikas,* in fact, becomes visible 'India leads' will again become a reality. The much-touted ordinary citizen is still reeling under the shocks of high prices, rampant criminalisation of daily life, casteism, unemployment, corruption at every level and almost total lack of security and governance. He does not understand the nuances of economic reforms. He is concerned with how are the promised '*Achche Din*' going to come and impact and better the quality of his life.

After seven decades of democratic rule and several bandied-about programmes, we have some 300 million people below the poverty line. In absolute terms, we have more poor people today than at the time of independence.

The same is true of illiteracy. More than a lakh of Indian villages still do not have drinking water. 'India leads' can become a glorious reality only when Prime Minster Modi's dreams of housing for all and a toilet in every house and hamlet and all-round cleanliness are realised.

The most tragic development for democracy has been the sharp decline in the strength and credibility of its institutions. Legislature threatens to become dysfunctional, the Executive suffers from unprecedented governance and ethical deficit. Of late, the Judiciary—the last sheet anchor of democracy and the Constitution—has also suffered great erosion in public esteem. Even the fourth estate—the media—has suffered an image deficit. The Union government tries to dominate and dictate to States and undermines democracy at the State level. Sometimes, Governors tend to ignore the elected State governments—the Chief Ministers and the Cabinets—and arbitrarily exercise powers in the matter of giving assent to Bills passed by the Houses of State Legislatures or reserving many of them for the consideration of the President, ie. the Union government. So long as this situation it not reversed, 'India Leads' is bound to remain a myth.

'India Leads' was a myth when successive governments were said to have got into and remained in power by buying support with money, ministerships bargained on not pursuing criminal cases and the like. The spectacle of unethically engineered or defection-manipulated majorities or of several successive hung Legislatures or coalition governments of disparate elements coming together solely for sharing the fruits of power and including some of the goon leaders with criminal records or otherwise doubtful antecedents, were all matters of grave concern. The price of legislators on sale was said to be running into several crores of rupees a man. The collective responsibility of the Council of Ministers at the Union level had become a sham for 10 years. What the then Prime Minister called the 'constraints of coalition politics' created a situation where to remain in power the Prime Minister and the larger coalition partner had to agree to be blackmailed by small parties demanding their pound of flesh, creamy portfolios and freedom to make money. Ministers spoke in different voices in utter violation of the concept of collective responsibility and disregarded even the Prime Minister. Without casting aspersions on any individuals involved, it may be seen that the Prime Minister himself was not an elected representative of the people. He was not the Leader of the House, not even the Leader of the Party. The Council of Ministers with the Prime Minister at its head was not, in practice, the supreme executive of the country. The National Advisory Council seemed to be in the nature of a super-cabinet. The institutions of the Prime Minster and the Council of Ministers were never so devalued or deinstitutionalised.

'India Leads' cannot be a reality so long as the conduct of our legislators, ministers and bureaucrats and the goings-on in the Houses of our legislatures continue to be matters of disgrace for the Indian democracy, some honourable exceptions notwithstanding.

Overall, however, 'India leads' is a reality because after all, we remain an open society and a federal polity. India is on the move. We are trying to move fast on the road to development with good governance. We are awake and seized of the problems that plague our nation.

Yes, we have problems. It is only the dead who have no problems. We are a living nation, pulsating with life. What is important is not the absence of problems and conflicts but the strength and stability of democratic institutions protecting fundamental human rights and changing and adjusting to the needs of society and their conflicts. That India survives as a united and a functioning democracy shows the inner strength and character of the people.

'India leads' became a reality when Heads of all the neighbouring SAARC nations attended the swearing-in ceremony of the Modi government in New Delhi, and again when the heads of ten ASEAN nations came as chief guests on our Republic Day on 26th January 2018, or when the Modi government quickly proceeded to build close pragmatic relationships with world leaders from countries like the US, Japan, Bangladesh, Nepal, South Korea, China, Mongolia, Australia, Israel and others.

'India leads' actually became a reality when the people gave a fresh proof of the strength and effectiveness of its democracy and threw out with a massive mandate a corrupt government and brought to power a new leadership committed to good governance and all-round, all-inclusive development. However symbolic, 'India leads' became a reality when 1960s onwards, Yoga became a craze around the globe and a multi-billion dollar industry in the US. 'India leads' became a reality when at the initiative of Prime Minister Modi, in December 2014, United Nations General Assembly resolved to declare 21 June as the International Yoga Day and when on 21 June 2015, 192 countries all over the globe celebrated this Day. The countries included several

Islamic nations like Saudi Arabia.

India will again lead if the tendency of centralisation of powers is curbed and greater autonomy is ensured to the States and from the States to local units in the Gandhian bottom-up, instead of the present top-down model. Delhi must agree to shed its extra weight. With economic liberalisation, political power and management rights must be restored to the people at the grassroots. The Union must concentrate only on the essentials. To preserve India as a Union of States, it is necessary to build it as a really cooperative federal Union or Union of autonomies with multi-tier government and sharing of power from the lowest grassroots levels to parliament and GOI.

India will lead again if the colonial model of administration and mind set is replaced by return of power to the people where it belongs.

India will lead if the people rise above their narrow self-interests, are prepared to remain vigilant and make sacrifices as responsible participants in democratic governance. India will lead if men of character and competence come forward to take responsibilities of being active participants in the democratic process and provide citizen-friendly good governance.

India will lead if the ordinary citizens feel secure and are assured a life of quality and dignity. India will lead and once again be the Vishwa guru if it returns to its own *dharma* of righteousness and spiritual prowess and her citizens relive the Gandhian values of *Asteya, aparigraha* and *tena tyaktena bhunjitha* instead of the pursuit of competitive consumerism, unsustainable consumption and hedonism.

Today, those in power are committed to cleansing the system to tackle the malady of tremendous governance deficit and the dwindling faith of the people in representative institutions, bureaucracy and even in the judiciary.

'India leads' will become a reality if the new leadership can tackle the reluctance of the political class to change the bureaucracy's love of the *status quo,* if the big fish found guilty of corruption and defrauding the public exchequer are quickly and decisively punished, and if the basic systematic reforms in the electoral and justice delivery system etc. are effectuated on a high priority basis. 'India Leads' will be a reality if even a quarter of the high expectations aroused are fulfilled partially. It has to be understood that no economic reforms, howsoever good and logical, shall succeed unless these are accompanied or preceded by essential political management reforms leading to good governance. The choice is between improving political management or accepting anarchy.

Concept of Good Governance

Going Back to Kautilya's Arthashastra

FOR SOME decades now, the issue of good governance has been in the forefront of political science discourses and discussions in the academia. The study of institutions that were relegated to the footnotes of history is back in reckoning and problems of good governance have come to occupy important spaces and have generated renewed interest. Both in the developed and developing parts of the world, there has been a welcome shift of focus from traditional concepts of government and politics to the concept of good governance, its attributes and imperatives.

Several studies have been taken up by various organisations in recent years. The world development reports, 1997 onwards have underlined the effectiveness of the state as an essential prerequisite for sustainable economic growth. The Bretton Woods institutions realised—even though very late in the day—that economic liberalisation reforms cannot succeed without first ensuring good quality and clean governance. In fact, the IMF made good governance a criterion for sanctioning loans.

There is nothing really new in stressing the principles and paradigms of good governance in political science. The concept in ancient Indian polity of the rulers being bound by *dharma* was precisely that of ensuring good governance to the people. Even though monarchy prevailed, there was no place for any theory of the divine rights of the kings or of arbitrary rule. *Rajdharma* was the code of conduct or the rule of law that was superior to the will of the ruler and governed all his actions. The *Jataka tales*, Shantiparva—Anushasanparva of *Mahabharata*, Shukracharya's *Nitisar,* Panini's *Ashtadhyayi, Aitreya Brahmana,* Valmiki's *Ramayana*, and not the least Kautilya's *Arthashastra* are replete with descriptions of tenets of good governance.

Western writers like Basham and Keith would like us to believe that India had had no school of political philosophy or anything like 'a serious theory of politics'. They forget that some 300 years before Christ, according to those well-versed in statecraft or science of government, *Rajvidya Vidam,* Kautilya 'churned the nectar of policy science from the ocean of *Arthashastra*'.

निति शास्त्रामृतं धीमानर्थ शास्त्रमधौ दधे

Kautilya's *Arthashastra* is a 'treasure trove filled with precious gems of wisdom'. The percepts and principles propounded by Kautilya have relevance beyond time and space. They have universal appeal and applicability. It is, however, necessary to relate them to modern times and concepts and to today's problems in each polity.

Kautilya deals extensively with the subjects of political economy and statecraft. *Arthashastra,* in its very nature, is a treatise on the policy of state administration rather than on the theories of origin and functions of the state. To the extent that it concerns itself with matters of good administration and how it should be run in the best interests of the people, *Arthashastra* is, for that very reason, among other things, concerned with matters of governance.

It may be said that Kautilya's *Arthashastra* is the first comprehensive treatise on politics in ancient India. But, *Arthashastra* itself begins with an acknowledgement that it is a compendium of several earlier *Arthashastras* and schools of thought in statecraft.

Artha is defined to mean material well-being of the people living on earth. *Arthashastra,* therefore, may be defined as the *shastra* that shows how acquisition and protection of earth and of its inhabitants is to be carried out. Normally this is the responsibility of the state. Therefore, *Arthashastra* becomes a book dealing with matters of the state, a book of *rajdharma* or *rajvidya.*

Following the analysis by Ghoshal, Kautilya's views on government can be grouped under three heads, viz the ruler (king), the officials and the mechanism of administration.

The first and foremost duty of the ruler is to ensure the protection of the people. '*Raksana*' or '*palana*' meant primarily the protection of the person and property of the people. The ruler must maintain order. Discipline lies at the root of all success. Disorder and offences against the law must be repressed without undue severity or leniency. Justice is the bedrock of society. Kautilya's whole concept of the duties of the rulers is positive and explicitly suggests improvement of every aspect of social life. The principle is the observance of the qualities of exertion, dutifulness, and impartiality culminating in a doctrine of the ruler's complete identification of his interests with those of the people.

Chapter V of Book I of *Arthashastra* concludes with the statement that a good ruler must be well-educated and disciplined in sciences, devoted to good governance of the people and bent on doing good to all people. These principles propounded by Kautilya stand the test even today and are a primary prerequisite for good governance.

Kautilya says, if a ruler is strong and full of energy, his people will be equally so. It is necessary that the ruler is always wide awake and alert. With the help of the Prime Minister, he is expected to keep a watch over the character and conduct of his ministers in charge of different departments of government (Chapters X and XIX, Book I). Kautilya is emphatic that before decisions of the state are made or any important administrative measures taken, they should be discussed in well-constituted Council of Ministers. He quotes Manu, Brihaspati and school of Usanas who believed that the Council of Ministers should consist of 12, 16 or 20 ministers but says that according to him (Kautilya) the Council may consist of as many Ministers as may be deemed necessary or affordable *(Yathasamarthyam).* (Chapter XV, Book I.) This view of Kautilya would have suited our politicians and parties who used ministerships to buy support. Accepting the recommendation of the National Commision to review the working of the Constitution (NCRWC), the Constitution (91st Amendment) Act, 2003 put a limit on the number of Ministers that could be appointed at the Union and State levels. Earlier there was a tendency to have jumbo Councils of Ministers. In some States, majority of the MLAs were made Ministers or holders of equivalent posts not because that many Ministers were needed or were actually affordable but because that was necessary to keep the flock together and sustain the government.

According to Kautilya, the ruler must follow the views and wishes of the friends and leaders of the people. One who fails to keep his promises to the people becomes untrustworthy. If the ruler works against the will of the people, then also he shall become unreliable. He should adopt the mode of life, dress, language and customs of the people he seeks to govern. He should follow the people in their faith with which they celebrate their national, religious and congregational festivals. The ruler must find his own prosperity in the prosperity of the people and must give priority to providing them with security and wellbeing. He should help the miserable, helpless and diseased people. (Chapter V, Book XIII.)

Kautilya goes as far as to lay down the daily routine for the ruler as part of his duties. He has to devote one-eighth of his time each day to attend to the problems and concerns of the common people. Kautilya says that a ruler (king) must 'never cause his petitioners to wait at the door, for when a king makes himself inaccessible to his people and entrusts his work to his immediate officers, he may be sure to endanger confusion in business, thereby cause public disaffection and himself become a prey to his enemies'. A good ruler is expected to himself attend to the problems *inter alia* of women, the minors, the aged, the afflicted and the helpless. All urgent calls, he must hear at once and never put off 'for when postponed, they may prove too hard or impossible to accomplish'. The ruler is bound by his vow to be always in readiness for action in the discharge of his duties. In the most categorical pronouncement of the principles of good governance, Kautilya says in the XIX Chapter of Book I:

प्रजा सुखे सुखं राज्ञः प्रजानां च हिते हितम् ।
नात्मप्रियं हितं राज्ञः प्रजानां तु प्रियं हितम् ।।

In the happiness of his people lies his happiness; in their welfare his welfare;

whatever pleases himself he shall not consider as good, but
whatever pleases his people he shall consider as good.

Thus Kautilya is in favour of a welfare state where the welfare and prosperity of the people—*(Yogakshema), Prajasukham* and *Prajahitam*—are the supreme concerns of the ruler. The ruler can have no likes or interests of his own.

Coming to the heads of departments and officers of the government, Kautilya's *Arthahsastra* lays down strict norms of conduct and control. If an officer fails in the discharge of his responsibilities any day, he would be fined twice the amount of his pay. It shall be the duty of the chief officer of each department to keep a watch over the performance of each person under his charge. Each department is to be officered by 'temporary' heads because 'just as it is impossible not to taste the honey or the poison placed at the tip of the tongue, so it is impossible for a government servant not to eat up, at least, a bit of the state revenue'. Kautilya speaks of 40 ways in which corrupt officers can cheat the government and the people. The *Arthashastra* goes on to say:

> *Just as fish moving under water cannot possibly be found out either as drinking or not drinking water, so government servants employed in the government work cannot be found out taking money for themselves. It is possible to mark the movements of birds flying high up in the sky but not to ascertain the clandestine movement of government servants.*

With a view to maintain probity in public service and to obviate chances of corruption among officers, Kautilya prescribes confiscation of their ill-gotten wealth, and transfer to another job 'so that they can't misappropriate government money or vomit what they have eaten up'. It is interesting to recall that the National Commission to Review the Working of the Constitution that submitted its report on 31 March 2002, recommended confiscation of ill-gotten or unaccounted wealth and property of public servants (just what Kautilya said in Chapter IX, Book II).

Kautilya is very progressive in his concept of marriage, divorce, remarriage, inheritance in family laws. He provides for the rights of women, welfare of prisoners, duties of citizens, consumer interest protection, fair dealings by merchants and artisans and other very modern concerns like forestry, environmental protection, water resource management, rights of the landless labourers and wage earners and punishment to the doctor for negligence in treating a patient. Discoverers of mines, precious stones, treasure-troves etc. he lays down, are entitled to a percentage share in what they discover. (Book IV, Chapters I and II.)

In Kautilya's *Arthashastra*, the Superintendent of Commerce is charged with the responsibility of *inter alia* supervising weights and measures to prevent deception by the unethical merchants. Punishment by fines according to a scale rising with the severity of the offence is laid down. The Superintendent of Commerce has to fix a profit of five per cent on local products and ten per cent on foreign products. Merchants making higher profits are to be punished. The sale of articles of quality inferior to what is claimed is punishable by eight times the value of the articles sold. Stringent punishment is provided for adulterators of goods and for middleman to cheat a merchant or consumer (Chapter II. Book IV).

Kautilya mentions 13 kinds of criminals who should either be banished or made to pay adequate compensation according to the seriousness of their guilt. He adopted the well-settled seven elements of state: *Svamin,* the ruler; *Amatya,* the minister; *Janapada,* the territory with people settled on it; *Durga,* the fortified capital; *Kosa,* the treasury; *Danda,* the army; and *Mitra,* the ally. The principle propounded behind these elements is that when they behave limb-like, they become an asset to the ruler. The ruler with the qualities of self-mastery can improve over the defective constituents but one wanting in this quality destroys even those that are wholesome and well-disposed. It thus becomes imperative for the ruler to protect and strengthen the institutions of the state that form its constituent parts. It also suggests the mutual interdependence of these elements of the state and the need for decentralisation of governance and devolution of power to the grassroots level of *Janapadas.*

Apart from giving guidelines on good governance, Kautilya also recognised the need of education of the ruler and administrators for developing their skills in statecraft. His education was not limited to teaching politics. He focused on the overall development of the personality of each person that enabled him to make reasonable judgements. The ruler, he mentions, who stands at the head must receive a thorough education and develop a character of austere virtue and self-restraint, and an all controlling sense of duty. It also enjoins upon the ruler a strict moral discipline as well as a control of the senses acquired by the study of sciences and the observance of their precepts. It was the first time that an integrated scheme of education for the ruling class was formulated.

Danda which literally means the policy of stick in Kautilya's theory holds a very important position. However, Kautilya is not for indiscriminate use of *danda.* He lays down principles and conditions under which and how *danda* should be applied. He mentions that while the lawful application of *danda* ensures the complete happiness of the individual, its unlawful or vicious application causes universal disaffection and its non-application produces anarchy symbolised by the law of the jungle. Judicious and reasonable application of the coercive power of the state secures the protection of the people and at the same time ensures the stability and prosperity of the state. Kautilya says unjust or indiscriminate use of *danda* may lead to revolt of the people against the ruler and the people may overthrow him.

The prime element in Kautilya's policy was the protection of the state and the people. His definition of security extends to the realm of the welfare of the people. The *Arthashastra* talks about the ruler's duty to protect the people from calamities by providing relief and from anti-social elements by punishing them.

Kautilya talks about planned settlement of the rural and urban areas with the objective of providing military, economic and administrative needs of the state. Here Kautilya is prudently advocating development strategies of harnessing and exploiting natural resources for the overall economic development and security of the state as well as to facilitate administrative and commercial objectives.

Though the *Arthashastra* lays down stringent policies of statecraft, it invariably follows the cardinal principle of protection and preservation of the state and its people. Nowhere does it allow the state to function in such a manner so as to create disaffection in the people. In the happiness of the people lies the legitimacy and the happiness of the ruler and to this end he is duty bound to perform all the duties of his *Rajdharma* required to keep the people happy. It propounds the fundamental good governance principle of accountability and of justice being the basis of lawful rule.

If a closer study of Kautilya's *Arthashastra* is made from this angle, it is believed, many a foundational norm behind the modern concept of good governance can be distilled from its *slokas* and passages.

There is much to take, in principle, from Kautilya's *Arthashastra* as a guidance point or reference for good governance. *Arthashastra* covers many aspects and propounds principles of such universal applicability the reference of which will undoubtedly enhance our present-day intellectual efforts towards policy-making for fulfilling the national agenda for good governance.

References

- Banerjee, Ajit M and Chandrasekaran, *Reviewing Governance - Issues and Options,* Tata McGraw Hill, New Delhi, 1996.
- Basham, A L, *The Wonder That Was India,* Fontana Books, Rupa and Co, Calcutta, 1982.
- Chopra, SK, *Towards Good Governance,* Konark, Delhi, 1997.
- Ghoshal, UN, *The History of Indian Political Ideas,* Oxford University Press, London, 1959.
- Kangle, RP, *The Kautilya Arthashastra Part III: A Study,* University of Bombay, Bombay, 1965.
- Kashyap, Subhash C, *Institutions of Governance in South Asia,* Konark Publishers Pvt.Ltd, Centre for Policy Research, New Delhi, 2000.
- Kashyap, Subhash C (ed), *Crime and Corruption to Good Governance,* Uppal, New Delhi, 1997.
- Kashyap, Subhash C, Towards Good Governance: *Need for Political Reforms, Indian Journal of Public Administration,* Vol XLIV, No3, IIPA, New Delhi, 1998.
- *Kautilya's Arthashastra,* translation by R Shamasastry, Mysore Printing and Publishing House, Mysore, 1915, 8th ed. 1967.
- Kulke, Hermann, and Dietmar Rothermund, *A History of India,* Routledge, London, (1986) 1998.
- Prasad, Beni, *Theory of Government in Ancient India,* Central Book Depot, Allahabad, 1968.

GOOD GOVERNANCE

Blueprint of Good Governance

Agenda for Political Reforms

IN THE midst of all the conflicts, controversies and bitter political battles, India is on the march. A process of churning is on. We can look forward to the future with pride. However, there is also cause for concern. Faith of the people in the quality, integrity and efficiency of governmental institutions still remains seriously eroded. Case for a review of the working of the institutions—Executive, Legislature and Judiciary—and for a wide range of political reforms is indisputable. Some rethinking is called for on the many promises made to the people and on the governments failure to work the political system we chose for ourselves. The time is ripe for a fresh look and for considering necessary systemic amends.

There is nothing wrong with the fundamentals of our political system of representative parliamentary democracy. But for the health and vigour of this system itself, it is of the utmost importance to constantly review and refurbish its structural-functional components, and from time to time to consider renewing and reinventing the entire gamut of its operational mechanisms to guard against putrefaction and decay.

Concept of Governance

In recent years, considerable attention in academia has been focussed on problems of realising good governance. The end of all economy and polity is social good and improvement in the quality of human life. Human beings are not to be considered as a mere resource for administration or development but they are the ultimate end towards which all administration, development etc. should be aimed. The watchword for Ashoka was *Yogakshema* or public welfare. And, this can be achieved only through good governance.

Governance refers to the manner in which power is exercised by governments in managing a country's social and economic resources. 'Good' governance is the exercise of power by various levels of government that is effective, honest, equitable, transparent and accountable. Besides the World Bank indicators of good governance encompassing democracy, transparency and accountability, it may be said that the whole idea of 'good governance' is that of a participative system in which those who are called upon to govern on behalf of the people are motivated with a will to giving their best, serving and doing good to the people, solving their problems and making their lives more liveable, satisfying and enjoyable. The essential prerequisites for quality governance are that the system should be good and suited to the needs, aspirations, background and ethos of the people concerned, and those selected for operating the system should be endowed with character and competence and motivated by the spirit of public service.

Since governance is the process of decision-making and the process by which decisions are implemented, an analysis of governance has to focus on the formal and informal actors involved in decision-making and implementing the decisions made and the formal and informal structures that have been set in place to arrive at and implement the decisions. Government is one of the actors in the game of governance. In urban areas the major actors constitute political parties, voluntary organisations, research institutes, religious leaders, finance institutions, the military etc. At the national level, in addition to the above actors, media, lobbyists, international donors, multi-national corporations, etc. may play a role in the decision-making process or in influencing the decision-making processes. In rural areas, for example, other actors may include influential landlords, associations of peasant farmers, cooperatives, NGOs etc. All actors other than government and the military are grouped together as part of the 'civil society'. In some countries, in addition to the civil society, organised crime syndicates also influence decision-making, particularly in urban areas and at the national level.

Some of the major characteristics of 'good' governance are—participation, consensus orientation, accountability, transparency, responsiveness, effectiveness and efficiency, equitability and inclusiveness and the rule of law. It ensures that corruption is minimised, the views of minorities are taken into account and that the voices of the most vulnerable in society are heard in decision-making. It is also responsive to the present and future needs of society.

The foundational norm of any democratic polity is that sovereignty vests in the hands of the people. Today, sovereignty of 'We, the people' stands grievously eroded. It has come to be widely believed that the administration has failed to meet fully the hopes, aspirations and requirements of the people. In this background what has become imperative is clean and quality governance as it affects the lives of the people.

Beside people-centred development, the balance among the Legislature, Executive and Judiciary has to be maintained in any constitutional democracy for good governance. Parliament and State assemblies legislate or amend existing laws; the executive in the form of ministers and bureaucracy administer laws and draft policy; The courts interpret the laws. The media, as the fourth pillar of democracy, is meant to serve as a watchdog and commentator. Good governance requires that all three organs of government stick to their basic duty or *dharma* and refrain from stepping on the other's turf. Whenever there is lack of harmony, smooth functioning of the government is affected.

Governance is viewed as the exercise of economic, political, and administrative authority to manage a country's affairs at all levels and as the means by which states promote social cohesion, integration, and ensure the well-being of their populations. It embraces all methods used to distribute power and manage public resources, and the organisations that shape government and the execution of policy. It encompasses the mechanisms, processes, and institutions through which citizens and groups articulate their interests, exercise their legal rights, meet their obligations, and resolve their differences. In terms of the UNDP's Policy Document (1997), good governance, therefore, depends on public participation to ensure that political, social and economic priorities are based on a broad societal consensus and that the poorest and most vulnerable populations can directly influence political decision-making, particularly with respect to the allocation of development resources. Good governance is also effective and equitable, and promotes the rule of law and the transparency of institutions, officials, and transactions. Governance encompasses the state, but it clearly transcends it by including roles for both the private sector and civil society organisations. The private sector has a crucial role to play in sustainable human development since it is the primary source of opportunities for productivity, employment, income generation, public investment, enterprise development, and economic growth. Civil society organisations facilitate public participation through social mobilisation. The capacity of governments to engage civil society is critical to a nation's capability to sustain political and economic opportunities and social cohesion. Sustainable human development is impossible without the participation of a number of actors and institutions.

Sustainable Human Development

Sustainable human development is defined as the process by which the range of opportunities and choices for people can increase and be expanded, while protecting those same opportunities and choices for future generations as well as the natural systems upon which all life depends. The expansion of peoples' choices is empowering when it increases their abilities to participate in the political, social, and economic forces of the society to free it from hunger, want and deprivation. This view of participation also means that there is mutual cooperation, and people work, interact and collaborate for development. That same expansion of choices and opportunities can also promote equity, including equity of access to services, goods, employment, income and technology. The needs of this generation must be met without compromising the right of future generations to realise their potential and enhance their capabilities free from poverty and deprivation.

Governance and sustainable human development can be seen to be indivisible. Governance in the *economic* setting has major implications for equity, poverty, and quality of life. Governance in the *political* setting is the process of decision-making to formulate policy and laws, which in turn has ramifications for security, equity, participation and cooperation.

Citizen-friendly Governance

Shorn of all jargon, for our model polity, good governance is citizen-friendly governance. The founding fathers of India's Republic built the entire edifice of her Constitution and democratic polity on the quintessential principle of sovereignty vesting in the people. Once freed from colonial rule, the people were expected to have ceased to be subjects of the foreign masters and become citizens of independent India. With the adoption of a democratic polity, the citizens were to function both as the rulers and the ruled. But, the transfer of power on the midnight of 14-15 August 1947 and our becoming a Republic on 26 January 1950 did not mean transfer of power to the people of India. Notwithstanding the significant progress and remarkable achievements of the nation on various fronts, the fact remains that the ordinary citizen of India is only very gradually beginning to feel the glow of freedom and the transfer of power to his/her hands.

The founding fathers of our Republic who gave us our Constitution were not oblivious of the imperatives of good governance for the success of Indian polity. Perhaps, the best blueprint for reforms needed to be urgently enforced is already contained in the 'principles' that Article 37 of the Constitution, ordained to be 'fundamental in the governance of the country'. Adherence to some of these fundamental principles of governance would require the state to secure:

- a social order for the promotion of the welfare of the people with social, economic and political justice for all (Article 38 [1]);
- minimisation of inequalities in income and elimination of inequalities in status, facilities and opportunities among individuals and groups of people (Article 38 [2]);
- right to adequate means of livelihood for all citizens—men and women equally (Article 39 [a]);
- opportunities and facilities for children to develop in a healthy manner and in conditions of freedom and dignity (Article 39 [f]);
- right to work, to education and to public assistance in cases of unemployment, old age, sickness, disablement etc. (Article 41);
- just and humane conditions of work and maternity relief (Article 42);
- a living wage for workers with conditions of work ensuring a decent standard of life and leisure (Article 43);
- childhood care and education to children (Article 45);
- raising the level of nutrition and the standard of living and to improve public health (Article 47);
- protection and improvement of the environment while safeguarding forests and wild life (Article 48A).

The source of many of our maladies lies in the disregard of the interests of the citizen. Civic sovereignty has got to be asserted and the citizen put at the centre of the political system and citizen-friendly governance brought about on a high priority basis. Above all, the citizens themselves have to realise their citizenship obligations and come forward to be active participants. Every citizen, in whatever position, has certain responsibilities towards fellow citizens.

In this connection, one also remembers the Blueprint of an 'Action Plan for Effective and Responsive Government' that came out of the Conference of the Chief Ministers of States in 1997. Only if it had been taken more seriously for implementation, things would have been very different today.

Citizenship Responsibilities

In a modern democracy, the role and responsibilities of a citizen are enormous. As the state in a democratic polity is the creation of citizens, it must afford them maximum opportunity of participating in the political system and of exercising not only rights but also their special responsibilities. Without them, a democratic polity will cease to function. In addition to requirements such as obedience to law and payment of taxes, which characterise all societies, democracy necessitates the citizens' active political participation and obligates the citizens to accept responsibilities. In a democratic polity, almost by definition, people are participants in the processes of governance. We, the citizens of India, must understand both the rights and the responsibilities that flow from our position as citizens. Unfortunately, we don't. The tasks of nation-building and economic development cannot succeed unless the citizens at large feel intimately involved, responsible and committed to contribute their mite in every way. To cast their votes and leave everything else to look after itself can be most suicidal for ourselves. Responsibility rests upon citizens to also exercise constant and organised vigilance over the conduct and activities of those elected to public offices.

Unfortunately, of late, there has been some rather disproportionate emphasis on the rights of citizens as against their duties, even though the traditions and temper of Indian thought through the ages laid greater emphasis on duties. The hope for building a united and integrated nation with dignity of the individual lies in the growth of institutions of civil society and the ability of us, the citizens of India, to rise above petty self-interests, identify the hard core of citizenship values enjoined by the Constitution and make a determined bid to work together to protect and promote them by contributing our mite. Every citizen must accept the position that as citizens all are equal, have the same rights and responsibilities and are entitled to equality before law without any discrimination. Each one of us must treat our fellow citizens as equals and must not discriminate between them on any grounds such as sex, religion, caste etc. Every citizen must enjoy the same fundamental rights of freedom of thought and expression, freedom of religion, freedom from exploitation etc. It follows that we must respect the freedom of all our fellow citizens and must do nothing which may result in personal exploitation of anyone.

The privilege of being citizens of the Republic of India makes adherence to citizenship values a matter of sacred obligation for all of us in whatever position. These values are rooted not only in our legal status as citizens but in the foundational norms which permeate the provisions of the Constitution. Citizens must respect citizenship values as these bring valuable rights and at the same time ordain required duties. As proud citizens we must realise that democratic way of life is the most civilised way because it is based on the dignity of every individual citizen. This also means that every citizen has to respect and protect the individual dignity of every other citizen.

Citizens voted to be in positions of power and governance must never forget that they are citizens first and always accountable, answerable and responsible to their fellow citizens at large. They must respect dissent, listen to complaints and never try to gag opposition. Certain standards of behaviour and discipline and of responsibility are essential to democratic ethos. Everyone must therefore imbibe a spirit of self-discipline and a sense of his or her responsibilities to his fellow citizens and society.

Right to vote under universal adult franchise gives to every citizen an opportunity to participate in the democratic process and to select the government. This right must be used not only to operate and defend democracy but also to make it more effective and meaningful. This is a tremendous responsibility. This right has to be exercised with meticulous care and careful thought, without fear or favour. Also, the more competent ones willing and in a position to be able to rise above petty self-interests and with a desire to sacrifice and to serve must come forward to more actively participate in the process as candidates and political activists. A full recognition of our democratic rights and responsibilities as citizens will automatically rid the system of corruption, criminalisation, money, muscle power and the like ills.

Universal adult franchise presumes an educated and wide awake citizenry. As Jawaharlal Nehru put it while speaking at a reception on 16 January 1955: 'Democracy only flourishes, as freedom only flourishes, when the responsibilities of freedom are understood and carried out. If the responsibilities are not understood and carried out, then freedom itself tends to slip away.' It is unfortunate that no systematic effort is being made to prepare the citizen for the discharge of this great responsibility.

Citizen and the State: The citizen needs to be restored to a position of pre-eminence at the centre of all state objectives and activities. Ways and means have to be found for reasserting the will of 'We, the People' over the organs of the state—Legislature, Executive and Judiciary—and restoring power to the citizen where it belongs. This would call for respect for citizenship values and emergence and strengthening of a civil society with an aware, awake, responsible and participant citizenry.

Constitutional democratic government has got to be limited government with state jurisdiction and role restricted to essentials. The state must function as a facilitator and infrastructure provider not only to business and industry but to the citizens at large and to the goal of improving their quality of life.

The citizen's role would have no meaning in a society where the citizens are not prepared to make sacrifices for protecting and promoting them or where they view them only in terms of their own interests and rights. The role of a citizen in the polity would imply all the rights, responsibilities and duties of citizens vis-a-vis fellow citizens, society at large and the state.

Exercise of the rights and responsibilities of freedom also involves a certain degree of tolerance of others and their opinions even when they strongly differ from ours. It requires the acceptance of unpalatable decisions taken democratically. The democratic method inevitably implies trying to understand each other's opinion, a certain give and take and a certain mutual adjustment.

It is only when we fulfill the basic duty of politics of restoring the power of the Constitution and its institutions back to their legitimate owners—the people—that things will begin to change. No reforms shall succeed and nothing can change unless the sovereign power is excercised by the people and they use it to discharge their citizenship responsibilities.

The most essential prerequisites for the success of any democratic polity are the willing interest, cooperation and participation of the politically aware, conscientious and intelligent citizenry in the affairs of the state, total respect for citizenship values, spirit of public service and dedication to the cause of democracy and freedom, protection of the civil and economic rights of fellow citizens and the full discharge of their duties and responsibilities by all citizens in whatever position.

Electoral and Political Party Reforms

The electoral and political party reforms considered necessary may be grouped under two major heads, viz. (1) practice and procedure related and (2) system related. Most of these do not call for any constitutional amendments. They are matters for political reforms which can be brought about through ordinary legislation or through rules, regulations and executive orders, provided that the political will gets crystallised with an agreement between political parties. The entire matter is in the legislative domain.

Election Commission: The superintendence, direction and control of election to the Houses of Parliament and State Legislatures and also to the office of the President and the Vice-President is vested in the three-member Election Commission. The Chief Election Commissioner and the two Election Commissioners are appointed by the President. It would be very desirable if this is done on the advice of a Committee consisting of the Presiding officers of the two Houses of Parliament. Ministers of Law and Justice, outgoing CEC and the leader of the largest party in the opposition in Lok Sabha.

The Election Commission's powers and jurisdiction are limited to holding elections and are specifically for the duration of the election process. While it is for the Commission to suggest the precise dates of election, it cannot defer elections indefinitely on grounds of law and order situation not being conducive to holding free and fair polls or such other things. The Commission's job is to hold elections and not to withhold them. In case of premature dissolution of Lok Sabha or a State Assembly, elections must be held as soon as possible and in any case, within six months of the date of dissolution of the House.

Representational Legitimacy: The most fundamental problem that presents itself in the present scheme of things is that of the representational legitimacy of the elected representatives of the people. As it is, the representative character of the representatives itself has become doubtful. Majority of them are elected by a minority of votes cast. In the three general elections before the 2014 elections, nearly 70% of them were elected by minority of votes cast. More votes were cast against each one of them than for them. There have been legislators elected who received less than 15 per cent of the votes cast.

The first-past-the-post system was adopted by us in the hope that it would help in building a more united Indian nation, that politics would grow on ideological basis and that a healthy two party system would develop. What happened was the reverse. The system proved to be terribly divisive. The society got more and more fragmented on caste, communal, linguistic and other narrower identity lines. It was naked vote bank politics that ruled the roost.

Clearly, if a candidate could win on less than one-third share of the votes polled, he did not need to generate a wider appeal. By making caste and community a factor in political power play, we made the divide even wider and deeper in Indian society and rendered it nearly impossible for Babasaheb Ambedkar's vision of a casteless and classless society ever coming true.

To ensure representational legitimacy to legislators within the existing system, it could be laid down that in order to be declared a winner, a candidate must secure a minimum of 50 per cent plus votes so that it becomes necessary for every winning candidate to woo more than his caste, community or narrow group vote bank and seek a wider consensus. If, in the first round, nobody gets over 50% then there should be a run-off contest the very next day or soon thereafter between the top two candidates.

Compulsory Voting: To increase the voting percentage and ensure wider participation, it is suggested by some that voting should be made compulsory. However, compulsion may be objected to on the ground of difficulties in implementation and the argument that the right not to vote is included in the right to vote. Also, it would be an infringement of an individual's freedom if someone is compelled to vote against his will. A better and more pragmatic alternative would be to make voting a fundamental citizenship duty in the Part IV A of the Constitution. Every voter should receive a certificate of voting. Certain incentives for voting and disincentives for not voting may be laid down. For example, it should be necessary to produce the certificate of voting for getting a passport, BPL Card, Ration Card, Driving License, IT rebate etc. These measures may easily take voting percentage to 90% or more without going for compulsory voting. An additional advantage in making voting a fundamental duty would be that the voter will realise that he is not conferring a favour on the candidate but exercising his duty as a citizen.

Frequency of Elections: No more a once-in-five-years affair, elections to some body or the other in one or the other part of the country have become an almost all-round-the-year activity entailing heavy expenditure and strain on security apparatus thereby adversely affecting the development agenda. As recommended by the National Commission to Review the Working of the Constitution, efforts should be made for simultaneous elections for all elective bodies all over the country once every five years.[1]

Independent Candidates: Something has got to be done to discourage independents in the Houses of State legislatures and Union Parliament and bring down their number by increasing the security deposits, disqualifying them for future elections if they get less than 5% of the votes polled and providing for their proposers and seconders being a certain number of Panchayat or Nagar Palika members.

Procedural Devices: In the area of procedural malpractices during election processes, the following need attention:

i. Foolproof method of preparing electoral rolls at the village and Nagar Palika or ward level and keeping them constantly updated. The same rolls to hold good for all direct elections from Panchayats to Parliament.

ii. Display of electoral rolls at post offices etc. in each Constituency Headquarters for public scrutiny.

iii. Authorising the Election Commission to take more stringent action in cases of electoral malpractices, and to take a decision with regard to countermanding the election or ordering repoll etc. and

iv. Security deposits of candidates securing less than 25% votes to be forfeited.

---

[1] See the chapter on 'Sumultaneous or Separate Electrons'

Role of Money Power: Cost of Elections

If the electoral process has to steer clear of tainted and motivated sources of funds, some of the following suggestions may need to be considered:

i. The cost of elections must be reduced. This can be done by changing the ground rules for electoral campaigns—partly by encouraging the use of electronic and digital technology to campaign at state cost and simultaneously by totally and effectively banning other overt and wasteful *tamashaas* (shows) of campaigning including the use of autos/buses to ferry people to election rallies . Wall writings, display of cut-outs, hoardings and banners, hoisting of flags (except at party offices, public meetings and other specified places), use of more than a specified number of vehicles for election campaign and for processions, announcements of publicity by more than a specified number of moving vehicles, holding of public meetings beyond the specified hours, display of posters at places other than those specified by the district/electoral authorities, should be banned.

ii. If possible, if not with immediate effect, then gradually, all elections from Panchayats to Parliament should be held simultaneously.

iii. No one should be allowed to contest from more than one constituency.

iv. Code of conduct should be made into a law and its violation should attract penal action.

v. Candidate must be required to clear all government dues and vacate unauthorised government accommodation etc. before being allowed to go to polls.

vi. A suitable law should be enacted, providing penalties against damaging or desecrating public or private property by candidates, political parties or the agents, through painting of slogans or erecting cut-outs and hoardings or putting banners and buntings.

vii. Legitimate sources for the essentially needed funds would have to be identified. Company and individual donations should be encouraged with higher limits placed on the maximum permissible amounts and liberal tax rebates must be allowed.

viii. In case the present ceilings are to be continued, they should be linked to the cost of living index so that they remain realistic. But, the expenditure incurred on a candidate's election by his friends, by the political party or by others should also be included while examining adherence to the ceiling. Full disclosure of the sources of election funds and audit of receipt and expenditure should be made compulsory.

Criminalisation: In the area of criminalisation of electoral processes and politicisation of crime, following suggestions deserve consideration:

i. *Disqualification of those charged with serious offences and derecognisiton of parties:* Once charges related to certain crimes have been framed by a court against a person, he should not be permitted to contest elections or continue as a member of any House unless cleared.

ii. *Speedy trial by special courts of cases involving candidates:* A potential candidate against whom charges have been framed by the police may take the matter to a special electoral court. This court would be obliged to enquire and take a decision in a strictly time-bound manner. Basically, this court may decide whether there is indeed a *prima facie* case justifying the framing of charges. If yes, the person should not be allowed to contest.

iii. The law should provide that whoever is convicted of any criminal offence by a court of law and sentenced to imprisonment for six months or more should be barred from contesting elections, for a period totalling the sentence imposed plus an additional six years.

iv. *Heinous Crimes:* Permanent disqualification for life of those convicted of heinous crimes.

v. *Caste and Communal Violence:* Statutory provision should be made prescribing imprisonment and disqualification for spreading caste or communal hatred during election campaigns.

vi. A question closely related to the criminalisation of politics is the issue of financing politics. For the last many years, a question that remains unanswered is regarding the financing of politics. For running a political party, for any political activity or for contesting any election to State Legislature or Parliament, tons of money is required. Almost everyone in politics needs it. Where is it to come from? Where does it come from? Nobody gives his hard earned, tax paid white money to parties or to politicians. Also, even black or tainted money can be expected only when one is part of the establishment as a Minister or a Member or is in a position to harm or help. And, elections are a tricky business. One has to prepare for the worst case scenario, particularly if one is a full-time professional politician or public man with no other known means of comfortable living to fall back upon.

While there are some excellent men and women of high calibre and great integrity in Indian political life today, the general, even though most unfortunate, perception seems to be that politics has ceased to be a vocation for sacrifice and service and has descended into being the most lucrative business with the highest ROI, for getting rich quickly. This problem is not peculiar to India. Even in the more advanced Western democracies there have been cases similar to ours. In UK, for example, payment of £1000 for a question resulted in the Nolan Committee Report and the introduction of the Register of Members' interests.

Almost all those elected to legislatures have to begin their legislative career with giving incorrect statements of election expenses. One may ask—if there is a general crisis of character in the nation as a whole in all walks of life and all professions, all-pervading devaluation of all values, if money, success and power, at whatever cost, become supreme concerns, can we blame only the legislators for all the ills? Is the problem not more fundamental calling for systemic rethinking and holistic reforms?

Political Parties

In the ultimate analysis, electoral reforms cannot be considered in isolation from other areas, in particular that of political parties. Although political parties were not mentioned in the Constitution until the fifty-second constitutional amendment enacted in 1985, the fact remains that representative democratic polity under the Constitution presumed a well-organised system of political parties.

Political parties are an important institution in any democratic polity. Both, the party or parties in power and those in opposition are essential to the functioning of a democratic government. It is for that very reason necessary that the parties themselves must be wedded to democratic principles and run democratically.

It is a common spectacle after every election that all the politics degenerates into purely personal struggles for Chief Ministership, Ministership or other lucrative offices with influence, status and power. No wonder people are beginning to lose faith in the system and in their representatives who are seen as not devoted to public service but engaged in seeking narrow personal ends of wielding power and amassing wealth with service to the people not being any part of their priorities. Representatives of the people losing the respect of the people should cause us the greatest worry if we are for preserving our hard earned freedom and democracy.

Concept of Opposition: The concept of official opposition in the parliamentary model is that of a part of the government in the wider sense. But in India, opposition has a tendency not to want to be a participant in the process and assume a share of responsibility. Every party, when in power behaves in a particular way and in quite a different way when in opposition. It would be most desirable that when in government, the party remembers that one day it may again be in opposition and when in opposition, it should be aware that it may have to assume the responsibilities of the ruling party tomorrow, and therefore, should behave today in the same way as it expects its opposition to behave. Thus, it is necessary for safeguarding freedom and democracy and their political institutions that the parties in power and those in opposition understand the delicate balance, accept each other's legitimacy and realise that they are not adversaries but partners with a common cause of serving the people.

In parliamentary polity, the main opposition has to be accepted and respected as a legitimate alternative and not to be shunned as an untouchable. It is in the mutual interest of major parties or national alliances to ensure that they remain the only viable alternative to each other. If we really believe in democracy and have faith in the people, no political party that gets the largest or the second largest number of elective seats and popular votes can be ignored or disregarded. It is dangerous for parliamentary polity to paint either of them as a villain. Also, it must be understood that the so-called regional parties are also national and equally patriotic in their perspective and that as partners in national alliances they can be as effective as any all-India party.

Law for Political Parties: Political parties should be institutionalised through a comprehensive legislation to govern and regulate their number and activities, lay down criteria for their registration and recognition as national or State level parties and their deregistration and/or derecognition in case of violation of norms laid down. The law should make it compulsory for the parties to maintain accounts of the receipt of funds and expenditure in a systematic and regular way. The accounts should also be compulsorily audited and made available to public for study and inspection. The proposed law should also provide for certain other matters like funding and democratic and clean internal functioning of parties. It should be laid down in law that no political party should sponsor or provide ticket to a candidate for contesting elections if he was convicted by any court for any criminal offence or if the courts had framed criminal charges against him. The law should specifically provide that if any party violated this provision, the candidate involved should be liable to be disqualified and the party deregistered and derecognised forthwith. If implemented, this would be obviously an effective check on criminals' increasing clout and control in political parties.

Regulating the Number of Parties: The number of parties registered with the Election Commission exceeds 1,800. Most of these do not participate in the electoral process and do not contest elections. Their registration is a cloak for driving some illegitimate benefits. Unless the number of political parties and/or alliances at the national and State levels is regulated by law, representational legitimacy of our legislators with a first-pass-the-post system cannot be assured. Also, no scheme of state funding can succeed. As such only recognised national parties and pre-poll alliances (ie. those that secure at least 10% of the votes cast) should be allotted common symbols to contest elections to Lok Sabha. State parties may be allowed common symbols to contest elections for State Legislatures and the Council of States (Rajya Sabha). This would, by prompting pre-poll alliances, automatically consolidate the vote and help in evolving some sort of federal parties or alliances providing more stable governments. There could be no difficulty in passing such a law in both Houses of Parliament because it is in the best interests of major parties.

Funding of Parties: Reform proposals in regard to political funding should revolve round (1) reducing costs, (2) better utilisation of funds, (3) curtailing influence peddling and political corruption, (4) strengthening public disclosure and transparency mechanisms with respect to the sources and the use of funds, (5) permitting higher corporate donations with higher limits and tax exemptions, (6) submission of false or incorrect returns bringing immediate derecognition of the party, and (7) bringing political parties under the RTI Act.

Seats for Women: Reservation by law should be made for at least 30 per cent of the organisational positions at various levels in every political party and the same percentage of party tickets for parliamentary and State legislature seats for women. Any failure to do so should hold a penalty for the party, that of losing recognition.

Training to Party Cadres: It is important that political parties in India realise the importance of imparting to their members necessary professional training in the modern techniques, tools and methods of political management, legislative functioning, leadership roles etc.

Parliamentary Reforms

As a first step, processes, control mechanisms, debating and decision-making procedures would have to be revamped and made faster. Floor management techniques would have to be professionalised at the level of whips, parliamentary officials and the Presiding Officers.

Building a better image of Parliament: Parliament connects the people and the government. It is necessary to establish a new rapport between the people and the Parliament. The two must be brought closer to each other. Parliament belongs to the people. It is ordinary people who have to be enabled to feel that they are participants in the decision-making and legislative processes, and that through Parliament their voice can reach the Government and that it counts. Parliament must have access to public opinion and the public must have access to the Parliament.

The people should know what their representatives are doing or not doing for them. Media—electronic and print—must be used effectively to highlight important issues for legislatures and legislators and to pursue and enforce their accountability to the people at large.

It is necessary that the press and public relations in Parliament are suitably reoriented and developed as a highly specialised and dynamic service, charged with the responsibility *inter alia* of educating public opinion in regard to the Parliament and its activities. Arrangements should be made for attending to enquiries from the public, publicising the telephone numbers and addresses from which information about Parliament and its activities may be sought while providing some public computer terminals and a more meaningful and communicative internet website from which any citizen can hope to get relevant information he may need regarding the Parliament and its activities, including for example, the status of pending legislation.

Improving the Conduct of Members: The already existing Code of

Conduct and Guidelines first circulated as early as in 1952 deserve to be observed. There is a strong need for MPs to invigilate themselves to uphold norms of parliamentary behaviour within and outside the Houses of Parliament.

Improving information supply: Parliament must build its own independent national information reservoir with a network of feeding and retrieval points. Developing an independent and transparent infrastructure of information support system in Parliament would have a profound effect on revitalising and transforming the institution of Parliament.

Nodal Standing Committee on Economy: Immediate steps should be taken to set up a Nodal Standing Committee on national economy, with specific subject-oriented study groups aided by experts and concerned with economic policy formulation and implementation.

Planning Legislation and Improving its Quality: Our legislation has often been criticised for hasty drafting and for its being rushed through Parliament in an *ad hoc* and haphazard manner. There is need for a dynamic—not mechanical—approach to legislative engineering and systematic programming of laws that may be proposed for enactment over a period of time. This can be done by (i) streamlining the functions of the Parliamentary and Legal Affairs Committee of the Cabinet; (ii) making greater use of the Law Commission; (iii) setting up a new Legislation Committee of Parliament to oversee and coordinate legislative planning; and (iv) referring all Bills to the Departmental Standing Committees for consideration and scrutiny, consulting concerned interest groups and finalisation of the 'second reading stage' in the relaxed atmosphere of Committees aided by experts, thereby reducing the burden of the House without impinging on any of its rights and improving the quality of drafting and content of legislation.

Setting up a Constitution Committee: Instead of the Constitution Amendments being presented to Parliament like ordinary pieces of legislation in the form of Bills for introduction, sometimes at very short notice, it would be desirable if Parliament is associated right from the initial stages of formulation of proposals for constitutional reform, ie. the actual drafting of a Constitution Amendment Bill may be taken up only after the principles involved have been thrashed out in a parliamentary forum and subjected to appropriate prior scrutiny by the constituent power. The proposed involvement of Parliament and a prior scrutiny can be achieved through the device of a Constitution Committee of Parliament. As an alternative, after a Constitution Amendment Bill has been formulated but before it has been introduced, it may be subjected to a prior scrutiny of the 'Constitution Committee'. If this is done, even the government will be saved many an embarrassment.

Departmental Committees and Improving Accountability: If the Subject/Ministry-based Standing Committees have to have real meaning and fulfill the purposes for which they were conceived and not to become a mere part that spoils the system and distribution of perks and benefits, they should embrace the entire spectrum of administration for an in-depth and continuous study.

Codifying Parliamentary Privileges: As a great institution, the Parliament should be able to take in its stride a great deal of the criticism and adverse comments against it. Privileges of Parliament are intended to be privileges enjoyed by Parliament on behalf of the people, to enable members to function freely and fearlessly, in the interest of the people. These privileges should not be allowed to become rights against the people. Time is now ripe for removing the existing uncertainty and anxiety of the press and the people through early codification.

Procedural Reforms: Rules of Procedure and Conduct of Business are meant for guidance, for regulating the business of the House and for facilitating the orderly expression of Members' views. Procedures must keep pace with the changing needs of the national economy, composition of Membership and the prevailing mood of the Members.

No single reform can provide a miracle cure. Also, parliamentary reforms cannot be effected in a hurry. We must proceed with care and caution and make a beginning by setting up a Parliamentary Reforms Commission or a 'Study of Parliament Group' outside Parliament as was done in the UK. before the comprehensive procedural reforms in the 1970s. Finally, of course, the Rules Committee or a Special Procedure Committee of the concerned House should examine all the reform proposals and report to the House on the matter.

Government

Electing the Leader of the House (PM/CM): If no party or pre-election alliance of parties secures a clear majority of seats in Lok Sabha or in any of the State Assemblies and the largest single party is unable to promise a stable government, the President or Governor, as the case may be, should ask the House to elect its leader just as it elects its Speaker. The person so elected may be appointed the Prime Minister/ Chief Minister. This can be done by the President/Governor sending a message to the House under the existing Article 86(2)/175(2).

When the simple question is that of determining the majority, the safest and the simplest course would be to hold an election on the floor of the House. It would also not be necessary then to seek a vote of confidence as, in effect, it would have been obtained in advance of the appointment through the process of election by the House itself. This would require neither an amendment of the Constitution nor of any law.

Vote of No Confidence: To ensure that the government so constituted will last for a reasonable period, once the Prime Minister/ Chief Minister is appointed and the government (Council of Ministers) duly constituted, it should be removable only by a constructive vote of no-confidence passed by a special majority. Under this scheme, the same motion which expresses lack of confidence in the Council of Ministers headed by 'A', should also contain the name of the proposed successor, 'B'. This will mean that there will be continuity in government and if the motion is passed, another leader will immediately take over. This will greatly reduce, if not completely eliminate, chances of getting into a situation where some forces join to bring down a government but are unable to provide an alternative, thereby necessitating frequent elections.

Public Administration

To make the administration citizen-friendly, mechanisms have to be developed for citizens' grievance ventilation and redressal. Politicisation of bureaucracy and interference of administration in the lives of citizens will have to end. Questions of appointment, promotion, transfer of civil servants and their interface with Ministers etc. have to be looked into, and healthy norms of accountability need to be established through necessary administrative reforms. Also, questions that deserve to be carefully considered include:

i. First and foremost, there has to be a change in the behavior and attitude of the civil servants. The civil servant must be trained to serve the people, inculcate a work culture and a spirit of efficiency and excellence. Also, we must rid the services of casteism, corruption and politicisation. Above a certain level—say the Joint Secretary level—all posts should be open for recruitment from a wide variety of sources including the open market. Officials, before starting their career, in addition to the taking of an oath of loyalty to the Constitution, should swear to abide by the basic principles of good governance including those of transparency and accountability. The administrative structure and systems have to be consciously redesigned. The specialist should not be required to play second fiddle to the generalist at the top.

ii. Denial of timely service to the public must be specifically made a serious offence of misconduct and subjected to summary and exemplary punishment. We must ensure better accountability procedures by curbing the tendency of having multiplicity of hierarchical levels, diffusion of responsibility and passing the buck. Where public servants cause loss to the state by their *mala fide* actions or omissions, they should be made liable to make good the loss caused and, in addition, pay damages. A more stringent law should be enacted to provide for forfeiture of the benami property of corrupt public servants as well as non-public servants. The Prevention of Corruption Act, 1988, should be amended to provide for confiscation of the property of a public servant who is found to be in possession of property disproportionate to his/her known sources of income and is convicted for the said offence.

iii. There is need to review the prescribed procedures for inquiries, punishments, appeals etc. to shorten their duration and to reduce the possibility of interlocutory delays or, more than one appeal. Constitutional safeguards to services under Article 311 may need reconsideration to ensure greater accountability.

iv. Supervision and inspection must be prescribed as primary duties of the higher echelons and negligence in this matter made a black mark for the purpose of performance evaluation and promotion. The reformed system should provide effective ways of prompt decision-making, quick disposal and avoidance of delays, misuse of discretion and attendant corruption.

v. A prominently displayed and widely published Citizens' Charter may be the principal declaratory mission statement on behalf of each department and office having dealings with the public. Such a declaration should list the services that are lawfully available, the charges to be paid if any, the time usually taken (same day in most cases), and it should further specify the point at which delays or harassment can be reported, or queries as to status of an application made.

(Some departments/offices in the States as also at the Union government level have come up with such charters but generally the progress has been slow. Also, adherence remains weak and the red tape is still strong. Also, all others, particularly those with direct public dealings need to issue and publicise their charters for the citizens.)

vi. At the points at which reports of crime, or of fear for safety of person or property are to be made, there must be a very clear enunciation of the rights of the complainant and, as a corollary, the rights of an accused person.

vii. The basic requirements for the success of the above prescriptions are:

   a. There should be true and effective decentralisation of powers and decision making, clear assignment of responsibility, decentralised decision-making and delegation of authority, transparency in administration and, bringing almost all rule-based non-discretionary powers for granting citizen services, down to the very cutting edge. In other words, the citizen should have to go to only one point where he would hand in his request and get the service he requires. Right to Information has been a great help but it has failed to usher in many expected benefits, such as speedy disposal of cases, minimising manipulative and dilatory tactics of the babudom, and, last but most importantly, putting a considerable check on graft and corruption.

   b. Full use of all the new and emerging technologies for more efficient governance. For every office having a large number of public dealings, schemes for total computerisation should be set in motion. Every citizen request (and report), should be entered into the system on receipt, and automatically go into a central data bank, as should the date of issue of sanction, permit, etc. Once the computerised system is established, there should be a central point of enquiry where, on giving particulars about a request or case, the reception desk should itself access the data bank on its computer, get a response about the status of the citizen's request, and give the citizen a printout with an indication about the time that would be required for fulfilling his request.

viii. The elimination of out-of-date and unnecessary laws is said to be already in process. This should be completed as quickly as possible. The same applies to redundant, or unnecessarily complex rules, regulations and forms so as to simplify matters for the citizen.

ix. Publication and printing of Acts, rules and regulations and guidelines for the citizen must be kept up-to-date and their availability singly should be an obligatory service of the government.

x. There is a need for rationalisation and drastic downsizing of the bureaucracy, cutting down the non-governmental functions of government and reducing the overall costs of administration at every level,

xi. It should be obligatory for bureaucrats at all levels to make a declaration of all assets and liabilities of self, spouse and dependents—declaration to be available to citizens on demand,

xii. It may be advisable to consider establishment of a Civil Service Board entrusted with transfers and promotions and of disciplinary matters affecting a person serving under the government.

xiii. The 1861 Police Act and old Police Manuals should be replaced. The Police Commission and Vohra Committee reports should be considered for early implementation. Police should be provided modern training and equipment, insulated from political interference and its senior officers held accountable for any lapses by the force. Those in sensitive posts should be assured a fixed tenure and law and order cadre, investigation branch, armed police and traffic police should all be separate structures. To strengthen the criminal justice system, Criminal Procedure Code and Evidence Act should be amended. Public grievance cells should supplement the vigilance cells within the Police Department.

So far as the administrative services at all levels are concerned, it is most essential that they move out of the colonial mind set of being the masters and rulers and assume the role of servants of the people to provide clean, transparent, citizen-friendly governance to all without any discrimination.

Union-State Relations

The federal structure in India has come to stay and needs to be strengthened. The central problem is not of Union-State relations now but of greater decentralisation of economic and political powers to lower and lower levels, with several tiers of functioning and people at the grassroots having real power, with the system growing up from there rather than coming down from above level.

Decentralisation: The only way to strengthen the Union is to make it lose its extra weight, to shed its monopoly of power in all areas and concentrate on essentials. With economic liberalisation must come decentralisation of political power and management. For example, whatever can be done by the local grassroots institutions like the village panchayats or municipalities, should be left entirely in their hands. This would be in keeping with what is now called the 'subsidiarity principle'. Government at a higher tier should have no power to remove or supersede a duly-elected government at a lower tier.

If we are really serious about providing multi-level governance and taking power to the doorsteps of the people at the grassroots level, the Constitution should clearly provide for distribution of powers between the Union, the States and the local governments of Panchayats and Nagar Palikas by suitably amending Articles 245, 246 and other relevant articles and the Seventh Schedule. It will certainly do no violence to the basic structure or features of the Constitution or to the parliamentary system. It has the potential to powerfully contribute to the needs of good governance and development.

Time has come for a comprehensive review of Union/State relations and Local Governance institutions. There can be no single universally applicable model. India's needs of stability, security and development demand a new marriage between unitary and federal polity so that both stability of the system and responsibility to the people are ensured. The new federalism should build a united nation of a large number of autonomies—not subordinates or subsidiaries—as federal partners at various levels. It would be a 'federal union' with multiple tiers of governance and sharing of powers from the grassroots of Panchayats to Parliament.

i. We should de-link the ethnic aspirations from political demands for separate states. On principle, smaller States may be better for good governance due to growing populations. A larger number of States may strengthen the Union. In some cases, instead of creating new States, sub-State and supra state structures may be created. Combined with strong zonal councils, this would lead to greater stability, more accountability, stronger Union and better administered, more developed or fast-developing States.
ii. Norms for Governor's appointments need revamping. Sarkaria Commission recommendations should be examined and implemented.
iii. Problems regarding Article 356 are only due to improper operation and interpretation of Articles 256, 257, 355, 356 and 365. These need to be read together under article 355. Without imposing President's Rule under Article 356, *suo motu* deployment of central para-military forces should be entirely in order.
iv. With liberalising economy, central control may get irrelevant. Income tax, corporation tax and indirect taxes can be moved to the concurrent list to facilitate harmonisation of taxes and a full VAT.
v. With a large number of smaller States and a four-tier system of governance, it may be possible to involve various groups in governance more closely and this may make the Union stronger and the nation more integrated, emotionally and culturally. Distribution of powers should be so designed that only the

most essential or minimum necessary powers are assigned to each higher level. For example, whatever can be done by institutions like the Village Panchayats or Municipalities, should be left entirely in their hands. Efficient bureaucracy cannot be a substitute for democratic decentralised government.

vi. Eleventh and Twelfth Schedule should be made mandatory and merged into a common list.

vii. In the North-East States, illegal migration must be checked. Local traditional institutions of government need to be modernised with gender justice for women and used as institutions of governance. Overlapping jurisdiction of State government, Autonomous District Councils (ADCs) and traditional system of governance and the problems thereof must be removed and jurisdictions of each clearly defined. Greater autonomy should be provided to ADCs by amending the Sixth Schedule. Problems with regard to participation of non-tribals in ADCs need to be addressed. Problems in judicial administration due to multiple overlapping jurisdictions of the traditional institutions, ADCs and the subordinate judiciary should be resolved and the emerging conflict between human rights and tribal rights and between conservation laws and tribal rights should be analysed and resolved.

Corruption

Corruption poses a serious challenge to development. In the political realm, it undermines democracy and good governance by flouting or even subverting formal processes. Corruption in elections and in legislative bodies reduces accountability and distorts representation in policymaking; corruption in the judiciary compromises the rule of law; and corruption in public administration results in the unfair provision of services. More generally, corruption erodes the institutional capacity of government as procedures are disregarded, resources are siphoned off, and public offices are bought and sold. At the same time, corruption undermines the legitimacy of government and such democratic values as trust and tolerance.

There is nothing entirely new in the corrupt conduct of public servants. Kautilya mentions forty ways of embezzlement of public funds.* What is currently talked about as corruption may be defined simply as lack of public and private morality and probity and of a sense of honesty and integrity. It is the abuse of public resources or position for private gain. Corruption may involve receiving illegitimate personal gratification for extending to another person illegitimate private benefit. Who can say with any honesty that even educational institutions, the academia or the media function with greater transparency, that the intellectuals do not sell themselves for project grants, foreign trips and the like or that any class can boast of better integrity or is inflicted with less corruption. Corruption has literally entered every walk of life, every profession and every area of activity. We all are guilty.

Corruption, delays, and harassment at lower levels of public dealing need to be attended to and remedied. Potent mechanisms have to be developed for citizens' grievance ventilation and redressal. Healthy norms of accountability of administrators directly to the people would have to be established through necessary administrative reforms. At present, the system is not even accessible to the ordinary citizen. As somebody said, the administrators—the officers and petty *babus*—treat the citizens as dirt.

Today, clean and quality governance has become a categorical imperative for our very survival as a democracy and a free nation. The most important task is that of cleansing the system and making the government and the administration really ordinary citizen-friendly. In the ultimate analysis, this can happen only if power is accepted, as Gandhi said, as a trust and an opportunity of service and politics and public administration themselves are viewed as a mission for sacrifice and service.

* See chapter 7

If corruption ceases to pay or yield rich dividends and if punishment becomes certain, swift, deterrent and really hurtful, corruption will certainly come down.[1]

Citizen and the Administration: If there is one area that affects the daily life of the citizen most vitally, it is where he or she has to come in direct contact with the administration at the ground level. Unfortunately, public administration in India, in its tenor and approach has largely continued to be colonial, one that suited the ethos and needs of the imperial masters and centralised authority. Far from being treated as the masters, the citizens are still treated as subjects and worse. The administrators or bureaucrats, instead of being at the service of the people, continue the colonial *mai-baap*[2] model.

In a democratic polity, the administration must be run by the citizens for the citizens. Corruption, delays and harassment at levels of public dealing need to be attended to and remedied on a high priority basis. No one should forget that the highest functionaries of the state—in the Executive, Legislature and Judiciary—are all appointed or voted to positions of power and governance as the servants of the people. They are citizens first and always accountable, answerable and responsible to their fellow citizens at large.

The elected rulers, viz the Ministers and the legislators and the administrators, have to be conscious not only of the fundamental duties of citizens at large but also of their own duties as citizens. It is one of their most fundamental constitutional obligations to be all the time aware of the fundamental rights of the citizens under the Constitution. For, wherever an obligation is cast on the 'state', it is for the citizens in positions of authority to implement it. Ultimately, the people will have to wake up and rise and armed with a full realisation of their responsibilities, they will have to assert their inherent sovereign powers to put the citizen at the centre of the political system and to bring about a citizen-friendly governance on a high priority basis.

---

[1] See chapter 10

[2] mother-father, a figurative usage

For this, of all the reforms urgently needed, highest priority should be accorded to electoral and political party reforms and these also we can begin by providing for greater representational legitimacy, simultaneous elections for Panchayats to Parliament, voting becoming a fundamental citizenship duty and enactment of a law for political parties.

The People: In a democracy, the real and the ultimate masters are the people, the citizens. Not enough has been done to educate or orient them to their responsibilities as voters and participants in the democratic process. There is no reason why citizens' vigilance groups and committees should not come up at every level and on a wide scale. The citizens need to be educated in and for democracy and constitutionalism and in the matter of their own citizenship obligations in a representative, participatory democratic polity. For, ultimately the responsibility to save freedom and democracy is that of 'We, the People of India'.

Nations are made only when people rise above their narrow self interests and are prepared to make sacrifices for their fellow citizens. Instead of devoting time to individual or group demands, we have to learn to give to the nation the maximum we can. Unless we, the citizens of India at large, are vigilant and conscious of our obligations as citizens, there is no reason why freedom and democracy should continue forever.

Democratic Governance

Space for the Underprivileged

OUR FOUNDING fathers resolved that 'We, the people of India', constitute ourselves into a Sovereign Democratic Republic, where all sovereign powers were vested in the people with no superior, internal or external, and where the people were their own masters and governed themselves through their representatives under a system they chose.

Basic postulates of a democratic order were that irrespective of religion, caste, creed, colour or sex and irrespective of the level of economic, educational or professional background, all citizens were equal before the law, all were entitled to be accorded equal protection by laws enacted by the State and there was no privileged class. Democratic polity also implied a faith that the people—whatever the state of development—were capable of understanding their best interests and taking their own decisions. Democracy substitutes methods of deliberation, debate and discussion for violent strife. In the struggle for power, the device of vote replaces use of force. Ballot substitutes the bullet. Also, democratic polity allows legitimate dissent and opposition to grow and prosper and even emerge as an alternative power centre to take over the reins of government constitutionally and peacefully. Every democratic system recognises the primacy of the will of the people. Behind every action of the executive or the legislative organ of the State, there is the will of the people which is the ultimate and final source of all authority. A democratic government has to function in accordance with the laws and with a full sense of accountability to the people through their representatives elected at periodic elections. The variant of democratic system chosen for us by the framers of our Constitution is that of representative parliamentary democracy where the Legislature and the Executive are not separate centres of power. They intermingle and merge. The executive government (Council of Ministers) comes out of Parliament, remains part of it and responsible to the House consisting of directly elected representatives of the people.

The biggest revolution after independence was the adoption of universal adult franchise. In the context of appalling poverty and illiteracy, it was an act of faith to give the right to vote to every adult citizen. The citizens choose their representatives to act in their interest. Problems arise when the representatives tend to act in their own narrow selfish interest instead of serving the interests of the people. Therefore, in recent decades, attention in the academia and among political activists has been focused on making representative democracy more and more participatory by direct involvement of citizens in matters of people's concerns. This is sometimes spoken of as empowerment of the people. Its main objective is that in matters affecting their lives directly, the ordinary people should come to have a greater say and a decisive voice. Participatory democracy is being considered more and more as not merely desirable but necessary. Under conditions of globalisation, where nation-level institutions of representation are being subordinated to hegemonic global power with the structure of political and economic decision-making more remote and alienated from people, the politics of participatory democracy has acquired a new relevance. Being a variant of participatory democracy, grassroots democracy is often identified with the struggle for empowerment and various micro movements brought about at the grassroots levels. It implies participation of the people in defining development goals and devising means to achieve them.

If after sixty-eight years of democratic government, we are talking about empowerment of the people, transfer of power to the people and of decentralisation of power to the grassroots, it is a clear admission of the fact that so far power was wrongfully centralised or that those in government were unlawful usurpers of the power and rights of the people and failed to provide democratic governance.

Concept of good governance evolved from the civil society's critical involvement with efforts to make representative democracy more meaningful and participatory, particularly with reference to what came to be called the underprivileged and marginalised sections of society. Governance and sustainable human development can be seen to be indivisible. Governance in the *economic* setting has major implications for equity, poverty, and quality of life. The needs of this generation must be met without compromising the right of future generations to realise their potential and enhance their capabilities that are free from poverty and the evil of deprivation.

Democratic government does not guarantee good governance. But, good governance is necessarily democratic governance and has, almost by definition, space for voice of the poor—the underprivileged, marginalised and deprived sections of society.

Among the foundational objectives of our polity, the founding fathers accorded the highest place to justice. The Preamble to the Constitution spoke of the resolve to secure 'Justice, social, economic and political' to 'all its citizens'. The rights of the common man were sought to be protected by an independent judiciary, provision of judicial review of legislation and validating of all laws subject to fundamental rights and assigning to the individual the right to move the highest court for the protection of one's constitutional rights under part III of the Constitution on Fundamental Rights was to be given.

Article 13 prohibits making of laws that are inconsistent with Fundamental Rights. Article 14 ordains the state not to deny to *any person* equality before the law and equal protection of laws. Article 21 guarantees rights to life and liberty which have been interpreted by the Supreme Court to include the right to live with dignity, right to education, the right to work and right to one's reputation. Article 22(1) *inter alia* lays down right to consult and to be defended by a legal practitioner of one's choice.

The Supreme Court had declared that the right to life under article 21 and right to equality before law under Article 14 included the right to legal aid. The court underlined the importance of access to justice to all citizens—more particularly to the poor and the marginalised—as an essential characteristic of democratic polity. It constituted itself into the supreme defender of the rights of the people and decided to extend its power to do justice in matters of public interest by entertaining Public Interest Litigation and providing access to justice to millions of the underprivileged who are unable to seek justice.

It was realised early in the history of independent India that while in theory access to justice and enforcement of fundamental human, rights were made equally available to all, the hard ground reality was that the vast majority of the poor, downtrodden, deprived, depressed, marginalised and the underprivileged, the women and the children were not able to seek or obtain either justice or enforcement of their fundamental rights. They suffered from ignorance and lack of financial means and legal assistance.

Considerable material was available in the United States and other countries in the West on Law and Society and on the commitment of democratic governance institutions in governmental and non-governmental sectors to resolve the problems of the poor and the underprivileged through access to law and justice mechanisms. While studying the material on the needs of legal assistance to the poor and the underprivileged in the affluent countries of the West, one is struck by the fact that their problem is of a small minority of the disadvantaged while in India it is the problem of the vast majority of people who are poor, illiterate and marginalized. Justice Brennan of the US Supreme Court said:

> Nothing rankles more in the human heart than a brooding sense of injustice. Illness we can put up with. But injustice makes us want to pull things down. When only the rich can enjoy the law, as a doubtful luxury, and the poor, who need it most, cannot have it because its expense puts it beyond their reach, the threat to the continued existence of a free democracy is not imaginary but very real, because democracy's very life depends upon making the machinery of justice so effective that every citizen shall believe in and benefit by its impartiality and fairness.

Justice Gajendragadkar had spoken of Indian democracy realising that 'the problem which concerns an overwhelmingly large number of its citizens cannot be successfully met unless it wisely uses its mighty weapon of law'—to provide equality of opportunity and economic justice to all citizens. However, Justice Gajendragadkar also warned us that mere passing of well-meaning laws could not be deemed to be a panacea. It was most generally believed in India, and not without legitimate foundations, that despite all the constitutional provisions of fundamental rights of non-discrimination and equality before law, the system worked unequally. The poor were unable to reach the courts and if they did, no justice could be expected when adversaries in the judicial process were not on equal footing.

In 1976, the Constitution was amended by the 42nd Amendment Act *inter alia* to include new Article 39A that obligates the state to ensure that the legal system promotes justice on the basis of equal opportunity and, in particular, to provide free legal aid by suitable legislation or schemes, to ensure that opportunities for securing justice are not denied to any citizen by reason of economic or other disabilities. A Legal Services Authorities Act, 1987, came after a decade of the constitutional amendment. Under the Act, members of SC/ST, women, children, industrial workers, persons in custody, poor, disabled and victims of human trafficking or of disasters are entitled to free legal aid. Under the Act, the government set up a Legal Services Authority at the Centre, State, District and Taluka levels. Legal Aid Committees were set up at the level of the Supreme Court and the High Courts. The Act gave statutory sanction to Lok Adalats. Also, under the PC sec 89, devices of mediation, conciliation, arbitration, Lok Adalats and judicial settlements are increasingly likely to be used for resolution of civil disputes thereby helping the poor and underprivileged to access justice without high costs and delays. Similarly, CrPC now provides for plea bargaining in certain criminal cases.

As part of its creative jurisprudence, the Supreme Court has assumed the responsibility of intervening *inter alia* in situations where the legislature and/or the executive fail to perform their duty, in particular, when they fail to protect the basic rights of the citizens like the right to live a decent life in healthy surroundings or to provide an honest, efficient and just system of laws and administration. What has come to be called 'Judicial Activism' was born as a corrective to inaction or failure of the executive and the legislature to provide clean, competent and citizen-friendly governance. Judicial activism in India, very largely, had its source in the introduction of Public Interest Litigation (PIL). In the beginning, the application of PIL was confined only to improving the lot of the disadvantaged sections of the society who, by reason of their poverty and ignorance, were not in a position to seek justice from the courts and, therefore, any member of the public was permitted to maintain an application for appropriate directions. The innovative judicial approach to 'Public Interest Litigation' came handy in cases of acute social injustice, economic exploitation, denial of human rights, corruption and other offences against public interest.

The 73rd and 74th Amendments to the Constitution constituted a milestone in the process of establishing decentralised democratic administration through local bodies and taking administration to the doorsteps of the people to ensure economic and social justice. The important thing was that the Panchayats were to be directly elected by the people like the Lok Sabha and State Assemblies. After the 73rd and 74th Constitution Amendments, there was some effort to give more space, voice, powers and responsibilities to local self-governing institutions through poverty alleviation, rural development and employment generation programmes more particularly directed towards the underprivileged. Panchayati Raj institutions were provided a substantial role in several programmes.

There was undoubtedly an impressive array of programmes to address the interests and needs of the underprivileged. On the whole, we can certainly take great pride in asserting

- that we have successfully worked the democratic system for sixty-eight years. As many as 16 general elections to Lok Sabha and many more to States Assemblies—largely accepted to be free and fair—have been held,
- that since the establishment of the Sovereign Democratic Republic under the Constitution, representative parliamentary democracy has remained vibrant and functional, and
- that there is enough to showcase the long strides from representative to participatory democracy and to democratic governance with considerable space to include the voice and interests of the underprivileged.

The new BJP led Government under the leadership of Narendra Modi has taken some fresh initiatives and tried to revisit and refurbish some of the earlier schemes to ensure that the thus far deprived and backward sections of the society benefit and are enabled to move upwards. Some of the new pro-poor social security schemes operational in favour of the poor are:

1. ***Atal Pension Yojana:*** All bank account holders aged between 18 to 40 years, by paying Rs 42 to 210 per month, can avail a monthly pension of Rs 1000 to 5000 from the age of 60 years.
2. ***Pradhan Mantri Jeevan Jyoti Bima Yojana:*** All bank holders aged between 18 to 50 years can get life insurance for Rs 2 lakhs on payment of only Rs 330 a year (premium deductable from the SB Account) ie. less than 1 rupee a day, with the insurance amount (2 lakh) payable to the family.
3. ***Pradhan Mantri Suraksha Yojana:*** All bank account holders aged between 18 and 70 years entitled to accident insurance cover of Rs 2 lakh for an annual payment of just Rs 12. Insurance covers death and permanent disability due to accident.

There is, however, another side to the picture. There is a wide gulf between the conceptual and the factual, between the rhetoric and the real. On principle, in a democratic republic, there is no place for any privileged class. But, in reality, things are different.

Notwithstanding the lofty norms of democratic governance, the poor, underprivileged people to not have the means to assert their legitimate authority against their exploiters and usurpers. Also, a question that can no longer be ignored is that of determining who is really underprivileged? In fact, the term 'underprivileged' seems to assume the legitimacy of a 'privileged' class while our democratic republican principles do not provide space for any privileged class. Also, how to ensure that the stigma of being the depressed and underprivileged does not become a matter of privileged status sought in perpetuity, or a vested interest is not created in permanently remaining maimed and disabled needing the support of crutches for all times. Ambedkar stood for a casteless society and was opposed to the stigma of depressed or Dalit becoming permanent.

The large number of poverty alleviation programmes and projects have consumed a sizeable portion of the national and State budgets but the results on the ground have been most disappointing. Many of the pro-poor programmes in favour of the poor were totally meaningless and actually often turned out to be anti-poor.

The really poor and deprived have hardly benefited from relief funds released in their names or from poverty alleviation programmes. Even where some benefits did reach them, most of it was grabbed by the privileged amongst them.

Under the camoflage of the slogans of one world and a global village, ordinary citizens instead of being the masters in a democratic polity were increasingly reduced to being mere consumers of goods and services. The result was a tremendous erosion in democratic rights and freedoms of the individual *vis a vis* the organs of the state, substantially reducing the space for the voice of the poor and the underprivileged. In the words of the former President KR Narayanan:

> We find that justice—social, economic and political—remains an unrealized dream for millions of our fellow citizens. The benefits of our economic growth are yet to reach them. We have one of the world's largest reservoirs of technical personnel, but also the world's largest number of illiterates, the world's largest middle class, but also the largest number of people below the poverty line, and the largest number of children suffering from malnutrition. Our giant factories rise out of squalor, our satellites shoot up from the midst of the hovels of the poor. Not surprisingly, there is sullen resentment among the masses against their condition erupting often in violent forms in several parts of the country. Tragically, the growth in our economy has not been uniform. It has been accompanied by great regional and social inequalities. Many a social upheaval can be traced to the neglect of the lowest of society, whose discontent moves towards the path of violence.

Democracy implies attention to the development and well-being of the poorest of the poor citizens of the nation. It must provide to the most marginalized and deprived sections of society equality of opportunity and the right to live with dignity and in freedom from want and fear. In the year 2000, the UN General Assembly set some Millennium Development Goals (MDGs). These included:

- Eradication of extreme poverty and hunger
- Achieving universal primary education
- Promotion of gender equality and empowerment of women
- Reduction in child mortality
- Improvement of maternal health
- Combating HIV/AIDS, Malaria etc.

The year 2015 was stipulated as the target for achieving these goals. Now, in 2018, when others are pursuing Sustanable Development Goals Agenda 2030, India is far behind the others in achieving any of these goals. Economic liberalisation and freedom to market forces has led to erosion of the workers' rights and to competitive consumerism with no thought given to the need for sustainable levels of consumption. The truth was that during the decade 2005-2014 unemployment increased, draughts and floods continued. While the granaries might have been full, the poor continued to die of starvation or commit suicides in increasing numbers. The number of landless labourers increased. Nobody talked of land reforms. The chief beneficiaries of various subsidies on fertilisars, diesel, seeds etc. were the big land owners. More and more agricultural land was being acquired by the land mafia for setting up industries, building shopping Malls, industrial townships, fancy housing complexes and tourist resorts. The poor and the deprived were the worst sufferers. The 73rd and 74th Amendment Acts failed to transfer real power to the grassroots in many of the States with the MPs and MLAs treating the new emerging leadership—particularly from the otherwise marginalised sections like women and SC/STs—as rival centres posing threats to their leadership.

Local matters must be left to be handled at local levels by the representatives of the people elected to the local bodies. Also, executive functions have to be left to executive agencies at concerned levels. The entirely unconstitutional Schemes like the MP and MLA LADS—Local Area Development Schemes with some hundreds of thousands of crores of public money involved each year—are an affront to the constitutional principles of distribution of powers between the Union and the States and separation of executive and legislative functions. Also, these schemes make the financially bankrupt PRIs look insignificant and powerless with each MP and MLA having large funds at his disposal (Rs 5 crore per year for each MP) for spending on local area schemes which are most legitimately the concern of PRIs under the 73rd and 74th Amendments.

To preserve 'India, that is Bharat' as a 'Union of States', it is necessary to work for building it as a 'federal union' or what Aurobindo referred to as a union of 'autonomies' with multiple tiers of government and sharing of powers from the lowest grassroot level of Panchayats to the Parliament and the Government of the Union. This would also be close to Gandhiji's model polity of concentric circles instead of the present pyramidical structure. Distribution of powers should be so designed that only the most essential or minimum necessary powers are assigned to each higher level. This would be in keeping with what is now called the subsidiarity principle. Incidentally, this would be the most rational and practical way of operationalising the Gandhian vision of a Constitution for India that recognises the sovereign power vested in the people at the grassroot level and building from below, in a bottom-up rather than top-down approach.

With nearly 20 per cent or one in every four law makers having criminal backgrounds, neither rule of law nor the freedom and security of ordinary citizens were safe. The most serious threat to the poor and the underprivileged having adequate voice in democracy, came from widespread corruption particularly during 2005-2014. The mother of corruption and criminalisation of politics was the system of electing our representatives. A candidate for election needed tons of money and plenty of muscle and mafia power and, both these come from the world of crime. Also, under our electoral system and 1800 registered political parties, some 70% of the winners had more votes cast against them than for them. Their representational legitimacy was therefore, very doubtful. Increasingly they came from the neo-monied classes. If the declarations made by the candidates were any guide, majority of them had assets running into crores.

The Constitution Commission had observed that the electoral process had not been able to keep out criminal, anti-social and undesirable elements from participating in and even dominating the political scene and polluting the electoral and parliamentary processes. The enormity of the cost of elections and electoral corruption was having deleterious effect on national progress and had led to the degradation of political processes to the detriment of common good.

The electoral system had proved to be terribly divisive of society on caste basis thereby further isolating and damaging the deprived and marginalised as mere vote banks with the leaders developing a vested interest in keeping them backward.

Democratic governance is not merely about having a government elected at periodic elections. For, elections can be and are manipulated through the use of flawed processes, money and mafia power. The weak, the poor and the underprivileged become pawns in power games and for petty temptations barter away their space to the marauders of democratic governance. If that were not so, with the vast majority of the people of India being in the category of the underprivileged, it should always be possible for them to occupy the largest space in democratic polity and to have their government catering primarily to their interests. But that does not happen and we are constrained to discuss the question of somehow providing them some space and some voice in democratic governance.

After all hope in the Legislature and Executive was lost, the Judiciary remained almost the last sheet anchor of the citizens' hopes. However, of late, even there things are no more rosy. The courts have largely failed to provide speedy and inexpensive justice to the people. In the words of the Constitution Commission, Judicial system has not been able to meet even the modest expectations of the society. Its delays and costs are frustrating, its processes slow and uncertain. People are pushed to seek recourse to extra-legal methods for relief. Trial system both on the civil and criminal side, has utterly broken down.

Costs of seeking justice are so high that ordinary citizens can hardly afford them. The lawyers are guilty of charging unreasonably high fees—many partly in cash—and having little interest in early disposal of cases. Not all lawyers conform to any professional ethics. On one pretext or the other, the advocates representing the parties keep asking for repeated adjournments and judges gladly oblige. Also, on the slightest pretext, the lawyers proceed on strike thereby paralysing the judicial process, causing delays and adding to the cost of litigation. In the higher judiciary the holidays, closed days and vacation days outnumber the working days.

It is good to be told that for violation of fundamental rights, one can go straight to the Supreme Court but how many of the poor and underprivileged can afford to have access to the Supreme Court? Can anyone seriously assert that justice depends today more on the merits of the case than on the means of the litigant? Can it be said that pitted against a rich adversary who has hired a costly advocate, a poor litigant fighting through a legal assistance advocate can hope to win on merits?

Referring to Article 141 of the Constitution, eminent jurist, Fali Nariman was constrained to remark that law's proverbial delays were not because there were too many laws but because there were just too many reported judgements and orders concerning them. The judgement factory has become over-commercialised and quite a large number of the 30 million pending cases can be attributed to this 'peculiar Indian malady of case law diarrhoea'. Despite the large pendency, our judges spend time writing 800-1200 page learned judgements, which instead of clarifying and declaring the law, confuse the ordinary citizens more.

The case for judicial reforms is today as much of a categorical imperative as reforms in any other sector. The legal fraternity has a great responsibility to ensure equal justice for all by ensuring that highest quality of legal aid is made available free in deserving cases through the scheme of legal assistance under the law. Merely celebrating Legal Assistance will not do. It is only when we fulfill the basic duty of politics of restoring the power of the Constitution and its institutions back to their legitimate owners—the people—that things will begin to change. However, no reforms shall succeed and nothing can change unless the sovereign power is exercised by the people and they use it to discharge their citizenship responsibilities towards fellow citizens, more particularly the underprivileged.

A Social Watch Report on Governance and Development *inter alia* concluded that the judiciary was by far the least accountable wing of the government while the effective use of PIL had in effect led to a scenario where the balance of power had shifted perceptively from the Executive and Legislature to the Judiciary. To quote the Report: The judicial system should be geared for providing a voice to the underprivileged and the less resourceful. This would entail providing all citizens, particularly the poor, access to justice.

Revisiting Corruption

Case for Systemic Changes

YEARS AGO, His Holiness, The Dalai Lama, in a Message said that systems 'based on democracy and individual liberty are the most suited to human needs'. But, he also added, 'the very conditions that allow for freedom in democracy are also open to abuse and provide greater opportunities for individual misdeeds. There is more chance of dishonest and deceptive behaviour'. The question, therefore, is 'how to find ways and means of preserving our democratic structures while at the same time devising strategies to curtail such harmful activities as bribery and corruption'? Freedom of speech and independence of the mass media should be used to expose 'duplicitous or dishonest' politicians, bureaucrats and others. 'We should have the courage to expose these shortcomings in society directly and clearly with sincerity and honesty'. That way, we can tackle 'acts of corruption and exploitation that sap the public good'.[1]

Corruption is nothing new. What is new is the scale and proportion of corruption cases and the social sanction that the corrupt rich and powerful command. Before the elections to the 16th Lok Sabha in 2014, we were privy to several scams relating to the Commonwealth Games, the 2-G Spectrum Licenses, the Adarsh Society, the LIC Housing Loans, the Lavasa Hill Station project, the Neera Radia Tapes and the heavily subsidised foodgrains meant for BPL families in UP that were being diverted for sale in open markets elsewhere. These were enough to put democracy in India to shame. Never before, in living memory in such a short span of time, so many scams of such mind-boggling magnitude had hit the headlines. What was even more disturbing was the fact that all these scams revealed only the tip of the iceberg. Much more was hidden below the surface. The Comptroller and Auditor General of India reported on mega scandals like those on hydrocarbon production sharing contracts, transfer of oilfields to Reliance etc. Many of the most corrupt are believed to continue to occupy high positions.

It is difficult to define corruption. In common speech, corruption connotes some form of moral delinquency or fall from rectitude. It signifies perversion of integrity by bribery or favour. 'In other words, any act of commission or omission by a public servant for securing pecuniary or other material advantage directly or indirectly for himself or his family or friends is corruption.' Political corruption may mean any 'improper or selfish exercise of power and influence attached to a public office or to the special position one occupies in public life'. As the first Central Vigilance Commissioner, Justice Nittoor Srinivasa Rao said:

---

1 From the Foreword to Subhash C Kashyap, (ed.), *Eradication of Corruption & Restoration of Values,* Sterling, New Delhi, 2001.

> It must be remembered that corruption or lack of integrity does not comprise only cases in which money or some material gain figures as consideration for doing something which is improper, but all acts by way of exercise of one's power or use of one's position in an improper manner with an ulterior object. In fact, power itself is more potent than material wealth and, even more than in the purely administrative field, the attainment of power of position and its retention by improper means becomes the object of ambition in the political field. If power of position is so acquired, chances are that it has been acquired for improper use and will be so used.

What is talked about as corruption may be defined simply as lack of public and private morality, probity and a sense of honesty and integrity. It is the abuse of public resources or position for private gain. Corruption may involve receiving illegitimate personal gratification to pass on illegitimate private benefit to another individual.[2]

The reality of corruption goes beyond time and space. The phenomenon is not unique to India or to our times. Also, it is not the monopoly of politicians or of any other profession. It is all-pervasive and omnipresent. Writing a few hundred years before Christ, Kautilya describes ways to embezzle public funds. Among other things, as punishment he prescribes confiscation of the entire ill-gotten wealth 'so that they cannot either misappropriate government money or vomit what they have eaten up'. In Kautilya's days corruption was not respected or accepted by society.

Edward Gibbon, summed up the reasons for the fall of Roman Empire in one word 'corruption'. In order to really understand the present-day phenomenon of corruption in India, we have to go

---

2 *Report of the Committee on Prevention of Corruption* (Santhanam Committee) Min Home Affairs, GOI, New Delhi, 1964; *Swarajya*, Annual Number, 1971.

back to its beginnings and growth at and after the transfer of power from colonial masters to Indian hands. We find Gandhiji upset with Congressmen trying to cash in on their sacrifices and penances by becoming Ministers, Members of Parliament and the like. While the Interim Government with Nehru at the head was in power, Gandhiji, writing in his dairy in Gujarati on 21 May 1947 said that if the Congress let the people down by becoming their overlord and arrogated to itself the position of a master instead of remaining their servant, 'A revolution will sweep over the country and the people will pick out the white-capped ones individually and finish them'. At his prayer meeting on 15 December 1947 Gandhiji said that he had heard from many trustworthy sources that corruption was on the increase. He wondered whether everyone will be 'for himself and none for India'.

On 11 January 1948, Gandhiji read out at his prayer meeting a letter that referred to the rot in the Congress and said that the people's representatives in the legislative bodies themselves resorted to corruption and crushed the people. They took money to get licences, indulged in black marketing of the worst kind, traded on ignorance of the masses, corrupted the sources of justice and forced the administration to transfer officers. The next day, on 12 January 1948, Gandhiji referred to a confirmatory letter received from an old friend who said that the behaviour of Congressmen in his province was deplorable. The taste of power had turned their heads. Several of the MLAs and MLCs were following the policy of 'make hay while the sun shines'. They made money by using influence in criminal courts and with administrative and revenue officers.[3]

Speaking on the midnight of 14-15 August 1947, Sarvepalli Radhakrishnan said:

'Unless we destroy corruption in high places, root out every trace of nepotism, love of power, profiteering and blackmarketing that have

[3] See Subhash C Kashyap, *Ministers and Legislators,* New Delhi, 1982.

spoiled the good name of our country in recent times, we will not be able to raise the standards of efficiency in administration as well as in production and distribution of necessary goods of life.'

Concluding the labours of the Constituent Assembly, its President, Rajendra Prasad, said on 26 November 1949: 'If the people who are elected are capable men of character and integrity they will be able to make the best even of a defective Constitution. If they lack these qualities, the Constitution cannot help the country. India needs today nothing more than a set of honest men.'

By 1963-64 things had come to such a pass that no less a person than the then Congress President, D Sanjivayya said on 31 July 1963, that 'the Congressmen who were paupers in 1947 are now millionaires and multi-millionaires. They own palatial buildings and factories... without having (had) any ostensible sources of such income'.[4]

It was represented to the Santhanam Committee that corruption had increased to such an extent that people had started losing faith in the integrity of public administration. The Committee was to report in 1964 that complaints against highly placed in public life were not dealt with properly enough to instill public confidence. This created cynicism and a belief that the governments were not against the corrupt if they had the requisite power, influence and projection.[5]

According to Gunnar Myrdal, 'As politics became increasingly concerned with practical issues, so the pressure of vested interests on the politicians grew stronger and with it, corruption and nepotism became profitable'. Politics became a gainful profession with high social status and opportunities to wield power as an 'avenue to privileges and patronage'. To be a politician came to be equated with

---

[4] Cf. Nirad C Chaudhuri, Corruption in Indian Politics, *The Hindustan Times*, May 5, 1968: '...in recent decades the common people of India have seen paupers acquiring immense fortunes by going into politics. They would not just believe that politics is not a more efficient and less laborious and risky means of making money than even the black market.

[5] Santhanam Committee Report, *op.cit.*

being 'a self seeker and opportunist'. Corruption was not only rampant but it was growing 'particularly among higher officials and politicians, including legislators and ministers'.[6]

Before the Emergency, in all discussions on corruption in public life, the common complaint, rightly or wrongly, was that corruption started at the top and that the men at the top were not serious about tackling the problem since they were themselves involved in one way or the other. Also, it was said that different standards of integrity were applied 'to the few at the top and many at the bottom'.[7] The greatest amount of resentment arose from the belief that Ministers found guilty of corruption or corrupt practices by Commissions of Inquiry, Tribunals or Courts went unpunished and could be seen in top positions in the country. As Dwivedy and Bhargava put it, 'It is not uncommon for a politician branded corrupt to continue to be a 'national hero.' Those found guilty or adversely commented upon, after disappearing from the scene for sometime or lying low for a while, reappeared often with added prestige and power.[8]

One of our most distinguished former judges of the Supreme Court, late HR Khanna was of the view that after the 1969 Congress split, 'political life in the country got amoralised and joining politics came to be looked upon as the quickest means of getting into seats of power and acquisition of wealth'. To quote Justice Khanna further:

> If there are three vices that are mainly responsible for eroding the moral values in the country, one would have no hesitation in pointing out a finger at lust for power, corruption and black-money. They are close allies of each other, work in

6 Gunnar Myrdal, *Asian Drama*, London, 1968, Vol.I, pp.261-63, 273, 291-92 and Vol. II, pp. 951-52.

7 John N Monteiro, *Corruption*, Manaktalas, Bombay, 1966, p.97.

8 *Economic Times*, August 5, 1971 and SB, Dwivedy and GS. Bhargava, *Political Corruption in India*, New Delhi, 1967.

> unison and have definetely spread their tentacles to almost all walks of life.
>
> Money was received by the politicians and other government functionaries in cash without receipt and it was ensured that the same was not reflected in the account books. As the level of corruption rose higher so did the incidence of black-money. Things came to such a pass that according to financial experts the incidence of black-money in India was the highest in the world and it exceeded the white legal money in circulation.
>
> As the heads of investigating agencies and vigilance officers owe their appointment and continuation in office to political bosses, the investigating agencies not only turn blind eye to lapses but quite often instead of detecting the crime and bringing the culprit to book they suppress the incriminating material and feel no hesitation in giving clean chits to the political bosses.[9]

On 23 March 1981, addressing a Conference of CBI officers, the then Prime Minister, Indira Gandhi, said that increasing corruption at various levels was a matter of major concern. There was a feeling among the people that those persons known to be corrupt escaped the clutches of law because of their position and influence while only the 'small fry are caught in the net'. In his oft-quoted remarks, Rajiv Gandhi said that of a rupee sent for the poor, only 15 paise reached the poor.

Much later, the then President, Narayanan, referring to corruption in public life, was constrained to observe that public office that was earlier regarded as a 'sacred space' was seen 'by an increasing number

---

[9] HR Khanna, 'Political Corruption' in Subhash C Kashyap (ed), *Crime and Corruption to Good Governance,* New Delhi, 1997.

of wielders of it, as an opportunity to strike gold and enjoy the loaves and some fishes' of power. It was a matter of the deepest regret that a great cynicism prevailed in the public mind about politics and administration.

All right-thinking citizens today feel deeply concerned about the dismal national scenario. Of the myriad problems facing us, the most disturbing is that of corruption. It has become one of the gravest challenges to Indian polity, society, economy and security. In terms of social values, corruption has come to have acceptability and respectability. In parts of India, it is said, there are fixed rates of bridegrooms openly quoted in relation to the bribe-potential in a particular service. Thus, an IAS sells for less than a Revenue Service or Customs officer.

As for economy, black economy and corruption are closely interlinked. Black economy plays a dominant role in the organised sector. A sizeable chunk of the black money is stacked in tax havens abroad. It is believed that India has more black money both within the country and abroad than any other country of the world and also that the amount of black money in the economy far exceeds the amount of white money. It is a matter of shame that the Supreme Court has had to set up its own Special Investigative Team to unearth black money stashed abroad in tax havens. It is believed that apart from other misuses, it is utilised for bribing and buying top politicians and funding terrorist activities. Corruption is thus a serious threat to national security and to democratic institutions.

As for individual safety, while no ordinary citizen felt secure anywhere, some of the most corrupt people who deserved to be behind bars, were among the most respected and feared and moved about freely under high category security provided by the state at colossal costs to the public exchequer.

The hard fact was that our society itself had been corrupted and had come to need corruption. Corruption had been legitimatised in public mind as a way of life and a lubricant for development. It was even described as a very secular, cementing, uniting and national integrational force. In the context of the economic culture of competitive consumerism, no other value system remained. Some of our most cherished values had also come to have a price tag. They had become saleable commodities. In a culture of poverty and shortages, an honest politician was seen as a good for nothing individual He could not help his supporters at times of their need. He swore too much by honesty. The story was told of an honest politician who said in his election speech that his old residential house still had a thatched leaking roof that he wasn't able to repair during two decades of his public life as a legislator. Speaking the next day, his opponent asked the constituents whether a man who could not repair his own house for 20 years could be of any help to them.

A very telling lesson in practical politics was once given by a senior Cabinet Minister of the Union Government in a private conversation. He said: 'What principles of probity are you talking about? I shall tell you what is real politics. In my constituency,' he said, 'every year there are floods. Unfortunately, there were none this year. All my workers are angry.'

Talking to the representatives of the people—the MPs and MLAs—one learned that overwhelming majority of constituents and other members of the public who visited them from morning and through the entire day came with illegitimate requests for favours that could not be met without compromising on probity and integrity. In such a scenario, how could people be expected to unite in a fight against all corruption. Also, sermonising apart, in an atmosphere where school admissions, seats in professional institutions, government jobs, contracts, postings and transfers were all bought and sold with hefty amounts, it was sheer hypocrisy to look for any probity, honesty and integrity in their conduct. Those who entered service by paying money had to recover their costs and more. How could we expect honesty from a government employee—a constable, a messenger or a *babu* —who had purchased his job at a high price? How could a school teacher who had to buy his position impart value education to his students? The legislators were no different inasmuch as they also had to buy their way to the legislature at a heavy cost.

When corruption comes to be regarded as a way of life and almost every ordinary citizen comes to believe that he or she can get nothing done—not even what he or she is 'most legitimately entitled to—without greasing palms, it is obvious that highest priority needs to be given to combating this problem as it affects daily life of ordinary citizens. That the malady of corruption has spread its tentacles wide and deep and extends to all professions and all walks of life hardly needs elaboration. Corruption in elections and in legislative bodies reduces accountability and distorts representation in policymaking; corruption in the judiciary compromises the rule of law; and corruption in public administration results in the unfair provision of services. More generally, corruption erodes the institutional capacity of government as procedures are disregarded, resources are siphoned off, and public offices are bought and sold. Corruption undermines the legitimacy of government and such democratic values as trust and tolerance. Also, those in power in the government are in a position to bargain for the best deal. They have almost unlimited means of bullying, breaking or buying support to remain in power.

It is said that the economic reform policy of liberalization and globalization had ended the license and permit raj. But, the ground realities were that in the new economic deal corruption in public life and in administration had got further compounded. The ancient Indian ideal of globalisation was expressed in *Vasudhaiva kutumbakam* meaning that the whole world was a family. The new Western concept of globalisation is of making the whole world a *mandi*—a market place—where everything is bought and sold. With the entry of players like the multi-nationals with their huge budgets and with all barriers removed and the market forces becoming the crucial determinants, corruption has gone 'big'. YC Halan writing on corruption a while ago said:

> Scams and scandals are the higher levels of corruption in which the elite and the politically and economically powerful, manipulate the system in such a way that money is siphoned off from state projects to their pockets. They being in powerful positions and having inside information play a safe game. Networking ensures that they are not caught or if the scandals are exposed they neither loose money nor their positions.
>
> The multinational corporations have revolutionized the kickback market. Competing for emerging markets in India they offer high kickbacks to bureaucrats and politicians in order to get a business deal through.[10]

More specifically recalling some of the main scandals that rocked Indian polity since Independence reference may be made to the Geep Scandal (1948), Mundhra Scandal (1957), Bofors Guns Deal (1987), Securities Scam (1992), Sugar Import Scandal (1994), JMM Bribes Scandal (1995), Fodder Scam (1996), Urea Deal (1996), CRB Scam (1997), Plantation Companies Scam (1999), Stock Market Scam (2001), Stamp Paper Scam (2002), Scorpene Submarine Scam (2005), Taj Corridor Scam (2006), Hassan Ali Khan Tax Evasion Case (2008), Army Ration Pilferage Case (2008), Rice Export Scam (2009), Orissa Mines Scam (2009) Koda Minng (2000) etc. According to an estimate by Prof TSN Sastry, the total amount involved in all known scam and scandals since Independence came to the staggering figure of Rs 910,603,234, 300,000 equivalent to 20.23 trillion US dollars. This

---

[10] Subhash C Kashyap, *Blueprint of Political Reforms*, New Delhi, 2003, p. 269.

is the figure from some years back.

Actually, in a democracy, nothing can be more tragic and cause greater worry than a situation where politicians—representatives of people— are regarded as corrupt and come to be detested by the people. But then politicians alone are not to be blamed nor is corruption confined to their ranks. It is there in the administration and is not confined to departments like the police and public works only any more. It has become all pervasive. This is so in the public sector and in the private sector, in labour unions, in professional bodies, in the functioning of NGOs, in business and in industry. Howsoever reluctantly one has to say this, not even the judiciary or the defence sector today can be said to be free from corruption. Also, who can say with any honesty that educational institutions, the academia or the media function with greater transparency, can boast of better integrity or are inflicted with less corruption. We are all guilty. We have, in some way, all become corrupt and there is a general devaluation of values all round. The system under which we live and the people who operate it, have nurtured an axis between corrupt businessmen, politicians, bureaucrats, police, smugglers and criminals. They together manipulate the system and monopolise power.[11]

The sources and causes of corruption are 'Systemic', Constitutional, Historical, Cultural, Sociological, Economic and Educational. The market-oriented consumerist value system, based on human greed, has made money, power and success at any cost our only concerns. To earn tons of money and get fabulously rich quickly or to gain power and position and be a success story in business, profession or politics, we are willing to compromise with principles of honesty and integrity and indulge in all sorts of corruption. To be able to form our governments or to stay in power and cling to our chairs, we are

---

[11] For the Vohra Committee Report, see Subhash C Kashyap (ed.), *Eradication of Corruption*, op.cit, Annexure 4.

prepared to be blackmailed and to buy support. We call it coalition *Dharma* or constraints of coalition politics.

The increasing disconnect between the people and politics and the visible anger against abuse and misuse of state power led to great dissatisfaction , anger, rise of extremism and potential for large-scale social turmoil and violence. The principal organs and functionaries of the state became self-serving and unaccountable, indulging in gross corruption of public funds. Often, people in positions from top to bottom were involved and scandals got exposed only when quarrels emerged on sharing the loot. It was both interesting and painful to listen to debates on the media between leaders of rival parties. The reply to charges of corruption was that the other side was also equally or more corrupt.[12]

When several scandals of horrendous proportions and the public outrage against them threatened to become unmanageable, debate on different drafts of yet another Lokpal Bill came handy as a diversion. All praise to excellent media management, corruption scandals receded to the background and an unprecedented elitist public-private partnership, Legislative Drafting Committee and differences on the draft provisions, hogged the headlines. While some of the euphoria generated by the campaigns and fasts for the Lokpal Bill had gradually withered away, the more fundamental issue of fighting the monster of corruption remained.

Any attempt to undetermine and denigrate established institutions of representative legislatures and independent judiciary could constitute a dangerous affront to all norms of constitutionalism, rule of law and parliamentary democracy of which we have been so proud. The remedy is to bring about some fundamental systemic political reforms. To reduce corruption at the political level, highest priority needs to be accorded to suitably reforming the electoral and political

[12] *South Asia Politics* (M), Vol. 9, No. 10, Feb. 2011, Editorial.

party systems so that more responsible, democratic and accountable parties emerge, men and women of better quality and character are elected and high values of service and sacrifice are restored to public life.[13]

The fact is that there is every need for huge unaccounted funds for political activity, party organisations and election campaigning. It is an important contributory factor in creating an environment of corruption, generating black money and promoting a parallel economy. There is considerable debate on the role of money power, muscle power, mafia gangs and criminals and the flow of free liquor during elections and the filing of false returns of election expenses. If actual expenditure is, say, Rs 1 to 5 crore or more, raising the expense limit to Rs 25 lakhs or 40 lakhs hardly helps. Also, the question remains: where do these lakhs or crores come from? Initially, it used to be the big industrialists and business houses who financed political parties because they needed licenses, permits and protection. For various reasons, these sources later dried up and the payments came to be made on job basis. Eventually, politicians turned to criminals.

- Criminals needed politicians' protection against the processes of law and, therefore, they paid them. They expected a good return on their investment.
- Politicians needed huge sums of unaccounted money for political activity, their parties, elections and for themselves. Nobody could pay hard-earned, white, tax-paid money to politicians; funds from the crime world alone came handy.
- Gradually politicians became subservient, dons of the crime world themselves entered politics and a phase emerged when politicians began seeking not only their help in terms of money but also their muscle power for winning elections and even for their own physical protection from rivals.

[13] Ibid., Vol. 10 no. 1, May 2011, Editorial.

A fundamental question is —if we need political parties —how are they to be financed, and if election business remains so capital intensive, where is the money to come from?

- from the crime world
- from contributions by citizens and party members
- from Governmental funding
- from pay-offs in contracts, arms purchases, licences, etc.
- from criminals, smugglers and the underworld
- from foreign sources—multinationals or various tainted official or unofficial agencies with vested interests and agendas.

In most of these cases, corruption is the inevitable concomitant. A way out can be found only by some fundamental systemic changes. Society runs on reward-punishment principles. If corruption ceases to pay, to yield rich dividends and if punishment becomes really swift, deterrent and exemplary, corruption would certainly come down. Ultimately the responsibility is ours. Various legislative and other methods and remedies have been suggested by experts, scholars, concerned citizens and public bodies for tackling the menace of corruption and bringing about some minimum necessary probity in public life and governance including the conduct of politicians and administrators. Some of these are summed up below:

- The mother of all political corruption and black money is our electoral and political party systems and therefore if the root cause has to be attacked, the first and foremost need is for systemic reforms in that area including a law for political parties.
- Those charged for corruption or moral turpitude should not be allowed to contest elections or hold any public office including membership of a legislature until cleared. Those found guilty should stand debarred from entering public life for 10 years. Those convicted of serious offences should be disqualified for life.
- In all cases of corruption, once the chargesheet is framed by the court, all the property of the accused must stand confiscated

until he is cleared.

- It should be made obligatory for every citizen going abroad to declare on oath that he does not have any foreign account or property in his name or in the name of anyone else, company or other entity, without prior GOI permission. If later, the statement is found to be false, all his assests should stand confiscated and all foreign accounts and/or property would be deemed to stand transferred to the state.
- Instead of diluting the present provisions of RTI Act, these should be strengthened to remove loopholes, pendency, delays in appeals and the reluctance of several institutions including political parties to give information under the RTI Act.
- The Lokpal Act must be made stronger and at once brought into operation. It must deal with all complaints and grievances of the people in regard to administrative delays, misuse of discretion and corruption at all levels but without in any way compromising the independence of the Judiciary or the credibility of representative institutions under the Constitution. In fact, the representative institutions deserve to be restored to a rightful level of public esteem. For Judiciary, setting up a separate Judicial Commission (or Judicial Lokpal) and the Judicial Accountability Bill should be expedited. For the conduct of Members inside the Parliament, article 105 should apply as hithertofore but parliamentary privileges must be codified forthwith as provided by the Constitution. Lokpal office must remain very modest, on the Swedish pattern and not become another huge Secretariat monster.
- Existing institutions charged with responsibilities of investigation etc. need to be freed from political control of parties in power. CBI should be reorganised under a Union law.
- State functionaries, including all elected people, Government officials, judges etc. should declare their assets and liabilities every year and put them in public domain.

- Citizens must be guaranteed by law, issue of ration cards, passports, tax refunds, house plan sanctions and a variety of licences, certificates etc. within strict time frames.
- Systemic political reforms are necessary so that corruption does not become uncontrollable because of 'compulsion of coalition politics', with small parties and independents playing the politics of brinkmanship, bluff and blackmail and demanding their pound of flesh.
- Anti-corruption laws for public servants should be made more stringent.
- Ill- gotten wealth and property must be confiscated.
- There should be a legally enforceable personal liability to pay compensation to the victim of corruption and administrative delay. Where loss is caused to the state itself through the corrupt conduct or *mala fide* action of a public servant, the latter must be made personally liable to make good the loss and pay exemplary damages.
- Report of the National Police Commission should be implemented, to begin with in Union territories and willing States.
- Political interference in administration should cease.
- Civil services should be de-politicised with transfers etc. being entrusted to a Civil Services Board.
- Laws, rules, regulations and procedures should be simplified.
- Downsizing the administration most substantially and computerisation of all records in the judiciary and in the government may help reduce corruption.
- Decision-making and regulatory functions of the State should be decentralised and made transparent.
- Government purchases, award of contracts and economic activity generally (eg. award of gas agencies and the like) should be completely depoliticised and debureaucratised.
- Judicial system should be drastically reformed to provide for

speedy and inexpensive delivery of justice.

The suggestions for laws that are enforceable and compliable in the field of ensuring greater integrity in governance can be multiplied but the problem of mounting corruption and erosion of integrity is not merely a problem of laws. The real problem is that those who can bring reforms and enact laws are the very people who have a vested interest in the *status quo*. Why should the beneficiaries of a corrupt system change it unless the public pressure becomes irresistible? This is a question yet to be addressed.

Glocalisation & Federal Governance

Indian Perspective

THE CONCEPT of 'Glocalisation' presumably had its origin in a Japanese business practice of manufacturing consumer goods in small localities in Japan with an eye on the global market. To attract the consumers in different locations all over the world and to maximise the sale potential, they tried to customise the goods according to local needs and beliefs in foreign lands. In the 21st century, in the matter of consumer goods, the place of Japan has been taken over by China and the clearest example of glocalisation is that of idols of Ram, Hanuman, Ganesh, Lakshmi and other Indian gods and goddesses sold in Indian towns and villages being made in localities in Communist China. Thus, in practical terms, Glocalisation may be said to have evolved as a strategy in international political economy to produce locally and sell globally. In other words, the idea of manufacturing nations was to convert the whole world into a global market for their goods. Political ramifications of Glocalisation lead us to questions of sovereign powers and governance in India at local grassroots and higher territorial, national, and ideally also global levels with multi-level federalism as the model. In recent times, social scientists world over have been grappling with centripetal and centrifugal forces being at work simultaneously with some nation states joining with each other to forge larger regional unions while some other states have been breaking up into separate smaller nations. Unifying and diversifying tendencies both have their logic and relevance in the national and international arena. On the one hand, we hear about the aspirations of one world order, global village and world federation and on the other equally strongly ideas of decentralisation, power to the people, grassroots democracy etc. are stressed. These contradictory global and local tendencies are sought to be subsumed under the very imaginative new concept of 'Glocalisation'. It recognises the equal legitimacy of both Global and Local and the imperative of merging and marrying the two.

In a normative sense, only multi-tier cooperative federalism can become a bridge expanding from the local all the way up to the global with the people at every level enjoying the fullest freedom and a sensation of sovereign power in their hands. Under the European subsidiarity principle as also under the Gandhian village-centric polity there is a bottom-up approach where power flows from the people at the bottom upwards. Whatever can be done at the grassroots level, only the local self-government institutions should have all the authority. What cannot possibly be handled at the local level that alone may be entrusted to the next higher level and so on upto the national and hopefully supra-national, regional and global levels. Underlying all this is the basic democratic principle of the right of all men to govern themselves as they like.

Federalism is not only a better way to democracy and world peace but it is the only way. A single centre of power as in a unitary state is antithetical to democracy. Federalism denies arbitrary powers in any hands and is based on the premise of distribution of sovereign powers. A lasting, secure and peaceful global order, therefore, must be crowned with a multi-layered federal polity. This, however, requires that we must agree on an approach under which all human beings are equal and equally free, and the earth and it's resources are the common heritage of all mankind irrespective of territorial, racial, religious, gender or other artificial man-made boundaries. For thousands of years, India also has had a concept of the world being One. It was that of *Vasudhaiva kutumbakam*—of the whole world being one family where there was a relationship of give and take, of sharing and caring with all the joys and sorrows being equally balanced for all the family members. It was very different from the modern concept of the whole world becoming a common market or mandi. With regard to Federal Governance in India, some conceptual clarifications may be flagged. Federal polity usually refers to the political system in a country with a rigid written Constitution defining and delimiting the powers and functions both of the federal legislature and government on the one hand and local or state legislatures and governments on the other. In a classic federation like that of the United States, sovereignty is divided between the federal and state institutions, both partaking of sovereign powers in their respective spheres.

A classic Federation, literally and historically is the result of an agreement. It is when two or more sovereign States resolve to surrender a part of their sovereignty and join hands to constitute a new union, a federal polity is born. It is a union without the constituting units losing their own identities. In fact, in a classic federation, the federal government enjoys only those powers that are by agreement surrendered to it by the units. However, there are also instances of some large countries where an existing unitary system may decide to share powers with the units under an agreed system of devolution or distribution of powers, for the sake of administrative convenience or to meet linguistic or ethnic demands. Canada and India are examples of such polities. But, in every case of federalism—classical or otherwise—(i) the Constitution occupies the supreme position. It is written and relatively rigid, that is, not easily amendable; (ii) there are at least two levels at which government functions. In other words, two separate governments—federal and state—coexist, and (iii) as the arbiter of any disputes between the federation and the units as also between the units themselves, the highest judiciary—federal court or Supreme Court—enjoys great authority and prestige.

Many countries which do not strictly fit in the definition of a federal polity and yet have many of its features are variously described by scholars as some kind of a federation or a polity covered by some variant of federalism. Today, one hears of all kinds of 'innovative' federalisms—cooperative, executive, emergent, responsible, parliamentary, populist, legislative, competitive, fiscal, restructured, reluctant or quasi-federalism are some of these. Mention is also made of federations without federalism.

Federalism can be both integrative and disintegrative. It may be used for integrating disparate and separate units and also for breaking up a united large nation into separate smaller autonomous units under a federal umbrella. Decentralisation of power and diversity may also contribute to national unity.

Ideally, Federalism is intended to keep different communities or divergent religious, linguistic, racial, tribal or other group identities united together under one nation state. Problems of social pluralism are sought to be resolved by an arrangement or agreement to arrive at a balance in sharing political power. Irrespective of any variant of federal polity, federalism is relevant only in a situation where the pluralism is territory based, where particular groups are concentrated in separate territorial units or where the societal diversities are territorially identifiable, definable and separable. Federalism as a political system can be a meaningful performer only for a society faced with territorial diversities. It is an arrangement between separate territorial entities to come together or to avoid break-up and stay united by sharing power through free democratic will. In a pluralist society, and in large nations with multiplicity of diversities, federalism is the only way to genuine democracy.

India's Constitution has been variously described as quasi-federal, federal with a strong unitary or procentre bias, federal in structure but unitary in spirit, federal in normal times but with possibilities of being converted into a purely unitary one during Emergency, etc. The fact is that it is difficult to put our Constitution in any strict mould of a federal or unitary type; it has features of both. It cannot be considered unitary because it provides, for example, for distribution of executive and legislative powers between the Union and the States and provisions affecting the powers of the States or Union State relations cannot be amended without ratification by the States. It cannot be considered strictly federal either because the residuary powers vested in the Union and territorial identities of the States can be varied by Union Parliament by ordinary legislation. The Supreme Court once called it 'amphibian.'

Reasons for this unique unitary federal mix are to be found in the constitutional history of India, the sheer size of the country and nature of her complex diversities based on religion, language, region, culture etc. There is perhaps no other comparable example of a classic plural society and a massive federal polity that is representative, republican and parliamentary, uniting and protecting under its umbrella numerous religious, linguistic, regional and other diverse identities. As has been well said, "India is a continental federal polity constituted into a single territorial sovereignty" as a result of historical forces.

The Constitution describes India as a "Union of States". A separate part is devoted to "Union-State Relations" meaning thereby that it is about relations between the whole and its constituent parts and not between the centre of authority and its peripheries. The Constitution makers avoided the use of words like 'federation' or 'Centre'. Actually, 'Central government', 'Central legislature', 'Central laws' etc. are an unfortunate hangover from the days of the centralised government during the colonial rule. A great deal of mischief in the quality of governance has been caused by the wrong use of these words.

Sources of conflicts in federal polities can be traced to differences based on ethnicity, religion, language, territory and culture. The single most important source of conflicts in federal societies is the tendency of the Union to dominate the units, to make them dependent and to treat them as subordinates and not as equal partners in government, and to work for centralisation of authority under a top down model.

We glibly talk of the 'transfer of power to the people' or 'decentralization of power to the grassroots' as if the power legitimately belonged to the bosses in Delhi or the so called 'centre' and now they were condescending to transfer some bits of it to 'We, the people' at the grassroots. In a democracy all the sovereign powers belong to the people and it is for them at the grassroots to hand over some of these to higher tiers in the wider interests of larger society and national and individual security.

Moving towards building a new balance of power in inter-governmental relationship requires a conflict resolution mechanism. In recent decades, conflict-resolution has developed into a distinct discipline in the academia and in policy studies discourses. In specific situations, nature of conflicts may vary and strong disagreements may emerge on grounds of ideologies, principles or differences of perception. Also, there may be areas of genuine conflict of material interests. The notion of Conflict Resolution (CR) may be distinguished from Prevention aimed at creating atmosphere as a preventive measure, Management involving gradual incremental change through continuing efforts, and settlement on an ad hoc basis. All these may be stages in CR or independent goals. CR involves dealing with the root causes of the conflict and eliminating them once for all through necessary systemic changes and restructuring institutions and relationships aimed at an honest Balance of Power between the union and the units.

In the context of Indian Federalism, it is important to revisit the areas of conflict in inter-governmental relations and secure a proper balance of power sharing between the Union and the units. The constantly evolving federal structures and innovative devices have proved to be very powerful. CR and power sharing mechanisms have been integral to national integration, democracy and good governance. In fact, the Constitution of India itself has been the most potent CR mechanism—founded on the spirit of accommodation, adjustment and respect for diversity—ethnic, religious, linguistic and others.

Whatever conflicts arose—and there were many major ones—were all sought to be resolved under the Constitution eg Tamil, Punjabi and North East movements for secession or independence or demands for new States. Geographic boundaries of the States have often been reorganised. In 1956, they were organised on linguistic basis. Several States were then created as needed. Later, more States were formed, eg Haryana, Himachal Pradesh, Nagaland, Manipur, Mizoram, Arunachal Pradesh and Goa. The ease with which the map of India has been redrawn and reorganisation of States effected during the last more than sixty years bears eloquent testimony to the unique resilience and flexibility of the political system and efficacy of its conflict resolution mechanisms. In 2001, 3 large States were bifurcated to create three new States of Jharkhand, Uttarakhand and Chhattisgarh to respect and encourage the local aspirations of the people. The latest addition is Telengana. Not all ethnic conflicts have been resolved. Movements continue for Vidarbha, Bodoland, Bundelkhand, and others. The process goes on. It is this dynamic process that is the source of the greatest strength to the system.

The number of States which was 14 has more than doubled. At present, the Union consists of 29 States and seven Union Territories. Some unique solutions of regional councils, development boards, etc. have been attempted with varying degrees of success. We experimented with Bodoland Autonomous Council, Darjeeling Gorkha Hill Council, Jharkhand Area Autonomous Council, Leh Autonomous Hill Development Council, Tribal Areas Autonomous District Councils in Tripura etc.

India's Constitution is replete with CR and power sharing devices like the Finance Commission, the Fifth and the Sixth Schedule, the Eighth Schedule, Reservations for SC/ST and Backward Classes. Also, we have the CEC, CVC, C & AG, CBI, CRPF and the like.

There are special provisions for creation of new States (articles 2, 3 and 4), adjudication of Inter-State Water Disputes, Inter State Council (article 263), Article 370 for J & K and articles 371 to 371-I for Maharashtra, Gujarat, Nagaland, Assam, Arunachal and Goa.

Some scholars have suggested that India be viewed as a civilizational State and not as a nation-state. Another suggestion has been that it be called a federal nation-state. We are, no doubt, a highly pluralistic society but our pluralism is not territory based. It is of a special kind. We have many diversities of various sorts pulling us at once in the same or in opposite directions. Indian society is fragmented and segmented at every level on different grounds. Our basic problem was never that of territorially based diversities or pluralisms. Our diversities are within and cut across territorial units. In a sense, our diversities themselves are plural and our pluralism is diverse, both horizontally and vertically. What seems to divide, also unites. In fact, our diversities are our greatest strength and a great cementing force for national unity. Diversity is not division and unity does not mean uniformity or conformity. Also, unity of India and integrity of the nation as concepts are very different from national or political integration.

When India achieved Independence or what is called transfer of power in the mid-night of 14-15 August 1947, unfortunately only the masters changed. The people did not feel the glow of freedom or transfer of power to their hands. The Constitution also continued the colonial model. Looked at from another angle, the people have to function through their representatives. The State leadership is the closest representative of the people. Each State leadership deserves to be respected by the Union government. If the leadership does not deliver, it is for the people of the State to wake up and act. If the people of the State allow themselves to be exploited by their leaders—whether they are tribal leaders or caste or community leaders—they can only blame themselves. If the caste, community and tribal leaders come to have a vested interest in not developing but in exploiting their own people then they become greater enemies of their people than anyone else. And, the solution has to be found by the people themselves in their own area. Many of the problems of the people and of polity—whether in the East or West, North or South—have to be solved in the area itself. In the North East, before India's independence, the traditional institutions gave them more freedom and power to take their own decisions at the grassroots level. Problems arise and a feeling is generated when somebody is taking away their freedom and independent identity. The question is where do we go from here? What is the way ahead?

Time has now come for a review of the union-state relations and local governance institutions. More innovative federal structures need to be devised. It is necessary to address the deep-rooted sources of conflicts. We have to go in for a different variant of the parliamentary system which is compatible with the new federalism, which should build a united nation of a large number of autonomies considered not as subordinates or subsidiaries but as federal partners at various levels, rooted in our culture, ethos and genius, and taking into account our weaknesses and needs of making the federal Union an ever-developing and lasting reality.

The honest and the practical way ahead is for the Union to lose its extra weight and shed its tendency to be the centre with monopoly of power to dominate over the units and the people. In short, the only way to preserve 'India, that is Bharat' as a 'Union of States' is to work for building it as a 'federal Union' with multiple tiers of government and sharing of powers from the lowest levels of Panchayats to the Parliament and the Government of the Union. Incidentally, this would be the most rational and practical way of operationalizing the Gandhian vision of a Constitution for India which recognises the sovereign power vesting in the people at the grassroots and building from below. Gandhi conceived public life as a mission of sacrifice and service and not as a lucrative profession. He advocated a less expensive election system linked with watchdog councils and separate elected chief executives at each local level. In the Gandhian model, the village is at the centre and all the power moves in a bottom-up (instead of the present top-down) approach. It travels upwards to the next tier of governance. There may be three or four tiers of governance represented by successive concentric circles with power at the highest level being limited to the minimum essential areas like national security, external affairs etc. This also represents the quintessence of the subsidiarity principle whereunder what cannot be done at the lowest level only is entrusted to the next higher tier.

Subsidiarity is not decentralisation of power. It is assertion of the power of the people. It implies autonomy at all levels in specified areas particularly at the grassroots level where the ordinary citizens come in direct contact with the government. Also, the citizens themselves have to realise that for democracy to have real vitality and vibrance, they have to be active and responsible participants therein.

Governance means dignity, development and growth of the individual to its highest potential. This calls for power being ultimately with the individual citizen. Struggles for separate identities or greater federalism in pluralist societies are often not a fight for social justice, for the promotion of the interests of the disadvantaged sections of society or for protecting the rights of the units against the Union. The real issue is not even that of separate cultural or ethnic group interests. The entire conflictual situation revolves round the issue of sharing the fruits of political power. Ethnicity, language, religion and the like are politicalised to be used merely as the means to legitimise one's claims in the struggle for political power. For any CR to succeed, we must transcend vote bank politics built on corruption, casteism, communalism, black money power, crime and cabal rule.

While, there is no dichotomy between a strong Union and

strong states, the way Union Governments have operated during the 68 plus years that have gone by and misused their powers blatantly for political and partisan ends, particularly under articles 352 and 356—Proclamations of Emergency and imposition of President's rule in the States—have weakened the case of the Union beyond repair.

Of late, the role and functioning of our Council of States which was conceived by the founding fathers as a federal house consisting of the representatives of the States has been considerably compromised on political, party and personal interest considerations of the rulers.

The Constitution Commission (2002) recommended (a) greater consultation between the Union and the States through the Inter-State Council under article 263; (b) establishment of an Inter-State Trade and Commerce Commission; (c) treating inter-State river waters as national assets and enacting legislation for dispute resolution; (d) appointing only persons of eminence and with detached outlook as Governors in consultation with concerned Chief Ministers and respecting their five-year term; (e) using article 356 only as a last resort after action under 256, 257, 355 etc. fails; (f) deciding questions of majority support only on the floor of the House; and (g) in case of a hung house, election of the Chief Minister by the House.

The federal structure has come to stay and needs to be strengthened. The States are more and more asserting themselves through their political clout. They are demanding ever more space and extracting greater share of powers of governance and financial resources. But, the central problem today is not of Union-State relations. It is of greater decentralization of economic and political power. It is heartening and nothing short of revolutionary that after the 73rd and 74th Amendments coming into operation, India has 3.50 million elected rulers—over a million of them women. But, the States, by and large, seem unwilling to transfer power lower down and the MPs and MLAs feel uncomfortable and threatened by the new grassroot leadership. The Union and the States should concentrate on essentials following the subsidiarity principle. With economic liberalization must come decentralization of political power and of management. Income tax, corporation tax and indirect taxes could be moved to the concurrent list. Government at each higher level may be chosen by and remain answerable to the lower level. Government at the higher level should have no power to remove or supersede a duly elected Government at a lower tier. If we are serious about providing multi-tier government and taking power to the doorsteps of the people at the grassroots, the Constitution should clearly provide for distribution of power between the Union, the States and the local governments making the 11th and 12th schedules mandatory. It would do no violence to the basic structure of the Constitution or to the parliamentary system.

When the basic units of the federal Union at the grassroots become small and autonomous, most of the conflicts related to ethnicity and quest for freedom may get resolved, and it may be possible to involve various groups in governance more closely and this may make the Union stronger and the nation more integrated, emotionally and culturally. There is every case for another SRC and creation of some 40-50 States of almost equal size and equal representation in one or both Houses of the Union Parliament. But, we should delink the ethnic aspirations from political demands for separate States. Apart from new States, Sub-State and Supra-State structures may be created to take care of common group concerns which cannot be handled at the level of the States. Combined with strong zonal councils, this would lead to greater stability, more accountability, stronger Union and better administered and more developed or fast-developing States. Norms for Governor's appointments need revamping. Sarkaria Commission recommendations should be examined and implemented. Problems regarding article 356 are only due to improper operation and interpretation of articles 256, 257, 355, 356 and 365. These need to be read together.

One alternative worthy of further examination may be of having Lok Sabha constituencies as administrative units and sub-districts and tehsils may similarly coincide with MLA constituencies. That way, in a multi-tier system it may be possible to involve various groups in governance and making the nation more integrated, emotionally and culturally. Some such innovative multi-tier federal structures may have the potential to resolve many of the conflicts in our polity and arrive at a proper power sharing arrangement in Union-State relationship.

Apart from restructuring the federal Union, we need administrative reforms, parliamentary reforms and over-all reforms for good and clean citizen-friendly governance. No single reform can provide a miracle cure. Ideally, simultaneous action on all fronts is required.

A great deal needs to be reformed in our politics but most of the desirable reforms can be brought about within the constitutional framework by mere political will, executive action or through ordinary legislation. In rare cases only, constitutional amendments may be deemed necessary. These can be enacted under the Constitution itself without violating its basic structure. And, in any case, Constitution also is only a means. The end is the freedom and the well-being of the people.

The ultimate way ahead would be to revisit Indian democracy and rebuild our federal polity on foundations of honest relationship between the Union and the Units with governments at all levels providing good people-centric governance.

Fortunately, the nation today is on the move and the leadership seems prepared to take difficult decisions. The time to act is now. Vested interests should not be allowed to come in the way. An early initiative may be of immense help in transforming the present national climate to one of hope, harmony and good governance.

INSTITUTION OF PARLIAMENT

Seven Decades of Parliament

Changing Character and Contours

THE FIRST Parliament of India came into being on 26 January 1950 with the commencement of the Constitution and birth of the Republic. This was the Provisional Parliament.[1] The first Constitution Amendment was passed during its life. In retrospect, one of the other significant events during the life of the Provisional Parliament was the *Mudgal case.* It was an indication of the high standards that the founding fathers wanted to establish that when HG Mudgal, a Congress member, was found to have used his position as a member to further the interests of the Bombay Bullion Association for a small money consideration, Nehru himself moved for setting up a committee to enquire into the matter and Mudgal lost his membership.

---

1 Also see the chapter on 'Functioning of Parliament'.

The first General Elections under the Constitution were held in 1951-52 and the bicameral Parliament with its two Houses—Lok Sabha and the Rajya Sabha—was duly constituted.

The first Lok Sabha (1952-57) was constituted on 17 April 1952. Its first sitting was held on 13 May 1952. Though elected by universal adult franchise and as such a truly representative body, the first Lok Sabha, in a sense, was highly elitist. It had a marked dominance, especially on its proceedings, of the people who had their education in prestigious and coveted institutions of learning either in India or abroad. Most of them came from urban backgrounds. The single largest professional group was that of lawyers. Although the House had a preponderance of graduates (37 per cent of the total membership), under-matriculates constituted the next largest group having 23.2 per cent of the total.

The average age of the members was 45 years and 8 months. The maximum number of members were in the age-group 50-55 years. Twenty two members forming only 4.4 per cent were women. It was a treat to hear some of the fiery speeches that came from women members. Renu Chakravarty, a communist member from West Bengal, distinguished herself as a great debator in the House having a 'strong yet feminine and musical voice'. She individually took the maximum time of the House. Other important lady members were Sucheta Kriplani, Rajkumari Amrit Kaur, Tarkeshwari Sinha, Vijayalakshmi Pandit and Maragatham Chandrasekhar.

With 364 of the 499 members being from the Congress alone, it was clearly a situation of one-party dominance. However, it could not be said that opposition was inefficient or was rendered ineffective by the large majority of the Congress. In actual practice, it always asserted itself and made its presence felt on every important occasion. On several matters, the Congress could not afford to ignore the opinion of opposition members. Nehru himself was known to respect the sentiments of the members on the other side, sometimes even against the wishes of the members of his own party.

Generally speaking, in terms of quality, the First Lok Sabha consisted of some of the most distinguished men and outstanding parliamentarians, all adept in parliament procedure, talented, accomplished and skilled in the art of parliamentary debate. The Congress party included, to mention a few by way of illustration, besides Prime Minister Nehru, other giants like Purushottam Das Tandon, Harekrishna Mehtab, SK Patil, NV Gadgil, Swaran Singh, R Venkataraman, NG Ranga, Seth Govind Das and Thakurdas Bhargava.

The list of the members from the opposition side was also no less impressive. It consisted of freedom fighters and powerful debators of a high order such as Acharya Kripalani, Ashok Mehta, SP Mukherjee, AK Gopalan, HN Mukherjee, NC Chatterjee, Renu Chakravarty, Meghanad Saha, HV Kamath, Sardar Hukam Singh and others. Each one of these men could be the pride of any parliament in the world. Ram Manohar Lohia was ruthless and brutal in his criticism of Nehru. It was a sight to see Nehru sitting in the House gracefully silent, relaxed and at times softly smiling and listening to Lohia accusing him of daily spending a huge sum on his lifestyle, his security, his dog etc. On his dog alone, Lohia said, Nehru spent 25 rupees per day when the average income of an ordinary Indian was hardly 25 paise per day.

The first Lok Sabha functioned at a time when far-reaching and important changes were taking place in the world. What was happening globally vitally affected India especially because she had just emerged from colonial subjugation and was taking her first steps towards rebuilding and rehabilitating the country's economy on a new basis. Legislation was adopted as the chief instrument of socio-economic engineering. It occupied about 48 per cent of the total time of the sittings of the first Lok Sabha. A large number of legislative measures ushering in great reforms in the social, economic, and political fields were brought on the Statute Book. Seven Private Members' Bills were passed. This remains a record inasmuch as the number has not been surpassed during any other Lok Sabha period.

The first Lok Sabha passed six (second to the seventh) Constitution

Amendment Acts. The Seventh Amendment was to give constitutional effect to the scheme of the reorganization of States.

During the years 1952-57, the House was in a formative period laying down healthy foundations for building the strong edifice of Parliamentary institutions and procedures. New situations had to be faced, fresh procedures evolved and appropriate rules laid down. And, in all this it fared very well indeed and passed on to the succeeding Houses high standards. Its working earned unanimous acclaim from experienced Indian and foreign observes. The *Manchester Guardian,* for example, wrote on 5 June 1954:

> Parliamentary institutions have not had good time in Asia... All that is happening in Asia throws a spotlight on Parliament in Delhi as one institution of the kind which is working in an exemplary way... Pericles said that Athens was the school of Hellas. Mr Nehru without boasting may say that Delhi is the School of Asia.

The second Lok Sabha (1957-62) deserved the credit of having given effect to a large number of legislative measures bringing about significant reforms in social, economic and political fields. Among the bills passed, four amended the Constitution (including the one incorporating Goa into the Indian Union). Two Private Members' Bills were brought on the Statute Book. For the first time, there was a joint sitting of both the Houses to resolve the deadlock on Dowry Prohibition Bill. The importance of the 'Question Hour' as a very potent parliamentary device for ensuring administrative accountability was highlighted by a question which brought to light the Mundhra Scandal and resulted in Minster (TT Krishnamachari)'s and ICS Secretary (HM Patel)'s resignation.

The opposition, though weak and fragmented, remained active and effective and never missed an opportunity to force a discussion.

On the other hand, when it came to preserving the prestige and dignity of the House, it remained united. When, in 1961, *Blitz* ridiculed an Opposition Member, Acharya Kripalani, the whole House stood up as one man. *Blitz* editor Karanjia was called to the bar of the House and reprimanded for breach of parliamentary privilege. Prime Minister Nehru himself was very accommodative of the Opposition point of view. Once he wondered how his government was being tolerated. If he was in the opposition, Nehru said, he could not tolerate it. Later, when Nehru did not accept an amendment moved by Rajaji saying that the majority was with him, Rajaji retorted, 'Majority may be with you but logic is with me', and Nehru gracefully accepted the amendment.

On the last day of the second Lok Sabha, Jawaharlal Nehru remarked: 'considering everything, we have done rather well, and considering the state of the world today when every other day we read about *coup d'etats* in various countries, it is surprising how we have carried on in our normal way'. It could be said the tenure of the second Lok Sabha represented the golden period in the history of Indian parliamentary democracy.

In the third Lok Sabha (1962-67), a remarkable change took place in the composition of the House. The lawyers, after having formed the largest group in the first and the second Lok Sabha, were pushed to the second position, the first position having been taken by the agriculturalists. The opposition members were even more active now. They included both—'the parliamentarians with excessive lung power' and the intellectuals who relied less on the volume of their voice and more on the cogency of points and their argumentative skills. Acharya Kripalani, Ram Manohar Lohia, Madhu Limaye and Minu Masani, were inducted through by-elections. Madhu Limaye proved very difficult to handle for Speaker Hukam Singh for in a Monsoon session he raised privilege issues almost every day, always in his loud and defiant voice.

When a member drew the attention of Acharya Kriplani to the fact that he was criticising a party that had attracted his own wife, the master of biting parliamentary wit, Kripalani retorted:' All these years I thought Congressmen were stupid fools: I never knew they were gangsters too who ran away with others' wives.

Treasury benches consisted of a number of people of equal oratorial capability, intelligence, sound knowledge and deep interest in parliamentary business. They were never silent spectators to whatever was happening around. On many measures proposed by the government, they fearlessly criticised, expressed genuine doubts, and sometimes even opposed government proposals. On many occasions, they joined opposition members in castigating the government for its fault or in demanding resignation of a corrupt or inefficient Minster.

The States Reorganisation Act, 1956 and the 7th Constitution Amendment redesigned the political map of India largely on linguistic lines. Value of Question Hour was vindicated when the Mundhra Scandal was unearthed by Feroze Gandhi's searching question. Powerful Minister TT Krishnamachari and ICS Secretary of the stature of HM Patel had to go.

The Chinese invasion in 1962 was a great shock to Nehru and a significant setback to his foreign policy. Krishna Menon's exit from the Nehru Cabinet was a unique example of Lok Sabha pressure working even in the face of Nehru's support for Menon. In another case, Minister KD Malviya had to resign when he was allegedly accused of having accepted money from a private party in return for official favour.

When Nehru tried to downplay the Chinese aggression by saying that in the area occupied by China not a blade of grass grew, the bald-headed senior Congress leader, Mahavir Tyagi quickly retorted:' Not a blade of grass grows on my head, shall you hand it over to China?'

Minister TT Krishnamachari had to resign a second time in 1965 for allegedly misusing his position. Still another Minister, GL Nanda had to go in 1966 for failure on law and order front in Delhi resulting in the death of seven people during the Anti-Cow Slaughter agitation.

After Nehru and then Shastriji's demise, Indira Gandhi became the first woman Prime Minister of India. An interesting development during the period was that the lawmaking function no more remained the major occupation of the House.

The fourth General Elections marked a watershed in Indian politics. Although the Congress Party retained absolute majority in the House, the losses that it suffered were the heaviest so far. The most important developments on the political and parliamentary scene in India during the fourth Lok Sabha (1967-70) period were the phenomenon of defections and party splits, of the Congress party losing its undisputed dominant position and of non-Congressism emerging as a rallying point for opposition parties.

The support of Indira Gandhi to VV Giri and his election as President, battle between Indira and the Congress syndicate, the controversy of conscience *vs* discipline, split of the Congress in the Gandhi Centenary Year (1969), the ouster of Morarji from Finance Ministership and the nationalisation of major banks, all had their impact on the functioning of Lok Sabha. The phenomenon of defections characterised the period. The House was dissolved prematurely on 27 December, 1970, and thus had a life of only 3 years, 9 months and 10 days.

The fifth Lok Sabha (1971-77) was significantly eventful. Some of the national and international events gave rise to serious debates, discussions and deliberations on the floor of the House. The Shimla Agreement in the wake of India's triumphant victory in the Bangladesh War generated a very lively discussion on the floor of The House. A plethora of legislative measures—some 482—were brought on the statute book. As many as 19 Constitution Amendment Bills were passed. These represented by far the largest number of such bills passed by any Lok Sabha. It was through the Constitution 35th and 36th Amendments that Sikkim was integrated with the Union.

Some incidents and developments that were bound to linger down in the memory lane were the introduction of a pension scheme for former members of Parliament, the Nagarwala issue where the Chief

Cashier of the State Bank of India made a payment of Rs 60 lakh on the basis of alleged oral instructions, and the persistent defiance of the Chair by distinguished members like Jyotirmoy Basu leading to suspension from the House. One also remembers the most heated discussion on the MISA and the long debate on the Import Licences case and the alleged role of the Railway Minister, LN Mishra and a member, Tulmohan Ram. The latter was said to have accepted a bribe for furthering the cause of applicants for import licences.

While a proclamation of Emergency issued earlier in December 1971 following the Pakistan aggression was already in operation, a fresh Proclamation was issued by the President on 25 June 1975, on grounds of threatened internal disturbance. Opposition leaders linked the declaration of a fresh Emergency with the Allahabad High Court's decision declaring the election of Indira Gandhi to the Lok Sabha void and disqualifying her 'from being chosen as, and for being, a member' of either House of Parliament or of any State Legislature for a period of six years. After a fourteen-hour debate, Lok Sabha adopted the resolution approving the Proclamation of Emergency. The most controversial of the decisions of the Lok Sabha were those extending its own life by two years and passing the far-reaching 42nd Constitutional Amendment. But before completing its extended term, the House was dissolved after being in existence for a period of five years, ten months and six days. The dissatisfaction with the Emergency measures and the movement led by Jayaprakash Narayan had made the position of the Congress Government very uncomfortable.

The fifth Lok Sabha left behind some bitter memories of the Emergency legislation, administrative excesses and political isolation of Indira Gandhi. However, there were many positive achievements too. The moments of greatest glory for the nation under the leadership of Indira during the same 5th Lok Sabha period, were the return of the Congress with more than two-thirds majority in Lok Sabha, the decisive victory over Pakistan, creation of independent Bangladesh, Shimla agreement, Indo-Soviet Treaty of Friendship, Sikkim becoming a integral part of the Indian Union, successful underground nuclear explosion establishing India's nuclear capabilities, etc.

The 1977 election brought to power a non-Congress government. But, it was a courageous decision on the part of Gandhi to accept the verdict gracefully, bow out of power and uphold the highest norms of parliamentary democracy. While the ruling party lost, freedom and democracy had won; the system had proved its legitimacy, vibrancy, resilience and vitality. It was established that even the most powerful could be defeated at the polls and transfer of power could be effected through constitutional and peaceful means. It was hardly a surprise, therefore, that the *New York Times* called the results 'an inspiration to all democracies' and US President, Jimmy Carter, in his congratulatory message said:

> The reaffirmation of the democratic process in India through a free, open and vigorous election had been an inspiration to Americans and to peoples in all parts of the world.

Some of the significant work done by the 6th Lok Sabha (1977-79) included an amendment to the Constitution (43rd) to revert to a five-year term for the Lok Sabha and State Assemblies instead of a six year term. Another comprehensive Constitution (44th) Amendment was passed to omit some of the amendments that were inserted by the 42nd Amendment during the Emergency. Almost the entire period was dominated by Janata Government trying to trace out and punish all those guilty of standing with Indira and responsible for the 'atrocities and excesses' of the Emergency period. The Shah Commission inquiry, the Maruti affair, the privilege issues against Indira Gandhi and in one of them, her warrant and arrest, jail and expulsion from the membership of the House, all were part of the same exercise.

Before the Janata Government could settle down to some positive business, serious fissures between the leaders and diverse groups constituting the Janata Party started surfacing. YB Chavan moved a vote of no-confidence in the Council of Ministers headed by Morarji Desai. It brought another non-Congress Council of Ministers, this time headed by Charan Singh who never faced the House and resigned. The 6th Lok Sabha was dissolved after remaining in existence for two years and a half only. The Janata experiment had failed.

The 7th Lok Sabha (1980-84) found Indira back in the saddle. The Congress (I) had avenged its defeat of 1977. Almost all other parties were in bad shape. The single largest group (39.3%) in the seventh Lok Sabha also continued to be that of 'Agriculturists'. In fact, right from the first Lok Sabha onwards, the strength of the agriculturists had been increasing in every successive House. The situation in Punjab dominated the proceedings of the House particularly during the last two years of its term. The Mandal Commission Report which recommended 27 per cent reservations for the backward classes was discussed in a marathon debate till late in the night in the Lok Sabha on 11 August.

On 31 October, 1984, the whole nation was shocked to learn of the dastardly assassination of Prime Minister Indira Gandhi by her own security guards on duty at her official residence. Rajiv Gandhi succeeded her as the Prime Minster. Held under the shadow of the assassination of Indira Gandhi, the 1984 elections gave a three-fourth majority to the Congress, which the party did not command even during Nehru's time. In every sense, the 8th Lok Sabha (1985-89) had a new look. In the International Year of the Youth, India had its youngest Prime Minister. Also, the House had some top stars from the film industry like Amitabh Bachhan, Vijayantimala Bali and Sunil Dutt.

The most distinguished characteristic of the 8th Lok Sabha was that an unusually large number of its members were really new. The eighth Lok Sabha had the distinction of having the largest proportion of educated members. More than 71 per cent were graduates or with higher attainments. The number of under-matriculates declined to 7.9 per cent to become the lowest in any Lok Sabha. In terms of professional background, the trend of the last few Lok Sabhas was continued and the agriculturists and lawyers continued to contribute the largest groups in the House. As many as 13 Constitution Amendment Bills were passed. Ten of these were finally enacted during its lifetime. The two most important amendments were those providing for disqualification of members on grounds of defection and reducing the voting age from 21 years to 18 years.

The Indian Post Office (Amendment) Bill, 1986 caused uproarious scenes in the Lok Sabha when it was taken up for consideration. It was, however, passed by both the Houses and sent to the President for his assent. Considerable public debate was generated on the issue. Finally, the Bill was returned by the President to the Government for clarification/reconsideration. It is significant that neither was assent refused nor was the Bill returned to Houses of Parliament. The Muslim Women (Protection of Rights of Divorce), Bill, 1986 generated lively discussions in the wake of the *Shah Bano case* and the Bill was passed at a marathon sitting on 5-6 May 1986 at 2.45 am.

The eighth Lok Sabha will be remembered in India's Parliamentary history for many important debates under various procedural devices. Some discussions were marked by pandemonia and procedural wrangles which also saw the suspension of 63 members of the Opposition on a single day—15 March 1989—for the remaining days of the week. The same was the case with discussions on the matter relating to the purchase of the 155 mm Howitzer guns from the Bofors company of Sweden.

Closely linked to the Bofors debate was the debate on the Report of the Comptroller and Auditor General of India on the purchase of these guns from Sweden. A record of sorts was created when the House was adjourned eight times on a single day—20 July, 1989. These developments ultimately culminated in *en masse* resignations by Opposition members from the Lok Sabha. 124 members resigned their seats in the House. Of these, 107 resigned during the Fourteenth Session (Part I) alone; 73 tendered their resignation on a single day—21 July, 1989. The eighth Lok Sabha verily was a historic House in many respects. It will be remembered for beginning the system of Departmental Standing Committees.

In the ninth Lok Sabha (1989-91) though Congress was still the largest single party, the number of parties represented was an all time record. There were as many as 24 parties. Also, it was for the first time that no party had secured a clear majority. A minority government of the Janata Dal was formed by VP Singh with the support of the BJP and the Left Parties from outside. The ninth Lok Sabha had the unique distinction of having the single largest party—the Indian National Congress (I) with 197 members—as the officially recognised opposition and the former Prime Minister, Rajiv Gandhi as the Leader of the Opposition with the rank of a Cabinet Minister to sit as the Leader of the Opposition in the Lok Sabha. The new members in Lok Sabha included Mayawati of BSP from UP, Uma Bharti of BJP from MP, Uma Gajapati Raju of Congress from Andhra, Subhashini Ali of CPI from UP, MJ Akbar of the Congress from Bihar and Atinderpal Singh, Simranjit Singh Mann and Bimal Khalsa (widow of Beant Singh, assassin of Indira Gandhi) from Punjab. Simranjit Singh never took his seat in Lok Sabha as he was not allowed to enter and take oath with a sword on.

The situation in Jammu & Kashmir, Punjab and Assam dominated the Proceedings. On 7 August, quite suddenly it seemed, VP Singh announced in the two Houses his government's 'momentous decision of social justice' on the report of the Mandal Commission. VP Singh's announcement, it was alleged, was politically motivated. Intense and massive agitation launched by the students, teachers, lawyers and others accompanied by self-immolation of young boys and girls on open streets virtually rocked the Lok Sabha.

The VP Singh Government could not complete even a year in office. Following the withdrawal of support by BJP and its allies in retaliation against the arrest of LK Advani and stoppage of his Rath Yatra to Ayodhya for construction of the Ram temple, it was obvious that VP Singh had lost majority support in Lok Sabha. However, he refused to resign and instead offered to prove his majority on the floor of the House. On 7 November, the motion of confidence was defeated by 356 to 151votes with six members abstaining. This established another record in as much as it was for the first time that the government was defeated on a vote of confidence. The President invited Chandra Shekhar to form the new government. However, his minority government was also short-lived.

On 6th March, Chandra Shekhar referred to the crisis created by the boycott by the Congress (I) Party and said 'I am unable to lead the government and propose to meet the President and offer the resignation of the Council of Ministers of my government'. The same day, the President in a letter to the Prime Minster, conveyed his acceptance of the resignation. The week-long political uncertainly was ended on 13 March, with the President dissolving the ninth Lok Sabha.

The biggest casualty during the ninth Lok Sabha period was institutional; the rules, conventions and time-honoured traditions in many respects were given a good-bye. There were more than the usual instances of pandemonia, noisy and uproarious scenes, walk-outs, crowding in the well of the House and raising of slogans, frequent adjournments and the like. When the ninth Lok Sabha was dissolved on 13 March, no less a person than the distinguished parliamentarian and socialist leader, Madhu Limaye, wrote that it had 'at last made its inglorious exit'. Limaye added, the entire tenure of the ninth Lok Sabha was disappointing and the last day was a day of national shame. At a time when the nation was passing through a grave economic crisis, Members were allowed to vote for themselves increased pension, allowances and facilities by relaxing rules. The most outrageous and indefensible of these was proportionate pension for life on completing only one year as a member. By this one act, the members of all parties proved that they were more concerned with petty self-interests than with the larger national issues and could not care less for public opinion or susceptibilities. A wave of nation-wide indignation followed the hasty adoption of the Bill by the two Houses. Eventually the President did not give his assent to the Bill. Secondly, financial business including voting on demands for billions of rupees for the Union, Vote on Account for 1991-92, Supplementary Grants for 1990-91 and the budgets of four States and one Union Territory under President's rule were passed within minutes without any scrutiny or discussion, making a farce of the role of Parliament. Also, as many as 18 Bills were passed again without discussion within less than two hours, setting a record of sorts but a rather dismal one.

Fortunately, the ninth Lok Sabha's tenure was brief. Experiment of minority governments run with outside support having flopped, the country was back at square one facing another general election within less than two years.

The tenth Lok Sabha (1991-96) was constituted under the shadow of the grim tragedy of the most gruesome and ghastly assassination of Rajiv Gandhi who was not only a candidate for Lok Sabha membership but also the most likely person to take over as Prime Minster after the elections. The tenth General Election was the most brutal and violent election in Indian history. Congress (I) emerged as the largest party in the House but a little short of absolute majority to form a stable government on its own. The sympathy generated as a result of the assassination of Rajiv Gandhi did add a few seats to the Congress (I) tally but it was not enough. The party was almost completely routed from two of the most populous States—UP and Bihar. The unanimous election of PV Narasimha Rao, first as the president of the Congress and then as the leader of the Congress Parliamentary Party and his appointment as the first Prime Minister of India from the Southern States strengthened the integration sentiment.

During the period 1991-1994, the Congress Government headed by Narasimha Rao strengthened its numerical position in Lok Sabha and acquired simple majority largely through managing splits in Opposition parties and allowing Opposition members to defect to its ranks allegedly through outright cash prizes and promises of ministership and the like. The defectors were not disqualified from membership as they were held rightly or wrongly to be covered by the provisions pertaining to splits in parties.

In an unusual move to placate members of Parliament and create greater vested interests in somehow continuing to be members for the full term, each member was allotted a crore of rupees each year to be spent under his directions in his constituency. From the procedural angle, the most noteworthy development during the tenth Lok Sabha was that of setting up a full-fledged system of 17 Departmental Standing Parliamentary Committees *inter alia* entrusted with the task of making an in-depth scrutiny of budget proposals and demands for grants.

The eleventh Lok Sabha (1996-97) had the distinction of more than half of its members being entirely new to Parliamentary life. They had never been members of a Parliament. Also, persons with criminal records had the largest ever representation in this House. Again, it would be remembered for the shortest ever life-span and the inability of political parties to form a stable government with support of majority of the members. As many as 28 political parties were represented in the House. We saw three governments and Prime Ministers come and go: Atal Bihari Vajpayee for 13 days followed by Deve Gowda and Gujral. It was a strange phenomenon that the two largest parties in the House—the BJP and the Congress—were outside the government while some 13-14 tiny parties of diverse and opposite persuasions cobbled majorities in the lust for sharing the spoils of power. Both Gowda and Gujral were members of Rajya Sabha. During the short life of the 11th Lok Sabha there were as many as four confidence motions moved by the Prime Ministers themselves.

The average age of the 11th Lok Sabha members was 52.82 years. Women members numbered 40 or 7.36 per cent. In terms of educational background, 77.36 per cent members were graduates or above. The largest single professional group continued to be that of agriculturists.

Indiscipline, disorder and pandemonia resulting in House not being allowed to function and getting repeatedly adjourned became routinised but the show lasted only 18 months. Be it as it may, the 11th Lok Sabha will be remembered for electing to the office of the Speaker for the first time a member of the opposition, PA Sangma who was also the first tribal, the first Christian and the youngest ever Speaker. At his initiative, a special 6-day session of the two Houses was held to commemorate the Golden Jubilee of Independence. For the first time in the history of Parliament, the Speaker delivered a speech in the House. He gave a clarion call from the Chair for a second freedom struggle.

It was an interesting coincidence that on his 50th birthday on 1 September 1997, both Lok Sabha and Rajya Sabha, as part of the celebrations of the 50th Anniversary of India's Independence, unanimously passed a historic resolution setting a national agenda of electoral reforms, transparency, probity and accountability in public life, preserving the authority and dignity of Parliament and all the political parties starting a powerful national campaign for eradicating criminalisation from politics and controlling population.

In the 12th Lok Sabha also, no party could secure a clear majority. A BJP-led coalition government headed by Atal Bihari Vajpayee was formed but it could last only for 13 months. Since no alternative government could be formed, fresh elections had to be called. The 12th Lok Sabha thus became the shortest lived Lok Sabha. Obstructions in the proceedings of the House, not allowing it to function and forcing frequent adjournments continued to be part of the strategy of the opposition. About 10 per cent of the time was taken up by them actually. A first during the 12th Lok Sabha was presentation of the budget at 11 am instead of the traditional time 5 pm.

In the matter of the background of members, 77 per cent of the members were university graduates or above. The number of women members had gone up to 44 or 8 per cent plus. Profession-wise the agriculturists continued to be the single largest group. For the first time, a member of the Scheduled Castes, GMC Balayogi of the Telugu Desam Party was elected Speaker.

At the beginning of the thirteenth Lok Sabha, Balayogi was again elected Speaker but due to a tragic accident he died prematurely and could not complete the term. Atal Bihari Vajpayee formed a coalition government of some 23 parties which despite many stresses and strains and a succession of crises continued and proved considerably stable with no alternative in sight. Fierce trials of strength were made on the floor of the House, first on the Prevention of Terrorism Bill and then on the motion on Gujarat. For the third time in the history of Parliament, the President had to call a joint sitting of the two Houses to pass the Anti-terrorism Bill. In March 2003, Vajpayee became the first non-Congress Prime Minister to have completed five years in office.

After the 2004 general election, the 14th Lok Sabha was constituted on 17 May 2004. It was dissolved on 18 May 2009. Sonia Gandhi was the leader of the largest party, the Congress and its Alliance, the UPA, but in a departure from tradition and precedents, it was not the leader of the largest party or alliance, but her nominee Manmohan Singh, a Member of Rajya Sabha, who was called upon by President Kalam to form the government. The leader of the largest party in Opposition (BJP), LK Advani was recognised as the Leader of the Opposition. For the first time, a communist Member of the House, Somnath Chatterjee was elected as the Speaker. The issue that generated much controversy was the effort, at retrospectively from 1959, legalising the illegality of members to hold offices of profit under the government by including a large number of such offices in the list of offices exempted from disqualification under the constitutional provisions. The Bill passed by the two Houses was returned by the President for reconsideration. The Bill was, however, passed again and when presented to him a second time, the President gave his assent.

In the matter of its constitution, the 14th Lok Sabha had the highest representation of agriculturists (41.88 per cent) followed by political and social workers (23.77%) and lawyers (12.26 per cent). It had about 50.46 per cent graduates. The number of non-matriculates came down to less than 3 per cent. Women members (46) constituted 8.48 per cent of the total membership. The time devoted to legislation came to only 21.63 per cent. The number of Bills passed were 247 that included two Constitution Amendments. The important pieces of legislation included (i) The Right to Information Act, 2005, (ii) National Rural Employment Guarantee Act, 2005, (iii) Protection of Women from Domestic Violence Act, 2005, and (iv) Disaster Management Act, 2005. The number of days on which the Lok Sabha had its sittings came to 332 in five years which worked out to less than 70 sittings per year, 20% of the time of the House was lost in disorder etc.

During the 14th Lok Sabha period Pratibha Patil was elected as the first woman President of the nation while Hamid Ansari became the Vice President.

Of procedural interest was the innovation of setting up some parliamentary fora on subjects like (i) Water Conservation and Management, (ii) Youth, (iii) Children, (iv) Population and Health, and (v) Global Warming and Climate Change. Each of them consisted of 31 Members—21 from Lok Sabha and 10 from Rajya Sabha. Different from Parliamentary Committees, the fora provided members an opportunity to informally interact with the concerned Ministers.

Parliamentary Museum set up during the eighth Lok Sabha period was relaunched. Also, as a first of its kind anywhere in the world, Lok Sabha launched a 24-hour TV Channel of its own—managed, operated and owned by it.

The 14th Lok Sabha shall be remembered also for the cash for votes episode where purchase of members for survival of the government was alleged.

Results of the general elections for the 16th Lok Sabha were declared on 16 May 2014. The 2014 election was the most expensive so far and as many as 342 members were elected with minority of votes cast. Incidentally, of the 242 BJP members more than half (142) had won with a majority of votes cast. Another noteworthy feature of the 16th Lok Sabha was that as many as 318 of the 543 members were entirely new to the House. For the first time after thirty years, a single party had returned with a clear majority and a massive popular mandate. BJP got 282 seats, Congress 44 and others 217. Congress had the worst ever performance. It could not get even the minimum necessary 55 seats to be recognised as a parliamentary party. As a result, there could be no Leader of the Opposition in the 16th Lok Sabha.[2]

In May 2015, when the 16th Lok Sabha had completed one full year of tenure. President Pranab Mukherjee summed up the performance of the first year of the 16th Lok Sabha when he said on 18 May 2015:

> Till now, the 16th Lok Sabha has sat for 90 days and passed 55 government bills; 24 bills were passed in the just-concluded fourth session. Further, the House sat late for 55 hours and 19 minutes in the fourth session to transact urgent government business. Seven hours and 4 minutes were sadly lost due to interruptions and forced adjournments. This is less than in many previous sessions.
>
> I am particularly happy the Constitution Amendment Bill related to the Land Boundary Agreement between India and Bangladesh was passed unanimously by both Houses of Parliament.

---

[2] See chapter on 'Leader of the Opposition'.

Process of Legislation

How Laws Are Made

FRENCH REVOLUTIONARY Mirabeau said: 'Laws are like sausages, you should never watch them being made'. Legislation or law making may seem to be a somewhat dull and drab business. If laws are made by the legislature, the law makers certainly find the business of law making uninteresting. Those who have seen Houses of Parliament at work would know that the legislative business is taken up only in the afternoon and usually the attendance at that time is the thinnest and interest minimal. It is not unusual to notice some elderly Minister or Member enjoying an afternoon siesta in the House when an important legislation is being debated. Interestingly, according to a ruling from the Chair, sleeping in the House is not unparliamentary, only snoring is .

The concept of law, as in the term 'Rule of Law' includes the objectives of natural justice, equity, individual honour and fair play.

It is quite conceivable that a law passed by the Legislature may be violative of the Constitution or of the principles of rule of law. This is what Mahatma Gandhi called 'lawless law'. Rule of law is to be understood as opposed to arbitrary rule of a person or party.

The modern concept of law is different from that under Austinian Jurisprudence. It is not that of a static and inert body of rules of action of general application and equal enforceability established by authority etc. Today we look at law as a complex dynamic process and a living organism that keeps growing, changing and getting newer and newer definitions through social urges, economic pressures, play of political forces, delegated legislation by the Executive, judicial interpretations etc. At every stage, in the process of implementation, law is being actually made and in effect modified. It is carried at an entrance to Yale Law School, 'Law is a living growth, not a changeless code.' We cannot attribute the act of law making to any one institution or body of people. All the three organs of the State—the Executive, the Legislature and the Judiciary—along with the society at large have a participatory role in the process. The Executive drafts the law and the Rules and later applies them, the legislature debates and approves and the Judiciary interprets and declares the law. In other words, law continues to be in the making after it is passed by the Legislature. It grows and may even undergo changes during the processes of operation. As someone said, laws made by the legislature are composed of words and words are as slippery as banana peel. They mean what they are interpreted to mean. Law is the expression of a principle of order to which we must all confirm in our conduct and relations as members of society and citizens in a democratic polity if social tensions and frictions are to be avoided.

In any organised society, law is employed to govern the conduct of the people to regulate the behaviour of everyone—high or low. Law has to settle disputes between individuals or groups through adjudication. The content and nature of laws in any society depend on the kind of need and complexion of the society. The ultimate aim, however, is to do justice. The end purpose of law is to provide justice to all individual and group interests. In one word, the goal of law is justice—social, economic and political. Rule of Law does not permit arbitrary rule of any person. Law has to discipline even state power and governmental authority if it goes arbitrary and violates individual freedom and rights.

If pursuit of justice calls for reinterpreting a law or changing its words and content, so be it. The supreme law, said Cicero, comprehended to mean something that confirms with the standards of justice, equity and good conscience. Laws emerge from the accumulated experience and wisdom of the past to meet specific situations at specific times.

As events occur, situations change; social-economic demands vary, laws have to be read as 'sorted, selected, moulded and adopted in subordinations to the ends of social utility, economic need and overall justice'. In other words, laws have to evolve according to the needs of time and place. For eg you may need to give top priority as law needs to adjust quickly to new institutions that arise and changing economic demands on the state may make restatement of some laws imperative. Also, to the extent that law is seen as a conflict resolution mechanism, fresh legislation may become necessary to resolve the emerging socio-economic conflict situations.

Generally, when we speak of law making or legislative process, our reference is towards statute law resulting from the exercise of legislative powers of the Union or State Legislatures. In that sense, law making is, by definition, the business of the Legislature and, on principle, it is often said to be its main function. In practice, however, over the years, there has been a fundamental change, both in qualitative and quantitative terms; legislation has ceased to be the predominant business of the Legislature. Also, the legislature is not the only actor in the drama of law making. Now-a-days only a small portion of the time of the Legislature is devoted to the business of law making. In fact, initiative in law making has largely moved to be with the Executive. In case of Parliament, during the period of the first Lok Sabha, nearly 50 per cent of the time was devoted to legislative business. This has since been brought down to nearly 12-13 per cent only. Also, there are other pre and post natal players in the game whose role has increasingly become more significant.

Parliament at best only discusses, influences, scrutinises and by putting its seal of approval legitimises legislative intent of the Executive expressed through Bills, Rules, Regulations etc. Its role in the legislative process thus is more legitimatisational rather than making the law

The story of law making begins in the Departments of the Executive much before a Bill comes before any House of the Legislature. It continues even after the Bill is passed into a law. Law also covers rules, regulations, by-laws etc. made by a subordinate executive authority under powers delegated to it expressly by the main statute. This is referred to as 'delegated' or 'subordinate' legislation.

In principle, legislative proposals emanate from social urges, felt needs and expressed demands of the people. In a welfare state with a democratic polity, the objective of legislation is to bring good to the people, to mitigate hardships, to resolve conflicts, to curb social, political and economic evils and to smoothen the road to social justice. Sometimes newer and newer social, economic, political or technological pressures necessitate fresh legislation or amendments to existing laws.

Article 13 of the Constitution of India declares all laws inconsistent with fundamental rights void and inoperative. It lays down that no law shall be made that violates or abridges any fundamentals right. Directive principles are in the nature of directives to the state meant to guide it *inter alia* in making laws with a view to secure a social order for the promotion of welfare of the people, ensure equality before law, empowerment of weaker sections, elimination of discrimination, prevention of concentration of wealth and means of production, elimination of exploitation, use of ownership and control of material resources for common good, protection of environment, forests and wildlife etc. The mighty weapon of law has got to be wisely used to restore balance to the economic structure and to remove the causes of economic tension from the political body of the community and to provide economic justice to the people. If the freedom of the individual and his rights need to be regulated in order to achieve social justice, then regulations are a part of the price that democratic citizens must cheerfully pay in order to sustain the democratic way of life.

Law needs to play an important role in building socio-economic justice. Legislation passed by elected representatives of the people in their legislature is the voice of the people. Under the scheme of the Constitution, it is entirely possible to bring about a social revolution through the processes of law.

Beginnings of a legislative proposal involving major policy issues may be traced to a promise made in the election manifesto of the winning party/parties, a policy decision/directive by the cabinet, an initiative at the level of the Minister, need felt by a Ministry/ Department, public pressure, popular demand or agitation, experience of the working of the existing laws, Judicial verdict.

The formulation of a legislative proposal implies a great deal of technical preparation and harmonisation of several competing claims, interests and other considerations. All the sources vital to legislation—technical data and statistics, accumulated administrative experience and expertise—are available only with the government. In all cases, as soon as a proposal is conceived, the steps that follow include:

> The concerned Ministry or Department examining the political, administrative, financial, economic or social implications of the proposal, Consultation with other Ministries of the Government of India or State Governments concerned, Obtaining the opinion of experts, where necessary, Interaction with professional and other interest groups such as business, labour, agriculture and industry, where deemed advisable, in-depth scrutiny of legal/constitutional aspects of

> the problem with reference to and in consultation with the Ministry of Law and/or the Attorney General, preparation of a self-contained Memorandum or note for the cabinet, consideration by the cabinet of the note mainly in regard to broad policy aspects involved, where necessary, reference to a Cabinet Committee or an *ad hoc* GOM for examination of the proposal in greater details, cabinet approval of the principle and the policy involved and, if deemed appropriate, requiring that the final draft of the Bill be submitted to the cabinet for detailed study and approval before being sent to a House of Parliament, drafting the proposed legislation in the form necessary for introduction in a House of Legislature ie. as a Bill.

Drafting a bill is handled by the government draftsman in the Ministry of Law and Justice. He is assisted by departmental experts and officials. The draft Bill prepared by the draftsman is examined by the concerned Ministry and administrative machinery in consultation with all other authorities likely to be involved in implementation. Sometimes, a Bill may have to be drafted several times. Only then does it get its final shape and is ready for introduction in the House of the Legislature.

Drafting a Bill is a highly technical job. It is a task of great responsibility and calls for high degree of legal acumen, mastery over language and experience and scholarship of a high order. The Draftman's job is very exacting. He must possess a wide and intimate knowledge of laws, leading court judgements, technical terminology and intricacies of the functioning of government departments.

A government Bill can be introduced in the House by the minister concerned. For this, a minister is required to give seven days' notice to move for leave to introduce the Bill. Simultaneously, two duly corrected copies of the Bill are sent to the Secretary of the House in which it is sought to be introduced. After the Bill has been found complete in all respects by the Secretariat, it is included in the List of Business on a date selected by the Speaker. Normally, copies of the Bill are made available to the members at least two days prior to the date on which it is proposed to be introduced.

The Three Readings: A Bill has to pass through different stages in the House before it becomes an Act. Each Bill undergoes three readings. First Reading, Second Reading, and Third Reading.

(i) *First Reading:* It is necessary to ask for leave of the House to introduce a Bill. After the Question Hour on the appointed day, the minister in charge of the Bill on being called upon by the Speaker, rises in his seat and says, '*Sir, I beg to move for leave to introduce the Bill...*'. Generally, the leave is granted by a voice vote and is rarely opposed. The Minister rises again to say, '*Sir, I introduce the Bill...*'.

Usually, the 'introduction' which is the 'first reading' of a Bill is only a formality and by convention there is no discussion at this stage. But, if introduction of a Bill is opposed on the ground that the proposed legislation is outside the legislative competence of the Parliament, the Chair may permit a full discussion in which the Attorney-General also may participate. The question is put to vote of the House thereafter.

After a Bill has been 'introduced' in the House, it is published in the Gazette of India. Even before introduction, a Bill can be published in the Gazette with the permission of the Speaker Chairman. In such a case, leave of the House to introduce the Bill is not necessary. In other words, the Bill does not have to go through the introduction stage.

(ii) *Second Reading:* Second Reading forms the most elaborate and vital stage in the life of a Bill because it is at this stage that it receives detailed and minute examination. The second reading or the consideration stage consists of two steps which may be called as the first Stage and second Stage.

The First Stage: The first stage involves the general discussion on the Bill as a whole where only the principle underlying the Bill is discussed and not the details of the Bill. At this stage, it is open to the House to refer the Bill either to a Select Committee of the House or to circulate it to elicit opinion thereon or straightaway take it into consideration.

Reference to Committee: A Bill may be referred to a Select Committee or a Joint Committee. The members of the Select Committee are drawn from among the members of the House where the Bill has originated. In the case of a Joint Committee, representation of members from Lok Sabha and Rajya Sabha, will be 2:1. The Chairman of the Joint Committee is appointed by the Presiding Officer of the House in which the Bill was introduced. These are *ad hoc* Committees which are appointed to consider particular Bills referred to them.

Bills may also now be referred by either House or its Presiding Officer to the new departmentally related Joint Standing Committees of the two Houses in accordance with the subject matter of each Bill.

The Committee considers the Bill clause by clause just as the House does. Amendments can be moved to various clauses by members of the Committee. The Committee can also take evidence from experts, associations or public bodies who are interested in the measure. Procedure for consideration of a Bill is the same as it is in the House. After clauses, Schedules, etc. have been individually considered and adopted by the Committee, the Lok Sabha Secretariat prepares a report for presentation to the House(s) which, in its turn, considers the Bill as reported by the Committee.

Eliciting Opinion: If a motion for circulation of the Bill for the purpose of eliciting opinion thereon is adopted, the Secretariat of the House circulates letters to all the State governments and Union territories asking them to publish the Bill in their Gazettes for inviting opinions of local bodies, associations, individuals or institutions concerned with the Bill. The period for eliciting opinion is generally specified in the motion for circulation of the Bill, but where no date has been specified, the State governments are asked to send opinions within three months of the adoption of the motion. After the opinions have been received, these are laid on the Table of the House followed by a motion for reference of the Bill to a Select/Joint Committee. It is not ordinarily permissible at this stage to move a motion for consideration of the Bill. The Bill again passes through the Committee stage and the Bill, as reported, is presented to the House.

After the report of the Select or Joint Committee on a Bill has been presented to the House, the minister may make any one of these motions—that the Bill as reported, be taken into consideration or that the Bill, as reported, be committed to the same Committee or to a new Committee or that the Bill be circulated or recirculated, as the case may be, for the purpose of eliciting opinion or further opinion thereon.

In case the minister prefers to move the motion that the Bill, as reported, be taken into consideration, a debate is allowed. The scope of the debate is confined to the Bill as reported by the Committee and the principle of the Bill is not open to discussion again, because the House, in effect, commits itself to the principle of the Bill when a motion to refer the Bill to a Committee is adopted.

The Second Stage: After the motion that the Bill or the Bill as reported by the Select/Joint Committee, be taken into consideration has been adopted, the Bill is taken up for consideration clause by clause. Each clause is placed before the House separately for discussion. Immediately after a clause is placed before the House, amendments thereto can be moved subject to the conditions of admissibility. The clause by clause consideration is often long and laborious as each clause is normally discussed separately and each amendment (except those withdrawn by the mover) is also discussed, adopted or rejected by the House. Amendments, if accepted, become a part of the Bill.

(iii) *Third Reading:* When all the clauses and schedules, if any, of the Bill have been considered and voted upon by the House, the Minister can move that the Bill be passed. At this stage, discussion is confined to arguments either in support of the Bill or for its rejection without referring the details thereto further than is absolutely necessary. Only verbal, formal and consequential amendments are allowed to be moved at this stage. Since the general principles of the Bill have already been agreed to and its details have also been examined, the third reading is seldom an occasion for a lengthy debate.

In passing an ordinary Bill, a simple majority of members present and voting is required. In a parliamentary system with the government enjoying majority support in the Lok Sabha, a Government Bill, therefore, has got nearly full guarantee of easy passage.

It is true that when a Bill is referred to a Parliamentary Committee, it is done so in a much amended form. Also, when the government is sure of itself, it may accept amendments even from opposition members. I recall this happening once when Pandit Nehru as PM was piloting a Bill.

Bill in the Other House: After the Bill has been passed by the originating House, it is transmitted to the other House for its concurrence with a message to that effect. Here, again, it goes through all the three stages. The House which receives the Bill can take either of the following courses:

(a) It may reject it altogether giving rise to a deadlock between the two Houses.

(b) It may pass the Bill as it is or with amendments. If it passes it as transmitted by the originating House, it goes to the President for his assent. If, on the contrary, it is passed with amendments, the Bill is returned to the first House. There the amended Bill is laid on the Table of the House. After two days, the minister concerned may move that the amendment(s) as proposed by the other House, be taken into consideration. If the House agrees to the amendments(s) proposed by the other House, the Bill is deemed to have been passed, as amended, by both the Houses. If, however, the originating House does not agree to the amendments proposed by the other House, the Bill is sent again to the latter to get its concurrence. If this House continues to insist on its amendments, the result is a deadlock.

(c) It may take no action on the Bill, ie. keep it lying on its Table.

In such a case, if more than six months elapse from the date it receives the Bill, a deadlock is deemed to have taken place.

Joint-sitting of the Two Houses: In case of a deadlock due to disagreement between the two Houses on a Bill, an extraordinary situation arises that is resolved by both the Houses sitting together. The Constitution empowers the President to summon a 'joint-sitting' of both the Houses for the purpose of deliberation and voting on the Bill; unless the Bill has already lapsed due to the dissolution of the Lok Sabha. Such a joint-sitting is presided over by the Speaker who is assisted by the Secretary-General, Lok Sabha. The joint-sitting is governed by the Rules of Procedure of the Lok Sabha. At the joint-sitting, only those amendments can be proposed which become necessary due to the delay in the passage of the Bill. The decisions at such sittings are taken by the majority of the total number of members of both the Houses present and voting. Thus, Lok Sabha, due to its numerical superiority may have a decisive advantage. The Dowry Prohibition Bill, 1961, the Banking Service Commission (Repeal) Bill, 1978, and the Prevention of Terrorism Bill 2002, were passed at joint-sittings.

Assent to Bills: When a Bill has been passed by both the Houses either singly or at a joint-sitting, the Bill is presented to the President for his assent. The President may assent to the Bill or withhold his assent. But since the President is a constitutional head, he would normally gives his assent.

When the President gives his assent, the Bill becomes an Act from the date of his assent. Instead of refusing to give his assent he may return the Bill with a message for reconsideration by the two Houses. If, however, the Houses pass the Bill a second time, with or without amendments, and the Bill is presented again to the President for his assent, he shall have no power to withhold his assent to the Bill.

Types of Bills

There are many variants, types and categories of Bills requiring different procedures for passage, eg:

Money Bills

The Constitution provides an elaborate definition of a Money Bill in article 110. According to this article, a Bill is deemed to be Money Bill if it contains only provisions dealing with matters of money—taxes, borrowing, expenditure, withdraw of money etc. all or any of the matters relating to:

- (a) the imposition, abolition, remission, alteration of any tax;
- (b) the regulation or borrowing of money by the government;
- (c) the payment of moneys into or withdrawal of moneys from the Consolidated or the Contingency Funds of India;
- (d) declaring a new item to be expenditure charged on the Consolidated Fund; and
- (e) any matter incidental to any of the matters specified in sub-clauses (a) to (f) of Article 110(1).

But a Bill shall not be deemed to be a Money Bill by reason only if it provides for the demand or the payment of fees for licence or fees for service rendered or by reason that it provides for imposition, abolition and regulation, etc. of any tax by a local authority or body for local purposes. It may be remembered that in case any question arises whether a Bill is a Money Bill or not, the decision of the Speaker will be final.

A Money Bill cannot be introduced in the Rajya Sabha. It can be introduced in the Lok Sabha only on the recommendation of the President. After a Money Bill has been passed by the Lok Sabha, it is passed on to the Rajya Sabha for its recommendations with a certificate by the Speaker that it is a Money Bill. The Rajya Sabha cannot reject a Money Bill nor can it amend it by virtue of its own powers. It must, within a period of 14 days from the date of receipt of the Bill, return the Bill to the Lok Sabha with its recommendations. The Lok Sabha may thereupon either accept or reject all or any of the recommendations of the Rajya Sabha. If the Lok Sabha accepts any of the recommendations of the Rajya Sabha, the Money Bill shall be deemed to have been passed by both the Houses with the amendments recommended by the Rajya Sabha and accepted by the Lok Sabha. If the Lok Sabha does not accept any of the recommendations of the Rajya Sabha, the Bill shall be deemed to have been passed by both the Houses in the form in which it was passed by the Lok Sabha (before the amendments recommended by the Rajya Sabha). Further, if a Money Bill passed and transmitted to the Rajya Sabha for its recommendation is not returned to the Lok Sabha within the said period of 14 days, it shall be deemed to have been passed by both the Houses at the expiration of 14 days. There is no chance of any disagreement between the two Houses in regard to Money Bills as in the case of an ordinary Bill, where the Rajya Sabha enjoys a co-equal power with the Lok Sabha. Hence, there is no provision of a joint-sitting in the case of a Money Bill. The approval of a Money Bill by the Rajya Sabha is, in effect, only formal and routine. In case of Money Bill, the President cannot send it back for recommendation. He either assents or may withhold assent (Article 111/200).

Financial Bills

The Constitution distinguishes Money Bills from the Financial Bills. Generally speaking, a Financial Bill may be any Bill that relates to revenue or expenditure. Besides providing for any of the matters specified in the Constitution for a Money Bill, it may also provide for other matters. For the sake of convenience, the Financial Bills may be devided into two categories:

Category A: Those Bills which make provisions for any of the matters specified in Art. 110 for a Money Bill but do not contain solely those matters, eg. a Bill that contains a taxation clause, but does not deal solely with taxation.

Category B: Bills containing provisions involving expenditure from the Consolidated Fund.

Difference between a Money Bill and a Financial Bill

The difference between a Money Bill and a Financial Bill, as provided in the Constitution, is merely technical. Accordingly, all Financial

Bills are not the Money Bills. Only those Finance Bills may be Money Bills which contain solely the matters specified under Art. 110/199 and which are, above all, certified by the Speaker to be Money Bills.

Besides, there is a slight procedural difference as far as the passage of Money Bills and Financial Bills through both the Houses is concerned. A Money Bill can be introduced only in the Lok Sabha on the recommendation of the President and the Rajya Sabha has no power to withhold its concurrence. A Financial Bill of category A, that is to say, any Bill which contains any of the matters specified for a Money Bill but does not exclusively deal with such matters, has two features in common with a Money Bill, viz. (a) that it cannot be introduced in the Rajya Sabha and also (b) that it cannot be introduced except on the recommendation of the President. But, it not being a Money Bill, the Rajya Sabha is fully empowered to reject or amend it as it does in the case of an ordinary Bill. Subject to the limitation that an amendment other than for reduction and abolition of tax cannot be moved in either House without the President's recommendation. Such a Bill has to go through all the stages in the Rajya Sabha as an ordinary Bill and in case of a disagreement between the two Houses, the provision of joint-sitting is resorted to for resolving the deadlock. It may be stressed that the provision for joint-sitting is not applicable in the case of a Money Bill.

Further, a Financial Bill of Category B containing, *inter alia*, a proposal that involves expenditure from the Consolidated Fund of India and also does not include any matter specified in article 110, is treated as an ordinary Bill and hence can be introduced in either House and the Rajya Sabha has full power either to reject or amend it. It does not require the recommendation of the President for its introduction. However, the recommendation of the President is essential for its consideration by either House. In other words, the President's recommendation is not a condition precedent to its introduction as in the case of the Money Bill and the Financial Bill of Category A, but in this case unless such recommendation has been received, neither House can pass the Bill. In all other respects, such a Bill is governed by the same procedure as an ordinary Bill, including the provision of a joint-sitting in case of disagreement between the two Houses.

Constitution (Amendment) Bills

The procedure for amendment of the Constitution of India has been laid down in Article 368. The power to amend the Constitution is vested in the Parliament. An amendment of the Constitution may be initiated by introduction of a Bill for the purpose in either House of Parliament. Such a Bill may be brought forward by the government or by a private member. Generally, Constitution (Amendment) Bills brought forward by ministers are introduced in the Lok Sabha. A Constitution (Amendment) Bill initiated by a private member, apart from being subject to the normal rules applicable to a private member's Bill, has also to be examined and recommended for introduction in the House by the Committee on Private Members' Bills and Resolutions.

Articles of the Constitution have been classified into three categories for the purposes of amendment:

(a) articles amendable by simple majority;
(b) articles that require special majority for their amendment; and
(c) articles that require a special majority as well as ratification by the legislatures of not less than one-half of the States.

Amendment by Simple Majority: A bill seeking to amend the following provisions of the Constitution requires only simple majority and such Bill is not deemed to be a Constitution (Amendment) Bill under Article 368 of the Constitution:

(a) admission or establishment of new States, formation of new States and alteration of areas, boundaries or names of existing ones (Art. 2, 3 & 4);
(b) creation or abolition of Legislative Councils in a State (Art.169);
(c) administration and control of Scheduled areas and Scheduled Tribes (para 7 of the Fifth Schedule), and

(d) administration of Tribal areas in the States of Assam, Meghalaya and Mizoram (para 21 of the Sixth Schedule).

A Bill providing for the formation of new States and for the alteration of areas, boundaries or names of existing States, can be introduced in either House of Parliament only on the recommendation of the President. Before he makes his recommendation, the President shall refer the Bill to the concerned States for eliciting their views within the period specified by him. He, however, is not bound by the views so ascertained.

The Parliament may pass a law to provide for the abolition or creation of a Legislative Council in a State, if the Legislative Assembly of the State passes a resolution to that effect by a majority of not less than two-thirds of the members of the Assembly present and voting. The Parliament may approve or disapprove of such resolution or it may not take any action thereon.

Amendment by Special Majority: A Bill seeking to amend any other part of the Constitution has to be passed by a special majority, ie. a majority of the total membership of that House and by a majority of not less than two-thirds of the members of that House present and voting. Strictly speaking, the special majority is required only for voting at the third reading stage of the Bill but by way of abundant caution the requirement for special majority has been provided for in the Rules of the Houses in respect of all the effective stages of the Bill.

Amendment by Special Majority and Ratification by States: A Bill seeking to amend the following provisions of the Constitution has to be passed by a special majority of both Houses of Parliament and has also to be ratified by the legislatures of not less than one-half of the States by resolutions to that effect passed by those Legislatures before such a Bill is presented to the President for assent.

(a) the election of the President (Arts. 54 & 55);

(b) the extent of the executive power of the Union and the States (Arts. 73 &162);

(c) the Supreme Court and the High Courts (Art. 341, Chapter IV of Part V, and Chapter V of Part VI of the Constitution);

(d) distribution of legislative powers between the Union and the States (Chapter I of Part XI and the Seventh Schedule of the Constitution);

(e) representation of States in Parliament; or

(f) the procedure for amendment of the Constitution itself (Art. 368).

The Constitution does not provide for any time limit within which the States must signify their ratification of a Constitution (Amendment) Bill, referred to them for this purpose.

Private Members' Bills—types of Bills

A Bill can be initiated either by the government or by any private member in either House of Parliament. Bills, thus, broadly fall into two categories (a) Government Bills and (b) Private Members' Bills. However, as things stand, in the Union Parliament no Private Members' Bill has become law during the last nearly four decades. All the laws that have found their way to the Statute Book have been Government Bills, and what we have discussed are only Government Bills.

In order to give opportunity to the people's representatives to express their views on various issues of public importance and persuade the government to formulate programmes and policies, parliamentary rules and procedures provide for initiation of legislation by private members also.

Discussion on Bills initiated by private members gives an opportunity to the House to come to terms with a problem and to discuss it in all its aspects. All shades of opinion of the House are made known to the government; it does not matter whether the Bill is finally passed or not. The purpose of focusing the attention of both the government and the public on the particular proposals contained in the Bill is attained. The government takes a policy decision on the subject of the Bill and presents its views before the House. The discussion helps the government to bring a comprehensive Government Bill on the subject, if necessary.

Two-and-a-half hours are allotted on every alternate Friday during a session for transaction of business relating to Private Members' Bills.

So far as the stages of a Private Member's Bill in the House and the general procedure are concerned, there is no difference between the Government Bills and the Private Members' Bills. There are, however, some special procedural features concerning Private Members' Bills in respect of the period of notice for introduction, restriction on number of Bills that can be introduced in a session by a member, Bills seeking amendment to the Constitution, relative precedence for discussion, etc.

A member who wants to introduce a Bill has to give one month's notice unless the Speaker or the Chairman, as the case may be, allows introduction at a shorter notice. The notice is to be accompanied by a copy of the Bill and an explanatory Statement of Objects and Reasons. Where a Bill, if enacted, is likely to involve expenditure from public funds, a financial memorandum giving an estimate of the expenditure involved and prior recommendation of the President/ Governor is appended to the Bill by the member. In case the Bill contains proposals for delegated legislation, a memorandum regarding delegated legislation is also appended to the Bill.

All the Bills due for introduction on a particular day allotted to Private Members' Bills are included in the List of Private Members' Business for that day.

In the Lok Sabha, however, bills seeking to amend the Constitution, apart from being subject to the normal rules applicable to Private Members' Bills, have also to be examined by a Committee of the House, namely, the Committee on Private Members' Bills and Resolutions and only those Bills which have been recommended by the Committee are put down in the List of Business for introduction.

By convention, a motion for leave to introduce a Private Member's Bill is not opposed. If a motion is opposed, the Presiding Officer may permit brief statements by the member who opposed the motion and the member who moved the motion and thereafter put the motion for decision of the House. Where a motion for introduction is opposed on the ground that the Bill initiates legislation outside the legislative competence of the House, the Chair may permit a full discussion thereon and thereafter put the motion for the decision of the House. If the motion is adopted, the member in-charge of the Bill introduces the Bill. Ordinarily, a member can introduce four Bills in a session.

In the Lok Sabha, after a Bill has been introduced and before it is taken up for consideration in the House, the Committee on Private Members' Bills and Resolutions classifies the Bills according to their nature, urgency and importance into two categories ie. category 'A' and Category 'B'. The time for their discussion is also allocated by the Committee. Bills classified in category 'A' have precedence over Bills classified in category 'B' for the purpose of consideration in the House. In Lok Sabha, the relative precedence of Bills in a particular category is determined by ballot. The Bills are included in the List of Business in the order of priority determined by the ballot. In other respects, the stages through which a Bill passes are the same as in the case of a Government Bill.

During the last 45 years, not a single Private Members' Bill has become law. The 14 Bills in this category that got to the Statute book in the first 18 years of the two Houses of Parliament (1952-1970) were:

i. The Muslim Wakfs Bill 1952 (Passed in 1954)

ii. The Indian Registration (Amendment) Bill 1955 (Passed in 1956)

iii. The Proceedings of Parliament (Protection of Publication) Bill 1956 (Passed in 1956)

iv. The Code of Criminal Procedure (Amendment) Bill 1953 (Passed in 1956)

v. The Women's and Children's Institutions (Licensing) Bill 1954 (Passed in 1956)

vi. The Code of Criminal Procedure (Amendment) Bill 1957

(Passed in 1960)

vii. The Salaries and Allowances of Members of Parliament (Amendment) Bill 1964 (Passed in 1964)

viii. The Hindu Marriage (Amendment) Bill 1963 (Passed in 1964)

ix. The Supreme Court (Enlargement of Criminal Appellate Jurisdiction) Bill 1968 (Passed in 1970)

x. The Ancient and Historical Monuments and Archaelogical Sites and Remains (Declaration of National Importance) Bill 1954 (Passed in 1956)

xi. The Hindu Marriage (Amendment) Bill 1956 (Passed in 1956)

xii. The Orphanages and other Charitable Homes (Supervision and Control) Bill 1960 (Passed in 1960)

xiii. The Marine Insurance Bill 1959 (Passed in 1963)

xiv. The Indian Penal Code (Amendement) Bill 1963 (Passed in 1969).

Of the above, the first nine were introduced in Lok Sabha and the other five in Rajya Sabha.

The post natal stage comes after a Bill is duly passed by the two Houses and with the assent of the President becomes law. It is concerned with how the law actually becomes operational. The law itself may provide that it will come into effect from the date of notification in the gazette. Also, it usually provides for rules and regulations being made by the executive to bring the law into operation.

Subordinate Legislation

Law-making is becoming increasingly complicated and technical; it is no longer a simple affair. In this situation, the Legislature has neither enough time to deliberate upon, discuss and approve all the necessary legal requirements nor the requisite expertise to work them out in procedural and technical details. A large volume of legislation always remains in arrears. It is, therefore, provided that the Legislature may delegate some of its power of legislation to subordinate agency. Consequently, the Legislature frames laws in general terms and leaves it to the government to make detailed rules and regulations within the limitations specified, and to carry out the objects of the legislation and to meet new situations not foreseen by the Legislature while enacting laws. Such rules and regulations made by a subordinate agency within the purview of the authority delegated by the Legislature, are called 'subordinate legislation'. It is sometimes described as 'delegated legislation' also in some states.

In India, this power of delegation is a constituent element of the legislative power as a whole. The Legislature is not competent to delegate to the Executive or any other body its essential legislative functions namely, the determination of legislative policy and its formulation as a rule of conduct. It is permissible only when legislative policy and principle are adequately laid down and the delegate is only empowered to carry out the subsidiary policy within the guidelines laid down by the Legislature. In other words, it can only utilise the other bodies or authorities to work out details within the essential principles laid down by it.

Subordinate legislation is sometimes denounced vehemently on the ground that it enables the administration to usurp the legislative powers of the Parliament and this leads to a 'new despotism' of civil servants who are not responsible to the Parliament or to the people directly. Such a blanket of authority could obviously enable the bureaucracy to do anything it liked. On the other hand, today it is impossible to completely avoid subordinate legislation. What is most essential, therefore, is continuous parliamentary surveillance and control over the exercise of the power of subordinate legislation.

Certain safeguards have been provided against the possible abuse of this power. For example, it is laid down that a Bill involving proposals for the delegation of legislative power shall further be accompanied by a memorandum explaining such proposals drawing attention to their scope and stating whether they are of normal or exceptional character. It has been further provided that regulations, rules and by-laws framed in pursuance of the legislative functions delegated by the Parliament to a subordinate agency, are laid before the House where amendments may also be moved. Thus the Parliament exercises scrutiny and control by asserting itself at these stages. Besides, all such rules and regulations are subject to examination by courts on the plea of *ultra vires* to the provisions of the Constitution. Above all, there is a 'Committee on Subordinate Legislation' in each House of the Parliament consisting of its members to see and report to either House whether powers delegated by Parliament have been properly exercised within the statute delegating such powers. It is the Committee on Subordinate Legislation which, in fact, appropriately guards against the possible assumption of arbitrary powers by the administration. It has all along endeavoured to see that all rules and regulations so framed, are not only laid before the Parliament without delay but that the Parliament has also the statutory right of annulling and modifying them.

Legislative Process at the level of the States is largely similar to that at the Union level except that most of the States are unicameral. Under our federal structure there is distribution of legislative powers between the Union and the States. State Legislatures can legislate only in the area of State and Concurrent Lists. In certain circumstances, Union Parliament can legislate on matters in the State List also and in case of conflict between Union and State laws under the Concurrent List, the Union law prevails. Also, Governor can reserve certain Bills for the consideration of the President before giving his assent (Art.200/201).

In actual practice, it is not always true that all the various stages of giving birth to a Bill are followed. In fact, there is a great deal of adhocism in the process of law-making at the pre-natal stage ie. at the level of the Executive Government. There is unfortunate lack of adequate legislative planning. Bills are often sought to be drafted in a haphazard manner, at short notice and sometimes are required to be introduced and passed in great haste, without the necessary scrutiny and debate. This inevitably results in ill drafted and faulty legislation. Once in 1991 on the last day of the 9th Lok Sabha, 18 Bills were passed in less than two hours without any scrutiny or Governer's assent which is necessary for a Bill becoming a law. Like the President, the Governor can also send Messages to the House in regard to a legislation or otherwise (Art.175) debate, setting a dismal record and making a farce of all the niceties of the Legislative Process. The Chemical Weapons Convention Act, 2000, after President's assent was reported to contain 40 errors (2001). The same year 33 Bills were passed in 32 hours. In some cases legislation was rushed through in a matter of minutes with just a few Members present. A crucial Bill on Bio-diversity was passed in 2002 in just 15 minutes. A Bill on non-productive assets of Banks was adopted with only 38 members present. In the Winter session of the 14th Lok Sabha in 2008, eight important Bills were rushed through in 17 minutes without debate. On the afternoon of 23 December 2008, every 2 minutes, a Bill was reported passed—9 Bills in 15 minutes. During the 15th Lok Sabha, 20 Bills were passed with less than five minutes of discussion. Rajya Sabha passed five Bills in less than five minutes.

In Lok Sabha, salaries or the Allowances of Ministers (amendment) Bill, the Commercial Division of High Courts Bill, the Constitution (scheduled tribes) Order (amendment), All India Institute of Medical Sciences (amendment) Bill were all passed in less than a minute. Parliament (Prevention of Disqualification) Amendment Bill, National Rural Employment Guarantee (amendment) Bill and few others took just two minutes in Lok Sabha and 21 minutes in Rajya Sabha. Once, when legislative business was being transacted the total number of members present in the House were eight of whom incidentally five happened to be Ministers and three Private Members.

There have been instances where the government has sought waiver of certain Rules in order to get a Bill introduced at shorter notice and passed with extra expedition. Also, on certain occasions the Secretariats of the Houses of Parliament have found and pointed out serious flaws in the draft Bills.

Most recently, during the 16th Lok Sabha, the constitutional amendment Bill in regard to the Indo-Bangladesh land boundary agreement on exchange of enclaves had to be passed a second time, all over again by the Rajya Sabha because of serious drafting errors. It was the 100th Constitution Amendment Act but at seven places it mentioned itself as the 119th Amendment which was the original number of the Bill when it was introduced.

The highly controversial Defamation Bill 1988 was sought to be introduced in Lok Sabha without even the copies of the Bill being made available to Lok Sabha Secretariat or Members as required under the Rules. This, of course was not allowed when the Bill was finally introduced in Lok Sabha; it was subjected to intense debate in the House and outside. It led to an unenviable situation. The Lok Sabha had to face the rare spectacle of the Press boycotting its proceedings and the Opposition staging a walk-out. For the first time, a Bill duly passed by Lok Sabha was not passed in the Rajya Sabha and was finally withdrawn.

Also, the two 1993 Bills drafted poorly and in apparent haste during Narasimha Rao's time seemingly seeking to delink religion and politics had to be given up after heated debate.

Parliament includes the President. The Postal Bill passed by the two Houses never became law because it was not assented to by the President. The Bill had caused uproarious scenes in Lok Sabha. The Bill was returned by President Zail Singh to the government for clarification/reconsideration in January 1990. Neither was the assent withheld nor was the Bill returned to the House for reconsideration. The Bill never became law. Much earlier at the very inception of the Republic, President Rajendra Prasad had stood against the Hindu Code Bill. Later President Venkataraman (1991) refused his assent to a Bill passed nearly unanimously by the two Houses of Parliament in a matter of minutes. President Kalam returned the Parliament (Prevention of Disqualification) Amendment Bill 2006 (Office of Profit Bill) for reconsideration. The Bill sought to protect with retrospective effect, from 1959, disqualification of 40 prominent MPs including Sonia Gandhi and Somnath Chatterjee. When presented after reconsideration the President had to give his assent.

There are also examples of the laws passed by the two Houses and assented to by the President that were either not brought into force for years or never, eg the Delhi Rent Control Act passed in early 1990s by the two Houses and assented to by the President but never notified and so it remained a dead letter. Benami Transactions (Prohibition) Act, 1988, duly passed by the two Houses but remained unimplemented because for 25 years no rules were framed. When vested interests fail to prevent passage of a Bill, they try to find out ways of keeping it ineffective through other means. Education was made a fundamental right by a constitutional amendment in 2003 but the necessary law to bring into effect was not passed till 2009 and actually it came into operation only after seven years ie. in April 2010. Still, who can say if illiteracy among the children has disappeared and all the children are going to schools.

There is every need for revisiting and revamping of the legislative process through a dynamic, non-mechanical, approach to legislative engineering and systematic programming of legislative proposals for enactment over a period of time. This can be done by (i) restoring and streamlining the functions of what used to be the Parliamentary and Legal Affairs Committee of the Cabinet; (ii) making greater use of the Law Commission; (iii) improving the quality of drafting and content of legislation; (iv) setting up a new Legislation Committee of Parliament to oversee and coordinate legislative planning; and (v) referring all Bills to the Departmental Standing Committees for consideration and scrutiny, finalisation of the second reading stage in the relaxed atmosphere of the Committees aided by experts thereby reducing the burden on the House without impinging on any of its rights and lastly, (vi) more seriously and meaningfully consulting concerned interest groups, CSOs and NGOs to cover the newly emerging so-called civil society activism.

Responsibility and Accountability

Concepts and Types

LITERALLY, 'ACCOUNTABILITY' connotes the practice or obligation to render accounts or the right to receive accounts. The servant to the master, the delegate or the agent to the principal and the subordinate to the boss has to answer for what he has done to discharge his assigned responsibilities. He has to give an account of the money put at his disposal—of what he has spent and how. Account is required to be given after the money is received and spent. In its very nature, accountability is *ex post* ie. after the event. Accountability is the process by which the principal supervises and controls the functioning and performances of the agent.

'Accountability' in the phrase 'Accountability to Parliament'

---

* See Subhash C Kashyap, 'Executive and Legislature Interface in the Indian Polity', *The Journal of Legislative Studies,* Vol. 10, No. 2/3.

refers to the accountability of the government or the administration to the people through their elected representatives in Parliament. Accountability in a democratic polity is the outcome of delegation of authority and responsibility. In parliamentary democracy, accountability means the power of calling the government to account.

Unfortunately, sometimes we use different words but mean the same thing while at other times we may use the same word but mean different things. In common parlance and political writings—even in parliamentary political science and constitutional law—terms like 'accountability', 'answerability' and 'responsibility' are used rather loosely and sometimes interchangeably. Also, we often speak vaguely of the concepts of administrative accountability, ministerial responsibility or responsibility of the executive to the Legislature without defining the terms and without seeking or providing the necessary conceptual clarification. Sometimes, 'accountability' and 'responsibility' are used as synonyms even though 'ministerial responsibility' or responsibility of the cabinet or Council of Ministers is a definite constitutional concept.

Types of Accountability

Accountability may take one of the following forms:

(i) Administrative accountability means the accountability of the administration ie. of the permanent services to the representatives of the people in the Houses of the Legislature (a) through the ministers as in the case of parliamentary questions or (b) directly as in parliamentary committees. The rationale for the accountability of the civil services is that while policies are initiated and formulated by the political executive and approved by the legislature, the actual administration and implementation thereof is in the hands of the permanent civil services. While money is sanctioned by the Parliament, it is expended by different departments. It is therefore for the concerned officers to account for it and justify that it has been spent in accordance with the sanction for the approved purposes.

(ii) Ministerial accountability flows from the concept that for everything that is done or not done in a government department, the Minister in charge is accountable to the Parliament. He is the link between the administration and the Houses of Parliament.

(iii) Personal financial accountability of Ministers means their 'obligation to make good any financial harm caused to the tax payer which results from their actions'. Although it exists in theory, it has ceased to have any practical relevance.

(iv) Penal accountability of Ministers casts an obligation 'to answer for criminal actions such as treason, misappropriation, encroachments on the freedom of the individual'. In some countries, the Parliament may act in a judicial capacity to take action against the Ministers on grounds of their penal liability for abusing the trust placed in them and harming public interest. In modern times, it still operates (more for the Head of the state than for Ministers) only in systems where there is separation of powers and the executive is not politically responsible to Legislature.

Ensuring Accountability

Accountability of administration is sought to be ensured through parliamentary devices. In the traditional parliamentary model, there are many ways of calling the administration to account. These include the Question Hour, the Committee scrutiny and the various devices for raising discussion on the floor of the House on matters of urgent public importance.

There is a great deal of ambiguity and semantic confusion in writings on Ministerial Responsibility/Accountability. The single most defining characteristic of parliamentary form of representative democracy is that the Ministry being the political Executive is accountable to the Parliament and can be voted out of office by it. People elect the Legislature, the Legislature throws up the Council of Ministers, individual Ministers are made responsible for their departments, the civil servants assist the Ministers and implement decisions. In elections, citizens are the principles who elect representatives to serve as their agents in Parliament. Then Parliament acting as the principal delegates authority to the agent, ie. the Ministers to act on its behalf under a set of rules by which the Ministers can be held accountable.

Civil servants implement legislation and advise and assist the Ministers as their agents. Thus, a chain of delegation in modern democratic governance shows who is responsible/accountable to whom.

Ministerial Responsibility

A more significant and constitutional term is 'ministerial responsibility meaning cabinet responsibility or the responsibility of the Council of Ministers. In countries with a parliamentary polity, the Ministers are usually responsible to the popularly elected House of the Legislature either individually or collectively or both. Ministerial responsibility to Parliament is sometimes also described vaguely (and perhaps not very accurately) as a type of accountability and called political accountability. Ministerial responsibility is not based on any objective assessment of civil or criminal offences but on the political opinion of the majority of the members of the House to which the Ministers are made constitutionally responsible. It is simply a matter of votes, of continuing to have or losing the confidence of the House. In the latter case, the cabinet must quit or fresh elections are called. This is, by and large, the position in countries that follow the Parliamentary system. The principle that has come to be widely established is that a government can continue in office only so long as it does not lose the confidence of the popularly elected House of Parliament. In case of parliamentary democracies with written constitutions, ministerial responsibility may flow from provisions of the Constitution. But, in fact, its sources may lie much deeper. First, it may be an invariable concomitant of the democratic theory of the sovereignty of the people.

To the extent that Parliament is the supreme representative institution and embodies the will of the people, it must be able to ensure that the government remains responsible to it and responsive to the needs and aspirations of the people. Secondly, it may be the most essential characteristic of parliamentary polity inasmuch as it presumes that the executive is part of Parliament; the relationship between the executive and the legislature is that of the part and the whole or the agent and the principal with the Ministers coming out of Parliament, remaining part of it and responsible and responsive to it, and in fact, representing Parliament in the Executive, guiding, overseeing and controlling the administration on behalf of Parliament.

Collective and Individual

Responsibility of Ministers may be individual or collective or both. Constitutions of more than thirty countries (including those of France, Israel, Finland, Italy, Japan, Mauritius, New Zealand, Portugal, Switzerland, Zambia, Zimbabwe, Malta and India) specifically mention that ministerial responsibility is collective which means that (a) irrespective of personal views or role in government, every minister has to own and defend the policies of the government, (b) in case of defeat on any major policy issue on the floor of the House, the entire Council of Ministers falls together and (c) any verdict of no confidence by the House on any issue or in regard to any department headed by one of the Ministers must lead to the resignation of the entire cabinet or the Council of Ministers.

Again in more than thirty countries (including Austria, Brazil, Denmark, Australia, Greece, Netherlands, Norway, Sweden, and UK), ministers are responsible both collectively for the policies and performance of the government and also as individuals for their own charge.

In the United Kingdom

British Constitution, known to be largely unwritten to this day, is the product of some fourteen hundred years' history. The Cabinet or the Ministerial system which now characterises it is however hardly 150 years old. Walter Bagehot's classic on *The English Constitution* (1865) was almost the first work to describe the Cabinet Government. The Cabinet system including the intricate relationship between the Cabinet, the Crown and the House of Commons rests almost entirely on conventions and practices that have little force in law.

The institution of Ministers and the concept of ministerial responsibility in UK had had undemocratic and feudal origins. Even as late as up to the 18th century, the Executive was the hereditary monarch. The Ministers of the Crown were his servants and were responsible to him alone. It was the monarch who delegated authority to the ministers. British Parliament itself was also a royal creation in origin and basically a feudal body.

Under the doctrine that 'the King can do no wrong', the King could not be held responsible in law for acts of the State. Since a peg was needed to hang responsibility on, the theory of ministerial responsibility was born. Every act of the State was supposedly taken in the name of the King but for any wrong committed in the process, the Minister of the department concerned was held responsible and not the King. To begin with, the responsibility was only legal and did not mean political responsibility to Parliament. Also it was only individual and not collective.

So long as the King/Queen was the real executive and the Ministers servants of the crown responsible to him/her, Parliament or the House of Commons (itself hardly a representative body of the people) viewed itself in an adversary situation and performed the role of the opposition. The recession of the King from politics and the advance of the principles of Cabinet Government were all slow processes and necessarily conditioned by the successive steps in the reform of Parliament and the extension of the electoral franchise during the nineteenth and twentieth centuries.

As power was transferred from the King to Parliament, political parties became strong and party governments followed, ministerial responsibility came to have a new connotation and until the 1930s, the cabinet could be said to have inherited the executive role of the monarch. Ministerial responsibility became political and only a question of commanding continued majority support on the floor of the House. A party majority could bail out a government on every issue. During 1945-1970, no vote was ever lost. Party cohesion was so close to 100 per cent that there was no longer any point counting it. Government with its party majority in a way had begun to control Parliament. Parliament (largely meaning the House of Commons) had become only a legitimatising body, giving the stamp of approval to proposals brought before it by the Ministers. Even administrative accountability became very limited if not marginal. So long as the government had a safe majority in the House, it could have the last word. Also, while a secure, stable and strong government could afford more substantial parliamentary scrutiny and accountability, a shaky, thin-majority, weak government always tried to avoid parliamentary scrutiny and accountability. Of course, it cannot avoid ministerial responsibility under any circumstance.

Nearly all the powers of the Crown are now exercised 'by or on the advice of the Ministers of the Crown' and the Cabinet is politically responsible to the House of Commons. Ministerial responsibility in UK, unlike India, is both collective and individual. The sanction in either case is the forced resignation of the government or the Minister as the case may be. Every government department is allocated to one or the other Minister who can then be held personally responsible to the House of Commons for all the actions in his department. The Minister is in charge and he can be attacked in or out of Parliament for what happens or does not happen.

Individual Ministers may resign because a Minister is unwilling to accept government policy and must, therefore, go to respect collective ministerial responsibility or because he owns personal responsibility for an error of policy or administration in the department under his charge. In 1982, a Minister had to resign for his statement in a rape case. Falklands war crisis led to the resignation of three foreign office Ministers. In 1986, Leon Brittan, Home Secretary (Minister), resigned as he was held responsible for the leak of a letter. The resignations of Michael Heseltine over the Westland Helicopters affair, Nigel Lawson over the role of Prime Minster's Economic Advisor, Sir Alan Walters and Sir Geoffrey Howe over European community policy, all highlighted the pitfalls and strengths of Margaret Thatcher's 'monocratic approach to Prime Ministership'.

In UK, the head of the administration is the Accounting Officer. The Permanent Secretary or Undersecretary is the Accounting Officer. That means all the moneys that are granted by Parliament remain under his control. The money is given for a purpose and he has to fulfill that purpose and account for it. The Accounting Officer has to appear in person before Parliamentary Committees to account for the money. That is why the Ministers do not appear there.

While Permanent Secretaries or Undersecretaries are thus accountable to Parliamentary Committees for explaining implementation, the Ministers are accountable to the Parliament for policies. Also, the administrators (civil servants) are to assist the Ministers in the business of government. They work in accordance with the Minister's instructions and rules and regulations. Minister is the link between the Permanent Secretary and the Parliament. The Permanent Secretary is responsible to the Minister and the Minister is responsible to Parliament. In this way, the relationship between the civil servants and the Ministers is governed by the convention of individual ministerial responsibility and provides a cloak of anonymity to the bureaucracy and departmental activities. The advice received by the Minister and the role played by the civil servants in the decision making is kept away from public gaze.

In practice, however, there has been a decline in the direct powers of the House of Commons to censure individual Ministers. Also, government departments have become so vast and their work so complex that the Ministers are not expected to be able to know everything or everyone in the Department. Therefore, a Minister now rarely resigns on grounds of any departmental failures. At best, he may consider himself responsible only for policy decisions taken by him. Ministers do not have to resign for faults of civil servants. They are only obliged to defend the officers on the floor of the House.

Ministerial responsibility is the foundation of administrative accountability to Parliament. It is because of ministerial responsibility that members of Parliament can demand from government, public explanation for its policies and actions. Ministers are answerable to Parliament for their conduct of public policy and administration. The doctrine therefore underpins all parliamentary procedural devices—debates on issues, various kinds of motions, questions and committee activity—that exercise scrutiny and ensure administrative accountability.

Argument for the doctrine of collective ministerial responsibility today is simple: sovereign powers of governance are exercised by Parliament through the Ministers responsible to it, particularly to the directly elected House of Commons. Under this view, the Ministers had no basis for their authority except the one given by or derived from the House of Commons. Ministerial actions, therefore have to reflect the wishes and views of the Commons. Ministerial monopoly of power is the only way to make power representative, responsive and responsible. Any public power not exercised by elected politicians or not under their control would be unresponsive, unrepresentative and therefore irresponsible. Collective responsibility implied that:

(a) major cabinet decisions were collectively taken,

(b) ministers argued in the cabinet but once a decision was made, every Minister had to stand by it and protect each other despite any disagreement,

(c) since responsibility in policy matters is collective, every Minister must support government policy and actions taken thereunder at least in public or resign,

(d) secrecy of cabinet discussions must be maintained as the authority of the cabinet and of the ministers concerned would be undermined if cabinet differences came in the open,

(e) the Ministry as a whole is responsible to the House and stands or falls together. The Commons is politically supreme and can, if majority of its members so decide throw out the government at any time. Defeat on an important issue or a vote of no confidence necessitates resignation of the Ministry or fresh elections.

Not all these conventions in regard to collective ministerial responsibility have been invariably followed. Thus, for example, there has been dilution of the cabinet secrecy norms with some ministers engaging in semi-public leaks of cabinet discussions and differences and some ex-ministers recording them in their Memoirs. On two occasions in the Labour Government of 1974-1979, the convention was actually suspended in order to allow ministers to vote against government policy in the House of Commons.

Although the convention of the Ministry resigning or asking for fresh elections in case of no confidence by the House of Commons remains intact, it is no more true that defeat on an important issue should also call for resignation.

As demands on government increased, only the most important matters percolated to the cabinet. Most decisions affecting a Department were taken by the Minister concerned. Also, a Minister had little time to participate in collective decision taking in regard to matters concerning other departments. Collective decision making has considerably dwindled. Even Prime Minister's interference is resisted by some Ministers.

In this scenario, the relationship between the minister and the House of Commons was getting governed more and more by the principle of an individual rather than collective ministerial responsibility. It is also important to reiterate that the cabinet as such has no legal powers. In law, it is usually the Minister who is responsible for actions of the Ministry. He has unlimited liability for political mistakes of his Ministry. Parliamentary statutes vest powers (unlike the position in India) in individual ministers. When the government takes on any new responsibilities by statute, powers to fulfill those responsibilities are granted to a minister with words like 'the Secretary of State shall have the power to ....'

Also, again under increasing constraints and complexities of governance, more and more decisions had to be relegated to the officials. Emergence of merit based civil service recruited through competitive examinations distinguished the neutral administration from the political executive. Interdepartmental coordination was largely handled at the level of officials. The officials were, of course, covered under administrative accountability to Parliament through the Minister and also directly. For example, the civil servants do appear before Committees and are accountable for the lapses of administration.

Some scholars talk of two different theories of ministerial responsibility in the UK. The 'Whig' theory emphasises political aspect of responsibility and holds Ministers or Ministry to be responsible for all State acts. The 'Peelite' theory on the other hand would like to use the concept of Ministerial responsibility to limit parliamentary scrutiny or administrative accountability to Parliament so that business of government is carried out more efficiently without interference. Peelites are committed to strong rather than representative government. (RAW Rhodes and Patrick Dunleavy, 1995).

Under the Whig theory, the Ministers were responsible because (1) they had the authority to take decisions, (2) they were accountable ie. obliged to give reasons, (3) they were culpable and could be blamed, sued, criticised and dismissed for wrong decisions, and (4) they were expected to act with rectitude.

In actual practice, there are difficulties in operating the Whig theory. In the context of cabinet, confidentiality and requirements of collective cabinet responsibility, it may not often be possible to discuss which decision was taken by whom. Increasingly it is being felt that it is very difficult for any Minister to 'carry the can' and own responsibility for a policy or action for which he himself was not responsible. Also, the vastness and complexities of administration today, requires the involvement of a large number of civil servants and it is not possible for the Minister personally either to monitor their performance or take responsibility for their acts. If Ministers are held responsible in such cases, the result would be either an unreasonable allocation of culpability on the Minister or an invitation to the Minister 'to interfere' in an agency's affairs.

The 'Peelite' theory is largely Tory. It emphasises stability (and not representation). Peelite aim is the preservation of executive power. 'Ministerial responsibility' under the Peelite perception meant that the executive (the Ministers) rather than the Parliament and the people were responsible for public policy. The stress was on 'responsible for' rather than 'responsible to' on authority and jurisdiction and not on accountability. Peelite theory would like the executive to possess authority independent of Parliament and the people on the ground, that cabinet and not the commons inherited the powers of the King. Party was also seen as a means of securing ministerial tenure rather than as a channel of expression of popular choice or representative urges. Questions of likely conflict between the right thing (rectitude) and popular thing have also been raised. 'Peelism' has been criticised by its opponents as tending to be an authoritarian doctrine of the strong rather than either representative or responsible government. To the Peelites who is responsible for what is a matter of private executive convenience. The Executive is seen as responsible for order and stability rather than for reflection of popular will. From ministerial point of view, it is Parliament and the electorate who are adversaries and not the civil servants.

Under the Peelite view, ministerial accountability is *ex post*. Parliament can exercise post mortem checks only and not participate in executive functions.

Both the Whig and Peelite views accept the Ministerial state and stand by the doctrine of Ministerial responsibility and parliamentary sovereignty.

The Ministerial responsibility doctrine offers the maximum flexibility. It can be a weapon at once of strong government and a representative, responsive, responsible, participatory system. In many ways, in recent years the concepts, conventions and traditional perspectives in UK in regard to the cabinet and ministerial responsibility have undergone considerable changes and the process of change continues. In fact, the British parliamentary theories and practices are very much in a flux particularly after UK joined the Europeans community. There is no single view or explanation shared by all. But, it can be said that the two major party system is essential for maintaining a clear location of responsibility. The styles of functioning of the two Prime Ministers—Thatcher and Major—also are a study in contrast in so far as these affect collective and individual ministerial responsibility. There is more openness and transparency now inasmuch as the erstwhile (until 1992) highly secret document on the 'Questions of Procedure for Ministers' (QPM) which stresses the collegiate or collective responsibility of Ministers, as modified by the Prime Minister's office from time to time, is now available to any citizen for a mere Pound 5 or so.

An important aspect to be remembered is that 'Ministerial responsibility' doctrine can also be used—and has been used—to blunt parliamentary scrutiny to deny information to Parliament. For example, in the committees of the House, senior civil servants may cite ministerial responsibility or demands of public interest to justify refusal to divulge the advice given.

In more state of the art terminology we can say that the choice today is between representative and good governance—a government responsible to the representatives of the people and one responsible for the good of the people. Ministerial responsibility may mean authorial power or representation and accountability—but if it is representational and participatory decision-making, how can the ministers take responsibility? At a time when the Constitution of India was being made by the Constituent Assembly, a writer of *English*

Constitutional History (1948) summed up the 'essential formula of the Constitution' as follows:

> The essence of the Constitution today is the temporary entrusting of great powers to a small cabinet or body of ministers (who are members of one or other of the Houses of Parliament) who are formally appointed to office by and dismissable by the King, but who are politically responsible to the electorate, through the House of Commons which is periodically elected on a wide, popular franchise, and who are legally responsible under the law and who are served by a corps of permanent civil servants.

During the last few decades (1978-2018), the Parliament has become more professionalised and specialised, has acquired resources and sharpened its devices to enforce better administrative accountability through improved scrutiny of the administration. This has been achieved largely through the House of Commons.

Departmental Select Committees were set up in 1979. These Committees have provided the means for more structured and continuous scrutiny of departments than was ever possible on the floor of the House.

Standing Committees and most Select Committees meeting in public sessions and broadcasting and telecasting House proceedings has helped not only accountability of the administration to Parliament but also generated a climate of accountability of Parliament to the people. Writing on the UK Parliament's changing role, Philip Norton said: 'Both Houses of Parliament are now more active than before and devote more energy to subjecting the conduct of government to critical scrutiny.'

Information and accountability to Parliament in the area of defence is still unsatisfactory although there is no need of conflict between legitimate needs of confidentiality and public accountability in the sensitive areas of defence. Defence Committee (HCDC) has become more effective as an instrument of ensuring accountability as time has gone by. HCDC has now become highly professionalised; it uses external advisers and has also developed its own expertise.

A major review of the working of the select committee system was undertaken by the Procedure Committee. It concluded that 'the improvement in the effectiveness of the scrutiny of Ministers is sufficient on its own to justify describing the change to a system of departmentally-related Select Committees as worthwhile and as a success' and that there had been 'solid, unspectacular but undeniable achievements.' However, a careful reading of that report does bring out some of the frustrations and concerns that were felt. The then Chairman of the HCDC, Michael Mates, gave evidence that the Ministry of Defence witness sometimes showed 'an unwillingness to answer frankly and in what seems to be a feeling that the less that is said to the Committee, the safer the Ministry of Defence will be. On certain occasion this has gone beyond acceptable bounds, with the stating of evidence that concealed a serious state of affairs. More frequently, it is a matter of wearisome generality or vagueness, or of trivial annoyances that make an inquiry more difficult, but which may be collectively infuriating.'

The Liaison Committee undertook another review. Michael Colvin stated in a submission to the Liaison Committee: 'the Defence Committee has not always found straightforward the process of obtaining information from the department it scrutinises. An added complication is that some evidence is submitted to the Committee in a classified form which cannot therefore be reported to the House.'

The HCDC gained a reputation for its low level of political partisanship, but has not been afraid to be quite blunt in its criticism of Ministry of Defence actions. There is already a valuable legacy of reports covering a multitude of diverse subjects. On a number of issues the committee has returned to review progress and harry the ministry for failures to take consequent action.

The HCDC took some fresh initiatives. Earlier, it used to rely upon four specialist advisors—one each from the Army, Navy and Air Force and a general advisor on defence and foreign policy. Now it hires a number of advisors. Also, the Committee is involved in pre-legislative scrutiny of legislative proposals and ratification of treaties. The HCDC broke new ground by conducting an inquiry as the strategic Defence Review was taking place. Evidence was taken of Secretary of State for Defence, two Defence Ministers of State, the Minister of State for Foreign Office, Chief of Defence Staff, Chief of Air Staff, Chief of General Staff, First Sea Lord and others.

Other Committees, such as Transport and Home Affairs, have a lesser security involvement. During the so-called 'Supergun Affair', both the Defence and the Trade and Industry Committees looked into the arm sales to Iraq. The Westland Affair even managed to attract the attention of three committees. The Defence Committee produced a report with the Trade and Industry Select Committee into 'Aspects of Defence Procurement and Industrial Policy' and held a joint meeting with the Foreign Affairs Committee at which the Hungarian Prime Minister and Foreign Minister were witnesses.[Bruce George and J David Morgan, JLS, 5(1)].

In India

The motivation, origin and content of the concepts of ministerial responsibility and accountability of the administration in India were entirely different and in fact, quite contrary to what happened in the UK. In the context of their sad experience of the arbitrary and irresponsible colonial rule, the leaders of the nationalist movement demanded institutions of governance that were representative of the people, responsive to their needs and urges and responsible to them through their elected representatives. What was called 'Responsible Governments' was first installed at the level of Provinces under the Government of India Act 1935. The Constituent Assembly opted for the Parliamentary System of Government because it preferred to have an executive that was responsible to the popularly elected legislature. This was the Indian concept of ministerial responsibility and clearly had its origin in democratic theory and the principle of the sovereignty of the people. In India we have no king who can do no wrong. The President can do wrong and can be impeached for violation of the Constitution.

Also, as things stand, again unlike the British, we have a written Constitution. The position, powers and interrelationships of different organs of the state and of other institutions mentioned in the Constitution are as defined and delimited therein. Article 75(3) provides that the Council of Ministers shall be collectively responsible to the House of the People (Lok Sabha). It would be seen that the responsibility of the Council of Ministers is only to the House directly elected by the people and not to Parliament as such. Also, the responsibility is only collective as against 'individual and collective' as in UK.

The most crucial feature of parliamentary polity is that the government or the real executive (meaning the Council of Ministers) is inside Parliament. It is sort of a grand executive committee of Parliament which consists of Members of Parliament made ministers and charged with the responsibility of governing the country on behalf of Parliament while remaining collectively responsible to Lok Sabha. The relationship between the Council of Ministers and the Parliament is that of the part and the whole or that of the delegate and the principal.

The constitutional provision regarding collective ministerial responsibility is operationalised through Rules of Procedure of Conduct of Business in Lok Sabha providing for a motion of no confidence.

Ministerial responsibility to Parliament or what is often termed parliamentary control over the Executive or the Government is based on

i. the constitutional provision of collective responsibility of the Council of Ministers to the popular House of Parliament; and

ii. the Parliament's control over the Budget.

In both these matters, ministerial responsibility or parliamentary control over the Executive is political in nature. The division in the House is on party lines. The answerability of the Executive is direct, continuous, concurrent and day-to-day. When Parliament is sitting, the continuance of the government in office depends from moment to moment on its not losing the confidence of the House of the People. The House may, at any time, decide to throw out the government by a majority vote, ie. if the ruling party or alliance loses the support of the majority Members of the House, its government goes. No grounds, arguments, proofs or justification are necessary. When the House clearly shows that it does not support the government of the day, the government must resign. While the government thus goes on grounds of ministerial responsibility to Lok Sabha, permanent services are not directly affected and administrative accountability is not involved.

While the Budget has to be approved and policies laid down by Parliament, administration and implementation of policies and programmes of the government falls upon the shoulders of the permanent services or the bureaucracy—the large staff of administrators, experts, technocrats and others forming the administrative apparatus. In every department of the government, administrative Head of the Department, the Secretary to the Government of India in the Ministry is the custodian of the money. He may be the drawing and disbursing officer. So, it is under his signature that all accounts are compiled, money is spent and policies are implemented. It is he, therefore, who is responsible if anything goes wrong.

Administrative accountability means the accountability of the administration to the Parliament. Parliament does not interfere with day- to-day administration nor does it control administration. Accountability to it is technical and ex-post facto, ie. after some thing is done, after action has ended. It is post mortem. It is not contemporaneous. It is not concurrent. Also, it has to be based on specific grounds. Under the Indian system, after a policy is laid down, a law is passed or moneys sanctioned, it is administration which is required to execute and implement. Parliament cannot itself administer nor can the Ministers. It is, therefore, the officers—and not the ministers—who have to explain, if things go wrong in the process of implementation. This they may do either directly as before parliamentary committees or indirectly through their ministers as in the case of Questions.

In a parliamentary polity, Parliament embodies the will of the people and it must therefore be able to oversee the way in which public policy is carried out so as to ensure that it stays in step with the objectives of efficient administration and the aspirations of the people as a whole. This in a nutshell, is the *raison d'etre* of parliamentary surveillance of administration. Parliament has to keep a watch over the behaviour of administration. It can enquire and examine *ex post facto* whether the administration in terms of its obligations under the approved policies and utilised the powers conferred on it for purposes for which they were intended and whether the monies spent were in accordance with parliamentary sanction. Administrative accountability in financial matters, in principle, is so rigid that if any amount has been spent in excess of the parliamentary sanctions, they may have exceeded the powers conferred on them, unless regularised by Parliament after satisfactory explanation. But, in practice, regulation is always allowed. This ensures that the officers function in the healthy awareness that they would be ultimately subject to parliamentary scrutiny and answerable for what they do or fail to do.

Parliament gets informed and administrative accountability is ensured through various procedural services. These services also constitute very potent instruments for effecting parliamentary surveillance over administration action. But, if Parliament does find the administration or any particular officer in the wrong, it does not directly issue any directions. It acts through the Ministers who alone are responsible. Devices available to ensure accountability include the calling attention notices and discussions on various motions, apart from questions.

On an institutional plane, another method of ensuring administrative accountability to Parliament is through the various Parliamentary Committees. Parliament conducts scrutiny of administrative decisions and action through three specialised committees—Estimates Committee, Public Accounts Committee and Committee on Public Undertakings. Apart from these Financial Committees, there are now 24 Departmentally Related Standing Committees and other scrutiny committees also to whom administration is answerable. We have the Committee on Government Assurances, Committee on Subordinate Legislation and Committee on Petitions. These Committees, specially the Financial Committees of Parliament, scrutinise closely the working of administration *ex post facto*. Their function in general could be said to be to criticise and review the whole range of administrative actions, to investigate and report on the economy, efficiency and propriety of expenditure and to suggest possible remedies for the shortcomings, if any. The role of Parliamentary Committees, therefore, is passive and not active in as much as they do not interfere in the process of day-to-day administration. (see Subhash C Kashyap, *Parliamentary Procedure, Law, Privileges, Practice and Precedents,* Universal Law Publication, New Delhi, 3rd edition 2014)

Parliament and Defence Policy

The Parliament's main means of influencing defence policy remains through its role in passing of the annual budget, the impact of debates in the Houses and through its various committees. The Departmental Standing Committee on Defence now examines the draft budget before commending it to Lok Sabha for approval. It tries to ensure accountability in the matter of defence policies and decision making. The Public Accounts Committee examines the effectiveness of Defence expenditure with the assistance of the Comptroller and Accountant

General (C&AG). The Estimates Committee examines the estimates usually of the preceding year. Although the committees have the right to demand information, it can be often denied on the ground of national security. Members of the Standing Committee on Defence have criticized the Government for 'secretiveness' in not apprising them of defence policy.

There is very little evidence of parliamentary involvement in defence technology issues. The avoidance of accountability in defence matters has created an adversarial relationship between the public interest institutions and interested public servants. Essential details that would facilitate public monitoring of decision making procedures and processes are available neither to the media nor to legislative bodies like the Standing Committee on Defence. The professionalism of decision making remains unmonitored and unverified. A culture of excessive secrecy has inhibited the development of an informed public debate on national security issues.

The 1987-88 parliamentary inquiry into allegations of bribes paid by the Swedish howitzer supplier Bofors to secure a major contract exposed the inadequacy of accountability mechanisms. The absence of parliamentary supervision results in such absurdities as a 5-year defence plan with no corresponding financial commitment. It has been suggested that to improve accountability in the area of defence, perspective and 5-year-plans should be subjected to parliamentary scrutiny and approval to ensure consistency between financial and defence planning. Also, there is a need for defence policy documents being issued from time to time for public debate as also more informed debate in the Houses of Parliament. As at present, most often all the debates in the area of defence are on issues of immediate concern and hardly on matters of long term relevance. There is need for developing greater governmental accountability to Parliament and in turn to the people to build public confidence in decision making. The Departmental Standing Committees are suitable instruments for the purpose but further reforms are needed to make the committee system really more accountable.

It has been suggested that for improved accountability, the Standing Committee on Defence could be restructured into smaller, more focussed sub-committees specialising in matters like security policy, defence management, internal security, financial planning etc.

It is important that the plea of national security does not become an alibi for avoiding accountability for institutional waste, fraud, abuse, professional neglect or inefficiencies. An attitude of evasion and a proclivity for inaction result from differing views of their own accountability among various committees of the executive and the legislature.

Need for efficiency, implying confidentiality in the interests of speedy decision making need not conflict with the requirements of accountability. Both are important. A balance has to be worked out. The challenge is to raise the level of trust between the government and the people represented by parliamentary committees and the civil society that would seek to establish whether variations from decision making norms are exceptions and not normal practice, that there are no extra-constitutional incentives at play which bypass the process or misuse it and the procedures and processes are reviewed to keep up with changes in technology and emerging threats. If the public or its elected representatives are unable to ask questions about the performance of security-related projects, the responsible government bodies lose not only public confidence but also their capacity to perform to their full potential. It does not mean that sensitive issues be laid bare to public scrutiny but the matter needs to be debated as to what is 'sensitive' and why.

Leader of the Opposition

Controversy in Sixteenth Lok Sabha (2014-19)

AT A time when the nation was passing through a critical phase, there was a dire need for a strong and stable government that could be expected to provide clean, citizen-friendly, development-oriented good governance. After the fiercely and bitterly fought electoral battle in 2014, democracy and people had won most decisively. This signaled a happy ending to the dirty politics of mutual brinkmanship, bluff and blackmail between the shaky ruling alliance and the so-called supporting parties. Another most welcome by-product of this election was the prospect of the much-sought 'two major party' system coming true. If the rules for recognition of parties were strictly enforced, we were actually left with only two national parties and in many of the States with only two or three regional parties. Hopefully, in the near future, with some political party and electoral reforms, the sad spectacle of our having over 1,800 registered parties could also change for a saner scenario.

There was however, one regret. While for the success of parliamentary democracy an effective opposition is as necessary as a functioning, strong and stable government, in the 16th Lok Sabha, opposition stood battered and badly decimated. Having been reduced to a dismal below-50 tally, the main party in opposition was not even entitled to have its leader recognised as the Leader of the Opposition. But, it was not as if there was no opposition in the present Lok Sabha. There were more than 200 members in the several opposition parties with their own leaders. It was just that, there could be no Leader of the Opposition in the rank of a Cabinet minister.

Since such a situation arose after some 35 years, we had become used to taking the existence of the Leader of the Opposition for granted. An uncalled for and unseemly controversy was created by those with vested interests. The non-recognition of the leader of the 44-member Congress Party as LOP was criticised as being motivated by political vendetta. Many questions were asked from different quarters with regard to the provisions applying to the recognition of the Leader of the Opposition with all the concomitants of the status, salary, allowances, perks etc. of a cabinet minister.

The well established principle and practice right from the First Lok Sabha period had been that the leader of the largest party in opposition was recognised as the Leader of the Opposition, provided that the party had a strength that could enable it to keep the House or constitute a sitting of the House which was one-tenth of the total membership, ie. the same as the quorum fixed for a sitting of the House. In the first Lok Sabha, the largest partly in opposition was the Communist Party with 30 members. It was recognised as a group and not as a party. In the 2nd Lok Sabha, no party had even the minimum required number of 30 for recognition as a group. In the 3rd Lok Sabha, the largest party in a opposition was again the Communist Party. With 34 members, it was recognised as a parliamentary group and extended certain facilities. In the 4th Lok Sabha (1967-70), the Swatantra Party secured 45 seats, one more than the Congress in the 16th Lok Sabha. It emerged as the largest party in opposition. It was also recognised only as group along with the Jan Sangh which had 31 members. Thus, during the period of the First to the Fourth Lok Sabha (1952-1969), there was no opposition party in the Lok Sabha with the requisite strength and therefore, there was no officially recognised Leader of the Opposition even though some very outstanding personalities occupied the opposition benches and led their parties.

In 1969, following the split in the Congress, Leader of Congress(O) with 60 members, Ram Subhag Singh became the first person to be formally recognised and given the status of the Leader of the Opposition in the 4th Lok Sabha. This lasted for about a year only. In the 5th Lok Sabha (1971-77), again, there was no party in opposition with one-tenth membership, hence there was no one recognised as the Leader of the Opposition. In the 6th Lok Sabha (1977-80) period, the Janata Party with 153 members became the ruling party while the Congress sat in opposition. Following splits in the Congress and Janata Party, Congress(I) with 58 members and Janata Party(S) with 68 members were both recognised as parliamentary parties. We had YB Chavan, CM Stephen and Jagjivan Ram as successive Leaders of the Opposition.

Again, during the 7th and 8th Lok Sabhas (1980-1989), there was no party in opposition with the requisite strength. No leader was, therefore, recognised as the Leader of the Opposition. Parties with 30 members or more like the Janata (S) with 41 memebers in the 7th Lok Sabha and Telugu Desam with 30 members in the 8th Lok Sabha were all recognised as groups only. During subsequent Lok Sabhas (9th to 15th), covering the period 1989-2014, since the requirement of having a strength of 55 members was fulfilled, we always had duly recognised opposition parties and Leaders of the Opposition who included Rajiv Gandhi, LK Advani, AB Vajpayee, PV Narasimha Rao, Sharad Pawar, Sonia Gandhi and Sushma Swaraj.

Until 1977, there were no emoluments of salary etc. attached to the position of the Leader of the Opposition. After the sixth General Election in 1977, which brought in the Janata Party government, the salary and allowances of Leaders of Opposition in Parliament Act, 1977, was passed. The Act extended to Leaders of Opposition in the two Houses, official status, allowances and perks like office facilities in Parliament House etc. equivalent to that of a cabinet minister.

The 1977 Act defined the Leader of the Opposition as that member of the Rajya Sabha or Lok Sabha who, for the time being, was the 'Leader of the Party in Opposition to the Government', having the greatest numerical strength and recognised as such by the Chairman/ Speaker of the Rajya Sabha/Lok Sabha. Although the definition in the Act did not spell out the ten per cent membership requirement, it was clearly implied in the required recognition by the Chairman/ Speaker. In the Lok Sabha, it was governed by Direction 121(c) which laid down one of the conditions for recognition as the party having 'at least a strength equal to the quorum fixed to constitute a sitting of the House, that is one-tenth of the total number of members of the House'.

If that was not enough, the Leaders and Chief Whips of Recognised Parties and Groups in Parliament (Facilities) Act, 1998, clinched the issue most decisively when it referred to a recognised party in the Lok Sabha to mean (vide section 2(b)(ii)) a party which has a strength of not less than fifty-five (55) members. It also provided for political parties in Lok Sabha having a strength of 30 to 54 members being recognised only as parliamentary groups. The law gives actual numbers.

The position under the law was thus conclusively settled, leaving no room for doubt or debate and no onus or discretion on the Speaker in the matter. It has been well said that the LOP 'post is not a product of the Speaker's subjective discretion but of time-honoured laws'. It is also true that the Speaker has simply not been vested with the power (or the option) to recognise anyone as LOP unless she/he fulfils the legal requirements. When the law is clear, there is nothing for the Speaker to decide or declare. The established practice is that the Speaker, on his own, does not make any declaration in the matter of recognising parliamentary parties or groups, she/he decides only when a formal request is made by the members concerned.

The position in the 16th Lok Sabha was that there were several leaders in the opposition heading their respective parties in the House, but there could be no officially recognised 'Leader of the Opposition' entitled to the status, salary, allowances, perks etc. equivalent to a cabinet minister.

While it was entirely within the jurisdiction of the Speaker to extend to any of the opposition leaders facilities like office accommodation in Parliament premises, some secretarial assistance, preference in seating arrangement in the House, speaking time in the proceedings etc. he could not legitimately waive or dilute the requirement of ten per cent membership. Also, if any effort was made by more than one party in opposition forming an alliance and electing a leader to constitute more than ten per cent and that way get around the requirement, it would have been most unacceptable and would have amounted to defrauding the public exchequer. Also, before someone could be recognised as the Leader of the Opposition, his party had to have the requisite strength. Alliances had no locus as a party.

It was asked what would happen to the laws/rules/conventions which provided for the Leader of the Opposition in Lok Sabha being a member of any Selection Committee /Collegium etc. for the appointment to offices like CVC, chairman NHRC, CIC, CBI Chief, Lok Pal etc. It should be quite clear that the concerned provisions can be easily modified to provide that in the eventuality of there being no recognised Leader of the Opposition, the leader of the largest group in opposition can discharge this responsibility. The very fact that in a couple of cases it was already provided that in the absence of a recognised LOP, the leader of the single largest group in opposition shall perform the role, shows that the situation of there being no Leader of the Opposition had been envisaged.

Lastly, it is important to remember that the parliamentary system works largely on precedents and practices. Since the First Lok Sabha came into being and during the entire period of 62 years (1952-2014), there were long periods when there was no Leader of the Opposition.

Also, no leader of a party with a strength of less than ten per cent of the total membership had ever been designated as the Leader of the Opposition. The ten per cent membership requirement was based on a deeper principle in parliamentary polity and history. Its roots can be traced to the British Parliament and the British Parliamentary System where the Opposition is considered 'Her Majesty's Loyal Opposition' or as a Government in Waiting and the Leader of the Opposition is supposed to be heading the Shadow Cabinet. The Leader of the Opposition has to be in a position to make the sitting of the House and if need be provide alternative government. It is for that reason that she/he is paid salary and allowances from the public funds and it is for the same reason that she/he has to satisfy the condition of being the leader of a party in opposition which has at least ten per cent of the members of the House on its rolls.

Unfortunately, in our Indian system, lawyers can always be found to agree to whatsoever be the client's case. To score political brownie points, an offensive was mounted after the 2014 May elections and an anti-BJP climate was sought to be created, as if the Congress was being denied its rightful claim to the LOP position. Actually, it was the people who had denied that position to the Congress by returning less than the minimum necessary numbers to the House.

When all the arguments under the Constitution and the law failed, some well-meaning leaders privately pleaded hard for recognising an opposition leader in the Lok Sabha as the Leader of the Opposition by the ruling party with the massive mandate showing large-heartedness, by extending to the leader of an opposition party the salary, perks and status of a cabinet minister. But, neither the government nor the Honourable Speaker had any inclination to be liberal to any party or leader at the cost of the public exchequer and in violation of the law.

Functioning of Parliament

Imperative of Effective Discipline

THE PRIMARY function of Parliament is to provide a government and to ensure good governance and rule of law. In parliamentary polity, the executive is part of Parliament and inside it. The text-book definition of Parliament as a mere law-making body no more holds good. It is often missed that a modern Parliament is much more than a legislative body. It is verily a multifunctional institution. Law making, both qualitatively and in terms of time devoted to it, is not even the most important of its functions. One of its crucial roles is to represent the people, to ventilate their problems and grievances and seek redressal by functioning as an effective link between the people and the government.

* Also see chapter on 'Seven Decades of Parliament'

The early decades after independence were the most eventful. Developments moved at hurricane speed. Centuries got compressed into years. India had to its credit many achievements. Several challenges of terrifying magnitude were faced by a functioning Parliament, within the democratic framework of constitutionalism. Some temporary aberrations like the Emergency notwithstanding, we were able to preserve freedom and rule of law and to bring about and maintain the unity and integrity of post-partition India. Representative institutions thrived and we grew as a stable, vibrant and functioning democratic polity.

However, there was another side to this. Soon, we were witnesses to a systemic decay and decline. Democratic values began getting devalued and institutions getting deinstitutionalised. By the time of the 14th and 15th Lok Sabha, things had come to such a pass that public thinking stood badly battered by the unprecedented spate of scams and scandals involving total governance deficit on all fronts. Faith of the people in the quality, integrity and efficiency of their elected representatives stood seriously eroded. Representative parliamentary institutions threatened to become dysfunctional. There was steep fall in the standards of conduct in public life. Loktantra tended to degenerate into loot tantra. Successive governments were said to have got into and remained in power by buying support with money, offer of ministerships, bargain on not pursuing criminal cases and the like. Huge sums of black money was believed to be stashed abroad. The general perception was that the government threatened some members with 'action under the law' while they kept threatening the government with withdrawal of support if they were not protected from the 'law taking its course'. Thus, there was mutual blackmail. The spectacle of unethically engineered or defection manipulated majorities or of successive hung legislatures or coalition governments of disparate elements coming together solely for sharing the fruits of power and including some of the alleged goon leaders with criminal records or otherwise doubtful antecedents, were all matters of grave concern.

The Houses, Committees and Members of Parliament are granted certain privileges to allow them unhindered freedom of speech and functioning in the discharge of their parliamentary duties. The basic law remains that all citizens, including MPs, are equal before the law. Parliamentary privileges do not exempt Members from their normal obligations to society which, in fact, should apply to them even more. Of late, there has been a widespread feeling of decay in the levels of conduct and etiquette followed by Members both inside and outside the Houses of Parliament. In the day-to-day functioning of Parliament, the observance by Members of certain rules regarding personal behaviour or etiquette is very important, not only for the smooth and decent conduct of the business of the House but also for upholding the dignity of Parliament and its members. A Member is not expected to use his privilege of freedom of speech to obstruct the business of the House. In any case, the exercise of every right and privilege is subject to the Rules of the House and the Constitution.

An overview of developments in parliamentary institutions since the first Lok Sabha reveals some interesting facts. The earlier Houses sat for long hours. The Opposition, though small in numbers, made valuable contribution to debates and had substantial impact on decision making. Parliament then could legitimately boast of having some very outstanding and accomplished parliamentarians who could do honour to any Parliament of the world. Again, when Lohia was pleading for Stalin's daughter Svetlana being given asylum in India on the ground of her marriage with an Indian, the charming lady Member, Tarkeshwari Sinha asked, 'when Dr Lohia was himself not married, how could he talk of conjugal sentiments?' Lohia immediately hit back: 'Tarkeshwari, when did you give me any chance?' Of late, such wit and humour in Parliament has become rare.

The number of days on which Houses of Parliament now sit each year and the time that is devoted to transacting business has decreased considerably in recent years. Even when they do meet, often little gets done. In the face of shouting, disturbances and disruption, total logjam prevails. It is recognised that the ugly scenes of indiscipline and indecorous behavior lead to waste of precious parliamentary time and loss of respect for the supreme representative institution. A resolution unanimously adopted by the two Houses of Parliament on completion of 50 years of Independence had pledged adherence to rules of decorum and discipline. Unfortunately, however, nothing changed. If anything, the situation became much worse. Sittings after sittings, almost entire sessions washed out and the drama costs the public exchequer several crores of rupees per day.

In a vibrant democracy and an effective functioning parliamentary polity, there can be nothing sadder than an increasing alienation taking place between the people and their elected representatives. Perhaps, the ever increasing number of members with the background of criminal cases against them has something to do with that. Today, we seem to be in a situation where sanctity of means has lost all value and relevance. If smugglers, gangsters, black-marketeers, foreign agents and any others from the world of crime can help put us in power, we are prepared to deal with them. We hear stories of leaders buying power by bribing the voters and fellow legislators. The people feel that many of the new breed of politicians in different parties have been selfish, power hungry, greedy, dishonest hypocrites and power merchants for whom the nation came last and the welfare of the ordinary people had least priorities. Their only concern was to amass wealth and get to and stay in power. They have been so busy in the struggle for power that they had no time or energy left for serving the people. In the words of a distinguished former President of India, they are 'no longer competitors in endeavour to serve the nation but are bitter enemies drawn in battle array'.

A very significant reason behind this state of affairs is the electoral process. Instead of being celebrated as festivals of democracy, elections have come to be regarded as battles. May be, there is nothing wrong in elections being fought vigorously and even bitterly. But, once these are over, parties and politicians are expected to return to civil parliamentary life and wait for another battle when it comes. A rather unseemly aspect of our elections is that these are going on almost all the year round in one or the other part of the country. Election campaign mood and rhetoric do not end even after the results of the general elections to Lok Sabha are announced. It should be possible for the present government to see reason and bring about some essential electoral reforms on a high priority basis including that of having simultaneous elections all over the country for all elective bodies from Pachayats to Parliament. While after the election, the leader of the party or parties commanding majority support in Lok Sabha forms the government at the Union level, those who fail to win majority support at the hustings should cooperate with the government in matters of providing good governance. It is important to remember that in parliamentary polity, the Opposition also forms a part of the government in the widest sense of the term. The people's mandate pertains to each of the Members elected. It is the duty of all the elected representatives irrespective of their parties, whether in power or in opposition, to ensure that Parliament functions, members discharge their responsibility to the people and decisions are made in the best interests of the people. Parliament functions through discussion and debate. After free expression of all views, decisions are taken by majority vote. As it is said in regard to British Parliament, 'the minority must have its say and the majority its way'.

Unfortunately, in the present climate of parliamentary indiscipline and confrontationist politics, a new Parliamentary Opposition Culture has developed under which those in opposition consider it their right to disrupt all business and not to allow the Houses to function. The deliberately adopted ugly Vote bank politics and strategy of negativism are directed at making Parliament dysfunctional in the hope of destabilising the government by blocking decision making on crucial issues of public concern. It is not realised that in the process, parliamentary democracy itself is threatened and it is we, the people, who suffer. The basics of the parliamentary system demand that at least matters of crucial national importance are kept above Vote bank party politics.

The financial cost of our parliamentary democracy has been rising to almost unaffordable and impossible levels. We may have to revisit and reinvent our democracy and bring about modifications based on our age old values and ideals. Parliament and democracy are tender plants and to save them, however idealistic and utopian it may seem, it has become a categorical imperative that politics must return to principles of being for service and sacrifice, to give one's best to the nation and take the least from it. Those in public life have to remember the Indian values of *asteya, aparigraha* and *Tena tyaktena bhunjitha.* The ruling party should propose a drastic reduction in the huge expenditure on Parliament and in the emoluments of members of Parliament and senior bureaucrats. That will send a powerful message to the people at large. In fact, I feel, instead of promising the moon, if we had asked for sacrifices and to use Churchill's words, promised nothing except 'blood, sweat and tears', the people would have responded better and cooperated willingly provided they saw similar sacrifice beginning at the top.

To function effectively, every institution has to follow certain rules of conduct and some basics of discipline. To what extent it is done depends upon the quality and character of the people who constitute the institution. What kind of people get elected depends very largely on the electoral system and processes followed. Notwithstanding the usual euphoria about our free and fair elections, our electoral system and processes have proved to be very divisive of society and unable to elect the right kind of representatives of the people. This has led to criminalisation of politics, politicisation of crime and generation of a black economy with tons of unaccounted money illegally kept in foreign banks and companies. If tickets to seek election to either House of Parliament have sometimes to be bought for crores of rupees; if election campaigns run with tons of black money and if democracy is on sale, it is natural that those with lots of black money and interest in good ROI (Return on Investment) will rush to buy them.

Also, an overwhelming majority of those elected had more votes cast against each one of them. Under the circumstances, they could be hardly considered legitimate representatives of the people. The National Constitution Commission (2000-2002) examined the matter in great depth and made recommendations in this regard. Unless the system is urgently revisited and reformed, only those with money and muscle power could constitute the category of winnables. Also, if one can very reasonably hope to win with a caste, community or other identity based vote bank of 15 per cent or so, why should he or she bother about the other 85 per cent? There is all the advantage in playing divisive politics and building separate identities. If the problem of unacceptable levels of parliamentary indiscipline has to be solved and effective functioning of Parliament has to be ensured in the interest of survival of our vibrant democracy, we must strike at the root of the malady and rush to reform the electoral system first.

Despite all its imperfections and failings, the present regime must act fast and hard. If after receiving such a massive mandate it failed to deliver, people would lose faith in the system. Democracy, Parliament and rule of law may not survive.

Logjam in Parliament

The JPC Report

Combating Corruption

IDEALLY, PARLIAMENT as the supreme representative institution of the people is expected to take serious note of the challenges posed to our polity by the giant scamsters. Members rising above their party differences should seriously deliberate upon the ways to quickly identify and punish the guilty and devise systemic reforms to prevent recurrence of such scams.

When the short (2010) winter session of Parliament began, it was foreseen as most likely to be stormy and full of turmoil. However, from day one, the proceedings of the two Houses were stalled. The entire winter session ended without transacting any worthwhile business. It was rendered almost completely dysfunctional. The ritual of laying down papers and the obligatory passing of supplementary grants was also a sham and a disgrace. Grants worth thousands of crores were declared as passed without debate, in the midst of din, by a voice vote, in a matter of minutes. It was a sort of new record that in 23 days, the Lok Sabha met for 7½ hours and Rajya Sabha for 2 hours and 44 minutes only. Both the government and the opposition were responsible for this parliamentary scam involving hundreds of crores of public money. There could be no better evidence of the low levels to which respect of Members for Parliament and public money had descended. The basic issues of large scale corruption soon receded to the backstage and a lot was focused on the parliamentary logjam.

The Opposition members were united in demanding the government to form a Joint Parliamentary Committee (JPC) for examining the allocation of 2-G Spectrum (second generation improved technology telephony) licences and other scams. They said that they would not allow the Houses to function unless this was agreed. The government was equally adamant on not admitting the Opposition demand. It said that the Public Accounts Committee (PAC) was the appropriate forum for deliberating on financial accounts and the report of C&AG. In any case, all the matters could be discussed on the floors of the two Houses. The government also offered to agree to a CBI probe under the supervision of the Supreme Court.

The Minister of Parliamentary Affairs argued against accepting the JPC demand on the ground that it was purely a political demand. This logic made no sense. First, if the demand was political, its rejection by the government was equally so. Secondly, Parliament itself was primarily a political institution meant *inter alia* for debating political issues. 'Political' cannot mean unreasonable or illegitimate. Thirdly, there were compulsions of coalition politics. Some of the problems arose when for formation of government in case of a hung House of the People, a price had to be paid to coalition partners/supporters, bargains had to be struck and often, the price demanded had to be paid in the form of creamy portfolios like telecom. In such a situation, corruption was inbuilt in government formation. It was known to the Prime Minister and others. It was understood and accepted as unavoidable in the best interests of power politics. Even the last resort removal of the Minister under attack through resignation perhaps became possible only after counter pressure and promise of support from a rival provincial satrap.

The Opposition felt that the JPC canvas could be vast while PAC probe would be limited in nature and the Ministers could not be summoned before it. As for the CBI Inquiry under the Supreme Court, it was very legitimately wondered how could the government make such an offer or interfere with the judicial functions and discretion of the court even though finally, the Supreme Court did agree for a CBI inquiry under its aegis. The Opposition asked what was so sinister about demanding a JPC probe. Its relevance remained even after the Supreme Court decision. After all, during the NDA regime in 2001, a JPC was quickly conceded by the Prime Minister to probe the Stock Market Crash Scam and related issues. The then Finance Minister, Jaswant Sinha and former Finance Minister, PC Chidambaram and Manmohan Singh, as also the Finance Secretary appeared before the Committee. A unanimous report was made and its recommendations were largely accepted.

The Opposition disowned responsibility for making the Houses dysfunctional. It asserted that it was the job of the government to ensure that Parliament functioned. All the efforts made by the trouble shooters and party managers at all-party luncheon meetings and otherwise failed to evolve a compromise. This was a clear failure of political and floor management skills on behalf of the government. The Speaker's last ditch effort also didn't succeed in ending the logjam. The fact of the matter was that those in Government and in Opposition were both equally responsible for the ugly impasse. There was an unnecessary, illegitimate and irrational tug of war in the name of the people. But, the people were nowhere in the picture. As usual, on both sides, political considerations and calculations of gain and loss had the upper hand. Perhaps, there was an unsaid long term political concern before the Government and the Opposition. Both had their eyes on the 2014 general elections. The Opposition would have liked to drag the matter on through the JPC device and the Congress feared a repeat of what happened to it after the JPC on Bofors. Also, perhaps the Congress was not sure of its allies and supporting parties.

The people were appalled and dismayed at the shameful levels and reach of corruption involving the UPA-II Government headed by Prime Minister Manmohan Singh and advised by the all powerful NAC. But, precious little was done by the Opposition to explain to 'we, the people' why it insisted on disrupting the parliamentary processes and proceedings of the Houses. The government side also failed to convince the concerned citizens about the justification, if any, for its so vehement and unrelenting opposition to conceding the near unanimous opposition demand. It is also feared that the deliberate dilly-dallying on the JPC demand could be to mark time to fudge records and buy and manage evidence.

Some of the information was being given out through blogs or TV Channels. But, the people were not taken into confidence. They needed to be informed about parliamentary processes, relevance and respective merits of different parliamentary committees etc. Even the media people kept enquiring about the difference between a JPC and the PAC being called upon to conduct the necessary inquiry.

It would have been best to use the fora of the floors of the two Houses of Parliament to talk to the people and educate them through parliamentary debates about the arguments of both sides. The Opposition leaders could place all the facts and arguments most forcefully and plead for the appointment of a Joint Committee of the two Houses. The government side could also justify its stand. The people could then form their opinion even though in a parliamentary system, while the Opposition has the right to have its say, the government, so long as it is in majority, should be allowed to have its way.

Parliament is the chief communication link between the government and the people. Close contact and an intimate rapport between the two is the quintessence of parliamentary polity. Parliament belongs to the people and not to MPs or parties. People must have access to Parliament. Unfortunately, in India today, there is a tremendous disconnect between the two. Things got worse when the Houses did not function and were shut against the people.

Under the Constitution (Articles 74-75), the Council of Ministers headed by the Prime Minister is 'collectively responsible to the *House of the People*'. If the Opposition was anxious to question the Prime Minister and nail his responsibility, the open session of the House of the People was the more effective and legitimate forum than a JPC. In the JPC, in any case, proceedings are in camera. No Prime Minister may like the idea of being summoned and questioned by a parliamentary committee but no Prime Minister can run away from the House either; questioning and indictment are in full public view before TV cameras.

In the context of Articles 74-75, again, it was clear that a Minister who ignored the Finance Ministry, disregarded the advice of the Law Ministry, flouted cabinet's decision and Prime Minister's own advice should never have been allowed to stay on as a Minister and indulge in wrong-doing that would result in massive defrauding of the public exchequer. Obviously, the Prime Minister could not disown all responsibility. He was the head and the responsibility was collective. It was a sad commentary if it was left to the highest court in the land to point out that the Prime Minister was disrespected by one of his own Ministers. The Constitution did not allow any dilution of collective responsibility of the cabinet or the clear responsibility of the Prime Minister himself. One wondered if some subtle and deeper politics was not involved, directed at a situation where Prime Minister Singh could be constrained to put in his own papers.

Also, why should the Ministers and the Prime Minister not be prepared to be questioned by Members of Parliament? They were all answerable to the Houses and a joint parliamentary committee was the two Houses in miniature or their microcosm. On the other hand, why did the opposition want to question them in the confidentiality of the Committee—JPC or PAC—behind closed doors, away from TV cameras and the limelight of public scrutiny. It may be of some interest to know that the nomenclature JPC or Joint Parliamentary Committee as such has *not* been mentioned in any constitutional or legal provisions or in the Rules of Procedure and Conduct of Business in the two Houses of Parliament. The term gained currency in the media during and after the inquiry into the Bofors scandal that broke out in 1987.

The device of parliamentary committees is intended to assist the Houses of Parliament in the efficient discharge of their functions. There are two types of Parliamentary Committees in India, viz (i) Standing Committees and (ii) *ad hoc* Committees. Standing Committees are those which are constituted by the House or the Speaker every year or from time to time, as the case may be and are permanent in nature. *Ad hoc* Committees are appointed for a specific purpose and they become *functus officio* as soon as they have completed the task assigned to them and presented their report. Standing Committees, amongst others, include the Financial Committees and Departmentally Related Committees. *Ad hoc* committees may be select or Joint Committees. A committee which consists of members of the two Houses is a Joint Committee. The Standing Financial Committee called the Public Accounts Committee is also a joint Committee in as much as members of the Rajya Sabha are also associated with it. All the Departmentally Related Standing Committees are Joint Committees.

The two Houses of Parliament have inherent powers to appoint special committees under special circumstances to examine and inquire into specific issues and report to the Houses. Apart from the Standing Committees, *ad hoc* joint committees of the two Houses have been constituted from time to time on various matters. All these technically were JPCs. It was, therefore, not correct to say that the JPC on Bofors was the first JPC or that there had been only four JPCs. Also, it was not correct to say that the four JPCs were total failures.

Any committee could only inquire and make recommendations. It was for the Parliament to discuss them and for the government to accept them and take appropriate action.

After Bofors, the nomenclature JPC had in practice come to connote an *ad hoc* joint committee of the two Houses formed for inquiring into a specific scandal of financial wrongdoing. A distinctive feature of such committees was their investigatory role. Of the oft-cited four such investigative committees in the past, the first was in 1987 on the Bofors scandal. After crusading for it and blocking Parliament for long, the Opposition boycotted the JPC on the ground that it was packed by Congress members. Even though the Opposition boycotted the JPC on Bofors, its inquiry led to mass resignation of opposition members and ultimately change of government. The cabinet itself was split with VP Singh putting himself up as a anti-corruption Messiah. The second JPC was formed in 1992 to investigate the Securities Stock Scam involving Harshad Mehta and other brokers. Parliament was largely paralysed for two weeks before the JPC was conceded. The third was set up in 2001 to investigate the Shares scam involving Ketan Parekh, Banks and corporate houses. The fourth JPC (20) was for inquiring into the use of insecticides in cold drinks. From 13 March 2001, Parliament was held to ransom for 9 days after the *Tehelka* expose. In April, after another week of adjournments, Congress Opposition demanded a JPC. On the issue of irregularities in defence purchases during the Kargil conflict, Opposition Congress again demanded a JPC. These demands, however, were not accepted. So far as political parties were concerned, they demanded JPC when in opposition and opposed it when in government.

A joint committee may be appointed on a motion adopted by the two Houses and may contain the names of its members. It may also be appointed by the Speaker of Lok Sabha and the Chairman of Rajya Sabha after mutual consultation. Members of some of the Standing Committees including the Public Accounts Committee (PAC) are elected according to the system of proportional representation by means of single transferable vote. This may be so even in the case of some *ad hoc* committees. But, even if the committees are constituted by the Presiding Officers, proportional representation of parties is kept in view and the numbers in committees represent the party position in the Houses, ie. by and large the ruling party or parties remain in majority in the committees as well. The Chairmen of Committees are generally appointed by the Speaker from among their members but sometimes a Committee may elect its own Chairman, eg Joint Committee on Salaries and Allowances of Members. In case of PAC, by convention, the Chairman is from the Opposition ever since 1967.

The Constitution *vide* Articles 148-151 provides for the independent audit agency of the Comptroller and Auditor-General of India (C & AG). In the Constituent Assembly, while moving to change the erstwhile designation of Auditor-General to Comptroller and Auditor-General, TT Krishnamachari, as a member of the Constitution Drafting Committee had said that the duties of this office were not merely of audit but also of exercising control over governmental spending.

Article 151 specifically lays down that the C & AG shall submit to the President reports relating to the accounts of the Union and the President shall cause them to be laid before both Houses of Parliament. Thus, to the extent that the executive is accountable to Parliament in financial maters, the C & AG works as the watchdog on behalf of Parliament. The effective functioning of the Public Accounts Committee depends largely on the assistance that it gets from the Comptroller & Auditor-General of India who is considered to be a friend and guide of the Committee. Soon after the reports of C&AG relating to accounts of the Union and also finance accounts of the Central Government and audit reports thereon have been laid before the House, the Committee determines from time to time the accounts and audit reports to be examined by it and the programme of the Committee is circulated to the Ministers concerned and C&AG to enable them to stay ready to appear before the Committee.

The main duty of the Committee is to ascertain whether the money granted by Parliament has been spent by the Government 'within the scope of the Demand'. The functions of the Committee extend, however, beyond the formality of the expenditure to 'its wisdom, faithfulness and economy'. The Committee is meant to act as a check not only upon extravagant, irregular or unauthorized expenditure, but also, within limits, upon unwise methods of management. Accordingly, in cases involving losses, nugatory expenditure and financial irregularities that are brought to its notice through the reports of the Comptroller and Auditor-General, the Committee may call upon the Ministry/Deptt concerned to explain what action, disciplinary or otherwise, it had taken to prevent a recurrence of the same. In such cases, it may also record its opinion in the form of disapproval or pass strictures against extravagance or lack of proper control by the Ministry or Deptt concerned. The Committee can also *suo motu* take up subjects not commented upon by the Audit. There have been occasions when the Committee has examined subjects not forming part of the Audit Report of C&AG.

In the case of the 2-G spectrum scam, the C & AG did his job and his report was laid before the two Houses. It had unearthed a major scam and pointed out blatant and substantial irregularities causing a loss of a mind-boggling amount of Rupees 1.76 lakh crores to the public exchequer. Without a public and transparent auction, the 2-G Spectrum licenses were given away to companies with doubtful credentials in 2008 at throwaway 2001 prices by Telecom Minister Raja. Two companies who bought the licenses for 1,500 and 1,600 crores, after a few weeks sold their stakes for 12,000 crores.

In parliamentary committees, ideally, the effort always is to function on non-party lines and take decisions unanimously or by consensus but the Rules provide for all questions at any sitting of a committee being decided 'by a majority of votes of the members present and voting'. On crucial issues involving party susceptibilities, it could not be easy for the opposition to have its way against the government. It was, therefore, wrong for the opposition to believe that they could compel the presence of the Prime Minister or other Ministers before the JPC. The majority in the committee could always overrule such suggestions. Also, under the Rules the question could be 'referred to the Speaker whose decision shall be final.'

While in the PAC, a Minister is not called before the Committee to give evidence or for consultation in connection with the examination of accounts, a Minister may appear before the Committee if the Chairman agrees. Also, it can be so arranged between the Speaker, the Committee Chairman and the Minister concerned that the Minister appears on his own. If the Opposition was somehow convinced that it should not appear to be stalling the proceedings of the Budget session and the government realised that it needed not to be seen as avoiding inquiry and answerability, there could be a way out of the impasse whereby the concerned Ministers and even the Prime Minister could appear before the PAC and the Committee could also go beyond the C&AG Report and take *suo motu* notice of allied issues. This only required an initiative from the Prime Minister himself.

Looked at from the angle of the Opposition, it was a golden opportunity to draw maximum political advantage by demanding good leadership, clean citizen-friendly governance and inclusive politics. They could make large-scale corruption a major issue and launch a massive campaign against it through speeches in parliamentary fora and on the ground all over the country instead of disrupting the functioning of the two Houses and thereafter sitting quiet sipping cups of coffee in the Central Hall.

While the parliamentary paralysis continued, the Supreme Court was also seized of the main issue of corruption in the 2-G scam. The CBI counsel had to admit before the Apex Court that the magnitude of the scam was mind boggling. When told of the 5000 calls recorded and 8000 documents seized, the Court asked the CBI Counsel not to beat about the bush when illegality was *prima facie* evident. According to reports, the Court castigated the CBI for tardy investigation and asked why the then Telecom Minister Raja and then Secretary Thomas had not been questioned and why FIRs were preferred against 'unknown persons' when C&AG—a constitutional authority—had already indicted the DOT and corporates for swindling pubic money. The Supreme Court questioned the legitimacy of the appointment of the CVC on the ground of pending charges against him and because of his controversial role as Telecom Secretary. It was most astounding and inappropriate for the Government Counsel to retort that in that case some of the judicial appointments could also be questioned. The Court, however, was forthright in posing the question of how could the CBI function under the CVC who had pending charges against him and who was the former Telecom Secretary. The CVC had only recused himself from overseeing the CBI in the matter of 2-G Spectrum Licenses. He made the interesting point that the charges against him were not of corruption but only of criminal conspiracy.

The saddest part of the debate in the media and among the pro-establishment pseudo-liberal intellectuals was that there was no willingness to call a spade a spade and outright condemn wrongdoing. Public cheating by those in power was countered and defended by pointing fingers at similar cheating by opposition parties when and where they happened to be in power. In other words, unable to plead innocent and not guilty, the guilty turned around and said that the others were also similarly naked in the *hamam* of politics. Party A accuses Party B of swindling public money and the reply of the accused is that you did the same. The blame game and defence strategy of counter offensive continued while the only losers were we, the people of India.

The ultimate question was whether the political class who were the largest beneficiaries of corruption had at last realized that enough was enough and the people were at last awake and not prepared to accept the sordid state of affairs any longer.

The Opposition pressure, strong observations from the Supreme Court and the relentless public outcry against huge corruption scandals at last had the necessary impact. Some of the most powerful had to go behind bars, the then rulers were thrown out decisively and had to bite dust at the hustings, licenses got auctioned bringing large revenues to the public exchequer. But, the battle against corruption has still to be fought and won.

Decline of Parliament

Road to Recovery and Reform

ALONG WITH good governance and erosion in the norms of the justice delivery system, the institution of Parliament also appeared to have suffered a sharp decline in various ways. Very little effort, however, was made to examine and analyse what really plagued the Parliament or to find out the reasons for the erosion of the traditional authority, high esteem and pristine glory of the institution of Parliament. We must deliberate on high priority basis why things came to such a pass? Perhaps, something can still be done to restore the legislature and legislators to their old glory and bring about a renaissance of democratic faith and parliamentary culture.

One of the most cardinal and fundamental functions of Parliament in a parliamentary system is to provide responsible and responsive representative government. In the words of the National Commission (NCRWC), one way to judge whether the system is working well or not is to see whether it has created governments that last their terms and succeed in providing good governance to the community. The overriding objective has to be to make both government and Parliament relevant to meet today's challenges that bear little comparison to those faced by our society in the middle decades of the twentieth century. The fundamental challenges are economic and technological. Parliament has to play a decisive role in refashioning the national economy, keeping in the forefront the ideals of a self-reliant economy that serve the real needs and aspirations of our vast masses. Parliament can play this historic role only if it consciously reforms its procedures and prioritises its work.

Until 1977, ie. for the first 30 years of Independence, Congress remained the dominant party with an undisputed majority. Interestingly, however, the opposition while small in number was more effective and had greater impact in the earlier years. Perhaps, it was so because of the high quality and character of membership on both sides and largely because a stable government and secure leadership could show greater magnanimity and accommodate opposition viewpoints without losing face. Attention needs to be drawn towards a distinct change in the content, canvas and culture of debates right from the early days of the first Lok Sabha days. In the earlier Lok Sabhas, there was much greater emphasis on discussion of national and international issues. Regional issues and local problems were left to be addressed in the State Legislatures. People would flock to hear Nehru initiate debates on international situation, on foreign affairs, etc. which were followed by high level discussions from a national angle. It seems that gradually but increasingly more regional and even local problems came to acquire greater relevance and importance for our members. What perhaps caused the greatest concern was not only the shift in emphasis but the fundamental change in approach and outlook as well. Sometimes it appeared as if we were more and more looking at national problems from regional, communal, linguistic or otherwise parochial angles rather than the other way round.

That representative democracy and parliamentary institutions have endured in India for seven decades, is a great tribute to their strength and resilience. There had, however, been in recent decades quite some thinking and debate about the decline of Parliament, devaluation of Parliament's authority, deterioration in the quality of Members, poor levels of participation and the like. One noticed a certain cynicism towards parliamentary institutions and an erosion in the respect for normal parliamentary processes and the parliamentarians. We had an unending debate in regard to the falling standards in the conduct of legislators as evidenced by poor quality of debates, niggardly attendance in the houses of legislatures, unruly behaviour of members, scenes of pandemonium and the like. Once a Lok Sabha Speaker said that he had to take aspirin tablets before taking the Chair. Legislatures having members with criminal records, sale and purchase of legislators to obtain majority and stay in power or somehow come to power and mortgaging the interests of the nation and of future generations for self-interests in the business of power politics had become the most common topics of popular discussion for years. The people were aghast and, and what was worse, they felt helpless.

Bashing Parliament and parliamentarians became a fashion with self-proclaimed intellectuals. This deserved to be deprecated because other institutions had perhaps declined more. But, it was true that in parliamentary polity, there could be nothing worse or more dangerous than the representative credentials of the representatives, with some honourable exceptions, becoming suspect and an increasing alienation taking place between the people and their representatives with the representatives losing the respect of the people. We were in a situation where sanctity of means had lost all value, meaning and relevance. If dacoits, smugglers, gangsters and foreign agents could help put us or sustain us in power, we were prepared to compromise with them.

The information explosion, the technological revolution, the growing magnitude and complexities of modern administration cast upon Parliament other vastly extended responsibilities. Inadequacy of time, information and expertise with Parliament results in poor quality legislation and unsatisfactory parliamentary surveillance over administration. Inadequacy of education and training in the sophisticated mechanics of parliamentary polity and the working procedures of modern parliamentary institutions have adversely affected the performance of both the legislators and the bureaucracy. Little effort has been made thus far to develop the essential prerequisites for the success of parliamentary polity—discipline, character, high sense of public morality, ideology-oriented two-party system and willingness to hear and accommodate minority views. Several of the archaic practices and time-consuming procedures most unsuitable for present day needs are being continued unnecessarily.

Members, irrespective of their party affiliations, have themselves become a new caste and parts of the establishment and co-sharers in the spoils. Again, some honourable exceptions apart, politics and membership of Parliament have emerged as a whole-time, highly lucrative hereditary profession for majority of those involved. Following the changed composition of the Houses, there has been fast devaluation of all the old values and increasing disorders and mayhem on the floor not only during the 'Zero Hour' but for the whole day and day after day. There is general apathy among Members, Ministers and public at large towards the work of Parliament. Absenteeism among members has assumed alarming proportions and defections for money and office have been a common phenomenon.

Legitimacy of government of representative institutions under the system are inextricably linked to free and fair elections and to the system being able to bring to power persons who truly represent the people's will and have the necessary abilities to govern. Therefore, as a first step, it would be necessary to reform the electoral system and the political party system. What is needed is a holistic approach to electoral reforms and a comprehensive legislation for the purpose.

Reforms and urgent remedial action seem imperative for

making parliamentary institutions and processes effective and potent instrument of ensuring sustainable economic growth so vital for the success of the economic policy of all inclusive development. Role expectation of Parliament is linked with the role perception of the State. Needs of development strategy should lead to cutting back on government involvement and drastic reduction in the role of the State in national economy. This should naturally get reflected in the reduced role for Parliament and its Committees. Also, their processes, control mechanisms, debating and decision making procedures would have to be revamped and made faster. Floor management techniques would have to be professionalised at the level of whips, parliamentary officials and the Presiding Officers. All this assumes the existence of a functioning Parliament.

For the Parliament, it is of the utmost importance constantly to review and refurbish its structural-functional requirements instantly and from time to time to consider renewing and reforming the entire gamut of its operational procedures to guard against putrefaction and decay. The case for reforming Parliament is unexceptionable and, in a sense, has always been so. The real question is of how much and what to change to strengthen and improve the system. We have to be clear about the precise need, the direction and the extent of the reforms that would be desirable at present. It is obvious that mere tinkering first-aid repairs and trifling cosmetic adjustments would not anymore be enough. What is needed is a full-scale review. We have to be prepared for fundamental institutional—structural, functional, procedural and organisational changes.

Nodal Standing Committee on Economy: Immediate steps should be taken to set up a nodal Standing Committee on national economy with specific subject-oriented study groups aided by experts and concerned with economic policy formulation and implementation. The study groups would make internal study reports to the main Committee based on operational research in performance evaluation against physical targets. The Committee would in its turn make annual reports to Parliament. These reports would prove valuable to various Ministries and Departments of the Government. Also, they would serve the purpose of constant vigilance and constructive appraisal directed at preventing erosion of credibility, plugging loopholes and strengthening the system as a whole. The Committee recommendations would help to evolve and adopt better means of monitoring, analysing and evaluating performance in implementing policies and prescribing correctives to ensure the best use of available resources. The *reports would provide valuable feedback to Parliament and should be discussed by the two Houses each year.*

Building a better image of Parliament: Parliament is the communication link between the people and the government. People talk of happenings in Parliament and of the members of Parliament as things quite remote and different from themselves. There is little consciousness of Parliament being their own and Members being from among themselves. A Senior parliamentarian (Hiren Mukherjee) speaking of 'Politics' generally, once bemoaned: 'It will not be very wrong to say, sorrowfully, that there never was a time in living history when politics and politicians were, almost rightfully, as denigrated, even degraded, and sometimes detested, in the eyes of our people as they are at the moment. It is necessary for Parliament to establish a new rapport with the people and convincing them that it belonged to them and not to MPs. The latter themselves are responsible to Parliament and to the people outside. It is ordinary people who must be enabled to feel that they are participants in the decision-making and legislative processes and that through Parliament their voice can reach the government and the public must be free to question it and expose it without being threatened under the law of parliamentary privileges. Once when somebody suggested that all the corrupt be dumped in the Bay of Bengal, an honourable member remarked: "I pity the Bay of Bengal. What will happen to it?" In its own long term interest, Parliament as an institution cannot afford to place itself beyond all scrutiny by anyone. There is every need for a parliamentary

Ombudsman. If stories that are current about payments demanded, offered or paid for—legitimate or not so legitimate—favours need to be thoroughly investigated and if untrue, publicly contradicted.

The people should know what their representatives are doing or not doing for them. Televising the House proceedings may not have improved the level of debates much but parliamentary politics has become more alive. Much remains to be done. Care has to be taken to see that televising of proceedings does not turn some members into demagogues and mountebanks playing more and more to the gallery and to the vast number of viewers and listeners all over the country.

It is necessary that the press and public relations in parliament are suitably reoriented and developed as a highly specialised and dynamic service responsible for educating public opinion on Parliament and its activities. Arrangements should be made for attending to enquiries from the public, publicising the telephone numbers and addresses from which information about Parliament and its activities may be sought, and providing some public computer terminals and a more meaningful, communicative and interactive internet website from which any citizen can hope to get any information and replies to queries and doubts he may have regarding the Parliament and its activities.

Panchayats and Parliament: The role of an MP must undergo change as a result of 73rd and 74th Amendments. The functions of Parliament and role expectation from Parliament should be transformed. Meticulous caution has to be taken to avoid any role conflicts between the Panchayats and Members of Parliament. Ideally, Members of Parliament are Members for the entire country and should concern themselves basically with the national issues leaving the local problems to the care of Panchayats and Nagar Palikas. Schemes like the one that placed five crore rupees each year at the discretion of each Member of Parliament to be spent on local projects are bound to create role conflicts and tensions. The MPs and MLAs LAD schemes are a fraud on the Constitution inasmuch they place many many thousands of crores of public money at the disposal of the legislators, nearly Rs 4,000 crore for MPs alone. It is an affront to the principles of distribution of powers between the Union and the States, assignment of certain functions to Panchayats and Nagar Palikas and distinction between the roles of the executive and the legislature.

The LADs schemes must be discontinued forthwith. Nepal had a similar scheme but their Supreme Court had declared it *ultra vires* under the then Constitution of Nepal.

Improving the quality of members: Quality of Members is the most important variable in the working of any Parliament inasmuch as a Parliament would be what its Members make of it. It is the primary duty of every member, irrespective of his party affiliations, to maintain and project a good image of the Parliament by his conduct both inside and outside the Houses of Parliament. Corporate image of Parliament is bound to remain poor unless the quality and conduct of Individual Members improves and every member is enabled to feel relevant and that he matters in what goes on in Parliament. Members of important Parliamentary committees need to lay down a strict code of conduct for themselves, never to ask the senior government officers appearing before the Committee for personal favours, avoid Committee tours unless really necessary and never accept any costly gifts, dinners, free transport, five star hospitality and the like while on tours.

Politics has become a highly professionalised business and should be understood as such. Irrespective of one's talents and professional background, every new member when he first entres a legislature feels completely lost in the dense forest of the mass of conventions, traditions, rules, regulations and formalities of highly sophisticated parliamentary procedures, processes and practices. Institutionalised arrangements are, therefore, necessary to provide the much needed professional training and orientation to every newly elected Member irrespective of his ideological or party affiliations. The curriculum should include, among other things, adequate knowledge of the political system, the Constitution, the Rules of procedure and Conduct of Business, the practices and precedents, mechanisms and modalities of the working of the Houses and the Parliamentary Committees, the do's and don'ts for members, the rules of parliamentary etiquette and the like. The emphasis should be on the practical know-how, the technicalities and the operational realities and the concrete situations and not the rule book.

The orientation seminars for new members that are now arranged have become too routinised, insipid and more in the nature of a ritual both for the participants and the organisers.

Reducing the Expenditure: Financial cost of Parliamentary democracy has been skyrocketing. During the last 70 years they have gone up by several thousand times. From some lakhs per year, the budget on the Union Legislature has gone up to thousands of crores a year. Also, the figures seem fudged inasmuch as much of the expenditure gets reflected under other heads. There is also the other thousands of crores kept at the disposal of members under the MP LAD Scheme etc.

A matter often raised is that of the salaries, allowances, amenities, facilities etc extended to members. Besides the members, we have ministers, Chairmen of Boards, Public Undertakings etc. and politicians occupying innumerable offices with Minister's status at the State and Union levels, each one costing ten to fifty times the cost of an MP. All this put together makes the cost of maintaining our huge army of all time professional politicians very heavy and hardly commensurate with the returns to society. While stressing the need for cutting down the overall administrative expenditure, we have to think of cutting down the mounting cost of democracy as well. There is a need to drastically slash parliamentary spending on various heads, even if the resultant economy in the context of the overall national budget, by convention, is not questioned or debated.

The Constitution Commission (NCRWC) had suggested a strict limit on the number of Ministers and equivalent posts both at the Union level and in the States. The Commission had suggested that the number of ministers should not be more than 10% of the membership of the popular House and the equivalent posts should be limited to 2%. The government did accept limit of 15% per cent (instead of 10%) on the ministers but no limit was placed on the number of posts of Minister's rank. Also, departments are created, merged or split from time to time. This causes confusion, instability, uncertainly and wasteful expenditure.

Another matter that would need to be addressed simultaneously is that of political activity having become terribly capital intensive. Running a political party, being an active politician and contesting an election requires tons of money. Where is it to come from? It has to be mostly black in India or abroad, and has to come from criminals, smugglers and the like. Now, why should they pay to send others to Parliament? Why should they not enter themselves? The result is that irrespective of their party affiliations the number of members with criminal cases pending against them has been increasing in the last three Lok Sabhas. In the 16th Lok Sabha it is said to have gone up to nearly 300.

Improving Information Supply: Information is power. For any effective surveillance over administration, Parliament needs information and its Members have to be fed with the latest information and kept updated regarding developments in all areas of parliamentary concern and more particularly in matters arising before their Houses or Committees. Parliament must build its own independent national information reservoir with a network of feeding and retrieval points. In this connection, computerisation of storage and retrieval of information in Parliament was well conceived. But much depends on the data files that are built and what is actually fed into the computer or the internet. Unfortunately, it seems there has been no qualitative change in the information gathering processes. Substantial data monitoring and analysis in regard to Parliament's and its members' own activities has got to be done in-house and not sourced out. Developing an independent and transparent infrastructure of information support system in parliament would have a profound effect on revitalising and transforming the institution of Parliament.

Planning legislation and improving its quality: Our legislation has often been criticised for hasty drafting and for its being rushed through Parliament in an *ad hoc* and haphazard manner. There is need for a dynamic—not mechanical—approach to legislative engineering and systematic programming of laws which may be proposed for enactment over a period of time. This can be done by:

(i) Streamlining the functions of the Parliamentary and Legal Affairs Committee of the Cabinet.

(ii) Making greater use of the Law Commission.

(iii) Setting up a new Legislation Committee of Parliament to oversee and coordinate legislative planning.

(iv) Referring all Bills to the Departmental Standing Committees for consideration and scrutiny, consulting concerned interest groups and finalisation of the second reading stage in the relaxed atmosphere of Committees aided by experts, thereby reducing the burden of the Houses without impinging on any of its rights and improving the quality of drafting and content of legislation.

Setting up a Constitution Committee: While executive power of the Union is coextensive with its legislative power, the constituent power under the Constitution belongs exclusively to Parliament. The responsibility of Parliament therefore, become much greater in the case of Constitution (Amendment) Bills. As such, instead of the Constitution Amendments being presented to Parliament like ordinary pieces of legislation in the form of Bills for introduction sometimes at very short notice, it would be desirable if Parliament is associated right from the initial stages of formulation of proposals for constitutional reform, ie. the actual drafting of a Constitution Amendment Bill may be taken up after a proposal is formulated but before it is introduced, it may be subjected to a *priori* scrutiny of the 'Constitution Committee'. If this is done, even the government would be saved many an embarrassment.

Also, where an enactment is placed beyond the power of judicial review by being included under the Ninth Schedule it may be desirable for Parliament itself to provide an alternative forum and remedy by way of review etc. to any aggrieved citizen. The proposed Constitution Committee may perform this function as well. In view of the fact that several laws are struck down by courts as being *ultra vires* the Constitution, it would be desirable to subject all legislation to prior scrutiny from the point of view of constitutional validity. Scrutiny by a parliamentary committee should help in ensuring that legislation purporting to be in furtherance of the Directive Principles does, in fact, have a reasonable nexus with the objectives in view and do not curtail the fundamental rights of the citizens beyond a measure that can be considered to be reasonable and strictly necessary.

Departmental Committees and Improving Accountability: The setting up of the subject based Departmentally Related Standing Committees has been the most historic development in recent years in the area of parliamentary reforms. Their number has grown to 24. This is perhaps too many. Three such committees were set up in 1989 on an experimental basis. Subsequently, the Rules Committee recommended ten Committees to cover all the Ministries and Departments. But, perhaps hard bargaining and needs for compromise and accommodation of various interests and considerations raised the number to seventeen and then to twenty-four.

Despite all the Standing Committees, it is reasonably well established that parliamentary scrutiny over public finance is at present inadequate and patchy and there is need for simplifying presentation of the budget. Also, for strengthening parliamentary control over the Executive, Committees should not become merely part of a spoils system and distribution of perks. These Committees were conceived as means for an indepth and continuous study and to provide:

(i) Close pre-budget-scrutiny of the estimates and complex expenditure plans (Demands for Grants) before they are voted on the floor of the House;

(ii) Concurrent and contemporaneous examination of the activities of government departments and matters of national concern in cool, non-partisan atmosphere;

(iii) Monitoring and evaluation of performance, relating financial input to the policy objectives and actual results to measure effectiveness, and detailed examination of supplementary estimates;

(iv) Feedback of valuable insight and information to Parliament and to the government to reappraise economic proposals;

(v) Closer and more competent scrutiny of all legislative proposals;

(vi) Review of the implementation of laws passed by Parliament in respective subject areas;

(vii) Leadership recruitment and training ground for higher responsibilities in government, participation by backbenchers and building a second line of leadership; and

(viii) Development of specialization and expertise among members.

Since the functions of every Ministry and Department are covered by the Departmentally Related Standing Committees and also in view of the proposed new Constitution Committee, Legislation Committee and the Committee on National Economy, it does not seem at all necessary to continue several of the existing Committees. This would rationalize Committee structure and above all lead to economy of expenditure under the head of Parliament and various Ministries of the Government.

The development of an integrated system of committees would reduce the pressures on the floor—cost of floor time may be estimated at being thousands of Rupees per second and strengthen parliament surveillance over administration. It would contribute to economy, speed, efficiency and smooth working both of Parliament and the government.

Parliamentary Control Over Borrowing: There is a need for stricter parliamentary scrutiny or control of public borrowing. Unlike UK, in India, until recently the constitution and the laws placed no limits on the borrowing powers of the Executive. Parliamentary approval for any amount of internal or external borrowings as such was not required except that it was part of the budget. This was a significant lacuna. Public borrowing is a charge on the future generations and must be duly controlled. It is a matter of some satisfaction that a Fiscal Responsibility Legislation is now in place.

Discussing Committee Reports on the Floor of the House: Under the present practice regarding not discussing on the floor of the House reports of some of the important Committees like Financial Committees, some very useful recommendations remain unappreciated and infructuous. It is time for modifying the practice. It would be most desirable to discuss as a regular feature all important reports of Parliamentary Committees particularly in cases of disagreement between the Committee and the Government.

Codifying Parliamentary Privileges: In a democratic society, any privileges for a section or class of the people are anachronistic, any undefined privileges like the privileges of Parliament are even more so. It is, therefore, of the utmost importance that the weapon of parliamentary privileges is used with great circumspection. As a great institution, Parliament should be able to take in its stride, a great deal of the criticism and adverse comments against it. Privileges of Parliament are intended to be privileges enjoyed by Parliament on behalf of the people, to enable members to function freely and fearlessly, in the interest of the people. These privileges should not be allowed to become rights against the people. Time is now ripe for removing the existing uncertainty and anxiety of the press and the people through early codification.

In the JMM case, the Supreme Court had acquitted the members who had accepted huge bribes for voting to keep the Narsimha Rao government going on the ground that it was covered by the privilege law in Article 105(2). However, immunity enjoyed by Members does not cover corrupt acts like accepting bribes for speaking or voting in the House in favour or against a proposal. The Supreme Court decision in the JMM case needs to be revisited and reversed at the earliest.

Procedural Reforms: Each House of Parliament is complete master of its procedure. The Rules of Procedure and Conduct of Business are intended to be merely for guidance, for regulating the business of the House and for facilitating the orderly expression of member's views. Precedents and conventions may not be allowed to become shackles to imprison and destroy the institution. Procedures must keep pace with changing needs of the national economy, composition of Membership and the prevailing mood of the Members.

(i) *Reorganising Parliamentary Time Table:* Houses of Parliament are proverbially hard pressed for time and find difficulties in completing their business despite long sessions and late hours. While Parliament must perform its oversight role and its weapons of open debate, scrutiny and accountability should not be blunted in any way, it has also to be seen that time-consuming procedures do not hamper the smooth transaction of public business. Assuming that the houses of Parliament return to normal functioning, most of the valuable time of the House is taken up by a variety of local and other unimportant issues, it may be in the fitness of things to suitably amend the Rules of Procedure in order to more firmly prevent Members raising in the House matters of local or limited interest with which the House as a whole is not vitally concerned. These may be raised in the committees. Similarly the many controversial issues that have come to be known as the 'Zero Hour' could better be dealt with in the Committees. It can hurt only those who are anxious to hog newspaper and TV headlines by creating scenes during the 'Zero Hour'.

The floor time ought to be better utilised for major policy matters, of vital national interest and important legislative and financial business. There is an urgent need to reorganise the parliamentary time table and rationalise the methods and procedures of the House. A better alternative to the present practice would be to allocate time to questions by writing their time slots.

(ii) *The Petitions Committee* needs to be strengthened and put to greater use. It has tremendous potential as a Parliamentary ombudsman. It may be advisable to pay greater attention to publicising the committee's existence and the scope of its functions.

(iii) *The Question Hour:* Each of the two Houses of Parliament devote an hour each day to questions. Quite often, as soon as the House meets, proceedings are disrupted and the Question Hour becomes a casualty. Referred to as the showpiece of parliamentary democracy, the Question Hour nevertheless reveals an inadequate appreciation among members of its real purpose and scope and of their own responsibility in the matter. Thus, instead of being an hour during which Questions are asked to elicit information from the government, in practice it may often become a discussion hour. While 20 Questions are listed for oral answers each day, usually not more than 4-5 are covered. Lengthy arguments and orations are made in the name of supplementaries with the actual questions being preceded by introductions and preambles. Often replies by Ministers also tend to be evasive or an exercise in the art of giving technically correct answers without, 'giving away' any information.

It is not unknown that very often Questions are suggested or drafted by persons other than the Members themselves. Sometimes, the Member giving notice is himself absent from the House when his question comes up for answer. In some cases, very extensive information involving considerable expenditure and effort in collection may be called for even though the benefits, if any, may not be commensurate with the costs. Also, the necessary top priority given to parliamentary Questions causes serious dislocation of normal work in the

Ministries and offices of the government. All this is not satisfactory and involves considerable waste of public money and parliamentary time.

(iv) *Adjournment Motions:* An adjournment motion is admissible if the matter sought to be raised is definite, urgent and one of public importance. When consent to raise a matter is refused, Members try to raise the subject-matter of their notices before the House and what follows often gives the impression of a tug-of-war between the Speaker and the Members. This is unfortunate and can perhaps be avoided if the Speaker concerns himself only with seeing if the cardinal conditions for the admissibility of an adjournment motion are satisfied. That is, if the matter sought to be raised is definite, urgent and of public importance, he should give his consent to moving the motion. Instead of taking it upon himself to be an arbiter of the relative merits or otherwise of the various adjournment motion of which notices are received and which are in order under the Rules, he may leave it to the House to decide if any of them and if so which one should be taken up for discussion by leave of the House being granted.

Discussion in the House, on a motion of adjournment or of a matter of urgent importance which may in any case, be uppermost in the minds of the members and of the people at large outside at a particular time, can do no harm. It may, in fact ease tensions and help to create a better and healthier atmosphere both inside and outside the House.

(v) *Absenteeism of Members:* Absenteeism of Members threatens to become a serious malady. Members for whom the quorum bells ring too often have a lot of pressures on their time and energy outside the House. In practice, the quorum requirement is often ignored by not questioning the quorum. There are occasions when the House is seen conducting important business with less than a dozen souls present. Suggestions have sometimes been made for reducing the present minimum ($1/10^{th}$) to

> constitute the quorum. What is required is ensuring better and longer attendance by the Members in the Houses or Parliament. The citizens have certain claims on their representatives and perhaps expectation of some minimum hours of presence in the house and some minimum hours of parliamentary work each day would be quite legitimate. Those members who are not so present in the House may, therefore, under their own self-regulatory procedures, lose their salary and allowances for the day. Some of these reform suggestions were made in the last Chapter of the concluding volume of *History of the Parliament of India* (6 vols.). Later, the National Commission to Review the working of the Constitution (NCRWC) fully endorsed and accepted these as their recommendations.

We can be legitimately proud of the reasonably successful working of Parliament during the last close to seven decades. However Parliament is relevant only as a dynamic institution ever adjusting its functions and procedures to the changing needs of the times. If democracy and freedom are to endure, if representative institutions are to be made impregnable, it is essential to restore to Parliament and its Members their traditional esteem and honour in the affections of the people. Reforming the Parliament is essential but Parliamentary reforms would have to be a part of an integrated approach to political and economic reforms, electoral reforms, judicial reforms etc. All aspects have to be taken up together in an integrated approach to political and economic reforms and as part of the overall review and comprehensive systematic reform agenda. Last but the most important pre-condition for even beginning to consider any reform agenda including the above is the need to first take out the institution from the ICU and again make it functional.

Relevance of Second Chambers

An Unsettled Issue

THE RELEVANCE of a second chamber has been one of the most controversial and vexatious questions of political science. The upper chamber is usually seen as a check on hasty legislation and majority despotism. In federal polity, it is considered specially relevant as the House of the States and a counter balance to the House of the people.

Leaders of India's freedom struggle were not unequivocally committed to a bicameral legislature. Gandhi was for a unicameral legislature. He said:

> "I am certainly not enamoured of and I do not swear by two Houses of legislature. I have no fear of a popular legislature running away with itself and hastily passing some laws of which afterwards it will have to repent. I would not like to give a bad name to, and then hang the popular legislature.

> I think that a popular legislature can take care of itself; and since I am now thinking of the poorest country in the world, the less expenses we have to bear the better it is for us."

Gandhi would have liked the Constitution makers to make the popular chamber as perfect as human ingenuity could make it but he wanted India to be satisfied with one chamber only. In the Constituent Assembly, there was considerable volume of opinion against having a second chamber as several members thought that a second chamber might prove to be a 'clog in the wheel of progress' involving avoidable expense and adding nothing to the efficiency of work. The justification for having a second chamber as stated on the floor of the Assembly, however, was that it was a check on 'legislation which might be the outcome of passions of the moment', that in the upper house, there would be 'dignified debates on important issues' and that the upper house would provide an opportunity to 'seasoned people who might be willing to participate in the debate with an amount of learning and importance' not generally associated with the house of the people. Also, as its name indicated, the Rajya Sabha was conceived as the federal house. *Rajyon ki Sabha* or the Council of States.

Very strong views were expressed in favour and against having upper houses in the Union and State Legislatures. As a compromise between strong views for and against bicameral legislatures, upper houses at the level of State Legislatures were made optional but at the Union level was considered essential as a house of the representatives of the constituent States, voicing their concerns and looking after their interests. In pursuance of the federal principle, the Rajya Sabha was conceived as the Council of the States as contradistinguished from the Lok Sabha which was to be the House of the people. While members of the Lok Sabha were to be directly elected by the people of India through territorial constituencies, on the basis of adult franchise, members of Rajya Sabha were to be elected by the elected members of the Legislative Assemblies of the States in accordance with the system of proportional representation by means of single transferable vote. In the case of Lok Sabha, any citizen of India could be a candidate. For membership of Rajya Sabha, a person had to be from among those 'ordinarily' resident within the territory of a particular State and only the elected MLAs of that State could vote for him/her to Rajya Sabha.

The foundational considerations were that the members of Rajya Sabha were to be the representatives and emissaries of the individual States and had to represent, safeguard and promote the States' interests. They could do so only if they were intimately familiar with their State and its problems and were ordinarily resident within that State. Members of Lok Sabha were visualised as representing the people and the nation as a whole and to look at problems from the all India and not States' perspective.

During the many years since the commencement of the Constitution, a practice had grown of some prominent leaders of all parties being accommodated in the Rajya Sabha through the back door after they lost election to Lok Sabha or opted out of Lok Sabha poll for whatever reason. Even if they were total strangers to a State, safe Rajya Sabha seats were found for them from the States where the party had a convincing majority or a sizeable membership in the Assembly. To fulfill the residential requirement, all that was considered necessary under the law was to get oneself registered as a voter in a constituency in the State concerned by making a declaration of being 'ordinarily resident' in the State at the given address. That in many cases, these declarations were false and were made willfully and in the full knowledge of the falsehood did not seem to bother the distinguished leaders including some supposed to be men of 'great integrity'. Some of those thus elected were senior national leaders but without any base anywhere in the country and with the least possibility of getting elected to any position from their own State. In fact, they might be *persona non grata* among their own people who were supposed to know them better.

Sometimes, a person was appointed a Minster without being a

Member of Parliament. In order to continue to be a Minister beyond six months he had to be elected as a Member. The backdoor of Rajya Sabha membership was often used for the purpose. Also there were occasions when political parties for their own reasons propped up minority community or caste show-pieces discredited and disowned by their own ethnic fraternity. Thus, what was intended to be a non-dissoluble permanent House of elders consisting of mature representatives of various States had become a House of patronage or a refuge of special types and a part of the spoils system.

It was gratifying to find that the Election Commission had taken some concrete steps to ensure that non-residents did not get enrolled as voters in States other than their own in order to seek election to Rajya Sabha from that State. The electoral registration officers were asked to really ensure that they were satisfied in the matter of claims regarding ordinary residence.

The jurisdiction of the Election Commission, however, began and ended with the election process. Questions of setting aside or invalidating any elections could be adjudicated upon only by the High Courts deciding election petitions which often took years. But, the Commission had certainly exposed the blatancy with which the premier national parties and illustrious leaders made a mockery of the law and used falsehood and other dubious means to get elected to Rajya Sabha.

The April 2000 biennial elections to Rajya Sabha and the controversies surrounding the defeat of party candidates, cross-voting and blatant use of money power to buy votes of legislators raised many questions and revived the debate regarding the very relevance of Rajya Sabha in our polity. One was reminded of the senior US Senator, late Claude Pepper, known among his friends as Red Pepper, who was a treasure house of anecdotes full of wit and humour. Many of his dining table jokes were on himself or the House to which he belonged. He narrated the story of a visitor to the US Senate who exclaimed: 'I had no faith in life after death until I saw the Senate'.

In India, even more than the *Lok* we think of *Parlok* and of life after death. Many of our leaders defeated at the polls for Lok Sabha or otherwise suffering political death, successfully seek resurrection in Rajya Sabha membership. It is said that not withstanding some very honourable exceptions, the House has become a refuge for rejected politicians and a hunting ground for money bags and manipulators. A prominent national daily said that soon Rajya Sabha membership may not be 'a mark of respect or stature' but simply of 'affluence and unscrupulousness'. It described Rajya Sabha as 'the most expensive club in India' but did not say that it was also the most paying.

As it happened, the level of debate in Rajya Sabha was hardly different or more dignified than in Lok Sabha. Unlike members of the earlier decades, present day members of Rajya Sabha, by and large, do not specialise in any subjects. Despite a higher minimum age qualification, membership of Rajya Sabha also does not necessarily consist of really senior or more seasoned, learned and experienced people. By and large, it is the parties that decide the composition of the House. It can hardly be contradistinguished from the Lok Sabha on the ground of being the House of Elders.

There is no real inner party democracy in any of our parties. Those who constitute the voters are not consulted or involved in selecting party candidates. Against their expressed wishes sometimes, outsiders are foisted by the High Commands. When there are no ideologically oriented parties and no principles are followed by parties or anyone else, how can the legislators alone be blamed? Free and fair election means full freedom to each voter to cast his or her vote freely, without any interference from any quarter and with the full assurance that the vote would remain 'secret'. Any open voting was bound to do violence to the fundamentals of our representative democracy and freedom of vote.

So far as cross-voting and violation of party directives were concerned, it was for each party to put its own house in order and bring its members around to abiding by party discipline. The malady of members selling their votes to the highest bidder raised a more fundamental question that could be hardly legislated upon or remedied through laws. We live in a society of competitive consumerism where quite naturally, money has become the supreme value. And, we have made membership of Rajya Sabha a highly lucrative, comfortable and secure (for 6 years) profession with plenty of opportunities to get rich quick. Unlike Lok Sabha, there is no risk of dissolution in the Rajya Sabha. The assured rupees five crores each year at the disposal of each member for a period of six years under the so-called local area development scheme is a great attraction and, of course, often a scandal and a fraud on the scheme of the Constitution. Interestingly, there were proposals to further raise the amount.

If elections to Rajya Sabha had to be made cleaner and the dignity of the House and its relevance to our federal democratic polity were to be restored, membership of Rajya Sabha (as of Lok Sabha) had to be made less attractive financially so that only those imbued with competence, some expertise, a spirit of service and with no personal axe to grind were chosen. Also, political parties had to become more democratic, principled, ideologically oriented, transparent and accountable. No candidates from outside the States concerned should be forced on them. If the Rajya Sabha had to have any relevance as the federal chamber or as the House of the States, only the residents of that State capable of representing the interests of that State and its people should be eligible to become its members. However, the way things developed, we moved in an entirely reverse direction. Some of the prominent members of the Rajya Sabha including one Prime Minister for two terms, got elected from States they had otherwise very little to do with before the election.

Under the Representation of the People Act 1951, originally a candidate for a seat in Rajya Sabha had to be an elector for a parliamentary constituency in the 'State or Territory' to which the particular seat pertained. He had, therefore, to be 'ordinarily resident' in the 'State or Territory' which he wanted to represent in Rajya Sabha.

Under an amendment to the Representation of People Act, 1951, it was asked if a candidate from one State could contest a Lok Sabha election from another State, why should similar freedom be denied to candidates for the Rajya Sabha polls? In the 2003 Amendment the position was changed. A person offering his candidature for election to fill a seat in the Council of States was now required to be just 30 years old and simply 'an elector for a Parliamentary constituency in India'; that is to say, he is no longer required to be an elector for a Parliamentary constituency in the 'State or Territory' to which the seat for which he is a candidate pertains. As a result, it is no longer required that the candidate for an election to fill a seat in the Council of States be 'ordinary resident' of the State to which that seat pertains.

Also, secrecy of ballot was always considered an essential concomitant of free and fair elections. The 2003 Amendment did away with the secrecy of ballot by providing for an open Ballot System on the ground that some members were reported to be indulging in cross voting for collateral and corrupt considerations and in violation of the directives of their party. The amendment made it obligatory for each elector for Rajya Sabha membership to disclose the way he had cast his vote to the representative of his party.

By a writ petition under Article 32, the 2003 amendments to the RP Act, 1951 on the above points were challenged as being unconstitutional and violative of federalism principles and basic features of the Constitution. The Supreme Court unfortunately found the petition devoid of merit on both the counts and dismissed it. It is difficult to agree with the judgement of the Court in this matter and one would wish that these matters are reviewed at the earliest opportunity for the following reasons:

(i) Once the vote has to be disclosed, it can no more be said to be free and fair;

(ii) Anti-Defection Law (10th Schedule of the Constitution) applies only to voting connected with the proceedings of the House. There has so far been no constitutional or legal provision laying down that party members have got to vote only in favour of the candidates of their party.

(iii) If the voting for Rajya Sabha seats has to be strictly on the lines of parties and their dictates, it is hardly necessary to have the formality of a vote, the parties can declare the list of those elected.

(iv) There is no guarantee that the parties would not indulge in the corrupt practice of selling their votes and seats to the highest bidders.

(v) The new dispensation has dangerous portents for our democratic polity and purity of elections inasmuch as the logic of the Court can easily and quite legitimately get extended to general elections to Lok Sabha and State Assemblies as well on the ground that there also votes may be cast on 'collateral and corrupt considerations' and many members of political parties also may be voting against their party candidates in different constituencies.

(vi) Looking at the genesis and growth of the concept of upper chambers in federal systems all over the world and more so of the concept of the institution of the Council of States in India during our long constitutional history and through the Constituent Assembly and its committees, one cannot easily stomach the argument that 'Council of States' and 'House of the People' are merely 'proper nouns' or that the declaration of law to the effect that the Council of States does not have to have 'the character of a body representing the States'.

(vii) It does not make much sense to elect 'representatives of States' or to provide 'representation to States' in the Council of States if in effect persons who have never lived in a State or Union Territory, who do not know its language and have little knowledge of its problems are the ones to be elected as per party wishes.

Politics must return to being for serving the people and not for enjoying power and looting the public exchequer. The 2003 Amendment passed by Parliament and the Supreme Court judgement upholding it have been most unfortunate inasmuch as these have legalised a patent malpractice and dishonesty at high places and sought to regularise and legitimatise the Rajya Sabha membership of all those elected on false declarations.

Second Chamber at the State level

The question of the desirability and utility of the second chamber at the State level has remained unsettled. Proposals have been made from time to time for the creation or abolition of the upper house. The controversy, however, was neither new nor unique to India. It has always and everywhere been a difficult problem in political science.

In the Constituent Assembly, while the idea of a second chamber at the Union level was largely accepted without much opposition, the provision for second chamber in the States was subjected to severe criticism. A prominent member of the Constituent Assembly described it as 'pernicious and vicious'. Another said that the second chambers would involve a substantial outlay from the public exchequer while they would only help party bosses to distribute patronage; their only other function would be to obstruct or delay needed legislation. The Provincial Constitution Committee of the Constituent Assembly after considering the pros and cons of the matter had decided that as a general rule there should be only one single chamber of the legislature in the States. Second chambers could be constituted in particular States only where very special circumstances required them. Constitutional Adviser, BN Rau and the Chairman of the Constitution Drafting Committee, Dr Ambedkar, more than once iterated that most States were expected to have only a single chamber. At the informal meeting of an elite group of founding fathers with Governor-General C Rajgopalachari, one last attempt was made to resolve the strong conflict of opinions in regard to the desirability or otherwise of having upper houses. At the end of the discussion, Sardar Patel, a down to earth politician and a man of few words, is said to have stood up to say: 'An unemployed politician is a social menace; we shall have two Houses.'

Under a compromise amendment, it was finally decided that the choice in the matter of having a second chamber would be largely left to the States themselves and that Parliament would decide to establish or to abolish the second chambers whenever requested to do so by the Legislative Assembly of the State concerned. Ambedkar made it clear that second chambers were being introduced purely as an experimental measure and only in those States whose representatives wished to have them. The whole trend of discussion appeared to be, in the words of Ambedkar, that 'the process of getting rid of the second chamber' should be facilitated. An amendment moved by Ambedkar, therefore, sought to authorise Parliament to create or abolish by law a second chamber in a State, if the Legislative Assembly of such a State passed a resolution to that effect by a majority of its total membership and a two-thirds majority of the members present and voting. That was accepted by the Constituent Assembly. It represents the present position and constitutes Article 169 of our Constitution.

In terms of political theory, bicameralism is traditionally based on recognition of distinction between the nobility and the common people and as such is against developments in democratic thought. In a sense bicameralism in its pure form is a dying phenomenon. There is a world-wide trend towards unicameralism. Several new constitutions have eliminated the second chambers altogether and most others have relegated them to an inferior or unequal position. Where they exist, the upper houses at best retain the power to delay—not to stop—legislation.

The lower house or the popular house has almost universally become politically dominant and constitutionally more relevant. It is much more so in a parliamentary form of government where it is only the popular house of the Legislature which can create and topple governments. The protagonists of a second chamber argue that the upper house is necessary in order to avoid hasty and harsh legislation and to act as a revising chamber. While the lower house, according to them, may have to play to the popular sentiment of the moment and may be swayed by its heat, the second chamber could work in a somewhat cooler and more detached atmosphere. It could introduce an element of sobriety and second thought particularly because there was no risk of a no-confidence motion on the floor of the second chamber. Also the elders could, perhaps in the best interests of the country, give a lead to, rather than be led by popular outbursts of the moment. In the context of present day realities, however, these arguments seem to lose much of their force. So long as the draftsmen are efficient and sincere and so long as the Ministers are unwilling or reluctant to accept in the Upper House amendments to proposed legislation, the second chamber can hardly be called much of a revising chamber. It can at best review or delay legislation. Under our Constitution, legislation can be introduced in either House and thus both the Houses function as the original and revising chambers equally. Also, the Governor of a State has the power to reserve, in effect, almost any bill for the consideration of the President. The discretion to decide which Bill should be so reserved vests completely in the discretion of the Governor.

As such, there is a mechanism already provided in the States for a check on hasty or harsh legislation. Further, as is well known, the atmosphere, the actual composition and the operational realities in the upper houses of our legislatures are hardly very different from those in the lower houses and from that point of view also, the upper houses do not seem to have continued relevance or legitimacy in our body politic. A second argument in favour of the upper houses relates to the measure of functional representation that they seek to provide.

Apart from the respresentation given to university graduates, teachers, local government institutions and others, the Governors can nominate to the upper houses distinguished persons from the fields of literature, science, etc. This enables intellectuals, scholars, scientists and artists to give to the legislature the benefit of their experience and wisdom without being required to face the rough and tumble of elections, which in any case they may not be prepared to do. This argument does have considerable force even though, of late, nominations to legislative councils and generally the whole composition of the upper houses have very often been criticised. The critics have said that instead of being a house for elders or distinguished men and women, the second chamber has tended to become a resting place for defeated politicians and for the parties providing political patronage to their favorites. It seems that historically one very practical justification and reason for some States in the Indian Union having decided to have second chambers was the need to accommodate the large number of political pilgrims who had got involved in the political processes of the national struggle for freedom due to the very nature of that struggle. It was necessary that the largest possible number from amongst them found berths in the centre or the periphery of political power. And in a parliamentary system, this could not be done without having two houses of Legislature.

So far as the text of the Constitution is concerned, the present position is very clear. The State Government or the State Legislature has no power to abolish or to constitute an upper house. However, if the Legislative Assembly of a State, by a resolution passed by a majority of its members and by two-thirds majority of those present and voting, recommends the creation or abolition of an upper house, the Parliament may by law do so and amend the Constitution accordingly. This can be done by the Parliament by a simple majority and is not technically to be regarded as an amendment of the Constitution requiring two-thirds majority. While Parliament is not bound to accept the recommendation, as early as on 8 April 1967 then Union Law Minister P Govinda Menon had made it clear in the Rajya Sabha that the Union Government would make absolutely no attempt to invade any of the rights of the State governments given by the Constitution and that whether a State wanted an upper house or not was entirely for the State Legislative Assembly to decide. The State Assemblies, he said categorically, could do away with the Legislative Councils by passing a resolution to that effect since they enjoyed autonomy in this regard and it was not for the Centre to contemplate any action in the matter.

It is time that a serious attempt is made to consider a reform in second chambers in the States unless we are resigned to or agreed on the gradual erosion of their utility and their abolition. Even though it may sound somewhat utopian, it seems that the best way to provide greater relevance and legitimacy to the second chambers in our political system would be to make them completely non-party forums with even greater functional, professional representation and interest-group orientation. The upper houses may be even smaller than what they now are. So far as possible, they might function without the floodlight of publicity and more in the nature of a reviewing committee consisting of experts, scholars, intellectuals and representatives of professional and other interest groups. The present higher age qualifications should give place to not only a literacy qualification but a qualification in terms of achievements and distinctions. Also, the interests to be represented should include not only what are commonly called the vested interests but also women, labour, agriculture, trade-unions, youth and various professional groups in different walks of life.

Legislators' Role and Functions

How to be an effective parliamentarian?

INSTITUTIONS OF parliamentary democracy today seem to be passing through more difficult times than ever before in history. The global trend is for becoming more populist instead of graduating to participatory democracies with the people themselves becoming active participants in governance and assuming more responsibilities as citizens at the grassroots with a bottom-up instead of a top down approach. In this connection the Gandhian model of concentric circles and European subsidiarity principle come to mind.

In principle, every member of Lok Sabha is supposed to represent the whole of India and not only his or her constituency. Similarly, a member of a State assembly stands for the whole State. Constituencies are only for purposes of electoral convenience. It is another matter that it becomes a practical imperative for every elected member to pay special attention to his or her constituency.

Modern legislatures have ceased to be mere law making bodies. They have become multifunctional institutions. In Parliament of India, only a small portion of the time is now devoted to legislative business. As for the role of individual members, during the last 48 years, not a single Private Members' Bill has become law. Perhaps, representational and grievance ventilation and redressal roles have become the most important both in qualitative and quantitative terms. Parliament represents the changing moods and needs of the people, Increasingly, it has become more of a microcosm and mirror of the people but also a barometer of their pulse rate. While the earlier Lok Sabhas were somewhat elitist bodies, with each successive election, the institution has been becoming more representative of the people at the grassroots. The same may be true of the State Legislatures.

An average member's own perception of his role is also that of a representative of the people. He sees himself as the chief communication channel and link or a transmission belt between the people and the Government. Many procedural devices are available to the member to raise on the floor and present to the government the problems of the people and seek their redressal. For, if the government is responsible to the legislature, the legislature and it's members are also responsible to the people. They have to understand and remain involved in what happens in their House, educate the people about its activities and project its proper image before the people as sort of PR men for the legislature.

Every member has to perform a very difficult role in his constituency, in the House and before the people at large. On the one hand, there is tremendous rise in the expectations of the people from their elected representatives; on the other, there is colossal erosion in the esteem and respect for them. People expect the Members to be models of good conduct and paragons of all virtues, devoted all the 24 hours and more to serving them. The constituents want their MP, MLA or MLC to solve all their problems, help them out of all difficulties including those with the law or the administration, attend all their social functions from *Namkaran* and *Mundan* of babies to marriages in their families, to take care of them in various ways when they visit him at the capital and so on. The same people who seek illegitimate and unjust favours later find it fashionable to blame the politicians for all the ills in society. In this context, we have to revisit the role of legislature and legislators and evolve principles and strategies for our legislators becoming more effective members of our respective Houses.

The most important functions of a modern legislature revolve round its role as a representative of the people—responsive to their woes and responsible to them for its own performance. Secondly, in a parliamentary system, the legislature has to provide the executive. The Council of Ministers has to come from the legislature. In parliamentary polity, government is part of the legislature. The Ministers are first members and then Ministers. Their primary loyalty is to their House. Some members become Ministers and that perhaps is the surest way to becoming more effective. But then, they become part of the government, of the executive, and no more function as ordinary members. Every private member, ie. a member who is not Minister, has to decide for himself or herself the area in which or the extent to which he or she would like to be more effective. It may be—

(i) In the House
(ii) In Committees
(iii) In the Constituency
(iv) In the State, the country and the party

Ideally, all are important and should be kept in view. But no one can perhaps be equally effective in all. Members anxious to make a mark in the House, particularly new Members, may find it most useful to spend long hours in the House and to use every procedural device to give a voice to people's problems and grievances, to raise matters of urgent public importance and issues of great concern to the people. Opportunities are available through Questions, Half-an-Hour Discussions, Calling Attention Notices, Short Duration Discussions, Resolutions, Private Members' Bills, Debates on Budget, Governor's Address, Adjournment Motions etc.

In order to be able to do so effectively, one has to be well-versed in relevant provisions of the Constitution, Rules of Procedures, parliamentary practices and precedents. It is most advisable to select some particular subject areas for specialisation through intensive studies and experience in the field. Some of the functions cannot or should not be delegated by the Member to someone in the staff, a babu, an agency, an interest group or the like. For example, notices of Questions or various motions have to be prepared by the Member himself based on his own knowledge and study and his perception of the issue. It is dangerous to sign any blank forms of notices.

To be an effective member, one invariably needs to be well versed in procedures and practices but these cannot be imbibed by anyone overnight. Howsoever talented and competent in his profession a person may be, when he comes to the legislature for the first time he is confronted with an entirely different atmosphere. He may feel lost in the dense forest of rules, regulations, directions, precedents, conventions, rulings, formalities and modalities of parliamentary procedure and conduct. Having made countless promises to the electors, the legislator is naturally anxious to voice their grievances and problems on the floor of the House. He has also to be seen to be doing so, forcefully and at the earliest. Also, having adopted public life and legislature membership as a profession, the legislator has every right to try to stay and progress in the profession.

The question before him is how to be effective as a legislator and also remain popular in his constituency. It is often the eagerness of the member to raise certain matters of concern to his people that land him in trouble in the eyes of the presiding officer and the rules. Often, his attitude may grow to be 'rules or no rules, I must have my say'. What use is his membership if he cannot express the woes of the people. In a parliamentary system, while government may ultimately have its way, members, whether in opposition or with the ruling party, must have their say. While knowledge of rules etc. no doubt, is necessary and important, the role of the presiding officer and of the legislature secretariat assumes tremendous importance. It has to be ensured that Rules serve the interests of all sections of the House and protect the rights of every single member.

Sometimes, ugly situations may arise because the Ministers do not do their home work, are not prepared with adequate replies or refuse to give information. At other times, depending on their numbers, the majority may try the steam-roller approach. Lastly, the media may also be blamed for giving prominence to those members who viölate the rules and create scenes. When a member who creates unruly scenes in the well of the House gets the news headlines, that becomes an incentive for similar conduct by other members. Those who deliver well-researched speeches hardly find a mention. Some Members point out that those who study the procedure carefully, do their homework and prepare their speeches with dexterity are neither noticed by the leadership nor by the media or the constituents, while those who make the right kind of noises and create scenes at the appointed moments get promoted to ministership or the like.

While there may be no soft procedural remedy under the Rules if some members in opposition decide not to allow the House to function as part of their political strategy to embarrass the government, members can be told how they can achieve their aim of raising a particular matter effectively within the rules and the need for the so-called indiscipline and defiance of the chair can be minimised. If we try to tell the members the need to strictly follow the rules in their pristine purity, they soon learn by experience or from their seniors that that was so much poppycock and that the way forward was at great variance from theory. Tearing of papers in the House is not permissible. Leaving the House immediately after delivering your speech is not in order. Slogan shouting inside the House is violative of the Rules. Every member is required to speak from his allotted seat. But, we all know that the practice in many such matters, is the reverse. All rules are flouted with impunity.

We need at various levels including those at party leadership and whips, intensive orientation programmes in the latest political management, floor management and conflict resolution mechanisms and techniques. Members need to be encouraged to decide for themselves the areas, subjects and government departments in which they wish to specialise to become more effective Members. At the Orientation programmes, the senior Members and experts can help new Members by telling them how it is terribly risky to sign on blank forms to give notice of Questions, Motions etc. Members have to be very careful where they put their signatures. They need to be told how in actual parliamentary life, they can get adequate opportunities of raising matters of concern; how, when and where notice under a particular rule should be given in order to be admissible; and getting the necessary priority, how a Question or Motion that may be ordinarily inadmissible can be made admissible by minor verbal changes. There are hundreds of tricks of the trade which cannot be found in any book nor can they be written about. These have to be imbibed by experience.

Some Members make their mark on the floor of the House and grow into outstanding orators and parliamentarians. It is seen that those who select some specific subjects, areas or particular ministries for study and specialisation prove to be better representatives and soon develop a reputation for their expertise. Also, the more effective Members are known to do their homework in connection with the proceedings of the House. When such Members speak they are listened to with great respect and attention.

One has to resist the temptation of earning easy publicity and headlines by shouting on the floor of the Houses, rushing to the Well, creating mayhem and pandemonium, breaking microphones, tearing papers and not allowing the House to function. In the long run these devices do not make a more effective parliamentarian. A Member has to try to master the art of debate, to put across one's point of view convincingly with facts and figures, with dignity, grace and self-confidence. One can be even aggressive in arguments but without being personal, bitter or biting. The chair has got to be respected by every member as the symbol of the authority of the House. Even as strategy, it is in the best interests of the career of a member to win a soft corner or healthy regard in the heart of the Presiding officer. For orderly functioning of the House, some of the effective parliamentarians have been known for their sense of humour. The ability to laugh, particularly at ourselves, can redeem sombre situations. Sparkling wit, enlivening sallies and brilliant repartees can diffuse tension, turmoil and turbulence in the House. Once in the midst of a very heated debate in Lok Sabha a member said 'Mr Kripalani is so bitterly criticising the Congress party which has attracted to its fold his own wife' Sucheta Kripalani. Acharya Kripalani, known for his wit, at once retorted:'Mr Speaker, so far I thought Congressmen were stupid fools. Now I know they are gangsters also who run away with others' wives.' The whole House burst into laughter. All the tension melted away.

On another occasion, the atmosphere in the House was very tense with Prime Minister Indira Gandhi speaking in a strong and angry voice. A seasoned parliamentarian on the opposition benches, Madhu Dandavate, interjected: 'Madam PM, recently when we saw you on the US TV channels, you were all smiles and looked so very charming. What has happened to you after your return to India?' Mrs Indira Gandhi herself joined in the full throated laughter that followed.

A casualty in recent years has been the relative absence of healthy wit, humour and sparkles of poetry in our legislatures. Writing the Foreword to the book on *Parliamentary Wit and Humour,* President Venkataraman said:

> 'The debates of the British House of Commons are replete with sparkling wit, enlivening sallies and brilliant repartees. Often times, they diffuse tension and bitterness during debates. It is this quality that has made the British Parliament a model for rest of the world… May the sparkle of humour…

> enliven (our) parliamentary proceedings and bring to hard and contentious debates, the eternal solvent of wit.'

As a liberating, exalting and creative force, humour is capable of reducing a turbulent and strained atmosphere caused by clash of ideologies and personalities to an amiable end by cooling tempers and resolving conflicts through processes of give and take, accommodation and adjustment.

Houses of our legislatures are living, vibrant, dynamic institutions, pulsating with life, full of vital energy and vigour. Some conflict of ideas, interests and struggle for power by various contending forces are natural to man. Verbal struggles on the floors of the Houses are better than physical strife on the streets, terror strikes or pitched battles. Debates in our Houses bring into the open the underlying tensions and resentments in society. Legislature becomes the legitimate arena for power struggle, for crystallisation of political activity or for acting out the conflicting roles and interests, eventually most often leading to some reconciliation. Some delicate problems do get resolved on the legislative floor. It has to be appreciated that on contentious issues, conflicting viewpoints and animated debates, some occasional interruptions, rise of temperatures and sound levels and heated exchanges between members representing the woes of the people only add spice and taste to legislative proceedings. Also, as has been light-heartedly said, when members fail to catch the eyes of the Presiding Officer, they may get agitated and take recourse to trying to catch his ears by shouting at the top of their voice. When all is said and done, it is now being increasingly recognised that the ugly scenes of indecorous behavior lead to waste of precious parliamentary time and erosion in the public esteem for the supreme representative institutions of the people. It has become a categorical imperative that all parties come together and arrive at a consensus on 'thus far and no further'. It is not difficult to recall the days and occasions when such lines were drawn during 10 to 11 hours through informal interactions in regard to contentious issues of the day. After strongly registering protests, houses were allowed to function and discharge their obligations to the people. Obstructing the arbitrary functioning of the government may be accepted but not rendering the House dysfunctional.

Both, those in the ruling party and those in opposition in the House have got to remember that their roles can be reversed. They would only be serving themselves if they behave as they would expect the other party to behave in their position. That way, members on both sides of the House can be really more effective and serve the people better.

Some members may not be so suited to or interested in being vocal on the floor of the House. They may prefer to be more active in the committees. In fact, it is possible to make more substantial contribution to public service by being effective Committee members. It is said: 'Legislature in Session is Legislature on exhibition while in Committees Legislature is at work'. Many members have built their reputations and political careers by being primarily effective Committee members. Committee work is a potent training ground for would be ministers. Also, Committees bring members in direct contact with senior officers which proves helpful to the members taking up causes of their constituents etc. Also, there are other mundane or not so mundane benefits of Committee membership and of being more effective there.

The third and in a way the most important area where every member would like to be considered to be most effective is the constituency work. Constituency image is particularly crucial in the case of MLAs in the States and MPs in Lok Sabha who are directly elected by the people. The most cherished profile of an elected representative in India is that of a helper and sharer of his constituents' personal anxieties and problems. A legislator is seen by the public as a Welfare Officer or 'case worker', as a sort of local ombudsman to whom they can take their complaints and grievances. Nothing can be more gratifying or fulfilling to the legislator himself than that he has been able to constructively contribute to the resolution of the problems of the community around him, not to speak of the accretion to his standing in the public eye. The common man, who still feels remote from the administration, wants some important person to take up his cause. And the legislator is regarded as 'a strategically placed intermediary between the people and the executive'.

The legislator should normally write or speak to the minister concerned regarding the grievances of his constituents. He may in case of a grievance of general character take up the matter at Question time or raise it in the House by other means. But all the individual cases cannot be brought before the House. If the legislator feels that the cause is just and legitimate but the normal channels would get delayed justice, he can even approach the civil servant concerned. There is no harm so long as the legislator only acts as a democratic link between his constituent and the administration. The overriding condition is that the legislator should never be seen to be misusing his position and influence to undermine the processes of law and justice.

A few other simple and practical tips for being more effective and popular in ones constituency may be mentioned.

First, it is vital that the member should have the reputation of being available and accessible to the people. The job of an MLA or MP requires that he should be travelling and moving around in his constituency almost all the time except when the House is sitting. The effort should be to cover every town and every village and meet as many people as possible including those who may not have voted for him. It is necessary that the team of his workers and supporters is kept intact and happy. But, on principle, after election the member represents all of the constituents and an image of one who cares for all including opponents is bound to pay rich dividends. During tours, the Member would naturally also inspect the progress of various welfare and development schemes including the utilisation of his own local Area Development Funds.

Secondly, the legislator is expected by his constituents to be a good and cool-headed listener and a sweet talker. Sweet tongue attracts and sustains many followers while even very well-meaning leaders become unpopular because of their overbearing manners. The public image of the Member is more important than the reality. And, the image has got to be that of an amiable, all the time available, accessible, easily approachable person committed to the service of the people.

Thirdly, it is important that the member gives the impression of being concerned with people's problems, of having within him a fire and a passion for service and a commitment to helping them all the time.

Fourthly, it might be much appreciated if periodically—preferably every three months or so—all the constituents are kept informed through a bulletin or a poster in the Panchayat Ghars or through meetings etc. of the work being done by their representative to improve the quality of their life, of how the funds at the disposal of the Member are being used, of what the Member is doing in the House or in the committees.

Fifthly, it cannot be forgotten that in order to be a successful, effective and ideal legislator one owes some fundamental obligations towards the State, the country and the Party to which he belongs. He is first and foremost a citizen of India and 'we the people of India' in terms of the Constitution, are one people. Also, as a member of Lok Sabha, one represents the whole of India and a member of the State Legislature; he represents the entire State and not merely his constituency.

Last but not the least important is the categorical imperative of remaining loyal to the party and its leadership and building an effective base of being useful to the party and devoted to its policies and programmes. For without the party support one cannot expect the party ticket next time and another term as a legislator—whether he was effective or not so effective.

Lastly, for being active in different areas, it is not an either/or situation. While focus and priorities may vary, almost every legislator has to prepare a healthy mix and adopt an integrated approach to all his functions. It is not easy but the legislator's job is not easy. It is difficult and onerous. Apart from other traits, it demands a very high degree of expertise in time management techniques.

Parliamentary Control Over Public Undertakings

Precept and Practice

PARLIAMENT IS the supreme representative institution of the people. The Prime Minister and all the other Ministers come from within the Houses of Parliament and remain responsible to Lok Sabha. Even the head of the executive and of the state, the President is a constituent part of Parliament. Since Parliament includes the President, members of the Council of Ministers and members of the two Houses, there is no separation of powers between the government and the Parliament. They are not separate centers of power. The Council of Ministers is a sort of executive committee of Parliament charged with the responsibility of governance on its behalf. On principle, the relationship between the government and the Parliament is that of the part and the whole. It cannot be adversarial. Parliament is constitutionally ordained to exercise overall control in matters of public policy, development and governance.

There is nothing entirely new about public sector enterprises in India. We find references to these, some 300 years before Christ in Kautilya's *Arthashastra*. State officers are mentioned as in-charge of managing the public sector industries of salt-manufacture, mining, coinage and gold. Under a nefarious, well thought out design, the British rulers had ruined Indian trade and industries particularly in steel and textiles for which Indian manufactured goods were world famous. The two world wars necessitated a rethink by the British in their own interest and for helping in their war efforts. In 1916, an Indian Industrial Commission was appointed. The report *inter alia* suggested that government must play an active part in the industrial development of the country. The emphasis was on 'those industries whose absence exposes us to grave danger in times of war'—the word 'us' obviously referring to the British.

During the Second World War, the existing industries worked to full capacity and some new industries were set up for supplying war needs. The defense industries and ordnance factories were to be owned and controlled by the state. Railway was already state owned.

When on the midnight of 14-15 August 1947, India achieved freedom from foreign rule and the leaders sat down to frame a Constitution, the most daunting problems before them were those of poverty, backwardness, underdevelopment and feeding the people.

On 6 April 1948, Shyama Prasad Mukherjee, the then Minister for Industries and Supply moved the first Industrial Policy Resolution which flagged the need for increasing production and the state playing 'a progressively active role in the development of industries' so as to quickly increase national wealth. The resolution said that 'state enterprises will, as a rule, be through the medium of public corporations under the statutory control of the Central Government who will assume such powers as may be necessary.' The industries were divided into three categories, viz. Public Sector, Mixed Sector and Private Sector. Mukherjee explained that the statutory public corporations would be run as business concerns. Thus, the necessity of the Public Sector was established along with mixed economy where the state and private sector enterprises would coexist.

The Constitution adopted on 26 November 1949 showed a tilt towards a socialistic pattern by emphasising social and economic justice in the Preamble and the Directive Principles asking the state to so direct its policy as to secure that the ownership and control of material resources of the community are so distributed as best to subserve common good and the operation of the economic system does not result in concentration of wealth and means of production to the common detriment (*vide* article 39(e)&(d)). Later, in December 1954, Parliament specifically accepted the principle of 'socialistic pattern of society' and on 30 April 1956, Prime Minister Jawaharlal Nehru mooted the second Industrial Policy Resolution. It was stressed that the objective was to generate more wealth and more production by the state itself speeding up industrialisation by particularly developing heavy industries and machine making industries in the public sector. The following decades came to be characterised as a period of 'the commanding heights of public sector enterprises'. It was said that the public sector was more concerned with strategic industries, public utilities, basic, heavy and essential industries, industries that could substitute foreign imports and industries which required huge investments beyond the capacity of private entrepreneurs. The public sector by definition was not supposed to be guided by mere profit motive and had to be ever conscious of public interest.

When the state controlled economy seemed to have reached a dead end, successive Messiahs of economic liberalisation reforms took over and India moved from socialistic pattern to an era of disinvestment, divestment, privatisation and public-private-partnership. Nevertheless, the public sector remains huge and its relevance and importance have not really diminished. Public Sector enterprises today exist in almost all countries of the world including those considered to be strong votaries of the capitalist ideologies. Even the most prominent advocate of free enterprise, the United States is known to be having a very large public sector.

In the debate on public sector enterprises, there is considerable semantic confusion in regard to their nomenclature. Also, some definitional and conceptual clarifications are called for. Different terms are in use. In parliamentary circles, the term in use is 'public undertakings'. The concerned parliamentary committee is also named Committee on Public Undertakings. It is often referred to as the PUC or Public Undertakings Committee. The Bureau in the Finance Ministry is named as the Bureau of Public Enterprises and describes public sector enterprises as Industrial and Commercial Undertakings of the Central Government. The first Administrative Reforms Commission had used the term 'Public Sector Undertakings'. Whatever term we use, public sector enterprises may be defined as autonomous or semi-autonomous corporations or companies established, owned, operated and controlled by the state and engaged in industrial and commercial activities.

The generic terms public sector enterprises or public undertakings cover several types of bodies engaged in industrial and commercial pursuits but the different nomenclatures used to describe them tend more to confuse than to clearly distinguish them. For example, terms like corporation and company are used interchangeably. It has been suggested that all statutory undertakings, eg LIC, CWC, DVC, IFC, FCI etc. could be called corporations. But, as it is, many undertakings set up as companies under the Companies Act, without any separate law at the back, call themselves by the more imposing name of corporation. This is misleading and makes determination of accountability to parliament processes a little difficult. In practical terms, there are three types of public undertakings—those set up by a Ministry of the Government ie. departmental undertakings; those set up under a separate statute by Parliament, ie. statutory undertakings; and those set up under the Law for Companies, ie. Joint Stock Companies.

There has been an unending debate on the nature, extent and limits of autonomy that public sector enterprises should enjoy.

Actually, it is very difficult to hold that any public sector enterprise is really fully autonomous. At best, it may be said to enjoy some operational freedom in its day-to-day working so that it has the necessary flexibility for being able to fulfill the mandate to follow business principles and serve the community. Operational autonomy is expected to help the top management to be enterprising and ensure economy and efficiency. Lord Keynes is often quoted to make the point that public sector enterprises cannot afford to forget that the criterion of action within their own field is solely the public good with motives of private advantage excluded and that these bodies are mainly autonomous within their prescribed limitations, but are subject in the last resort to the sovereignty of democracy expressed through Parliament.

It needs to be clarified that there are some fundamental differences in the concepts of responsibility, accountability and control.

In the context of public sector enterprises, to speak of parliamentary control may not be justified except in a very loose and general sense. Parliament does not control these enterprises or their functioning nor does it have the means or the legitimacy to do so. It is an executive function which is in the domain of the government. Normally, every public undertaking is under the administrative control of a Ministry and a Minister is responsible for it before Parliament. Parliamentary Committees can hold the administrative heads of concerned Ministries or/and the top management of the undertakings accountable before them but they cannot interfere in the day-to-day functioning of the undertakings or control them by issuing any orders, directions etc. It is for the government, through the concerned Ministry to do so, to call for reports and issue necessary directions with a view to exercise control over them.

Parliamentary concern in public enterprises flows from:

1. Parliament being the supreme representative institution in matters of public policy,
2. Public funds being involved,

3. The motive being not merely to earn or maximise profit but to serve some public purpose and meet some social objectives. Public enterprises were conceived of as major instruments of socio-economic engineering undertaken by the government.

It is, therefore, important for Parliament to exercise necessary surveillance and ensure full accountability of public undertakings to Parliament. As instruments of public policy, enterprises are clearly accountable to Parliament because, Parliament has the right to call for information in regard to the functioning and performance of these undertakings, to summon the top government officers of the controlling Ministries and the top executives of the industries before its Committees, particularly the Public Undertakings Committee. It is unfortunate that sometimes the chief executives of some of the big public enterprises resent Parliament calling them to account as undue interference in their working or an affront to their operational autonomy.

In case of departmental undertakings, unquestionably the degree of governmental control and accountability to Parliament are almost total. The state is the sole policy maker, shareholder and banker. It is for the government and Parliament to decide how much control and accountability are compatible with efficiency of these undertakings.

Statutory corporations are created by Parliament and the law setting each one of them lays down the objectives, the powers and the levels of autonomy and limitations thereon. It is axiomatic that with public policy, public funds and social objectives involved, there can be no question of Government giving up its control completely or the Parliament not holding them to account within the parameters of the law. Usually, the running of the statutory undertakings is entrusted to their management. While policy making powers remain vested in the government, the government does not interfere in the day-to-day administration of the undertaking. Also, Parliament by a self-denying ordinance, as it were, debars itself from interfering in the day to day affairs of the public undertakings. Thus, a statutory undertaking may be said to enjoy considerable autonomy in its operations so long as it fulfils the social and public interest objectives and financial obligations for which it has been set up under the framework of the Act and government policy. While that is the formal position, the ground realities are that so far it has not been possible to strike a balance between the level of autonomy desired and the control and accountability deemed necessary.

In the case of the third category of undertakings which are joint stock companies created by the government under its executive powers, the Company Law applies. The government controls both policy and management. In situations of failure, the dividing lines between the responsibility of the Company management and the controlling Ministry of the government are found to be very thin for Parliament to ensure adequate accountability.

The parliamentary procedural devices that are called into service for calling to account public undertakings generally are:

Parliamentary Questions
Half-an-Hour Discussions
Calling Attention Notices
Debate on the Budget and more particularly on Demands for Grant
Debate on the President's Address
Debate on Bills and Amendments
Discussions on matters of public interest under Rule 184
Short Duration Discussions on matters of urgent public importance under Rule 193
Parliamentary Committees particularly the Committee on Public Undertakings and the JPCs

Questions are perhaps the most potent parliamentary procedural device for ensuring accountability to Parliament and exercise surveillance over administration. Questions are asked about losses, wastes, production shortfalls, delays, staff matters etc. The best example of the efficacy of the Question procedure in the context of public sector undertakings was a question asked in regard to the LIC investments which brought to light the Mundhra Scandal and resulted in a powerful cabinet minister and an ICS Secretary losing their jobs (1957-58).

All the procedural devices have been used from time to time to highlight malfunctioning of Public Undertakings and efforts have been made to call them to account through discussions on the floor of the Houses of Parliament under various Rules. The most specialised and effective device for ensuring the accountability of public undertakings to Parliament however has been the Committee on Public Undertakings (PUC or CPU).

The question of an institutional mechanism for exercising parliamentary scrutiny over the public undertakings was first raised in the Public Accounts Committee in 1950-51. It was repeated in its 1952-53 Report. There was a move in Lok Sabha in 1953 for a separate committee for public undertakings. The Rules Committee favored the move. Prime Minister Nehru observed that there should be overall control of Parliament over autonomous and semi-autonomous corporations but he said he was against any interference in their day-to-day working.

The demand for a separate committee was revived in 1956, In 1957, Speaker agreed to a sub-committee of the Estimates Committee. In 1959, it was given powers of a parliamentary committee to call for papers and persons. On 18 November 1963, Lok Sabha passed two motions for setting up a separate Committee for Public Undertakings. Rajya Sabha concurred on 2 December 1963. The first Committee on Public Undertakings was constituted on 1 May 1969, with 10 members from Lok Sabha and 5 from Rajya Sabha. Rules were suitably amended to provide that PAC and EC would not examine those undertakings that are marked to Public Undertakings Committee *vide* Rules 312 A and 312 B and Schedule Four.

In 1973, in view of the increase in the number of undertakings, the membership of the PUC was increased to 22—15 from Lok Sabha and 7 from Rajya Sabha—at par with the PAC. The members are elected by their respective Houses by proportional representation by means of single transferable vote. The Chairman is nominated by the Speaker from among the Committee members.

The functions of the PUC and the procedure for examination of public undertakings by the Committee are laid down in detail in rules 312A and 312B, Schedule 4 and the Internal Rules of Procedure. The Committee can call for papers and persons.

The 4th Schedule to the Rules lists the undertakings to be examined by the Committee. These include (1) 11 Statutory Corporations, (2) all the govt. companies formed under the Companies Act and whose annual reports are laid before houses of Parliament and (3) 4 Departmental Undertakings.

The Committee is required to examine the reports and accounts of the undertakings and reports of C & AG on undertakings with a view to determine whether 'the affairs of the undertakings are being managed in accordance with sound business principles and prudent commercial practices', provided that the Committees shall not interfere in matters of major Government policy and matters of day-to-day administration.

After examining the audit reports or otherwise, the Committee at the beginning of each year selects the undertakings or subjects for examination. The concerned administrative Ministry is asked to supply preliminary material for study. On the basis of questions that arise from study, further materials are asked for and then a formal questionnaire is prepared for the evidence of representatives of the ministry and the undertaking concerned. The Committee also invites memoranda from non official organisations and experts from Chambers of Commerce and Industry, trade organisations, private sector companies and others like the workers' unions.

Study groups are appointed and sometimes even sub-committees are formed for in depth examination of issues. The Committee undertakes tours for on the spot study of the working of public undertakings.

The Committee calls officers of the Undertakings for giving evidence before it in regard to detailed working of the Undertakings. Thereafter officers of the Ministry are called for discussion of policy matters *separately*. Sometimes different pictures emerge—one may blame the other for failures and non-delivery.

The Committee takes the assistance of C & AG. It deliberates in camera with no outsiders present. All decisions in the Committee are taken by consensus or majority. Report is presented to Lok Sabha and also laid on the Table in Rajya Sabha. By convention, reports are not discussed in the House. Minutes are also laid on the Table. Report is sent to the Ministry. Action Taken Reports are also laid on the Table.

But, there is another side of the story which is different from the formal or theoretical position as it exists under the rules, the laws and the Constitution. There are serious limitations to the Parliament's role in exercising surveillance over Public Sector Undertakings. Parliament cannot and should not try to 'control' their working while the Public Undertakings must at all times remain accountable to Parliament and its institutions. There are some unresolved difficulties like who is to determine and how, what are 'sound business principles and prudent commercial practices'. It is open to much academic discussion. Similarly, if increased production and maximisation of profits are not the criteria, it is difficult to judge efficiency of any undertaking. There are no clearly defined standards of economy and efficiency. In fact, the malaise is much deeper. Deliberating on Parliamentary control over Public Enterprises is difficult at a time when Parliament is not able to control itself. It has become largely dysfunctional. Its credibility and even representative credentials are at the lowest levels. There is a widening gulf and disconnect between the Parliament and the people it is supposed to represent.

The two major parliamentary devices are the Questions and Public Undertakings Committee. A great deal of time and money is spent in the Ministries and undertakings preparing replies to Questions. But day after day, Question Hour is not held, whole days of parliamentary sittings and sessions are washed away, thanks both to the government and the opposition. Also, the Members often may not take their responsibility in regard to giving notice of Questions seriously. As for Committees, the original intent was that parliamentary committees would function on non-party lines, away from the glare of publicity to really help by nailing the shortcomings and faults in administration and in the public sector undertakings. In the present scenario, we are witnessing the demise of all semblance of parliamentary committee culture with members divided on party lines and even the impartiality of Chairmen being sometimes questioned. Not only efforts at consensus building seem to have been given up, even peaceful decisions by majority are becoming difficult.

On another plane, it may be said that public enterprises are national assets created with public funds. Besides meeting social objectives and contributing to nation's industrial and economic growth they must be sources of surplus by maintaining the highest standards of economy and efficiency. Public enterprises are expected to augment revenues of the state. It would be sad if the public undertakings are made losing concerns through mismanagement of their resources—funds and facilities—are abused and misused for personal and party ends by the politicians in power treating the public enterprises as their monopoly milch cows, pocket boroughs or as tools like the CBI and the Police.

Honourable Members of Parliament

Emoluments and Perks

THE QUESTION whether our Honourable Members of Parliament are underpaid or overpaid has never been satisfactorily settled. That in their own perception there is always case for upward revision of their emoluments and facilities is borne out by the fact that, on an average, almost every second year, Members have been voting for themselves enhanced emoluments and perks.

The Union Government was earlier reported to have worked out a proposal for setting up an independent emoluments commission to recommend appropriate salaries, allowances and other perks for members of Parliament. The proposal was approved by the All India Whips Conference including the Chief Whips and Whips of various political parties. This was welcome news.

At present our law-makers, both at the Union and State levels, are the only group of people paid from the public exchequer who determine their own salaries, allowances and other perks and thus become judges in their own case. This is clearly violative of the basic dictum that any outgo from the public funds has got to be with the approval of an authority other than the one likely to be benefitted therefrom. In fact, during the period of the 14th Lok Sabha also, the idea of setting up an autonomous Salaries Commission for MPS was accepted by the government in principle but nothing came out of it.

After the latest (w.e.f. 1 April,2018) hike in the salary and allowances of members of Parliament, it seems obvious that there is no intention of changing the status quo and appointing any independent emoluments commission since, as reported, now it has been provided that all the allowances will increase after every five years starting from 1 April, 2023, on the basis of cost inflation index. The decision will be conveyed to the Parliament's Joint Committee on Salaries and Allowances of MPs for making amendments in the relevant Rules.

Article 106 of the Constitution provides for members of Parliament being 'entitled to receive such salaries and allowances as may from time to time be determined by Parliament by law'. Until Parliament made such a law, members were to be paid the same emoluments as were applicable to members of the Constituent Assembly. Consisting of some of the most distinguished and talented persons, the Constituent Assembly paid no salary to its members. They received only Rupees 45 per diem for days of the sitting to cover daily cum conveyance allowance. As a token gesture in the context of the hard economic situation of the country, the members voted for a cut even in this paltry sum and, therefore, Rs 40 per day only was the consolidated per day allowance paid to members of the Constituent Assembly/Parliament till Parliament passed the Salaries and Allowances of Members of Parliament Act, 1954, providing for a salary of Rs 400 per month and a daily allowance of Rs 21 per day. Ever since, it has been a record of members repeatedly revising their emoluments upwards irrespective of the then prevailing economic conditions of the country and poverty of its people. The 1954 Act has been amended 29 times. Although the Constitution mentioned Parliament passing a law only in regard to 'salary and allowances', Members later sanctioned to themselves a pension also. The relevant law is now called the Members of Parliament (Salaries, Allowances and Pension) Act.

Fears were expressed in the Constituent Assembly that the Constitution that they had framed might give rise to a new class of professional politicians which could be its undoing inasmuch as they would try to become parasites on society and begin to live on their ministership, membership of legislatures etc. with nothing else to fall back upon. The fears seem to have come true. Now, every MP is entitled to a basic salary of Rs 1,00,000 (one lakh) per month, Constituency Allowance of Rs 70,000 per month, Office Expenses Allowance of Rs 60,000 per month. Furniture Allowance paid for the term has also been increased to Rs 1,00,000 (one lakh) and for the days of sittings of the House, Committees etc. (or when required to be on any other work connected with parliamentary duties like attending a parliamentary seminar or the like), a Daily Allowance of Rs 2,000 per day. In addition, every member is entitled to an interest free loan for Conveyance, Rs 50,000 for I-pad, exclusive Medical Facilities of the highest class (including well equipped medical centre in Parliament premises) and travel facilities in the highest class in rail, by air (34 air tickets for member and spouse or companion and additional 8 air tickets for spouse on her own), steamer or road plus liberal travel allowances. Every member gets a railway pass for self and spouse/ companion for travelling air-conditioned First Class free any number of times anywhere to anywhere within the country. A separate pass for the spouse is also available. Besides, one other person can travel with the member free in ACII class. Every member gets without any charge 40,000 kl of water per year, 50,000 units of electricity per year, installation of several phones with 1.5 lakh phone calls per annum, all free. Besides, every member is provided free residential accommodation in New Delhi. For luxurious flats there is no charge and for bungalows only a nominal fee is charged. Their market rentals would run into several lakhs per month. Besides, some members were reported to be living in the luxury of 5-Star Hotels even after a year of election on the plea that the houses allotted to them had not been vacated by earlier occupants or were under repair etc.

There are myriad other facilities and perks provided by members to themselves. These include foreign travel on duty by air in First Class with Daily Allowances etc., Clubs, common rooms, bank, post office, transport, LPG service, Super Bazar etc., access to stenographic, computer, research and reference services, exclusive air and rail booking offices, and other facilities in Parliament premises, Diplomatic Passports, relief in regard to income tax liabilities, free quarterly laundry services for household furnishings etc., supply of free furniture at residence and so on. Special protocol arrangements of Reserved Lounge, tea etc. are made at airports. Also MPs are exempt from paying toll tax on highways. It was in the news all over the media that heavily subsidised food of the highest quality was served to Members in Parliament house at ridiculously low rates making it the cheapest quality food anywhere in the world. The subsidy ran into crores. In fact, the variety of perks flowing from membership were difficult to list or document in terms of what these actually cost.

Above all, every member has Rs 5 crores per year at his/her disposal under what is called the MPLADS (Members of Parliament Local Area Development Scheme). There has been a pressing demand to increase the amount many fold. The Scheme is basically unconstitutional as being violative of the principles of federal polity and separation of Executive and Legislative powers. That, however, is another issue calling for a separate analysis in depth.[1]

After ceasing to be member of either House of Parliament, under a 2003 law, every ex member receives a handsome pension for life

[1] See Chapter on 'MP LAD SCANDAL'.

without requirement of any minimum period of service which, in effect, means that if one has been a member even for one day he would be entitled to pension for life. On the death of a member, the spouse or dependent is paid a family pension.

History of sorts was made in 1991, on the last day of the last session of the ninth Lok Sabha, when the two Houses of Parliament, each within a matter of minutes, without any debate or dissent, near unanimously adopted a Bill *inter alia* providing pension to every former member even if he had put in only one year's service in Parliament. It aroused considerable public indignation and disdain and generated loud protests from some concerned citizens and the media.

Some strong articles, editorials and letters to the editor appeared in national dailies. A strong plea was made by the present writer to the President not to give his assent to the 'outrageous' Bill. Subsequently, two articles were also published in national dailies (FE and HT). Extracts follow:

> Popular indignation apart, the President might be well-advised to return the Bill to the Government for reconsideration of their advice in regard to assent under Article 74 Proviso. There would be no question of the Bill being returned to the Houses of Parliament under article 111 as that article does not apply to the situation and under that article presumably, the President has to function on the advice of the Council of Ministers.

Inasmuch as the amendment regarding pension being made payable after a year's service was not accompanied by the required presidential recommendation, it was inadmissible and should have been ruled out of order. Its admission being violative of Article 117 of the Constitution and Rule 81 of the Rules of Procedure and Conduct of Business in Lok Sabha, would be another reason in favour of the desirability of the President returning the Bill to the government.

There was already the Postal Bill precedent.

For what they did, members of the Ninth Lok Sabha should hang their heads in shame. By this one act, they proved that they were more concerned with self-interest than with national issues and could not care less for public opinion and susceptibilities.

President Venkataraman had referred the constitutional /legal aspects in the matter to the Attorney-General for his opinion. The Attorney-General upheld the objections and agreed that Article 117(1) had been violated and as such the amendment was vitiated. Although, the Attorney-General was understood to have provided an escape by saying that if the President so wished he could still give assent to the Bill and no illegality would be involved. The President in his wisdom, however, decided to do no such thing and after about a year the Bill was finally returned to the government without the President's assent. The Rajya Sabha was informed that the President had withheld his assent. The Bill did not become law. The public exchequer was saved from being defrauded. This, in fact, became the only example of a Bill almost unanimously passed by the two Houses not being allowed to become law because of the President not giving his assent.

To recount an article by the author then published in *The Hindustan Times:*

> 'When the highly obnoxious Bill was passed it made news but when it was not assented to and therefore did not go on the statute book, it hardly attracted much media attention.'

Later in 1992, there was a similar situation in the State of Bihar. An article by the author published in *The Hindustan Times* said *inter alia:*

> The Laloo Prasad Government may be accused of many things but never of failing to provide good Press copies or newsworthy stories. The latest is the one concerning the two Houses of Bihar State Legislature passing within a matter of

minutes two Bills to substantially enhance the daily allowance, travelling allowance, pension etc.

The Bihar case was very similar inasmuch as both the Bihar Bills were financial Bills. They were passed in great haste by both the Houses. The Governor's prior recommendation for their introduction required under Article 207(1) of the Constitution had not been obtained. It was expected of the Governor to follow the precedent set by President R Venkataraman, show some sagacity and act with firmness by withholding his assent to the Bill. It was a matter of some quiet satisfaction that the Bihar Governor seemed to have listened to the voice of sanity and the two Bills could not become law.

The 2003 law was far more obnoxious than the ninth Lok Sabha bill inasmuch as not even one year's service was anymore required to entitle an MP for life pension. Any period, even a day was enough to make it a charge on the Consolidated Fund of India during the entire life time of the Member and also to take care of the survivors in the family through family pension. Yet, unlike 1991, the passing of the Bill and its enactment seemed to have met a conspiracy of silence all round.

In 2004, one of the most highly revered national icons, Late Nanaji Deshmukh, himself a distinguished member of Parliament, wrote 'with a feeling of deep anguish and sorrow but out of a sense of responsibility' that while fellow countrymen were toiling under extreme poverty and unemployment, our 'so called representatives' were 'getting richer and richer' and 'shamelessly piling up more burden on the country by increasing their own perks and perquisites'. This brought our democracy 'to disrepute and shame'. The 1954 Act, he said, had undergone 25 revisions till 2002 and the salaries and allowances of members had gone up ninety times during the first fifty years in utter violation of all principles of financial propriety. The approval of Parliament was always a mere formality with all parties of different hues fully supporting more and more for themselves even though they might not otherwise allow the Houses to function to debate and pass measures of common public good.

At a time when the salary of a member was only Rs 12,000 per month, Nanaji had estimated that the direct monthly expenditure on an MP was at least Rs 3 lakh per month. Himself an MP, he knew first hand. On that basis, the present monthly cost of an MP must work out to close to some 10 to 15 lakh per month or more, which would be few hundred times the *per capita* income of an Indian. Any increase in the emoluments of MPs immediately impacts States and if the expenditure incurred on State legislators is also taken into account, the cost of Indian democracy would be seen to be colossal. No wonder, we are witnessing an erosion in the popular esteem for the politicians and a widening gulf between the people and their elected representatives, notwithstanding a few honourable exceptions.

In the context of the recent non-functioning of the houses of our legislatures, the poor record of the conduct of members generally, the fact that the numbers of multi-millionaires and persons with criminal background have been increasing in Parliament and the fact that during the last nearly 48 years not a single Private Member's Bill has been passed, it is not surprising if any proposal to further increase the pay and perks of MPs meets with public frown and results in a serious backlash.

As for what would be an appropriate payment for members for the services that they render, the present writer has been suggesting that if they are paid a salary of Rs 3 to 5 lakh or more per month with all special perks and free or highly subsidised facilities withdrawn, the public exchequer would be a gainer. The frequent increases in the salaries and perks of members have contributed to the decline of Parliament and it's members in public esteem. The National Commission to Review the Working of the Constitution (NCRWC) reporting in 2002 said that a matter affecting the image of our legislators concerned the salaries, allowances and perks that from time to time they voted for themselves. There could be differences on whether members were underpaid or cost too much but it was a legitimate public expectation that membership of Parliament should not be converted into an office of lucrative gain. It must remain an office of service.

It is well-known that so far as members themselves are concerned, they feel they are woefully underpaid. They want more and have their own arguments. Also, in this matter, all members speak in one voice, irrespective of parties they belong to. On the other hand, the people at large are not convinced. They feel the payments and perks available to members are already too high and disproportionate to the services they render to society today. The people have seen paupers getting rich quick in politics and ever after living luxurious lives like princes of old and refusing to reveal their assets or sources of wealth and income within India and abroad, some honourable exceptions again notwithstanding. Also, if payments are really so low, why the terrible scramble for tickets and their alleged sale and purchase for crores.

Any effort to compare the payments to our legislators with those of the senior-most civil servant (Cabinet Secretary) or with the emoluments of members in other more affluent countries would be most illogical. It is *infra dig* and odious for members to want to be at par with a bureaucrat. In any case, it is only one—the seniormost in civil service—who gets that salary at the fag end of his professional career of three decades plus. Also, unlike an MP, a bureaucrat is a whole time government employee. As for payments to members of foreign parliaments, these would have to be seen in relation to their GNP, GDP and the *per capita* income of ordinary citizens in those countries, the exchange value of currency and it's purchasing power in particular countries.

On a point of international comparison, it may be incidentally pointed out that in many countries including UK, Canada, Australia, Japan, USA, Austria, Belgium, Ireland, Netherlands, Zimbabwe etc. members contribute to their post-retirement pension fund. The contribution is deducted from their salaries every month. On ceasing to be members and on reaching a specified age of retirement

(65, 67 or other), they receive pensionary benefits in proportion to this monthly contribution and on the basis of a certain number of years of parliamentary service. India is unique. The members make no contribution at all and no old age for receiving pension is prescribed. Also, there is no condition of any minimum period of service in Parliament. If a person becomes a member at the age of say 26 years and remains a member only for a day or a few days, he would be entitled to pension for life, to family pension etc. right from that young age. This is against all concepts of pension which is, by definition, supposed to be an old age protection and security.

In a democratic polity, nothing can be sadder than the representatives of the people losing the respect of the people by repeatedly and too frequently voting for themselves high emoluments and all sorts of perks. If freedom and democracy have to survive, it is imperative that the esteem of the people for their legislators is restored before it is too late and this can happen only when the legislators realise that it is not in their own long-term interests to unabashedly refuse to place any limits on the loot of people's hard-earned money. A stage now seems to have come where politicians themselves realise and accept that there has been a steep erosion in public esteem for them and something has got to be done to restore public faith in their worth to society. The most important single factor responsible for this state of affairs is that politics is believed to have ceased to be for sacrifice and service and is increasingly seen as a lucrative profession, business or career that gives power, pelf, perks and position and chances of getting rich quick. Every politician has to ask himself and honestly answer the question why he is in politics. With the present government wedded to principles of good, clean, corruption free, citizen-friendly governance in power, if ever there was an ideal time to make sacrifices and make a new start in public life, it is now. One way of really tackling the menace of corruption also would be to make political offices and memberships of legislatures less lucrative financially and attractive only to those dedicated to the nation, committed to sacrifice and service and with no personal axe to grind. Simultaneously, it would have to be made less expensive to be in politics. Let us all agree to give up the competition for demanding and trying to extract the maximum from the nation and instead take a vow to give our best. All this may seem idealistic but nothing less will do today.

Not increases but voluntary cuts in salaries, allowances, travels, seen and unseen perks and subsidies of members of Parliament themselves need to be announced. The oft-repeated suggestion of 'No work, No Pay' to members also needs consideration. It is all well to ask ordinary citizens to sacrifice for the poor by surrendering gas subsidies but a beginning ought to be made by the people's representatives by surrendering the many of the extraordinary perks and subsidies enjoyed by them. Sacrifice must begin and seen to begin at the top with Honourable Members of Parliament. The lead given by them is bound to impact the legislators at the level of States. Also, this would win tremendous goodwill and acclaim from the people. As the very first step, a wide national debate would be in order.

Cash for Questions

Expulsion of 11 Members

IN THE series of sting operations, a sensational camera expose of 11 MPs allegedly taking money for asking parliamentary questions was the hottest news in the closing month of the year 2005. Strangely nicknamed 'Duryodhana', the undercover operation raised more questions than it answered. The statistics regarding party affiliation of 11 MPs were not really relevant because conductors of the operation claimed to have more up their sleeves. According to them what was put in the public domain 'cannot be construed as the entire gamut of facts' and they had 'more interesting material'. This was enough to keep many other members and parties on the tenterhooks with the Damocles sword hanging over their heads. Was there a second list and, if so, was it being used for blackmail and making big money? It could perhaps never be documented but the fact was that the mentioned second list and the 'more interesting material' was never brought to light.

The eleven alleged bribe-takers were caught not by any official law enforcement agency, crime branch of the police or anti-corruption squad but by a private body in (Communication) business. This gave rise to questions in regard to the morality and motivation of 'Duryodhana'. Were the operators moved only by altruistic high patriotic motives of serving the nation and public interest? The criminal act of bribery involved a giver and a taker, one who tried to tempt and the other who yielded. Both were equally guilty.

Could we not legitimately expect greater transparency in the operation? For example, what was the total number of MPs approached? How was the list of those approached prepared? What sampling techniques, if any, were used? Was it random or representative sampling? Did it extend equally to the ruling party and opposition MPs? It was important to know all that to dispel doubts regarding only a few being specifically targeted or entrapped. Selective indictment or selective justice was bound to seem unfair and prove counterproductive. Did people not have the right to know how many of the MPs approached refused to take the bait and be bribed? If all the other 775 MPs were found to be immune from temptations of such money, should they and their number not have been specifically mentioned while branding 11 as the black sheep? Also, was there no one in the list of those approached who could haul up 'Duryodhana' for attempt to bribe an MP and for serious breach of parliamentary privilege? Both the Parliament and the law of the land could have then punished 'Duryodhana' appropriately.

Could it be said that the whole exercise resulted in catching some small fries from the back benches while the big sharks escaped or were kept outside the net? Many politicians were said to be on the regular pay rolls of different interest groups including business groups and crime syndicates. But why single out politicians, many others in honourable professions got paid in the name of retainership fee, consultation fee, service charges and the like, not for professional services or expertise but for acting as middle men, fixing deals, influencing high ups and getting legitimate or not so legitimate things done.

Even in the more advanced Western democracies there had been cases similar to ours. In UK, for example, payment of £1000 for a question resulted in the Nolan Committee Report and the introduction of the Register of Members' interests.

Almost all those elected to legislatures had to begin their legislative career with giving incorrect statements of election expenses. One could ask, if there was a general crisis of character in the nation as a whole, in all walks of life and in all professions, all-pervading devaluation of all values, if money, success and power, at whatever cost, had become supreme concerns, could we blame only the legislators for all the ills? Was the problem not more fundamental calling for systemic rethinking and holistic reforms. The National Commission on the Constitution (2002) made some far reaching recommendations and presented a blueprint of needed reforms. These were still relevant and needed to be considered on merits.

As for the expose by 'Duryodhana', the response of the Presiding Officers of the two Houses and of the parties was prompt, swift and most exemplary. Nothing better could be asked for. In Rajya Sabha, the matter was referred to its Ethics Committee presided over by an Hon'ble Member of the seniority and eminence of the Dr Karan Singh. The lone Rajya Sabha member involved in the expose was suspended. In the Lok Sabha, Hon'ble Speaker asked its ten Members to abstain from the House till their cases were finally settled. Presumably following the 1951 precedent in the HG Mudgal case, a Special Committee was appointed to enquire into the cases and report to the House before the current session concluded. The Hon'ble Member Pawan Kumar Bansal, appointed Chairman of the Committee, was already the Chairman of the Committee of Privileges.

The Special Committee reported with extreme expedition and the Lok Sabha equally promptly decided to expel from membership of the House all its ten members involved. The Rajya Sabha did the same in regard to the one member from that House. It was one of the swiftest operations to punish members of Parliament.

There was no substance in the argument that Privileges Committee was the only legitimate forum to consider such matters. However, it would have been certainly better if the non-party character of the process was maintained and reasonable time and legal assistance was allowed to the errant members to defend themselves. Some other queries were raised in the media in regard to the action against Members adjudged guilty of conduct unbecoming of Members of Parliament, and of lowering the dignity and committing contempt of their respective Houses by accepting financial gratification for asking questions in Parliament. Did the Houses of Parliament have the power to award to its members the ultimate penalty of expulsion from the membership of the Houses? According to the treatise on Parliamentary Procedure,[1] the House did have the power to punish its Members by suspension and expulsion from membership. There were clear precedents including the case where former Prime Minister Indira Gandhi was expelled from membership and also sent to jail for committing breach of parliamentary privilege and contempt of the House.

But there was divergence in judicial opinion. According to one High Court (Madhya Pradesh), the House of a legislature had the power to expel a member while according to another High Court (Haryana & Punjab), such a power did not exist. The uncertainty was set at rest when the matter of the expulsion of 11 MPs in the 'cash for questions' case was taken to the Supreme Court. It was held on 10 January 2007 that the Legislature had the power to suspend as also expel its members *(Raja Ram Pal vs Speaker Lok Sabha)*.

In fact, there was every case for the Supreme Court reviewing its ruling in the Narasimha Rao case letting off the bribe-taking JMM MPs on the ground that under Article 105, members taking bribe

---

1 See Subhash C Kashyap, *Parliamentary Procedure,* Universal, New Delhi, 2006 (2nd Edition), pp. 638-639 and 719-720.

for voting in the House could not be proceeded against in any court. Bribe-taking could not be deemed to be part of the proceedings of the House nor could it be construed as anything said or vote given in Parliament.

Members and Offices of Profit

Law and Practice

DESPITE ALL that has been written and talked about the issue of the office of profit under the government constituting a disqualification for membership of Parliament, this whole business still seems to be surrounded by smoke and shrouded in mystery. The need for an objective presentation of the constitutional position seems obvious. 'We, the people of India' should know what it is all about.

Article 83 of the Constitution lays down the qualifications for membership of the two Houses of Parliament. In order to be eligible to be chosen as a member, a person must be a citizen of India and not less than 30 years of age in case of Rajya Sabha membership and not less than 25 years of age in case of Lok Sabha membership. Additional qualifications may be prescribed by law.

Under Article 102, a person shall be disqualified for being chosen as and for being a member of either House (i) if he is not a citizen of India or otherwise owes allegiance to a foreign state, (ii) if he is an undischarged insolvent or one declared by a competent court to be of unsound mind, (iii) if he holds any office of profit under the Union or a State Government other than the office of Minister or any office exempted by Parliament by law, and (iv) if he is otherwise disqualified under any law made by Parliament. Also, a person may be disqualified on grounds of defection under the Tenth Schedule which was added to the Constitution by the 52nd Amendment.

If any question arises whether a member of either House has become subject to any disqualification, it shall be decided by the President after obtaining the opinion of the Election Commission and in accordance with that opinion except in case of disqualification on grounds of defection where the matter will be decided by the Speaker of Lok Sabha or Chairman Rajya Sabha as the case may be (Articles 102(2) and 103).

The job of Parliament and its Members is to represent the people, to lay down policies, to make laws and to exercise surveillance over executive action. With the exception of Members who become Ministers, other Members are not expected to exercise any executive powers by accepting any office of profit under the government. If those charged with the responsibility of overseeing the executive, themselves become part of the executive establishment or become beholden to the executive for an office of Profit under the Government, obviously they cannot be expected to faithfully perform any worthwhile oversight functions. That is why, Article 102 of the Constitution provides that apart from certain other things, holding an office of profit under the government would constitute a disqualification for membership of Parliament. Giving a somewhat arbitrary power to the Parliament/State Legislatures, it is provided that any offices can be exempted from disqualification.

A Member, Jaya Bachchan, was in March 2006 divested of her Rajya Sabha Membership by the President on the advice of the Election Commission as per Article 103 of the Constitution. Several other cases were also reported to be pending when the two Houses of Parliament passed a Bill to retrospectively prevent the disqualification of a large number of Members who were alleged to be occupying high offices of profit under the government. These included the then Speaker of Lok Sabha, Som Nath Chatterjee and leader of the ruling United Progressive Alliance, Sonia Gandhi.

The occupants of the offices of profit tried to escape disqualification by resigning. The question arose whether a person would be allowed to take an escape route through the backdoor, avoid the likely stigma and other consequences of disqualification and package his subterfuge of resignation as an act of sacrifice? Could the resignation be accepted before the proceedings were concluded by the Election Commission and decision announced by the President? Also, what happened to the period during which the alleged office of profit had been held, authority exercised and benefits drawn? Even after resignation, should the question not have been settled by the Election Commission whether the position of office of profit under the government enough to disqualify a Lok Sabha member? In 1951, when Nehru moved for the expulsion of H G Mudgal, the House deprecated the attempt of the Member to circumvent the effect of the motion under consideration by resorting to the resignation route and resolved that by resigning, Mudgal committed contempt of the House and aggravated his offence. However, in this case involving several heavyweights, all the objections and legal consequences were sought to be resolved by giving the Act retrospective effect from as far back as 1959.

The President, Dr Kalam, however, returned the Bill to the Houses of Parliament for reconsideration. When the Bill, after reconsideration was again presented to the President under Article 111, he gave his assent after a few days and not before the government announced the appointment of a parliamentary committee to consider the issues raised by the President.

Constitutional provisions for State Legislatures corresponding to Articles 102 and 103 are Articles 191 and 192.

The Parliament (Prevention of Disqualification) Act, 1959 (amended from time to time) declares the offices of profit under the government which do not disqualify the holders thereof for being chosen as, or for being, members of Parliament.

The term 'office of profit under the government' has not been defined in the Constitution or the Representation of the People Act, 1951, or the Parliament (Prevention of Disqualification) Act, 1959. The Courts or other authorities have, however, stated in this connection certain broad criteria:

Office of Profit

(i) The essential characteristics of an office of profit are (1) it involves an appointment by the State in one form or the other, (2) it carries emoluments payable mostly periodically, (3) it is for a limited period, (4) it is terminable, (5) it is not assignable, (6) it is not heritable, (7) the holder of the office must be *sui juris*.

(ii) Profit in Article 191 (Article 102 for Parliament) of the Constitution of India does not necessarily mean any remuneration in cash but it certainly means some kind of advantage or gain which can be perceived. But, the mere influence which one gains by virtue of his position as member of a Committee which has no remuneration attached to it is not an office of profit within the meaning of Article 191 of the Constitution, and the member of such a Committee would suffer no disqualification by being a member thereof.

(iii) Profit connoted the idea of pecuniary gain. If there is really a gain its quantum or amount would not be material but the amount of money receivable by a person in connection with the office he holds may be material in deciding whether the office really carries any profit.

(iv) The emoluments attached to the office may be in the nature of pay, salary, honorarium, fees, daily allowance, travelling allowance etc. Where salary is attached to an office, it immediately and indisputably makes the office an office of profit.

(v) If consideration is paid in the shape of remuneration, ie. sitting fee, or attendance fee, it becomes a profit inasmuch as it does not even purport to cover any actual expenses. Such consideration or remuneration should be deemed to constitute 'profit' even though on detailed accounting it may be found that no financial advantage has in fact been gained by the member in question.

(vi) Travelling and halting allowances received by a member of an Area Committee are not remuneration but represent reimbursement of out of pocket expenses and a member of an Area Committee does not, therefore, hold an Office of Profit within the meaning of Article 191 of the Constitution and is not disqualified for membership.

(vii) According to the Parliament (Prevention of Disqualification) Act, 1959, if a person is not entitled to any remuneration other than compensatory allowance as defined in section 2(a) of the Act, he will not incur disqualification for receiving that remuneration.

(viii) In order that an office may be an office of profit, it is not necessary that there must be some sort of regularity of income. Neither is it necessary that there should be actual making of profit by the incumbent; it is enough if the holder of the office may reasonably be expected to make a profit out of it.

(ix) For the purpose of deciding the question of disqualification, so long as any profit was attached to an office, it did not matter whether the profit had in fact been appropriated or not. Therefore, there was no distinction for the purpose between the members who drew the allowances and those who did not. Some offices may be considered offices of profit even if the actual payment of emoluments attached might have fallen into disuse.

Under the Government

(i) The source from which a person receives profit is not the sole test as to whether he holds an office of profit under the government within the meaning of article 102(1)(a) of the Constitution. The power to appoint and remove is also one of the tests and if a person is appointed by the government to an office of profit and is removable by the government from the office, he would be a person holding an office of profit under the government even though he is not paid out of the government funds.

(ii) The power conferred on the State government to exercise control and supervision over the working of the University will not make the University, or its officers, subordinate to the State government in the sense that they would be disqualified to be chosen as and for being members of the State Legislature. The Vice-Chancellor is appointed by the Governor in his capacity as Chancellor of the University, distinct from his office as the head of the Executive, and the appointment cannot be deemed to have been made by, nor can the office of the Vice-Chancellor be said to be under the State government by virtue of the appointment having been made by the Governor in another capacity.

(iii) The power of the government to appoint a person to an office of profit or to continue him in that office or revoke his appointment at their discretion and payment from out of government revenues are important factors in determining whether that person is holding an office of profit under the government, though payment from a source other than government revenue is not always a decisive factor.

(iv) A person serving as a teacher in a school receiving grant-in-aid from government does not hold an office of profit under the government merely because the school receives grant from the government for payment of a portion of the dearness allowance and the pay. The real test would be whether the government of the State had the power to remove a person from office. If so, it must be held that the person holds that office under the government of the State and this is irrespective of whether the salary attached to the office is paid by the State or paid out of some other funds.

(v) To determine whether an office is under the government, it is not necessary to see whether the government has some disciplinary or supervisory powers over the incumbent of the office.

(vi) For holding an office of profit under the government, one need not be in the service of government and there need be no relationship of master and servant between them. Several factors enter into the determination of this question—the appointing authority, the authority vested with power to terminate the appointment, the authority which determines the remuneration, the source from which the remuneration is paid, the authority vested with power to control the manner in which the duties of the office are discharged must all co-exist and each must show subordination to Government and it must necessarily follow that if one of the elements is absent, the test of a person holding an office under the government, Central or State is not satisfied. The source from which the remuneration is paid is not decisive. Whether stress will be laid on one factor or the other will depend on the facts of each case.

(vii) The disqualification of a person who holds an office of profit does not cease on his submitting an unqualified resignation of his office but only when his resignation is accepted by the proper authority.

For all the parties and beneficiaries of governmental offices of profit, the options were two. One based on constitutional morality and political principles where the office of profit under the government should be strictly defined and clearly delimited in the Constitution itself and holding any such office other than that of a Minister or some parliamentary office, should invariably disqualify the holder from membership. Alternatively, the Union Parliament and all the State Legislatures had to bring legislation to protect holders of all such offices. The second option prevailed. The States were competing with each other in rushing to pass legislation in unseemly hurry to exempt all and sundry offices from disqualification. Politicians in all parties would like to continue to profit from the loot of public exchequer. The consensus for sharing the booty may be a blatant fraud on the Constitution and on 'We, the people of India' who are completely insensitised to assert and speak up.

Lobbying by Members

Members' Conduct, Privileges and Interests

DURING THE 15th Lok Sabha period, a Union Minister of State in the Ministry of Environment and Forests, wrote to the Speaker Lok Sabha and the Chairman Rajya Sabha raising some vital issues involving the conduct of Members. He complained that some of them were acting as lobbyists, either to promote the interests of their own concerns or for others. The Minister pointed out how his own Ministry was sought to be pressurised by some Members to further certain interests. The matter had serious ramifications and called for a national debate.

That such things happened had always been widely suspected. The Minister's allegations, however, were vague, in very general terms and not actionable. If anything, they tended to further erode the falling respect and esteem of the people for their own elected representatives. It was very much like some academics and social activists alleging that politicians were corrupt and source of all our societal ills. Perhaps, the hangover of the Minister's own academic past got the better of him to make such remarks. Unless the precise names were given and specific instances cited with proper documentation and evidence, no meaningful action could be expected to follow the Minister's epistles to the Presiding Officers.

In all fairness to the Members of Parliament and parliamentary institutions, the Minister should have come forward with facts and details of the information in his possession so that appropriate action under the Constitution, Laws and Rules of the Houses could be initiated to ensure that our elected representatives—Hon'ble Members of Parliament—did not degenerate into serving their own personal or family business interests or becoming power brokers, middlemen, influence-peddlers, liaison men, commission agents or lobbyists for vested interests.

One view that was advanced and debated was that Members of Parliament worked under tremendous pressures. They are approached by many people for help because of their legitimate communication links with the Parliament and the government. Often, the Members have to write to the Ministers. It should be entirely the responsibility of the Minister to have the matters examined and decisions taken on merits.

Communications from honourable Members of Parliament are entitled to due respect in the chambers of Ministers. But, that also casts a tremendous responsibility on the shoulders of the Members. They should not blindly sign any missives to Ministers. As for Members trying to directly influence government officials, that is entirely impermissible.

In some quarters, it is advocated that in the context of economic liberalisation and free market policies adopted by us, lobbying should be accepted as an essential concomitant and legalised on the US pattern. In the United States, almost every interest group has its lobbyist on the Hill to protect and promote its interests in the portals of the US Congress and in the government. The lobbyists have to be registered under the Registration of Lobbies Act. The lobbyists interact with Members of the Congress and build pressure groups to influence policy in the interest of their clients. Sometimes, these pressure groups and lobbies play a more potent role in policy formulation, legislation and implementation than even the political parties. No wonder the lobbyists in the US are some of the most highly paid people.

Here again, our situation in many respects and our polity are very different from the United States. In the context of vast sections of our people still suffering from poverty, backwardness and deprivation, it would not at all be possible in foreseeable future to have lobbyists for all interest groups. Any law permitting lobbying would only legitimatise and promote some of the most unfair practices including payment of bribes and commissions. The lobbyists would become the middlemen. The dividing line between a lobbyist and a broker is very thin.

In our parliamentary system, several procedural devices are available to Members to seek information from the Ministers and to raise matters of public importance in the parliamentary fora. Every Member is a Member of the Parliament of India. He cannot be confined to concerns of his constituency. He can raise matters of concern to any or every part of the nation and pertaining to the public interest of any section of the people. But, if a Member of Parliament has any personal, direct or pecuniary interest in any matters coming up before the House or a Committee of which he is a member, he is expected to inform the Speaker/Chairman of his interest in advance of his taking part in the concerned proceedings.

Under Rule 255 in the Lok Sabha, objection may be taken to the inclusion of a member in a Committee on the ground that the member has a personal, pecuniary or direct interest of such an intimate character that it may prejudicially affect the consideration of any matters to be considered by the Committee. If the Speaker holds that the member, against whose appointment objection has been taken, has a personal, pecuniary or direct interest in the matter before the Committee, he shall cease to be a member thereof forthwith. For the purposes of this rule, the interest of the member should be direct, personal or pecuniary and separately belong to the person whose inclusion in the Committee is objected to and not in common with the public in general or with any class or section thereof or on a matter of state policy. There have been several instances where action has been actually taken by the Speaker.

Under Lok Sabha Rule 371, vote of a Member on the floor of the House may be challenged on the ground of personal, pecuniary or direct interest in the matter. The Speaker shall decide whether the vote of the member should be disallowed.

Norms of Parliamentary Decorum and Etiquette to be followed by Members are contained in the code of conduct which is part of the Rules of the House (Rules 349 to 359 & Directions 115 A and 115C, Lok Sabha). But, this largely covers the Members' conduct in the matter of the maintenance of parliamentary decorum in the proceedings of the House.

Besides, under the law of parliamentary privileges flowing from Article 105 of the Constitution, any misconduct in the presence of the House or a committee thereof, including that by Members themselves, constitutes a contempt of the House. Members found guilty of such contempt can be punished by admonition, reprimand, suspension from the House for a particular period, commitment to prison or even expulsion from the House.

Members generally are expected to so conduct themselves as to maintain the dignity of the House to which they belong and not to indulge in any conduct unbecoming of Members of Parliament or inconsistent or derogatory to the dignity of the House. Thus, it is considered the duty of each member to refrain from any course of action prejudicial to his privilege of freedom of speech in the House. It is irregular for a member to enter into any contractual agreement with an outside body, controlling or limiting his complete independence and freedom of action in Parliament.

The extent and amplitude of the words 'conduct of a member' have not been defined exhaustively, but it is within the powers of the House in each case to determine whether a member has acted in an unbecoming manner or has acted in a manner unworthy of a Member of Parliament. Thus, even though the facts of a particular case do not come within any of the recognised heads of breach of privilege or contempt of the House, the conduct of a member may be considered by the House as unbecoming and derogatory to the dignity of the House.

The first such case which is often cited occurred as early as in 1951 during the Provisional Parliament period. The House decided on the 24 September 1951 that the conduct of a member (HC Mudgal) in undertaking to canvass 'support' and to make 'propaganda in Parliament' on behalf of the Bombay Bullion Exchange, in return for financial or business advantages, was 'derogatory to the dignity of the House and inconsistent with the standard which Parliament is entitled to expect from its Members'. The House by a resolution determined that Mudgal deserved expulsion from the House.

During the 8th Lok Sabha period (1985-89), 96 notices of questions relating to drug manufacturing companies, their products and formulations for different dates were received from seven members. From the format, language and typing of those questions it appeared that the source of all of them was the same and they appeared to be rather sponsored questions to lobby for or against certain multinational drug companies. The questions instead of asking information gave information and no public interest appeared to be involved. It also appeared that the medium of question procedure was being abused and therefore was violative of Rules (Rule 43 (1)). All these notices were disallowed.

Again, a large number of questions relating to drug manufacturing companies, their products and formulations from almost the same set of members were received. Except a few which were found admissible on merit and were accordingly admitted, all other questions were disallowed. Some of the members represented against disallowance of their questions. These members were asked to see the Speaker. Only one member turned up. He was told by the Speaker to desist from accepting questions from private companies indiscriminately and without personal scrutiny.

During the 14th Lok Sabha period, in a sensational expose on camera, ten Members of the Lok Sabha and one Member of the Rajya Sabha were shown on TV as accepting money for asking questions in Parliament. On 23 December 2005, motions were passed in the two Houses expelling all the 11 Members from their respective Houses for conduct lowering the dignity and credibility of Parliament.[1]

There are many established parliamentary customs and conventions which a member has to make himself familiar with. These customs and conventions are based on the past precedents, the rulings of Presiding Officers and on the unrecorded traditions of Parliament. These are put together in a Handbook for Members and *inter alia* include:

- Information given to Members in confidence or by virtue of their being members of Parliamentary Committees should not be divulged to anyone nor used by them directly or indirectly in the profession in which they are engaged, such as in their capacity as editors or correspondents of newspapers or proprietors of business firms and so on.
- A member should not try to secure business from government for a firm, company or organisation with which he is directly or indirectly concerned.
- A member should not give certificates which are not based on facts.
- A member should not unduly influence the government officials or the Ministers in a case in which he is interested financially either directly or indirectly.

---

[1] See Chapter on 'Cash for Questions'.

- A member should not receive hospitality of any kind for any work he desires or proposes to do from a person or organisation on whose behalf the work is to be done by him.
- A member should not in his capacity as a lawyer or a legal adviser or a counsel or a solicitor appear before a Minister or an executive officer exercising quasi-judicial powers.
- A member should verify the facts before proceeding to take action on behalf of his constituents.
- A member should not elicit any official information in an unauthorized manner by inducing a government employee to give information to him which in the course of his normal functions he should not give, nor encourage any such person to speak to him against his senior officials on matters of public importance and policy.
- A member should not write recommendatory letters or speak to government officials for employment or business contacts for any of his relations or other persons in whom he is directly or indirectly interested.
- Members should not take action on behalf of their constituents on some insufficient or baseless facts or without verifying the veracity of facts nor should they allow themselves to be used as ready supporters of individual grievances. If the legislator feels that the cause is just and legitimate but the normal channels would get delayed justice, he can approach the civil servant concerned and bring the matter to his notice, but with decorum and in a manner not in any way amounting to pressurising or exercising undue influence.
- Conduct of a member involving corruption in the execution of his office as a member is treated by the House as a breach of privilege. Thus, acceptance of any fee, compensation or reward in connection with the promotion of or opposition to any Bill, resolution or matter submitted or proposed to be submitted to the House or any Committee thereof is a breach of privilege. It

> would also be a breach of privilege and misconduct on the part of a member to enter into an agreement with another person for any reward to advocate and prosecute in the House the claims of such person.

The Handbook also provides details of the appropriate procedure for Members communicating with Ministers, whom to write for seeking information, for complaining etc. If a Minister says that any member was trying to influence him or lobby for any private party, he should be asked to substantiate his allegations with specific references to the names of Members and details of their attempts to influence him or his Ministry officials. If that is done, it would be a fit case for further action and can be referred to the Ethics Committee or the Privileges Committee of the House concerned or even a Special Committee may be constituted to inquire and report to the House. The House can then discuss the report and decide upon appropriate action to be taken against the Members found guilty of conduct unbecoming of Members of Parliament. If any bribery or other corrupt practice violative of any law including IPC, Prevention of Corruption Act etc. is involved, the Members can also be hauled up by the law enforcement agencies of the State and proceeded against like any other citizen. One can only hope for appropriate action being taken against any Members guilty of conduct unbecoming to them.

Mplads Scandal

Fraud on the Constitution

THE COMPTROLLER and Auditor-General of India (C & AG) has repeatedly commented adversely on the utilization of funds under the Members of Parliament Local Area Development Scheme (MP LADS). Simultaneously, there were pressing demands from MPs to substantially increase the amounts available under the Scheme. The UPA II Government had increased the amount from Rs 2 to 5 crores per year for each member.

No wonder if the increase was perceived as an attempt to bribe the MPs *en masse* and add substantially to their vested interests in the continuation of the House in the face of threats of no confidence moves in the government.

Sometimes, the history does repeat itself. For the first time in 1993, a person publicly asserted that he had personally handed over to the then Prime Minister a suitcase containing a sum of Rs one crore.

The allegation of such corruption at the level of the Prime Minister shocked the nation. The accusation of Rao accepting a crore of rupees was dismissed as wild and baseless. But before 1993 was out, a crore of rupees from the public exchequer were placed at the disposal of each Member of Parliament every year. There may be no connect between the two events but one remembers that besides the one crore in a suitcase episode, the newspapers at the time were full of stories regarding the securities scam and the JPC report thereon. Astute political manipulation and allurement of huge amounts of money and ministerial berths were believed to have succeeded in securing the necessary defections and defeating the no confidence motions.

It would be difficult to assert that it was a mere coincidence that just before the JPC report was about to be discussed on the floors of the two Houses of Parliament, another JPC report—this one on the Salaries and Allowances of Members of Parliament—was laid on the tables of the two Houses. Besides recommending many other generous perks, the Committee asked the government to provide Rupees two crores per year for each member of Parliament to be spent on development works in his/her constituency/district solely at his/her discretion. In a unique show of solidarity with his fellow members and prompt decision-making, the Prime Minister at once announced in Parliament on 23 December 1993 a sort of interim Action Taken Report when he promised a gift of rupees one crore per annum to be placed at the disposal of each member. It was a question of somehow pleasing and placating the MPs. As if the existing perks and payments and other direct and indirect financial benefits of membership were not enough, an additional vested interest in continuing to be members at all costs was created lest some members got ill-advised to try to topple the minority government on the Securities scam issue and the JPC report thereon. The hint of the likely losses on dissolution of the Lok Sabha was clear. If one were to remember the damp-squib that the following discussion on JPC report turned out to be, the conclusion was obvious that the hint went down well.

A point was made that after all this money was not going to be physically handed over to the MP. But, people had come to know only too well what percentage, if any at all, of the sum spent in their name, actually ever reached them. Also, one asked if the money was not meant in any way as a perk or payment to MPs, how and why did it flow from the recommendations of the Committee concerned with their Salaries and Allowances.

Narasimha Rao succeeded in taming the Opposition and making all the protests against corruption non-issues. Things had come to such a pass that there could be no politics and no party activity without tainted money. In any case, if the then Finance Minister of the country (Manmohan Singh) was 'not prepared to lose his sleep' over the multi-crore securities scam, members could not be expected to sacrifice their membership—the hen that laid a golden egg every day—merely on the issue of corruption. The badly besieged Manmohan Singh government not only multiplied many times the salaries, allowances and perks of all members but added to the crores at their disposal under the LAD Scheme.

The scheme does serious violence to our Constitution, to its federal principles, to the distribution of powers between the Union and the States and more specifically to subjects assigned under the XI and XII schedules and to the much bandied about new Panchayati Raj institutions established under the 73rd and 74th Constitution Amendment Acts. Members of the Union Parliament should have no role in the exclusive domain reserved for the States by the Constitution. It is difficult to appreciate with what legitimacy can a member of the Union Parliament be allowed to meddle with development priorities in areas which belong almost entirely to local bodies or to State legislatures. Individual members of Parliament dictating in towns and villages which drain, road or bridge or school building should be built and when and where, would make a mockery of the basic features of the Constitution. Further, if one looks at Articles 243G and 243W and the 11th and 12th Schedules of the Constitution, it would be clear that almost all the items mentioned in the Guidelines figure in the domain of Panchayats and Nagar Palikas. And, as such, MPs should not meddle in those matters. As it is, sometimes an MP—a member of the Union Parliament—has more funds at his disposal for attending to Municipal or Panchayat needs than those bodies themselves. Federalism and decentralization of power to the grassroots through the 73rd and 74th Amendments thus becomes a facade.

Under the foundational principles of parliamentary polity and the Constitution, while the government is collectively responsible to the Lok Sabha, Members are not to exercise any executive powers. LADS vests almost exclusive discretionary powers in individual Members to select projects for implementation in their constituencies and sanction expenditure thereon from public exchequer. This clearly makes MPs wield executive powers and tends to blur all distinction between executive and legislative authorities.

A Member of Lok Sabha has, at his or her disposal, a sum of *Rs 25 crore* during the 5-year term and a Member of *Rajya Sabha has Rs 30 crore* during the 6-year term to win favours, build vote banks and ensure electoral support by suitably obliging the influential sections of the electorate. At the time of the following elections, the sitting MPs would come to have an illegitimate advantage over their rivals at the hustings. There would be no level playing field and no equality of opportunity to new candidates or, in a collective sense, to parties in the opposition.

It is true that the Supreme Court in its wisdom declared MPLADS fully constitutional but the arguments against it remain. The highest court in the land can also sometimes go wrong and one can only hope that it would correct itself at the earliest opportunity.

It is argued by some friends that the guidelines provide enough safeguards like members recommending items only from the planned schemes. In fact, these are hardly likely to dent the fundamental farce. It seems the Scheme was born in sin and was actually intended to be misused. While some MPs are known to have maintained reasonable transparency in utilization of funds and made real good use of LADS, the scheme remains a clear fraud on the Constitution. With nearly 800 members of the two Houses of Parliament, and with the State Legislatures also having similar schemes for their members, the total outlay for all the LADS would come to staggering figures of hundreds of thousands of crores per year.

LADS has generated widespread corruption and blatant misuse of public funds. It has not been possible to develop any monitoring mechanism. There is near total absence of accountability. The State Legislatures cannot sit in judgement over the acts of Union MPs. The Parliament will not hold its members to account and, in fact, it cannot because the LADS is implemented by the States and concerns State subjects. The scheme has not attracted enough media attention; this may be because of the very widespread vested interests shared by legislators, bureaucrats, babus, contractors and others. It is time that the law makers see the writing on the wall and not take the people for granted for too long.

SOME EMINENT PARLIAMENTARIANS

Jawaharlal Nehru
Artificer of Parliamentry Democracy

The Colossus

AFTER FIFTY years of Jawaharlal Nehru's passing away, his ashes, as he had desired, were flown and scattered all over the vast land of the nation including the heights of the Himalayas and immersed in the Ganges to mingle with the earth and waters of the country he loved. In his will and testament, Nehru got very poetic and emerged as an individual most passionately and emotionally attached to the sacred river representing the age-old culture and heritage of India.[1]

During the year 2015, the nation celebrated the 125th birth

[1] See Subhash C Kashyap, 'Jawaharlal Nehru: From Far and Near: Some Recollections' in *Witness to History*, Nehru Centre, Oxford, New Delhi, 2011.

anniversary of Nehru, the first Prime Minister of India. Of late, one hears some criticisms and even derogatory references to Nehru. Of course, like anyone else, Nehru also made mistakes and had his weaknesses. But, his detractors are actually moved very justifiably by the blatant injustice done to other great leaders of the freedom struggle and nation builders like Sardar Patel, Subhas Bose, Jayaprakash Narayan and others. For they are all our national icons and not the property of any party. I believe it is in that spirit that the Government of India also embarked upon an impressive programme of activities for the 125th birth anniversary celebrations for Nehru.

Without getting involved in different party perceptions or controversies between the admirers and detractors of Nehru, I would like to put down for the younger generations some anecdotes based on personal interactions with him. I can brag about being among those leftovers of destiny who had seen Nehru in flesh and blood and, what is more, had occasions to sit with him and talk to him. My first glimpse of Nehru was when sometime in 1936-37 he visited our hometown and the procession carrying him stopped on the doorsteps of our house. Many ladies and children had assembled there. Nehru offered to walk in but my mother conducted an *aarti* at the entrance itself and presented him a bag containing donations collected for Congress funds. As a child of 7-8 years, I remember I was charmed by the most handsome man I had seen. The procession ended in front of the municipal hall in a large public meeting addressed by Nehru. I was with my father, himself an active freedom fighter and Congressman. I saw an elderly man trying to help Nehru to take off his Peshawari shoes. Nehru brushed him aside and scolded him for his slavish behaviour. Although it was a rally of mostly illiterate common folk of a small town, Nehru's speech was full of references to great things that were happening around the world and the poverty and backwardness of India. Referring to the non-violent freedom struggle under Gandhiji, he recited two lines I have not forgotten. They ran somewhat as follows:

Hamne manzilen tay ki hain kuchch is tarah,
Ham chale chalkar gire, gir kar uthe, uthkar chale.

As I look back, it seems to me the villagers only looked at the charming Kashmiri face of this prince among patriots and felt enamoured without understanding much of what he had talked about. Apparently, one of the secrets of this man's popularity was the charm of his personality and the aura built around it. Later, when I was in intermediate classes at the Meerut College and active in the Students Congress, Nehru visited the city as part of his whirlwind tour during 1945. We, the student activists, worked with the local Congress leadership. Ch Charan Singh was the DCC President. Nehru arrived by road, very much behind schedule, late in the night. Wearing a black sherwani, he moved past the guard of honour presented by the college girls. We could see him putting his hands in the sherwani pocket and take out a few grams to munch on. Suddenly, he stopped and started admonishing the organisers for keeping the girl volunteers waiting until such late hours in the night. Next day, in a pilot jeep we went ahead to be at the venue of the next meeting on the village side. As the road connectivity was poor, I saw Nehru walking with us through the fields to the meeting venue. My father had given me a Kodak Brownie box camera as a birthday gift. I was carrying it with me. Somehow, quite impulsively, I started aiming the camera at Pandit Nehru with a view to take a snap. He looked at me, smiled and proceeded to give me my first lesson in the art of photography. He said the camera lens must not face the sun. For a good photograph, the sun should be behind. Nehru stood in the shade under a tree, posed for me and asked me to shoot. Encouraged, I requested another favour for an autograph. He got angry and said 'you also need an autograph' and threw away the new autograph book. I never had one either before or after.

I cannot forget a small incident during the walk with Nehru through the fields. A village boy, about 9-10 years old, was walking with us. I noticed that Nehru instinctively came close to putting his arm affectionately over his head but quickly withdrew. Perhaps he had noticed how dirty and dusty the boy's head was. It indicated some inner conflict between Nehru's socialistic instincts and his aristocratic Western upbringing. The day's tour ended at a large rally near Ghaziabad. The enthusiastic crowd was anxious to get near the volunteers. Nehru himself jumped from the podium over the heads of the jostling crowd. Soon, order was restored. This had become a well-tried Nehru strategy of crowd management. What a contrast from independent India where all the security arrangements are directed towards keeping the crowds away from the leader. The Gaziabad meeting was followed by tea at which prominent citizens, industrialists and Congress leaders were present. When the party was on, one noticed Nehru suddenly put up his two hands and jump over to the other side. He was perhaps tired of the formal ambience and the playful child within revolted.

Nehru felt invigorated in the midst of a crowd. He was not a great orator, in any case not in Hindi. He often rambled in halting Hindustani like a teacher anxious to explain things to children. But, he connected with the people very well. They heard him spellbound. While speaking, he was also thinking with his audience.

After joining the University at Allahabad in 1946 and having read more of Nehru, I felt Nehru was more of a well-bred Englishman who had made the discovery of India. With all his scientific temper and secularism, Nehru was spiritual at heart even if not religious. He was proud of India's ancient heritage of rich culture and philosophy. He found great solace in Vedanta and Buddhism. Nehru visited our University and addressed the students. The meeting was followed by an At Home for the guests with the office bearers of the University Union. For me, it again became a memorable occasion when Nehru taught me some table manners like never to peel a fruit for another person and not to pass anything across the table.

As is well known, Nehru was a little temperamental and could easily get upset and angry. However, he cooled down equally fast. I remember how he was annoyed with a student at the University campus for walking ahead of him and repeatedly aiming his expensive camera at him. Nehru snatched the camera and threw it away. The student, known as a good photographer and physically a little lame, walked away muttering, 'If the Prime Minister has such a temper, God save the country'. The same day, the boy was invited to Anand Bhawan and Nehru personally presented to him a nice new camera. It is another matter that the proud boy politely declined to accept it.

Later on during 1949-50, I was President of the Allahabad University and was residing in the GN Jha hostel. One fine morning I heard a knock at my hostel room door. Lal Bahadur Shastri, then UP Police (Home) Minister was standing there with DM Bhargava and others. 'Panditji wants you at Anand Bhawan, come right away', Shastriji said. When we finally met, incidentally only at the airport, Nehru said he was coming to Allahabad again next month and would like to address the college students from all over the district. For long an Honorary Member of the University Union and with the University campus almost next door neighbour of Anand Bhawan, Nehru was very well aware of the geography and logistics of the university. He indicated in great detail what arrangements were to be made, where the dais was to be built etc.

On the appointed day, more than a lakh students turned up. Suddenly, it started raining heavily. Despite being fully drenched in torrential rain, the crowd remained unmoved and fully disciplined. Nehru sent Munshiji (as Nehru called Shastriji) to see the state of affairs. After he returned fully satisfied and reported, Nehru came. Most unruffled by the continuing rain, and drenched himself, Nehru was in a very joyful mood. The Vice-Chancellor who was also present on the dais tried to protect the Prime Minister from rain by holding an umbrella over his head. Nehru curtly brushed him aside while pointing towards the huge gathering of young students—boys and girls—who were also braving the rains. Nehru spoke for over an hour in the pouring rain. He spoke about the work the Constituent Assembly was doing. In my youthful exuberance, I had the audacity to speak after him and also to criticize the government, particularly for not having allowed the Asian University Students Conference. He heard me in good cheer, all the time with a soft smile, intervening only once when he took the mike from me and clarified that he was told that the government did not find the time opportune and the proposed conference could certainly be held later. I can never forget the courtesy and the consideration extended to me by PM Nehru when with prior appointment I called on him at his South Bloc office. I was merely a student, but the PM talked to me with indulgence, stood up and came upto the door of his office room to see me off.

Joining the Lok Sabha Secretariat as an officer on the research side early during the First Lok Sabha, I saw for some 11 years Nehru functioning as the Leader of the House. When Nehru passed away in May 1964, I was working as in-charge of the five-volume study on the framing of the Constitution under the guidance of the Shiva Rao Committee. Nehru had taken keen personal interest in the project. Only a few hours before we got the shocking news of his demise, we had received a letter dated 24th May 1964, saying that he would try to send a Foreword by the end of the year. This was presumably one of the last papers signed by him at Dehradun.

Nehru was invariably present in the House during the Question Hour and through all major debates. His presence in the House for long hours had a sobering effect on all other members. While sitting in the House, he would dispose off a large number of office files—a habit that I hurriedly picked up from him and followed during the seven years of my functioning as the Secretary General of Lok Sabha.

Nehru played an outstanding role in building our parliamentary institutions and establishing lofty conventions, practices and precedents. On two occasions, he sort of clashed with Speaker Mavalankar. One was in regard to the issue of Ordinances and second was on not being allowed to make a second statement in the House. On both the ocassions, Nehru yielded to the Speaker. Nehru's punctual and graceful entry with respectful bows to the Chair and to both sides of the House, even during his last days were moving experiences for those who witnessed the scenes. I recall one day when I was checking the display of teleprinter news items, to my utter surprise, I found the Prime Minister standing by my side and asking about the latest news. Obviously, those were different days with no computer, internet, TV or mobile. Once, the PM needed some information urgently. To save time, he himself walked into a Lok Sabha Secretariat Branch. The Staff were awe struck and lost their nerve until the old Section Officer stood before the PM with folded hands and requested him to leave so that the staff could quickly trace the relevant papers for him. We are unlikely to see such a spectacle again.

I was myself witness to some unforgettable debates in Parliament. For example, the ruthless and brutal criticism by Ram Manohar Lohia, comparing the average daily income of an Indian with the daily expenditure on Nehru's dogs. Nehru sat smiling through all this and more. It was normal for Nehru to sit through strong attacks on him and his government and at the end deliver his spirited reply sometimes even admitting gracefully that some of the criticism was justified. One remembers the firm handling of Kripalani's motion on General Thimayya's resignation and Nehru's unequivocal declaration that in India, civil authority would always reign supreme. Once, when Atal Bihari Vajpayee made an unsparing verbal attack, Nehru not only patiently listened but at an evening reception the same day, without any bitterness, spoke to him. Nehru once told the Lok Sabha:

> 'Parliamentary Democracy is a delicate plant and it is a measure of our own success that the plant has become sturdier during the last few years. We have faced difficulties amid great problems and solved many of them. But many remain to be solved. If there are no problems, that is a sign of death. Only the dead have no problems.'

A question is sometimes asked: In the cacophony of discordant voices, what is Nehru's main legacy? When Nehru himself was asked that question, he replied: 'Hopefully, it is four hundred million people capable of selecting a leader for themselves and governing themselves.' Nehru made unique contributions to the freedom struggle. A legend in his time, he left many legacies for India and for humanity at large. In his own words, a queer mixture of East and West, out of place everywhere, at home nowhere, Nehru had to make a Discovery of India but he is very legitimately credited with having played the most dominant role in nation building as the prime artificer of parliamentary democracy in India. He laid firm foundations of space and nuclear research including scientific, technological and industrial infrastructure and is rightly regarded as the builder of modern India. Nehru was the chief architect of independent India's foreign policy based on the principles of non-alignment, prohibition of nuclear weapons, disarmament, co-existence and world peace. In the words of Prime Minister Rajiv Gandhi:

> The early years of free India were the years for institution building and laying the firm foundation of principles from which we could draw strength in our endeavours at building a new India. In these formative years, Jawaharlal Nehru's was a contribution of lasting significance in articulating and shaping the principles of democracy, socialism, secularism and non-alignment. These are principles upon which India has continued to build. They constitute the pillars of our nationhood.
>
> The Constitution that guarantees every citizen his rights; Parliament which represents the voice of the people; the multiparty system which enriches democracy; an Independent judiciary which guarantees impartial justice; a free press which can effectively reflect the concerns of the people—all these institutions were nurtured in their early years by Jawaharlal

> Nehru. He ensured that they take deep and firm roots and become a part of Indian democracy, a part of our way of life.[2]

For Nehru's critics, on the other hand, there are as many negative legacies of Nehru. They are said to include the partition of India, problems with China and Pakistan, the inspector and license raj in the name of socialistic pattern of society resulting in poor record of development and widespread corruption and much else. Above all, Nehru is blamed for the Kashmir problem, divisive politics and electoral system and for politicisation of minorities as vote banks.

It may be said that Nehru's unique role in building the great Parliamentary system has not received due attention from scholars. Again, writing the Foreword to a book on the subject[3], the then Prime Minister, Rajiv Gandhi said that Nehru's name will forever be linked with the history of parliamentary democracy. The reverence in which Nehru held the authority of Parliament and the conventions he helped to shape, enabled our democracy to take such deep and sure roots. Nehru built the infrastructure and the grand edifice of Parliament, brick by brick. He made Parliament a 'potent instrument of nation building, social engineering, economic reconstruction and national integration'.

As one irrevocably committed to parliamentary democracy, Nehru respected the Houses of Parliament and the Opposition even though throughout the period of his premiership, opposition in Parliament was very small in numbers and was not officially recognised. He encouraged dissent and invited and welcomed criticism. Once, when a no confidence motion was moved against his government, he appreciated it and said he thought such occasions were good for the

---

2 Subhash C Kashyap, *The Political System and Institution Building under Jawaharlal Nehru,* National, New Delhi, 1990, Foreword

3 Subhash C Kashyap (ed.), *Nehru and Parliament,* Lok Sabha Secretariat, New Delhi, 1986.

government. On another occasion, he once said: 'After all that has happened in recent months, I do not know how I am tolerated. If I was in the Opposition, I could never tolerate this government.' Only Nehru could use such strong words against himself and the government headed by him. Sometimes, while replying to debates, he would begin by saying that there was some truth in the opposition criticism.

Nehru's role in making the Constitution of independent India is also not appropriately appreciated. It is surprising that not enough attention has been paid in our academia or elsewhere by way of carrying out the necessary researches to assess the unique contribution of Nehru to the philosophy, framing and working of the Constitution. He was almost the sole author of the concept of the Constituent Assembly. He played a dominant role at various stages of Constitution-making.[4] In the words of Justice Krishna Iyer:

> The voice that mattered most, the views that prevailed most, the principles that were ultimately readily accepted and the direction of the Constitution and its dimensions and values in its final shape, were largely of one person, Nehru.

The then Prime Minister, Indira Gandhi, writing a Foreword to my book on Nehru and the Constitution said:

> The spirit of our Constitution bears the imprint of his (Nehru's) inspiration even though the forms might have been devised by professional lawyers.

It was largely due to Nehru that the Constitution adopted by the Constituent Assembly on 26 November 1949 was above all a

4 For further study see Subhash C Kashyap, *Jwaharlal Nehru and the Constiution*, Metropolitan, New Delhi, 1982. Also see Subhash C Kashyap, *Indian Constitution Conflicts and Controversies,* Vitasta, New Delhi, 2010, Chapter 9.

consensus document. Thereafter, for fourteen years (1950-1964), Nehru as the Head of the Government was responsible for working the Constitution. The way he worked the Constitution gave it shape, meaning and content. In fact, the Constitution was being made as much during 1950-1964 as it was during 1946-1949. During his premiership, as many as 17 constitutional amendments were enacted. Nehru was a strong advocate of the need for flexibility in the Constitution. No Constitution, howsoever good, could bind succeeding generations. In order to be lasting, it must be amenable to change in accordance with changing societal needs and aspirations.

When the nation celebrated the 125th birth anniversary of Nehru, it was pertinent to recall, among other things, his role in the evolution and operation of the Constitution not only as a matter of historical interest or to pay homage to the great builder of modern India, but because Nehru's vision and views, and his words and warnings on the crucial problems of Indian polity are as relevant today as they were when he moved in flesh and blood and guided the destiny of the nation. What he told the Constituent Assembly, he could as well be saying today:

> At present the greatest and the most important question in India is how to solve the problem of the poor and the starving. Wherever we turn, we are confronted with this problem. If we cannot solve this problem soon, all our paper Constitution will become useless and purposeless.

One is constrained to ask, whether after 68 years of the working of the Constitution, the problem of the poor has really been solved? If the Constitution has failed to deliver, it is for the researchers and scholars to decide if any culpability in this matter attaches to Nehru or the Constitution or both. It is true, recently, many expectations of better days were aroused. Fortunately, the people have not lost hope and are prepared to wait, but failure would spell disaster for freedom and democracy.

Sardar Patel

Builder of the Indian Union

Pragmatist and Patriot

THERE IS increasing competitive clamour to usurp Sardar Vallabhbhai Patel's legacy. It is necessary to look beyond the controversies and view the great artificer of post-Partition India in proper perspective. Before Independence, the Congress was not so much a political party as a national movement and an umbrella organisation for adherents of diverse ideologies. Among the most outstanding leaders of the freedom struggle and one of the founding fathers of the republic, Patel belonged to the whole nation. It would be puerile and futile for any party today to claim proprietary rights or a monopoly over his legacy. If parties otherwise opposed to each other come forward to commemorate his role in building the nation, it should be a matter of joy for all.

Patel was not a romantic idealistic visionary but a down-to-earth realist. He did not like going out of the way to appease the Muslim

League. Rajmohan Gandhi says: 'Unlike Jawaharlal, who sometimes imagined Hindu-Muslim unity when it did not exist, Vallabhbhai was frank about the reality. Also, he felt it unnecessary to give "secular" wrapping to his utterances… Vallabhbhai never tried or claimed to represent Muslims and he found it natural to speak as a Hindu.'

The mayhem unleashed in Bengal under the name of 'Direct Action' by Jinnah was followed by massive Hindu reaction. Patel noted that it was a good lesson for the League, because he had heard that the proportion of Muslims who had died in the aftermath of 'Direct Action' was much larger. In the communal carnage in Noakhali, Hindus were forcibly converted to Islam or killed and temples were destroyed. The Hindu reaction, again, was massive. Many Muslims suffered in UP and Bihar. Speaking at the Congress Session at Meerut, Patel advised the advocates of Pakistan to follow methods of love and peace. He added that 'sword will be met by the sword'. With the constitution of Pakistan, he hoped the rest of India could live in peace.

As chairman of the Advisory Committee on Fundamental Rights, Minorities etc. in the Constituent Assembly, Patel played a crucial role in discarding separate communal electorates, reservations and quotas. He said: 'When Pakistan was conceded, at least it was assumed that there would be one nation in rest of India—the 80 per cent India—and there would be no attempt to talk of two nations here also'. Patel was forthright in saying that all those who believed in the two-nation theory had no place in India and should move to Pakistan. He told the Muslims pointedly: 'For God's sake, understand that we have also got some sense… There will be no injustice done to you. There will be generosity towards you, but there must be reciprocity. If it is absent, then you take it from me that no soft words can conceal what is behind your words. Therefore, I plainly once again appeal to you strongly that let us forget and let us be one nation.'

Patel sometimes joked that Nehru was 'Congress's only nationalist Muslim'. The self-proclaimed secularists of today should take note of Patel's real views and decide if they wish to own his legacy to the exclusion of all others, or if they are willing to accept him in totality. Patel was a proud Hindu, but it would be wrong to think that he was anti-Muslim, communal or anti secular. Patel stood for equal political rights for all citizens. While their religious, linguistic or other minority rights must be respected and protected, Patel was opposed to any political rights being sought or granted on grounds of such belonging. He did not agree with BM Birla's suggestion that India be declared a Hindu state. The state, he said, must exist for all, and protection of minorities was also its responsibility. For him, radical ideology took a backseat. He said he did not believe in any caste or community, the entire country was his village. He believed that stability was a precondition of development and it could come only when there was unity. Speaking in the Constituent Assembly on 25 May 1949, he said that, 'It would be in the interest of all to forget that there is anything like majority or minority in this country and remember that in India there is only one (Indian) community.'

When, in 1950, Nehru wrote to Patel about their differences, Patel said: 'Our secular ideals impose responsibility on our Muslim citizens in India—a responsibility to remove the doubts and misgivings entertained by a large section of society about their loyalty founded largely on their past association with the demand for Pakistan and the unfortunate activities of some of them.' In one of his last speeches on 7 October 1950, Patel summed up his stand by saying: 'Every Indian citizen, whether Hindu or Muslim, will have to behave as an Indian, and the sooner they realize this the better.' The nation today needs to see Patel in the correct perspective, without allowing politicians to appropriate his legacy, pandering to vote-banks.

Dadasaheb Mavalankar

"Father of Lok Sabha"

IN THE history of Parliament and parliamentary democracy in India, the name of Ganesh Vasudev Mavalankar—called with affection 'Dada Saheb'— shall always be remembered with great respect. The contribution of Mavalankar to laying sound and solid foundations of parliamentary polity in India was the most significant and substantial. No wonder, Nehru himself called him 'Father of Lok Sabha'. Today, when we find several of the present-day Speakers in the country being openly accused of playing politics and taking partisan stands to make or mar the fate of governments, it is specially relevant to remember the first Speaker of Lok Sabha who established the highest norms as a parliamentarian and as a Speaker. In fact, he could be a role model for Speakers anywhere in the democratic world.

Mavalankar's was a many-splendoured personality. His contributions to national causes and service of the people were diverse and multifarious. He was a great parliamentarian and the first Speaker of independent India. He was indeed a born Speaker. During the nearly two decades of his tenure he remained a legislator, he almost never sat in any House as an ordinary member. He was always Mr President or Mr Speaker. Congratulating Mavalankar on his election as Speaker of Lok Sabha, Nehru referred to his vast experience and said that the first Lok Sabha was fortunate to have a Speaker of his calibre 'to guide us, and if we go astray, to pull us back where necessary, to admonish us and to check us.'

I might, in all humility, add some bits of personal reminiscences and impressions connected with Dada Saheb Mavalankar and his Speakership. I have had the proud privilege of seeing and knowing all the Speakers of Lok Sabha so far—some from a little distance and others fairly closely. When with the background of a university teacher with some academic pretensions, I joined the Parliament Secretariat as a young officer, Dada Saheb Mavalankar was the illustrious first Speaker of Lok Sabha. In his case, my impressions were largely formed from (i) viewing him function as the Presiding Officer from the Lok Sabha Galleries, (ii) the couple of occasions when he addressed the officers and staff, (iii) a solitary meeting with him in his Chamber and (iv) his orders, notings and remarks on the files that moved up to him and came back. As a junior officer, I could expect or ask for no more.

I vividly recall his impressive—somewhat awe-inspiring—personality. A great administrator and disciplinarian, he believed in building one unified hierarchy in the Parliament Secretariat with unity of command. Although under his stewardship there was large expansion in the Secretariat and the staff strength grew from a paltry fifty to about five hundred, he himself never recommended a single person for appointment, thereby laying firm foundations of an efficient Secretariat built on respect for merit. He delegated authority and placed the fullest faith in the Secretary, MN Kaul, and his Joint Secretary Shakdher. The two worked in such close unison that they were often considered two bodies with one soul and one mind. They were the eyes and the ears of Dada Saheb. Once while addressing us, he called Kaul and Shakdher as his two sons in the Secretariat. In fact, for all of us in the Secretariat, he was truly a father figure, rather a *Pitamaha.* We all felt proud that we were working for and under a great Speaker and one who was among the galaxy of great men the country was fortunate to have had at that time in history.

Dada Saheb always insisted upon 'an independent Secretariat for Parliament' for the simple reason, he said, 'that the Speaker, as representative and head of the Legislature, must have the help and advice of people who do not feel themselves suppressed because of the powers of the executive government, who will give advice and put through the work irrespective of frowns and favours.' He also said:

> If my Secretary were to advise me on the admissibility of a question or the admissibility of a motion keeping in view as to what the Prime Minister will think of his advice, I think the purpose of having an independent Secretariat is lost. Our business is to uphold democracy.

The *Mool Mantra* that Dada Saheb gave to all of us and that permeated, in a very real sense, all our working and thinking in those formative days was that of not being influenced by any considerations of fear or favour. To all new entrants to the service of Parliament Secretariat he simply advised adherence to principles of freedom, faith, objectivity and speed:

(i) Think and act freely without fear or favour,

(ii) Have faith and confidence in your colleagues—delegate and assume responsibility at every level,

(iii) Be objective and non-partisan—amidst politicians and politics but above all party and political considerations,

(iv) Be quick in disposal, do not delay, do not pass the buck or toss the files, take responsibility and decide; in parliamentary work delay is inexcusable and time factor is often the most important.

It is these cardinal principles that laid the foundations of an independent and efficient Secretariat of Parliament and developed a distinct culture for parliamentary officials quite different from the culture of the executive bureaucracy.

Despite a rather tough exterior, Dada Saheb was a warm-hearted man. While speaking at the Silver Jubilee celebrations of the Secretariat, he assured all the officers and staff that every employee of the Secretariat was free to express his views. I remember, once sometime in 1955, I put up information copies of some research brochures on which I had worked and advance printed copies of which had just then arrived. The file went up the hierarchy. The then Secretary, Kaul, marked it to the Speaker. It came back to my desk on the same day with some very kind words of appreciation and encouragement. I knew I had received the blessings from the *Pitamaha*, Dada Saheb.

Dada Saheb had ambitious plans for a separate Parliament Library Building. I can recall attending a meeting held in the Speaker's Chamber to discuss the matter. It is another matter that for some reason, Dada Saheb's wish of Parliament Library Building did not materialise for long. It was a matter of some satisfaction that more than three decades later, as Secretary-General, I had something to do with laying the foundation stone for the Library Building by the then Prime Minister, Rajiv Gandhi.

I have some impressions also of the conduct of the proceedings of the House by Dada Saheb. He had insisted upon the House functioning with the highest standards of dignity and decorum, that the members from all sides of the House comply with the rules and regulations, conventions and precedents. In a House which consisted of great stalwarts, both on the Government and Opposition benches, and some very distinguished and difficult members, he would stand no nonsense. No one—Minister or other member—could walk up to the Speaker's Chair to have a word with him or the like. They could meet him only in his Chamber. In the House, if they had something to say, they had to do so through officers at the Table to whom they could talk or send notes. No member could be seen walking between the Chair and a member speaking at the time. No shouting, yelling, reading of newspapers, talking among themselves or otherwise disturbing the House by indecorous behaviour was tolerated.

In the best tradition of British Speakers, Dada Saheb spoke very little in the House. He sat in the Chair with a quiet dignity and there was something majestic about him. His demeanour inspired a sense of awe and commanded instant respect. Whenever he opened his mouth, he was heard in silence and obeyed. When he called 'Order, Order' in his firm voice, it was like the falling of a hammer and dead silence descended on the House. It was inconceivable that any member would remain standing or speaking after he had signalled them to stop and take their seats or when he himself stood up. To an occasional recalcitrant member who disturbed the orderly proceedings or continued to stand or speak, one stern look from the Speaker was enough to send waves of admonishment and obtain immediate compliance of the Chair's wishes. When the Speaker stood up, it was the ultimate signal for all others to sit down and to listen to the Chair in silence and with reverence. On his part, Dada Saheb had a mastery over the rules and procedures. He listened to various points of view and then made up his mind and gave his decision. Once he did that, nothing could change his mind. He did not allow his ruling to be questioned or discussed directly or indirectly. It was extremely rarely that Dada Saheb was seen on his legs in the House. It was hardly needed. Those times were very different.

Speaker Mavalankar was very particular to impress upon the Ministers that it was in their own interest and in the interests of the Government to respect the parliamentary procedures and practices, the rules and conventions and never to forget that the Ministers themselves were first Members of Parliament, part of Parliament, subordinate to Parliament and answerable to Parliament.

On principle, Dada Saheb could measure swords and afford to disagree with the mightiest and the greatest. He could refuse to allow Prime Minister Nehru to make a second statement in the House the same day as it was then not permissible under the rules. He could join issues with the Prime Minister in the matter of issue of Ordinances and question the desirability of agreeing to the prorogation of the House merely because Government wanted to issue some Ordinances. When it came to the rights and prestige of the House *vis-à-vis* the other House in a matter of privilege, he could firmly disagree with the views of the Prime Minister and establish a convention for dealing with matters involving members of one House in cases of alleged breach of privilege of the other House. The convention lasts to this day and is followed.

However, the Speaker could do little alone if there was not at the helm of the government and as the Leader of the House the great democrat and respecter of institutions and parliamentary traditions, Jawaharlal Nehru, who was quick to remind the Speaker himself how to retain the dignity of his office *vis-à-vis* the Prime Minister. Although they often met socially, Dada Saheb as Speaker scrupulously avoided calling on the Prime Minister. And, once when the Speaker wanted time to see the Prime Minister, it was the latter who reminded Dada Saheb that when the Hon'ble Speaker wants to see the Prime Minister, it is for the Prime Minister to go to the Speaker's Chamber and see him there after finding out *his* convenience. This is the stuff of which greatness takes shape, this is how parliamentary history is made and how great traditions are built.

Sarvepalli Radhakrishnan

Contribution to Parliament

SARVEPALLI RADHAKRISHNAN, a multifaceted personality, with an uncommon brilliance, excelled in many fields in a way rarely paralleled in history. We have had the proud privilege of having philosophers, intellectuals, teachers, scientists, politicians, religious gurus and other eminent men and women down the ages. But, Radhakrishnan was not only an eminent teacher and a reputed philosopher but also a skillful diplomat and a statesman of the highest order. In his later years, when he was elected to the august office of the President of India, he brought a rare grace and dignity to it by virtue of his deep scholarship, knowledge and wisdom. It was rightly said that we had the philosopher-statesman of Plato's conception occupying the highest office in the land.

He was, above all, an intellectual par excellence with rich background and experience, insight and knowledge of affairs in the

East and the West, the past and the present and with an uncanny vision of the future. A multi-dimensional personality like him cannot obviously be discussed in all aspects within the limits of one write-up. Here, therefore, the attempt is only to present a glimpse of the contributions that Radhakrishnan made to the Indian Parliament during his stewardship of the Rajya Sabha as its Chairman even though he continued to play a vital role in Indian Parliament even after ceasing to be the Vice-President and hence, the Chairman of the Rajya Sabha. For, thereafter, he was the President of India.

Radhakrishnan was never a Member of Parliament though he was in Parliament for 15 long years. From 1962 to 1967 as the President of India he was a constituent part of Parliament and, earlier in 1952, elected by the members of both the Houses as the first Vice-President, he became the *ex officio* Chairman of Rajya Sabha and presided over its deliberations for ten long years—the formative years of our Parliament and parliamentary democracy in India. The nation was indeed fortunate to have him as the first Chairman of Rajya Sabha because it was he who gave the much-needed shape and direction to the role and functions of that House. While felicitating Radhakrishnan on his election as Vice-President and Chairman of Rajya Sabha, Nehru had said:

> Sir, I should like to say a few words, not of congratulation to you on occupying this high office, but rather of congratulation to the House that we have the privilege of having you here to guide the deliberations of this House as well as, if I may say so, to help us in a multitude of ways in another high capacity.[1]

As the presiding Officer of Rajya Sabha, Radhakrishnan lent great dignity to the Chair. With his witty and humorous remarks he maintained and sustained the lively debates and they were sufficient to

---

[1] *RS Deb.*, 16.5.1952, cc. 32-33.

evoke restraint both in the treasury and the opposition benches. Under his stewardship the debates were marked by positive traits so essential for any healthy discussion.

Function of Parliament

Presiding Officers in various Houses of Legislatures often spend a lot of their energy and lung power trying to prevent Members saying something. This becomes a contributory cause for indiscipline and indecorum. Members insist upon saying what they want to say despite the Chair not allowing it for they deem it their fundamental right to express the woes of the people and their views freely in Parliament. Radhakrishnan was very clear in this matter. Speaking on the functions of Parliament, he said that it must 'express, not suppress, social discontent… It acts as a liaison between the people and the state.' Radhakrishhnan, a great advocate of not forgetting the ethical part in politics, instructed the people's representatives that 'the decisive consideration should not be whether we do anything popular but whether we do the right.'[2]

The path of righteousness was as virtuous in politics as in religion. It was Radhakrishnan, who for the first time, expressed the firm view that members of Parliament should be given proper training for their effective functioning in the House. 'They must have a thorough knowledge of the Constitution, especially the Directive Principles, which form our 'national *dharma* or righteousness'[3], he said.

Radhakrishnan was an ardent supporter of the Second Chamber in Parliament. A Second Chamber, he felt, was essential for preventing hasty legislation. In India the two chambers are equal in status and in most of the functions. The Rajya Sabha is not merely a revising chamber as in some other countries; it is complementary or equal to the Lok Sabha because all bills (except money bills) can originate in either House.

---

[2] S Radhakrishnan, *Occasional Speeches and Writings 1956 to 1957,* Vol. II, p. 289.

[3] Ibid., p.290.

While presiding over Rajya Sabha, Radhakrishnan acted with intrinsic and manifest non-partisanship, fairness and impartiality, with ill-will to none and good-will to all. Being a supporter of parliamentary democracy, he stressed the importance of the right of the opposition to freedom of thought and expression. While vehemently supporting the minority opinion in a democracy, he once said:

> A democracy is likely to degenerate into a tyranny if it does not allow the opposition groups to criticize fairly, freely and frankly the policies of the Government.

At the same time, he warned that the right to criticism should not degenerate into willful hampering and obstruction of the work of parliament. He conducted the business of the House in such a manner that both the ruling party and the opposition were fully satisfied. Pandit Govind Ballabh Pant, the leader of the House in the Rajya Sabha, congratulating him on his election as Vice-President for a second time, said:

> You have treated every Member of this House with tender consideration and even affection. The proceedings of the House have been conducted by you with unerring dignity, grace, imperturbable patience and, if I may say so, gentleness. The rights and privileges of the Members of this House and of everyone of us are in your safe keeping, and we could not have thought of a better and safer custodian and guardian.[4]

VK Dhaga, from the opposition, similarly observed:

> I would say that you as the Chairman of the House never allowed anyone in the Opposition to feel that you ever have

[4] *RS Deb.* 13.5.1957, c. 3.

> been partial in any way in the matter of giving the rulings. We feel completely secure that with you in the Chair, complete impartiality will be maintained and that we need not be afraid of anything. You have in this House lent charm, grace and dignity on many occasions.[5]

Rulings and Directions

His rulings and directions as the Chairman of Rajya Sabha have gone a long way in establishing sound parliamentary traditions and healthy precedents. He had a conviction that we should develop our conventions and traditions in consonance with our past while remaining fully responsive to our changing needs. Without going into the details of various rulings of historic procedural interest delivered by him, it must be pointed out that he was not for referring to or copying the Westminster procedures. He firmly observed:

> I am not referring to what May's Parliamentary Practice may have said. Why should we always be bound down by the practice followed elsewhere? We are an independent House and we follow our Constitution and Rules of Procedure.[6]

Power, Prestige, Rights of Rajya Sabha and its MPs

It was through his rulings that Radhakrishnan emerges as a zealous guardian of the position of Rajya Sabha. He never compromised on the dignity of the House. Once, when Prime Minister Nehru made a statement about a bill having been passed by Parliament while only Lok Sabha had passed it, he made a strong observation and said:

> Under the Constitution, Parliament means both the Houses, Lok Sabha and Rajya Sabha. Without the concurrence of the

---

5 *Ibid.*, cc. 4-5.

6 *Ibid.*, 12.2.1959, c. 446.

> House, no bill can become law. An act of Parliament means something that is agreed to by both Houses and assented to by the President.[7]

It was due to his efforts that members of Rajya Sabha could become members of the two important Financial Committees of Parliament, viz the Public Accounts Committee and the Committee on Public Undertakings, with full rights. Also, through his efforts and initiative, certain principles for handling privilege matters involving members of the other house were established. He believed that the two Houses and their members were entitled to equal respect.

At the same time, Radhakrishnan did recognise the limited powers of Rajya Sabha in certain matters. He never favoured the idea of pretending to claim power over such matters and usurping the powers of Lok Sabha. Thus, when a Member raised a point of order regarding the Income Tax (Amendment) Bill, 1952, contending that it was not a money bill, the Chairman ruled out the point of order and held that the Speaker's endorsement in this regard was final and conclusive.

Right Precedents

Radhakrishnan was always keen to establish right precedents. For instance, on 4 May 1959, he ruled out an objection to a discussion on Tibet as an internal affair of China. He said: Under rule 148 of the Rules of Procedure of the Rajya Sabha, discussion may be raised on any matter of general interest. We are discussing only the situation arising out of the recent events in Tibet or, in other words, the impact of that situation on India. Therefore, it is admissible.[8]

Wit and Humour

As Chairman, Radhakrishnan was at his best in conducting and

---

[7] *Ibid.*, 16.8.1956, c. 1353.

[8] *Ibid.*, 4.5.1959, c. 162832.

regulating the proceedings, more particularly in tackling vocal members with amazing tact, skill and gentleness. During difficult hours, he would diffuse the tension with his great sense of humour and ready wit. When a Communist Member objected to a Minister using the word 'God', Radhakrishnan ended the controversy by his humorous observation that even Khrushchev had used the word 'God' in the UN Assembly.[9]

Once disallowing a point of order, Radhakrishnan in his characteristic gentle voice, observed: 'If we begin breaking the convention, the breaking would be the convention.' In another instance, when Prime Minister Jawaharlal Nehru was replying to a question, Bhupesh Gupta rose to ask a supplementary and said, 'Let me ask a relevant question. Is the Prime Minister....' Before he completed the question, Radhakrishnan commented, 'for the first time he is going to ask a relevant question.'[10] The House burst into laughter at this humorous and witty dig at the great parliamentarian that Gupta was. Once, after a question on setting up a Yoga Institute near Jammu, Bhupesh Gupta continued to ask the same question again and again, Radhakrishnan advised Gupta to resort to a good 'yogic exercise of stop talking for half an hour.'[11]

Many more instances can be cited when his unfailing sense of humour instilled a sense of loyalty to the Rules of the House and near guarantee of dignified behaviour from all the members. Nobody took any offence against his rulings or comments.

Firmness as Presiding Officer

While witty and humorous and anxious and generous to give everyone a chance to speak, Radhkrishnan was also firm in ensuring that no member crossed the limits imposed by the Rules or the decorum and

---

[9] Cited in Sudarshan Agarwal (ed.). *Dr. Sarvepalli Radhakrishnan: A commemorative Volume 1888-1988* (New Delhi, Prentice-Hall, 1988), p. 123.

[10] *Ibid.*, p. 118.

[11] *Ibid.*, p. 119.

propriety of the House. He held that merely informing the Chair was not enough. A member must have specific permission of the Chair to be able to speak on the floor of the House. He combined firmness with flexibility, caution with freedom and strength with safety. While latitude for the present need was allowed, no license for the future was given.

Again, he was always conscious and particular about maintaining a high standard in the debates and whenever there was any deterioration in it, he used to caution members about the importance of preserving the dignity of the House. Once, in the year 1955, after a heated discussion, the Chairman was constrained to observe:

> We want to maintain the good name and dignity of the House. Every one of us is interested in that as much as I am. I do not want it to be said that sometimes those discussions suggest that we are not behaving like serious, responsible members of Parliament, but rather like irresponsible professional agitators… we must be careful and preserve our good name and our dignity.[12]

Radhakrishnan never hesitated to remind members about their duties and responsibilities. One day the House had to be adjourned for want of quorum. He said on that occasion:

> I notice that for the first time during these seven or eight years, our House had to suspend business on Friday for lack of quorum. Membership of the Rajya Sabha is an honour and a distinction. It also carries with it responsibilities and obligations. If you do not carry out the latter, you damage your honour and your distinction.

[12] *Ibid.*, p. vi.

In short, it was a blessing for the people of India to have such a personality at the helm of affairs. Far from remaining a mere emollient of the constitutional mechanism, Radhakrishnan made his position one of immense significance to the nation. This was largely due to his individual qualities of independence, insularity and objectivity. In fact, he wielded more influence than power and even the most irrepressible spirit in the House did not venture to challenge his rulings. So high was the esteem in which he was held, that at his request, the Opposition leaders even withdrew their amendments that they had moved to the Motion of Thanks on the President's Address.

In this context it would be pertinent to quote the impressions expressed by some of the leaders on Radhakrishnan when they bid farewell to him in the Rajya Sabha on his retirement from the Chairmanship in order to take up the exalted office of the President of India. Jawaharlal Nehru, while speaking on this occasion, said:

> Today, I believe, is the last day when we shall have the honour of you presiding over this House. Henceforth you will preside over a more important organisation, ie. the nation itself. We are on the one hand a little sad at your leaving us here, because you have made this House with yourself as the Chairman rather a unique place and have converted it into a large family, sometimes apparently quarrelling but really a family under your guidance. On the other hand, Sir, we are of course glad that you are going to the highest office that this country has to offer and we are quite sure by being there you will exercise your charm to convert this huge nation also into a large family, what we call national integration.[13]

[13] *RS Deb.* 11.5.1962, c. 2937.

Bhupesh Gupta observed:

> ....We have always treated you as something more than a mere Presiding Officer who knows how to combine his leadership and guidance with high intelligence, good humour, tolerance and above all, with the awareness that the democratic opposition has a significant creative role to play in the fashioning of our parliamentary institutions. In the course of ten years you have, Sir, helped to build up certain traditions and ways peculiarly of your own and which are not mere copy book repetitions of either the May's Parliamentary Practice or what is said in the rigid lifeless rules and procedures.[14]

To sum up, Radhakrishnan played a significant role in setting parliamentary norms, particularly, in establishing conventions and precedents, in maintaining the dignity and decorum of the House and its members and in ensuring the high quality of parliamentary debates. His contributions to the Parliament of India in its formative period shall always remain memorable and inspire us and many coming generations.

[14] *Ibid.*, c. 2939.

Govind Ballabh Pant

"Great Son of the Himalayas"

The father figure—as I saw him

I[1]

A DISTINGUISHED son of the Himalayas, Pandit Govind Ballabh Pant was in every sense a heavyweight and a truly towering personality. One of the greatest patriots, he influenced and inspired several generations of men and women in UP and in the rest of the country.

It is a great privilege to be able to pay humble homage to a man revered by me since my early childhood. Having been born in a family of freedom fighters, I spent my formative years in the midst of intense struggle and under the benign shade and shadow of titans like Pantji. I am proud to be able to claim being among those fortunate ones

1 Largely based on the transcript of a film interview given by the author to Prakash Jha.

who not only interacted with Pandit Pant but who also received and enjoyed endearing affection and fatherly love from this great and good man whom I can place second only to Pandit Jawaharlal Nehru. I also had the privilege and the pleasure of seeing something of Pantji as a freedom fighter, as the Chief Minister of UP and then as the Union Home Minister. This happened because of my family background and then the circumstances of my own later life and career, first as an active youth leader and President of the Allahabad University Union and then as a humble servant of the Parliament of India.

Pantji and the other Congress leaders used to visit our house quite often. I remember an incident of 1936-37, when at almost midnight Pantji came to our house with some 20-25 other Congressmen. All the family members including children woke up. Almost the first thing that Pantji told my father was that all the 20-25 people were coming after touring a number of villages and were very hungry and that whatever was readily available in the House should be brought. My mother and my grandmother, who were alive then, quickly got ready. All the different flours of wheat, bajra, makki and channa available were mixed together, *Chapatties* were prepared and brought before Pantji. He enjoyed them very much and was full of appreciation for the strange mix that he had never tasted before. We were all moved.

It was possible to provide 20-25 beds and beddings for all the guests. It was winter. A bed was set up for Pantji and arrangements made for all his colleagues on the floor. Makeshift beds of grass called *Pural*, were made to provide warmth in the large rooms called *dalans*. A couple of *angithies* were also kept nearby to keep them warm as there were limited quilts and blankets to provide to everyone. I believe more than one person slept under one covering and that way they spent the night. Pantji insisted that he would sleep on the floor along with the other workers and he did. Early morning before any one of the children awoke, they were all gone.

Another incident I recall of Pantji is of the period after Independence. He had come to our town. A Reception Committee was set up and a huge reception was arranged. My father was not in politics any more. A Gandhian idealist, he had retired from public life soon after Independence in August 1947. Also, unfortunately at the time of Pantji's visit my father was down with fever. When the Reception Committee and other Congressmen received Pantji outside the city, he asked for my father. He was told that my father was unwell. The Reception Committee had arranged a procession, a large procession with Pantji on elephant back. Pantji sent his son, Raja (KC Pant) in the procession and he himself came to our residence, sat with my father and for more than an hour kept talking to him—asking about his health and trying to persuade him to again get active in politics. He told my father that winning the freedom was only half the battle, the real task of reconstruction and nation-building was only beginning and good men must not withdraw from public life. My father, however, had different views. He said, 'It may be a very narrow or limited view, but so far as I am concerned, I believe the job for the likes of me is over. Now it will be a fight for loaves and fishes of office for which, in all humility, I am not suited'. I do not know, rightly or wrongly, but my father refused to be convinced. He lived to be 94, kept serving the people in his own way until the very end in 1984, took no part in politics but always cherished his association with genial giants like Pandit Nehru and Pantji.

These two incidents of my father's association with Pantji reveal his great human qualities. The fact that despite his weight and size and his pre-eminent position as leader, he refused to sleep on a *niwar* bed offered to him but insisted upon sharing the floor with the Congress workers, speaks volumes of his humanism and of how he cared for his party workers. Again, it was no easy decision and not an ordinary gesture when he eschewed the proposal of being taken through the city at the head of a huge procession on elephant back getting hailed by cheering crowds and groups of people assembled on the two sides of the road, on roof tops and tree tops anxious to have his *darshan*. Instead, he preferred to visit an ailing Congress worker and spend an hour with him. It showed his human touch in political life and his love for his colleagues and for even ordinary party workers. That is what made him loved and respected by the people, by all his colleagues, by partymen and even by opponents.

Pantji's head used to shake because of the injuries sustained by lathi blows during the freedom struggle. As a result, even while in his fifties, Pantji looked relatively older. But, he was always full of youth and energy and the shaking of his head did not in any way diminish the dignity with which he spoke. In fact, it added to it. As workers in the student movement we were inspired by him and felt enthused by the ideas he expressed. He was one of those senior leaders who were respected by the youth for their ideals, their values and their sacrifices.

During 1946-1953, I was at the University of Allahabad, the same University from which Pantji had taken his postgraduation degrees. Incidentally, in 1949-50 I was President of the University Union and Executive Chairman of what was then called the All India University Students' Organisation. We had proposed to convene an Asian University Students' Conference. For some reasons, the government did not want that kind of a conference to take place at that time because, as Pantji later explained to me, there were developments in China and in other countries that perhaps made it inopportune to convene such a conference at that time. We had some sounding from the government about its not being advisable at that time; the government was opposed to it but did not want to say so openly. It should have been given up, perhaps, but as young men and student leaders we decided to go ahead. We continued to give statements to the press and kept writing to the Government of India and to the UP government hoping that either they allowed the Youth of Asia to meet or openly came forward to disallow or ban the proposed meet.

One fine morning, I got a telegram from the Chief Minister's office—I think it was CD Pande who sent it—asking me to come to Naini Tal and see the Chief Minister. I went to Naini Tal. I remember his residence which was on a height. We were seated in a very large drawing room. I found a number of people sitting on the floor which was well carpeted. There were some sofas all around. With a strange sense of self-respect, as a student leader, I did not like to sit on the floor and hence sat on one of the sofas. When Pantji came, I found that almost all those present touched his feet; some of them in fact fell at his feet. Pantji sat on the central sofa on which five people could sit. However only Pantji was seated on it. None of the others including some senior Ministers, leaders and workers would dare sit by his side. Since I was seated on the sofa and perhaps was the only one to do so, he enquired about me and I introduced myself. He called me and made me sit by his side on his large sofa. Thereafter, he started asking about my family and me. Then he very quickly moved on to trying to make me understand as to how it was not advisable to hold the conference at that time and how it was not in national interest. Within a couple of minutes, Pantji decided to get up. I also stood up and we both started moving out. We came to the lawn and he continued talking about the conference. I remember with great fondnes, how he admonished and scolded me but there were also moments when he talked to me very lovingly, affectionately, and tried to persuade me. I can never forget the suave pleadings and the firm admonitions and above all, the fatherly affection with which these were administered to me. When I write these words I still feel his loving hand on my shoulders and shall continue to feel it so long as I live.

Once, when I went to Pantji's residence at Naini Tal, it was early morning. We were waiting for him in his drawing room, I decided to get up and come out; by chance I saw that a big heap of files was being carried to the first floor, from one room to the bathroom. A few seconds thereafter, Pantji followed wearing a big leather belt round his waist presumably because he had some hernia trouble. Pande told me that it was quite usual for him to dispose of a large number of files in the bathroom. That made a great impression on my young mind; he would not waste even the minutes spent in the bathroom. Every morning Pantji first disposed of urgent official work and then he did his pooja (prayer and worship). Only after that he came out to meet morning visitors. While waiting for Pantji, we could hear him recite *mantras* and *shlokas* in a sonorous and sweet voice with the ringing of bells. A very secular person, Pantji in his personal life was highly religious, God fearing, and a devout Brahmin.

He was one of the most distinguished products of the University of Allahabad and almost passionately loved the university till his last day. He never refused any invitation to visit the Allahabad University. I remember that when he was the Chief Minister of UP, we invited him to visit Allahabad to address the University Union. He agreed. Purushotham Das Tandon and Pantji, both were present at the University meeting. The very first thing that he said in his speech was that when he came to the University, he again became a child and wished to sit among the students rather than on the stage. In the course of that speech, I remember he narrated how during his student days, he and Purushotham Das Tandon, apart from politics and national struggle, also took part in dramas. Once when *Merchant of Venice* was staged, Pantji was the hero and Tandon played the role of Portia. None of us knew about it. Tandonji had by then a white beard and enjoyed the thought that at one time he had played female roles with Pantji.

Pantji is widely known, apart from many other things, as a great administrator. He was one of the most distinguished Chief Ministers that any State in India ever had. The special mark of his administration, to my mind, was the humane touch he gave to it. It was said that he was one Chief Minister who knew every District Magistrate in the State by name; it was remarkable how the Chief Minister could remember the name of every single District Magistrate. He not only remembered their names, but in many cases, the names of their family members as well. Once, when Pantji was visiting Allahabad, we had gone to receive him at the Amousi Airport. The District Magistrate, (subject to correction), was, I think, one Bhargava. As soon as Pantji alighted from the plane, he called Bhargava by his first name; not only that, he immediately asked him about the well-being of his wife who was perhaps not well. Then he asked him about his children by name. Such a gesture coming from the Chief Minister could not but move any district magistrate or administrator anywhere. I believe the way he talked to Bhargava, he could be talking the same way to many other district magistrates all over the State.

I remember once I happened to be in Lucknow when Pantji was the Chief Minister. The Lucknow University students were on strike and were agitating with a long charter of demands. The students came in a large procession to the Council House. There was a lot of police bandobast. But the students, agitated as they were, were threatening to break the police cordon and enter the Council House. It was becoming difficult for the police to control that crowd. One of the officers approached Pantji. He asked them to open the gates of the Council House and allow the students to come in and be seated. The Assembly was not in session then. There was a big hotel near the Council House at that time. Within minutes, some trucks full of cold drink bottles arrived and the drinks were served to the students. All this time, Pantji remained in his chamber meeting people and doing his office work. After an hour or so, he sent word that three or four leaders of the students could come and see him and tell him what their demands were. When those leaders came, Pantji gave them piece of his mind and thoroughly scolded them for unruly behaviour. By that time, the crowd had already dispersed and those three or four students, after getting scolded went back. I do not know what happened thereafter. But that was Pantji's way of handling a difficult situation.

It hardly needs to be said that Pantji was one of the greatest parliamentarians we ever had in this country. In fact, I believe he would rank among the very best in the world. Having been in the secretariat of Parliament right from the time of the first Lok Sabha, I had the privilege of seeing him function in parliament right from the time when he came to Delhi as Home Minister in 1955. I particularly remember the way he handled the very difficult subjects of States' Reorganisation, Punjabi Suba agitation and the Official Language issues.

I remember, as a young officer, I was then in charge of Parliament's Research Service and we prepared a brochure on the States Reorganisation Commission Report containing press comments and so on. Pantji had the greatness of mentioning it on the floor of the House in his speech; he gave full-throated praise to the brochure.

Pantji's way of dealing with the Opposition was really great. He would disarm his critics by beginning with an acceptance of their arguments and by praising their points of view. And then, gradually, slowly, one by one, he would demolish all their arguments and would make them feel that there was no substance in anything that they said. It was important that his demolishing of arguments did not leave any rancour or bad feeling behind. He spoke with grace, friendliness and understanding even of the Opposition's view-point and the Opposition in return appreciated his remarks and accepted them.

It is with sadness that I remember the day when the news of Pantji's passing away reached us. Very honestly, I felt as if a very close and elderly relative from the family had passed away. At that moment somehow, I did not think of Pantji as a great parliamentarian, as a great administrator, as a great patriot, as a Great Chief Minister or as a great Home Minister. I thought of him as a person to whom I and each member of my family somehow felt very close. For each one of us, it was a personal loss.

Pantji as the Towering National Leader

Unfortunate by, studies on Pant have not received adequate academic attention. There has been no proper scientific appraisal of this great man and his work to the cause of our nation and its people.

Govind Ballabh Pant was one of the foremost leaders of our freedom struggle. Like Jawaharlal Nehru, he was a fine product of the Gandhian age. His politics was, therefore, politics moulded by that age, representing in full, the moral norms and ethical values of Mahatma Gandhi. It was the good fortune of Uttar Pradesh that such a stalwart of the stature of Govind Ballabh Pant guided its destiny at the most critical period in its history.

At the time when Pantji took up the Chief Ministership of UP, after independence, the state had to encounter the problems bequeathed by the partition of the country. When the provinces of the North Eastern Frontier, Punjab, Bengal and to a certain extent even Delhi were in virtual flames with the worst type of communal riots and killings, UP remained largely unaffected. Credit for this goes to the deft handling of the situation by the Pant government. A staunch secularist, Pant, along with his Home Minister Rafi Ahmed Kidwai, took the strongest measures to ensure that there was no communal holocaust in the State. An outstanding achievement of the his government was that it could not only rehabilitate a large number of refugees who came in the wake of partition, but also successfully keep the State away from communal disharmony and religious fanaticism.

Pantji was the Chief Minister of Uttar Pradesh for over nine years from 1946 to 1954, and during this period he could provide the State and the people a stable government efficient in law and order and known for its administrative soundness. An administrator *par excellence,* he believed that administration should be ever-responsive to the call of the times and the changing needs of the people. In his scheme of administration, the human factor always had a pivotal role. As he once said:

> The problem of administration is not mechanical. It is psychological. Perhaps it is more than that. It is human and unless everyone connected with administration is imbibed with sympathy and understanding, it is difficult for administration to yield the results which the people have a right to expect.

Pantji was one who believed that the sole goal of government was the public good. Man was created not to serve government; rather government was created to serve man, to protect him and his rights. A democrat and socialist to the core, he always strove for a welfare state.

He new fully well that democratic socialism alone could ensure justice for all. The agrarian reforms which he had effected in the state of Uttar Pradesh, in fact, speak not only of his abiding interest in the well-being of the peasantry, but also of his democratic socialistic credentials. Under the stewardship of Pandit Pant, Uttar Pradesh was first state in India to have successfully abolished the zamindari system. The existence of the zamindari system was obstructing the progress of agriculture in the State. Pant could foresee that the abolition of the system was, therefore, a prerequisite for the release of the productive forces of the economy to be followed by adequate agrarian reforms. His government thus enacted the UP Zamindari Abolition and Land Reforms Act, 1950 which abolished the zamindari system from July 1952.

Many were the difficulties the Pant government had to encounter. There was the problem of a uniform system throughout the State. There was confusion about the ultimate form of land tenure. On top of it all, the validity of the Act itself was challenged in the highest court of the land. And when the Act was declared invalid by the Supreme Court, the zamindars started leasing out their lands to frustrate the law. To counter this, the government came with a new Act which was passed on 21 May 1952; it invalidated all such illegal transactions. The Zamindari Abolition Act was certainly a very complex piece of legislation inasmuch as it involved so many people and vast areas of land. But it was a great achievement of the Pant government that such a revolutionary change in the socio-economic sphere could be accomplished peacefully and democratically. As a result, the government could assume effective and direct relations with the peasants in regard to their holdings.

Pantji attached the utmost importance to the development of democratic institutions at the grassroots level. He believed in the decentralisation of power. One of the very first acts of Pantji on his assuming the office of Chief Minister of UP in 1948 was to declare the avowed objective of his government to go in for a panchayat in every village which was vital for village upliftment. The Etawah Project, associated with the name of Albert Meyer, which set the pattern for all community projects, was started with the whole-hearted support of Govind Ballabh Pant. It was a project intended to establish an integrated approach with village level workers as the main instrument of social transformation. And ultimately, it became the prototype for Community Development and National Extension Service in our country.

Under the Pant government, the State of UP witnessed all-round progress. The UP Plan of 1950 in the formulation of which Pantji had a major role was a modest one by any modern standards. But it laid a solid foundation for the economic development of the State. Statistics are revealing. From Rs 86 crore, the allocation of the plan rose to Rs 132 crore and the State's national income rose from Rs 1,308 crore at the time of independence to Rs 1,562 crore in 1952. Despite the population increase, the per capita income also registered a growth from Rs 218.7 crore at the time of independence to Rs 241.8 crore five years later. The road construction programme was completed a year ahead of schedule. Considerable progress was achieved in the construction of houses for industrial labour. Intensive work was done under the Community Project Schemes covering more and more areas. The most noticeable advance was made in the sphere of agriculture. Food production increased substantially. The State irrigation projects had progressed satisfactorily and, in fact, it was this that played a significant role in helping the State attain the planned target of additional food production. Uttar Pradesh not only became self-sufficient but was also able to assist the deficit areas of the country. Pantji can rightly be called the maker of modern Uttar Pradesh.

In the political life of Uttar Pradesh, Pantji was the most formidable figure. As a matter of fact, from the day he became the premier of the United Provinces to the day he relinquished the office of the Chief Minister of Uttar Pradesh in 1954 to join the Union Cabinet, his position remained unchallenged. There were, of course, occasional criticisms against him, but these took place mostly in the Uttar Pradesh Congress Committee, rather than in the State legislature. But Pantji could maintain his supremacy in UP politics, especially in the Congress Party by virtue of his integrity, ability and most important of all by his democratic temper. In the fluctuating fortunes of politics, he remained a strong pillar. The economics of factional politics could never overwhelm the idealism of his politics. He never had any group of his own, not even a Kumaon group. He transcended all groups in politics. It was only natural then that he could maintain a subtle discipline in the party organisation, in the legislature party and in their inter relationship, and above all, in the politics of the State itself. It was Pantji's phenomenal success as the Chief Minister of UP and his administrative acumen that prompted Pandit Jawaharlal Nehru to bring him to Delhi as the Home Minister after the death of Rafi Ahmed Kidwai. As Home Minister, he was a second Bismarck and he could successfully complete the work of consolidating the integration of India, the great heritage left behind by Sardar Patel. His outstanding achievement was the able and statesman-like manner in which he maintained peace and law and order in the country. After Sardar Patel, he was one of the greatest Home Ministers that we had in post-Independence India.

It would be an incomplete exercise if we attempt to assess Pantji just in terms of his contributions to UP as Chief Minister alone. He was one of the greatest leaders of our country who contributed much to the development of parliamentary democracy and the institution of Parliament. He believed in liberty and equality and attached great importance to a free press. He had the highest respect for even the opposition and considered constructive criticism as an essential ingredient for the success of democracy.

As a parliamentarian, he had few parallels. The dexterity and skill with which he took part in parliamentary debates was remarkable. He was not only an able debator but could also marshal facts most vehemently and formidably. In an easy-flowing style without any bitterness or rancor, he could always successfully meet the arguments of his opponents. He was invincible he was in his arguments and this made even the Opposition to have the highest regard and respect for him. Be it in the State legislature or in Parliament, he was consulted and his guidance sought on all vital matters.

Like Sardar Patel, Pantji was head and shoulders above many of his contemporaries. Apart from all his work and achievements in public life, he was known for his intensely humane qualities which endeared him to every Indian. As Pandit Jawaharlal Nehru said:

> Govind Ballabh Pant is a big man, tall and heavy of body and slow of movement. He is a son of our mountains and carries something of their imperturbability about him. I had sometimes seen him irritated and angry, but I have never seen him lose his temper. He and I had shared together lathi blows of the police in 1928 and we had also had adjoining cells in prison. A man of outstanding ability, he was the obvious leader of the Congress Party in our province. It was an aggressive party, more so than in any other province, and not easy to manage. But by his unfailing good humour and tact and his amazing patience, he surmounted every obstacle and was liked even by his critics and opponents. He is not a revolutionary type and his whole bent is towards constitutional activity. But, like so many others in India, circumstances have compelled him to other causes. The chief criticism made of him has been that he is too good, too soft. He is indeed the perfect gentleman.

Ram Manohar Lohia

Bold and Outspoken

AN INTELLECTUAL giant nothing short of a genius, an accomplished parliamentarian with a keen sense of wit and humour, a selfless and fearless fighter, a colourful personality, a brilliant and engaging conversationalist and, a man with strong likes and dislikes. A person with a vision, along with Nehru, Jayapraksh and Narendra Deo, Ram Manohar Lohia was among the most endearing leaders that I have had the pleasure of knowing.

His greatest contribution was that of giving a new Four Pillar political philosophy, the concept of a total revolution—social and economic—and a perspective of 'Economics After Marx', of equal irrelevance of Capitalism and Communism. Lohia also created a bunch of committed young leaders. He could have contributed to the nation much more if only he had survived a simple operation at the government hospital since named after him. He laid special emphasis on social justice and massive employment generating small scale enterprises and development of appropriate technologies and new small unit machines to serve their needs.

Lohia's 'spirit of constructive militancy' and permanent 'civil disobedience', could inspire a movement against the menace of corruption. A patriot and a fighter for the values and ideals of freedom, democracy and socialism, Lohia was endowed with a sharp intellect of the biting variety. While he lived, he was something of a rebel and a stormy petrel in Indian Politics.

Lohia had an uncanny sense of humour. Once when he returned from one of his jail terms during Nehru's Prime Ministership and was asked about it, he jocularly remarked with his characteristic twinkle in the eye that the father sends me to jail but the daughter sends me packets of nice mangoes. Although an incorrigible lifelong bachelor, Lohia had many charming friends—Indian and Foreign—among the fair sex. Short statured, dark-complexioned and in no way very shapely, there was something of a magnet in his personality that attracted people, particularly women and the youth. He was very sweet and endearing in his personal relationships. He made friends easily and won an army of admirers all over the country and abroad most effortlessly.

Lohia's ancestors were Marwari businessmen settled in UP. He was educated at Akbarpur in UP and at Bombay and Calcutta and later took a doctorate from Berlin. Among the founders of the Congress Socialist Party in 1933, Secretary of the Foreign Affairs Department of the Congress Party during 1936-38 under Jawaharlal Nehru's presidentship, among the top heroes of the 1942 Quit India Movement, Lohia suffered imprisonment on more than two dozen occasions—many of them after independence. In 1947, Lohia was in the forefront of the founding of the Socialist Party with a distinct identity of its own. In 1948, it separated from the Congress completely. In 1952, Lohia became the General Secretary of the Praja Socialist Party which was formed later after a merger of the Socialist Party and the Kisan Mazdoor Praja Party (KMPP). In 1955, Lohia parted company with the PSP (Praja Socialist Party) of JP (Jayprakash Narayan), Ashok Mehta and others and formed a separate Socialist Party of India under his own chairmanship. Although there was tremendous affection between JP and Lohia, in many respects, particularly temperamentally, the two were each other's opposites. JP was highly cultured, sophisticated and gentle. Even his angry outbursts were in remarkably cool tones and tenor. Lohia had no liking for cultivated bourgeois manners. He was forthright to the extent of being blunt. He could be hard hitting in speech and never hesitated to emit fire and ridicule against his adversary.

Lohia never accepted the partition of India, and in fact till his death he remained a votary of the union of India and Pakistan in a confederation. His concept of the Independent Indian Republic included the freedom of the French and Portuguese possessions in India as also of Kailash and Mansarovar in Tibet.

Lohia had a facile pen and wrote a large number of articles, monographs, pamphlets, editorials and books in Hindi and English. Not exactly a Hindi enthusiast like Purushottam Das Tandon or Seth Govind Das, Lohia was strongly anti-English. 'Removal of English' as a top-priority programme was a matter of genuine conviction and commitment for him.

Lohia was a powerful orator. He carried the audience with him and knew how to modulate his style according to the needs of the situation and the nature of his listeners. In 1949-50, speaking at the Allahabad University Union, he created a tremendous impact on young hearts and minds. At one stage during his Hindi speech, he referred to a thrilling experience in Thailand when late in the night in his Hotel, he heard a Hindi film song being sung some distance away. With great gusto, Lohia recited the lines '*Gaon Ki Yeh Chhoriyan, Doodh ki katoriyan*' and sent the youthful audience into ruptures and rhythmic clapping.

Although a Gandhian in many ways and a believer in decentralisation of political and economic power, cottage industries and non-violence, Lohia did not very much bother about the outer trappings of Gandhian life like travelling in third class railway compartments. He travelled first and loved the good things of life. Even the very serious-minded Acharya Narendra Deo could not sometimes resist taking a dig at Lohia's taste for female company and a life lived in style.

A great lover of folklore and a *Ramcharitmanas* fan, Lohia often spoke of the tremendous potential of epics like *Ramcharitmanas* for moving the masses. He was totally opposed to caste hierarchy based on birth. He favoured more than equality to be extended to women, backward classes, Scheduled Castes, tribes and minorities. For, mere equal treatment was not enough. The aim was to bring up the down-trodden people to the general level by providing them better opportunities and creating a new class of people. On another plane, Lohia believed that a separate *biradari* or a new caste of Members of Parliament and State Legislatures was developing. They claimed all sorts of privileges and facilities not available to the common citizens of the country. And this created a wide gulf between them and the people they claimed to represent. Actually, the moment a person became a member, he joined the new elite class of MPs and they all behaved alike, irrespective of their party affiliations. Lohia often lamented that Parliament had little use for him because it was irrelevant as an instrument for bringing about the seven-point revolution that he wanted. For the same reason, he had little patience or use for the highly sophisticated and complicated rules of procedure that prevented the Members from raising on the floor of the House the woes of the people.

Lohia's famous seven points for revolution sound so contemporaneous today that they need recapitulation. These were (1) equality between men and women, (2) non-discrimination on grounds of colour of the skin, (3) special opportunities for the backward and non-recognition of caste based on birth, (4) freedom from foreign rule and setting up of a democratic order, (5) ending inequalities in accumulation of wealth and bringing about economic equality and planned growth in production, (6) privacy of citizens and democratic order, and (7) complete disarmament and recognition of *Satyagraha* as a legitimate weapon.

Lohia's theory of equidistance was based on the belief that both communism and capitalism were two sides of the same coin. Also, he was the author of the strategy of non-Congressism which had the effect of harvesting the anti-Congress forces and installing non-Congress governments of United Fronts in several States in 1967 and soon thereafter. Lohia was for reduction and rationalisation of governmental expenditure in the interest of overall efficiency and development of agriculture and industry.

He left behind no family and no property but his thoughts have not only survived but really proved to be more relevant after his death. In fact, it is during the last few years that Lohia can be said to have arrived. Lohia's creed has only now come of age. It is another matter that many leaders who now claim to represent him are more of an antithesis of his vision and views.

During his lifetime, many socialist friends betrayed Lohia and now many years after his death, some of his self-proclaimed adherents are betraying his thoughts and polluting the values of decency and socialism by their politics, personal conduct and lust for money and power. What better evidence of this could be cited than that of the MPs again and again voting for themselves higher pay, allowances, many perks and life-long pensions. This would have seemed scandalous and inexcusable to Lohia. According to a journalist friend who talked to Lohia a few days before his death, Lohia had complained that nobody listened to him. Perhaps those who are now trying to build edifices and memorials in his name and garlanding his pictures and statues on his birthdays were the people who listened to him the least.

Purushottam Mavalankar

Ability to Stand-up and Say "No"

DIOGENES, A philosopher in ancient Greece used to roam the market place of Athens full of men, in broad daylight, with a lantern in hand. When once asked about what he was searching for, he replied: 'I am looking for a man. Men are so rare these days'. Since those days, men have become rarer.

A noble son of illustrious parents, Purushottam Ganesh Mavalankar was indeed a man the whole nation can be proud of. He was a good man, a gem of a man, a superb human being. Words fail to describe him.

A handsome and charming personality, Mavalankar(Jr) was endowed not only with brilliance of mind and love for learning but qualities of heart that endeared him to one and all. There was a radiance and sublimity in his ever smiling face. Highly cultured and polished, he was amiable and suave in manners and a good friend. But, he was also a no-nonsense man and could get angry at any attempt to mislead him by falsehood or cunningness.

A true patriot, parliamentarian and political scientist, Mavalankar was also a public man and a politician but of a different vintage.

Socrates said, 'When the conscience is sick, you must stand up even if the whole world is against you'. And Mavalankar literally stood up to be heard and counted on the floor of Parliament more than once during the Emergency aberration in the history of India's democratic experiment even when he knew that the might of the state and the majority of his peers in Lok Sabha were against him.

Elected to Lok Sabha as an independent candidate, Professor Mavalankar remained above political party considerations and took an objective stand on every issue on merits and according to his own insights.

He very scrupulously maintained his independence in Parliament and outside. He never succumbed to the lure of office of Minister or the like even though it could be his for the asking only if he was willing to give up his 'independent' status and join the Party.

Mavalankar never spoke in Parliament merely to gain media attention and publicity. He always followed rules of parliamentary etiquette and decorum and never spoke without prior study and preparation. Naturally, therefore, he was widely respected and heard with attention.

While he was conscious of his duties to his constituents and performed them to the best of his ability, while functioning in Parliament as a Member of the House of the People, he meticulously considered himself to be a Member of the Parliament of India charged with the responsibility of thinking of the problems of the people of the entire country from an overall national perspective.

A man of principles in politics may appear to be a contradiction in terms today but Mavalankar was one such. He contested election for a seat in Lok Sabha and won. But unlike almost all other members, he did not have to begin his parliamentary career with a lie in the return of election expenses filed with the Election Commission. He had kept his election campaign expenditure strictly within the prescribed limits. No camouflage of expenditure by fans or friends was indulged in and there was no question of a political party spending anything on his election because he was not any party's candidate. When Professor Mavalankar found that it was no more possible for an independent with modest means to contest an election, he decided to withdraw from parliamentary politics. Even persuasions from friends did not work as he was not prepared to compromise with standards of rectitude and integrity to collect and spend tainted money to contest elections. Today, when public life has become synonymous with contesting elections and to fight an election to Lok Sabbha, on an average several crores are mentioned as the minimum necessary, Mavalankar's feat may appear to be a piece from some fiction but it is true and very much from a real life story.

A second instance of adherence to principles that comes to mind is that of the stand taken by Mavalankar on the issue of Members of Parliament voting for themselves post-retirement pensions for life. It may be recalled that a Bill for the purpose was brought forward and passed during the Emergency. Earlier, when a State Assembly had passed a similar Bill, Mavalankar had written to Prime Minister Indira Gandhi how it was 'wrong in ethics and improper in law' for the members to vote for 'all past, present and future MLAs of that State for the benefit of receiving life pension'. He further wrote: 'I cannot understand how elected members, in their capacities as chosen representatives, go about providing for their future in such a manner. I am sure you will share my disgust with such a piece of legislation which is both unusual and unfortunate.' Mrs Gandhi replied that the point was well taken and that it was 'difficult to justify such a law at a time when there is need for utmost economy and austerity.'

Obviously later, Indira Gandhi forgot all this. But not Professor Mavalankar. He stoutly opposed the Bill for pension for MPs. He believed:

> Membership of a representative assembly must not become a professional career, much less a potent instrument for profiteering for the daredevils and the pushing souls!... Parliamentary and public life is an avenue and an opportunity to serve the people, it can never be a job or a profession in the ordinary or routine sense of the term earning a pension on retirement! An MP's work is a calling, a challenge, and not job or a profession.

Not only did Mavalankar oppose the Bill, even after it became law, he refused to draw throughout his life any pension from the public exchequer. Under the law, he could have drawn handsome monthly pension for some 25 years. In contrast, in subsequent years, members have only been increasing their perks, monthly payments and life pensions unashamedly. Once the members of Parliament in the two Houses went so far as to adopt unanimously, within minutes, without debate, a Bill allowing life pension only after one year's service as an MP. It was the ninth Lok Sabha and one looked in vain for a Mavalankar to stand up. While in retreat at his home in Ahmedabad, he must have shuddered to read about it in the newspapers.

A student of the legendary Prof Harold Laski, Mavalankar (Jr) established the Harold Laski Institute of Political Science at Ahmedabad under his dynamic and activist Directorship. A large number of events were regularly organised at the institute and many monographs published. It was a pleasure to see the very well maintained library of the Laski Institute. However, some years back when Mavalankar's health did not any more allow him to attend to the work of the Institute, he closed it. He took meticulous care to return by cheque to all the Life Members proportionate amount of the subscription paid by them. Who would bother to think about such things today?

If a portrait of an ideal parliamentarian is to be painted or a model presented through a study, Mavalankar's name would emerge as an eminently suitable choice. His conduct as a practitioner of healthy value-based politics with a spirit of sacrifice and service can be a worthy example for the present and future generations. His own greatest ambition and hope in all humility was that his work and speeches in Parliament, to use his own words, 'may keep the Torch of Freedom burning a little more against any tornado of authoritarianism, and may help light up the path of democracy all the time.'

I have very fond memories of my personal association and long friendship with Purushottam Ganesh Mavalankar. I had the privilege of having been with the Parliament right from the days of the venerable first Speaker, Dada Saheb Ganesh Vasudev Mavalankar. At first, as a young officer in Parliament, I saw Mavalankar (Jr) usually from a distance when he visited Parliament during Dada Saheb's time or when his mother was a member or even later. My first close personal contact with him was when I was invited to inaugurate a Seminar on Youth Unrest at Baroda and he was in the Chair. This was in 1967. Thereafter in 1971, he joined the Parliament as a Member of Lok Sabha and for some six years we met often and discussed many matters of national and parliamentary concern.

Even when he ceased to be a Member, we continued to meet at Delhi, Ahmedabad or elsewhere during personal visits and sojourns or at Seminars and Conferences. I remember that he always agreed to my requests to write articles or papers and to come to participate in seminars and symposia until his health deteriorated and it became difficult for him to write or travel. It was a pleasure and privilege for me and my wife to pay our respects to the revered mother of Mavalankar (Jr) at 'Gopika'. Later she was honoured at a special function at the Central Hall of Parliament House and she honoured us by a visit to our official residence at Aurangzeb Road in New Delhi. My wife and I also remember having enjoyed the hospitality of Mavalankars (Purnima and Purshottam) at 'Gopika'.

One of my proudest possessions is the book titled *No, Sir*, authored by PG Mavalankar and presented to me with an affectionate inscription by 'Purnima and Purshottam Ganesh Mavalankar' on 22 August 1979, at New Delhi. During his lifetime, he wanted me to deliver the first lecture in the Professor Mavalankar Lecture Series. Neither he nor I could imagine that its postponement would make it a Memorial Lecture. It is with sadness that I recollect my share in the postponement. For, if I had known that he was preparing to leave us, I would have done anything to come to Ahmedabad to once again speak with him while he was adorning the Chair. But, now having known Anand and Ashutosh, I fervently believe that both Dada Saheb and Purshottam Mavalanakar are present and alive in them. May they live long.

MISCELLANY

National Resurgence from the North-East

Past, Present and Future

THE SUN rises from the East. It always will. If the preambular objective of the 'unity and integrity of the nation' enshrined in the Constitution has to be achieved, and if the vision of national resurgence has to materialise, we need to begin from the North-East. If we really want to develop better social communication between the people inhabiting the North-East and those in the rest of the country and create a climate of real pan-Indian fraternity, the New Delhi colonial mindset of regarding the North-East territory as being theirs—the approach that it belongs to them—must change and be transformed into generating among those in the North-East—tribals and others—a feeling and belief that the entire country belongs to them, that it is inalienably theirs and that it is as much for them as for other citizens to fight for its security, unity, integrity and well-being.

The North-East

What we have come to call the North-East of India includes the seven States of Assam, Nagaland, Manipur, Tripura, Meghalaya, Mizoram and Arunachal Pradesh. Although geographically not contiguous, Sikkim is also in the North-East and is, therefore, now often added to the list of the seven sister States. It would be wrong to regard the North-East as a monolith. It is not a single homogeneous political or ethno-cultural entity. Its population is very heterogeneous. In ethnic, religious, cultural and linguistic parameters, North-East is as diverse and plural as India itself. It is composed of numerous—some 250—tribes, sub-tribes and close communities. Their customs and traditions, languages, icons and beliefs vary widely. The number of live dialects is estimated to be nearly 400. There are differences not only between tribals and non-tribals but also between tribals in hills and tribals in plains. There are disputes between different States and tribes. Assam has boundary disputes with almost all its neighbours. There are differences among tribes and sub tribes. Even among insurgents and undergrounds, there are numerous separate groups. Also, there is sizeable non-tribal population of people from outside the North-East. Within the States, none can be said to be inhabited by a single tribe or ethnic group. On the other hand, they and tribes that cut across State boundaries, eg the Nagas spread over beyond Nagaland are demanding an enlarged homeland that covers all the Naga inhabited areas. North-East is not a tribal majority area. Assam and Tripura are dominated by non-tribals and even in others, all tribals are at best 60% only.

The Past

Traditional tribal cultures predate the arrival of the British and are an inseparable part of Indian culture. The known history of these regions goes back to some two thousand years. It is noteworthy that people here also had a sense of history. This is borne out by the Buranjis maintained by the Ahoms in Assam or Cheitoron Kumbaba by the

Manipuris in the early years of the Christian era. In 1228 AD, Tai Prince Chowlung Sinkapha was attracted to what he called the land of Golden Gardens. He sowed the foundations of the kingdom of Assam by bringing together under its umbrella the people inhabiting the lands of the present seven sisters. The Ahoms ruled for nearly 600 years. They were known for their all inclusive approach, for respecting separate identities and promoting a policy of coexistence of different tribes and communities.

Before the British, all the tribes and clans enjoyed primordial independence even if it meant perennial fights with each other. A major effort to integrate all the areas in the North-East was made by the British colonial rulers. Besides the sizeable tribal population in Assam, there were the 'excluded and partially excluded areas' that were placed under the personal rule of the Governor. Also, there were areas along the frontiers which were covered under the North-East Frontier Agency (NEFA).

When India's independence and partition came in 1947, the tribal people of the North-East were anxious to preserve their distinct identity and culture.

The founding fathers of India's Constitution appointed a special Sub-Committee to study and examine the prevailing administrative set-up and institutions among the tribal people of North-East India. They recognised the necessity of a different political and administrative machinery for the areas in the then Assam inhabited by Hill tribes. Articles 244 and 275 and the Sixth Schedule made appropriate provisions with the objective of (a) maintaining the distinct customs, socio-economic and political culture of the local people, (b) preventing their exploitation by the more advanced neighbouring people of the plains, and (c) allowing the tribal people to develop and govern themselves according to their customs, traditions and practices through their representatives—elected or selected. Autonomous District Councils were provided so that the Hill tribes could freely manage their affairs in their own way and work out ways and means to protect and safeguard their traditions, customs, languages and dialects, culture and ethnic identity.

As at present, Schedule Sixth contains provisions as to the administration of Tribal Areas in the States of Assam, Meghalaya, Tripura and Mizoram. Fifth Schedule applies to Scheduled Tribes and Scheduled Areas in other States. On the whole, the Constitution puts great premium on the protection of the identity and rights of the tribal people.

It may sound ironical but as the Meghalaya Governor Moosahary once said, it is a fact that distance between the North-East and India increased after Independence and Partition in 1947. Partition snapped the rail route of transportation to and from NE region to rest of North East through West Bengal. It was later connected by laying a track through the narrow corridor linking Assam with West Bengal. The problem of land hunger and the continuous movement of populations to the lush green pastures of North-East became more acute and created and continues to create serious demographic distortions. Traditional cultural identities felt threatened when in disregard of the ideals of unity in diversity, coexistence and non-interference in each other's beliefs, efforts were made to assimilate peaceful smaller cultures into the larger and dominant groups. Anyone who has travelled through the interior areas of the States in the North-East and interacted with the common people—specially the youth—at the grassroots level would agree that they are simple, peace-loving and extremely hospitable and inherently friendly people.

The Present

In the recent past, most unfortunately, North-East evoked images of turbulence, violence and insurgencies. It was considered to be somewhat separate and remote from rest of the country. The people in the North-East themselves felt isolated, neglected and discriminated against. But things are changing. Even in antiquity when the concept of a nation State was not known, the consciousness of India as a geographical unit and as one civilizational and cultural continuum existed. Ancient history and mythology present enough evidence of close links between what we call the North East and other parts of India.

The basic problem in the North-East today—as in the rest of India—is that of tremendous governance deficit. There is a disconnect between the people and their own elected representatives. Militancy and insurgency are also perhaps only volcanic eruptions against lack of governance and widespread corruption. While some of the insurgency groups may be really inspired by an ideology or the urge to fight injustice, there may also be others for whom, like politics today, it is another lucrative business or industry for earning quick and huge amounts of money. Because some have amassed lot of wealth, those left behind feel more wronged and exploited. The youth in the North-East have the same problems, ambitions and success orientation as the youth elsewhere.

The senior administrator, Toki Blah has flagged the point that the traditional democratic systems in the North-East were based on values of participation, truth and intense community spirit of social cohesion and of sharing and caring. They were inclusive and had great integrative potential. In the NE, life of the people revolves round their communities. Traditional democratic practices are averse to monetary value system and to concepts of majority rule. On the other hand, the present democratic politics, electoral and party systems are terribly divisive, breed corruption and insensitivity and lead to a disconnect between governance and politics. Political parties, need for vote banks, role of money, muscle and mafia power, criminalisation of politics etc. have made efficient delivery systems and people-centric governance impossible. While, in recent years, there has been some progress and perceptible affluence has come, the problem of evolving an effective delivery system and management mechanisms remain. Obviously, there is a need to revisit the functioning of the traditional democratic institutions and marry them with modern institutions under the Constitution. Also, there is every need to redefine the meaning of development for the North-East, to work for better resource management and internal resource-generation.

As things stand in the North-East, the present system is seen as divisive, breeding corruption and insensitivity. There is tremendous dichotomy and disconnect between the ethos and aspirations of the people and the prevailing political processes along with a complete disregard of the security, well-being and interests of the people and their urge for preserving their traditions, culture, values and democratic institutions. The crux of the problem is multiplicity of agencies, overground and underground, creating administrative bottlenecks, shifting of responsibilities, colossal expenditure and frittering away of scarce resources on too many delivering too little to serve people's interests. There is a total lack of performance and of accountability. It is necessary to consolidate and rationalise the existing governance mechanisms to maximize benefits to the citizens, to work for good citizen-centric governance which delivers on development while protecting the traditions, culture, democratic institutions and identity of the Hill tribes. In fact, there is every case for redefining the meaning of development. Mere receipt and expenditure of large funds are no indicators of people-centric development leading to a better quality of life and a better sense of human happiness and over all security.

Look East and Act East Policy

North-East is the only region in the sub-continent which borders on several Asian nations like Myanmar, Bhutan, Nepal, China and Bangladesh. That makes it important from the angle of national security. The 1962 Chinese aggression forcefully underlined the security issue. North-East has almost become a corridor between South East Asia, China and India and can play a vital role as a bridge between India and South East Asia. India's more than two decades old Look East Policy (LEP), the much enhanced interest and strategic participation by India in the ASEAN now made more meaningful with

Modi's call for the Act East policy make the North-East of India a more important player as a gateway to farther East. AEP is bound to impact the development story of NE. The cultural and racial ties of the NE people with the SE can also be seen as a positive asset opening up better trade and strategic advantages. In the words of Late PA Sangma:

> India's Look East Policy has to look to North-East first. Today, one-third of India's trade volume is with South East Asia which has emerged as the largest trading partner with India but it has had no impact on the country's North-East. India's Look East Policy is meaningless if it does not have any impact on the region.

This is despite the fact that much more cross-border trade is known to be illegal and not part of the official records. Suitably legalising it would be to the advantage of all the countries involved.

The location of NE naturally makes the area strategically important in geo-political terms both externally and internally. But, it should not become a pretext for New Delhi to centralise power in its hands and seek to control the NE. Many problems in federal polity have their source in the so-called centre trying to dominate the constituent units or impose its will in matters outside its jurisdiction. The approach of the UPA government buying support to protect its tottering coalition governments was also to prove counter-productive in the long run.

Without undermining the separate identity and autonomy of the States, some thinkers advocate coming together and integrating the seven or the eight States of the North-East into a NE Economic Union that would be able to exert more pressure on New Delhi in favour of demands from NE. There are others who plead for economic integration of NE States with their SE neighbours. Thus, the North East Council Act provided for setting up a North East Council with equal representation of all the eight States. The Council was to prepare a regional plan of economic development of all the NE States. The North-East Council and the Ministry of North Eastern Region speak of their own road map of development in the following words:

> The development vision should be based on the needs and aspirations of the people. They are tired of insurgency, lack of governance and stagnation. A strong NE can engage with global economy.

Nagaland Chief Minister, Neiphiu Rio, pleading for stepping up infrastructural development, had once suggested construction of a highway along the Indo-Myanmar border which could 'not only open the area for trade and economic development, but will also serve as the highway for patrolling the international border and for checking illegal trafficking of drugs and arms through the famous Golden Triangle'.

Similarly, the then Union Minister, Jairam Ramesh had said that, 'for India's North East, the future lies in emotional and political integration with the rest of the country and economic integration with the rest of Asia'. Even from outside, there had been powerful voices in favour of NE emerging as an economic entity in its own right. The Kunming initiative by China proposed 'an economic integration of Yunnan Province, Myanmar, India, NE India, and Bangladesh—a sort of sub-regional grouping in a larger regional trading agreement.'

It is most unfortunate and a sad commentary on our policy makers that more than two decades after the announcement of Look East Policy, and now the Act East Policy, North-East is still far from benefitting. The progress on building the necessary infrastructure to make North-East really a Gateway to the East is woefully slow. However, there are ample indicators of the approach and agenda of the present Modi Government having a better hold on the problems and the importance of the States in the North-East of the country. There is evidence of genuine anxiety to ensure that the road to South East Asia passes through the North-East. Earlier , the effort appeared to be to bypass North-East. According to a write-up, even though India's relationship with ASEAN had been raised to a strategic partnership, the pace of infrastructural development remained low and below the national average, despite all the priority promises under the Look East and Act East policies. Upto 2014, only 400 km of the 621 km Assam portion of the East-West Corridor was completed. Besides, most of the Integrated Check Posts and border trade points on international border in the North-East were yet to see the light of day. With all it's vitality and charm, hopefully, North-East will no more consider left out, underdeveloped, disturbed and alienated.

The Future

Unfortunately, in 1947, power was transferred by the British colonial masters to a political party but the people did not feel the glow of freedom or the transfer of power to their hands. This was much more so in the North-East. In fact, many of them felt they had more freedom earlier, that the traditional institutions gave them more freedom and power to take their own decisions. As someone said, during the British rule, the Commissioner played tennis and allowed the people to live their lives. Some of their freedom and identity is allegedly being taken away under the slogans of democracy, development and national integration. Undoubtedly, this has got to change and fundamental restructuring and reorientation of the administrative system would be necessary. Traditional community institutions have to be identified, respected and empowered to take decisions. To say that any negotiations can takes place or changes considered only within the Constitution of India is meaningless and makes no sense. The Constitution has been amended 99 times—on an average, once in every seven months—and can be amended again and again, if national interest requires. It is only fair that we look ahead and put all our might to ensure that consensus is built on plan for the regeneration of India in the North-East. In all humility some other suggestions may be offered. These are both a political and a strategic necessity and a pre-condition for economic growth, trade and industry.

It is necessary that the North-East is no more seen as remote and inaccessible. It should be opened up with much improved connectivity, internal and external and infra-structural facilities. Railways and roads need to be considerably expanded. Improving rural connectivity would also help promote higher agricultural productivity in the food sector. Contacts—individual and group—between intellectuals and professionals—administrators, agriculturists, lawyers and others—need to grow much faster. North-East should be brought closer to the over-all consciousness of the rest of the country. It is even more important to throw open the rest of India to the North-East and its youth. The extent that it has happened in recent years, is a welcome sign. Those in North-East must feel that they have as much right over everything everywhere in India as any other citizen anywhere in the country. If that happens, the rhetoric would yield place to an agenda of development and attending to the problems of backwardness, unemployment, lack of industry and infrastructure and delivery of inexpensive and prompt justice. Illegal migration needs to be dealt with firmly and without Vote bank considerations. It is most desirable to improve the detection and deportation machinery. It has been presumably been responsible for the NE population rising at a rate faster than all-India average.

The most foundational premise of democracy is that sovereign power belongs to the people. If so, people everywhere, in every part of the country, at every level, should be able to govern themselves as they like, through institutions of their own choice. Top-down models of power-sharing and of development have failed. Imposition from above proves most painful. The only way is to work for a Gandhian bottom-up instead of the present top-down model of local autonomies going up to evolve into a multi-tier federal or confederal polity with the maximum power remaining with the lowest unit or the people at the grassroots, whether it is a traditional democratic institution, an Autonomous District Council or a Panchayat. The European model of the subsidiarity principle comes also very close to the Gandhian concept of concentric circles. Only what cannot be done at the lower level should be entrusted to the next higher level with power at the top remaining minimal and in limited areas like foreign affairs and defence. The overall shape of the polity may be that of a Union of autonomies at various levels. This would take care of all fears of attempts at assimilation or submergence of tribal or sub-tribal identities.

North-East is one of the most beautiful, enchanting and endearing areas of the country. The exquisite ambience, fascinating environs, wild life, unique flora and fauna, green hills, radiant rivers and charming people have tremendous potential to make North-East a great destination for both domestic and foreign tourists. In a sense, NE is also a land of mystery. Besides this prospect of the North-East developing into an Asian tourism hotspot, the advantage of English education, facility in that language and computer literacy can help the North-Eastern youth to develop information technology business parks and make their area an international IT hub with plenty of BPOs (Business Process Outsourcing) and KPOs (Knowledge Process Outsourcing) all around. Also, there is considerable scope for trading in organic agricultural and horticultural products, medicinal and herbal plants, floriculture, handlooms and handicrafts. The area is rich in natural resources that are awaiting to be harnessed for the well-being of the people. Besides many minerals, crude oil, forest wealth, coal, building material, arable land, paddy, tea plantations etc. North-East has plentiful water as well which is increasingly becoming a resource of overriding importance. NE can legitimately claim records of the highest rainfall and of being recipient of billions of cusecs of rain water. It is said that in 21st century water may become a commodity as precious as petrol. NE can also develop as a store house of renewable hydro-power.

Our age-old principle of Unity in Diversity has to be understood in the right spirit and needs to be reinforced. Diversity is not necessarily divisive. Unity does not mean uniformity. In democracy, existing diversity has to be accepted and rejoiced at for it's potential to lead to unity. In India, diversities of various sorts are misused by parties and politicians for building their vote-banks. On the other hand, multiple diversities can be used also as a source of great strength for the unity and integrity of the nation. Diversity in the North-East, as in the rest of India, has to be respected as an existential reality but it cannot be forgotten that the aim is unity and that is what is meant by the principle of Unity in Diversity.

Actualisation of the potentialities of the North-Eastern region of India to contribute to the strengthening of the nation calls for an understanding of the ethos and needs of the people in the States in the region, ensuring good governance, peace, rule of law, respect for traditional freedoms and institutions, end of insurgency and extortions and above all a bottom up approach of power in the hands of the people at the grassroots level. Now, with the BJP in the government in majority of States in the North-East as in the rest of India and also at the Union level, one hopes the present leadership should be able to achieve its avowed goal of less government and more governance and of taking all the people together on the road to development (Sabka sath sabka vikas). We can then look forward to realising the long-term vision of the emergence of the new India rejuvenated by the rays of the sun rising from her North-East.

East Meets West

The Shifting Focus

ON THE somewhat abstract and abstruse theme of East meeting West, what immediately comes to mind are the oft-quoted lines of Rudyard Kipling:

Oh! East is East and West is West
And never the twain shall meet

What is not so-often quoted are the lines that follow:

But there is neither East nor West
Border, nor breed, nor birth.

One also remembers Northrop's book, and his epistemological concepts. For him, in Eastern thought, world is an "undifferentiated aesthetic continuum" with reality being"all connected and unified"while in Western thought reality is represented by separate, well differentiated objects. In the East, it is done by intuition and in the West by postulation.

Ravi Shankar Foundation's official fusion music recordings with the Beatles are also titled, 'East Meets West'.

The earth is round and moving. What is West and what is East depends upon where the viewer is. If he keeps moving West, he shall reach what now is East to him and vice versa.

East is more ancient by many thousands of years. When East meets West, Swami Vivekananda, Aurobindo, Ravindranath Tagore, Radhakrishnan, Md Iqbal, Yogananda Paramhansa, Gandhi, Nehru and others emerge. It is another matter that the last named, Nehru, was not so much from the East. He was more of an English gentleman who had later to make a discovery of India, looking at India's past and present through a Western prism.

In the words of Aurobindo, 'East and West have always met and mixed more or less closely, they have powerfully influenced each other and at the present day are under an increasing compulsion of Nature and Fate to do so more than ever before. There is a common hope, a common destiny, both spiritual and material, for which both are needed.'

It is important for all nations to understand the urgency of meeting the crisis of our times and fulfilling their common destiny. While the West has made more significant strides in modern Science and technology including pursuit of material progress, the Eastern mind and particularly we in India remained more wedded to spiritual pursuits, development of higher consciousness and unraveling the secrets of the self. The West has concentrated more and more on the external world while the East has been concerned with the supreme truth of the spirit, with self within as the sole reality. The Western man looked outside and tried to understand the phenomenon while the Easterner looked within and got involved in analysing the Self.

When the West came to India, it conquered, colonised and plundered the people. When the East landed in the West, it carried the message of universal brotherhood, spiritualism, respect for all religions and Yoga. For close to a thousand years, India was subjected to barbaric invasions from the West and for a similar period, she was subjugated by different colonial masters from the West as well. One invader took great pride in having killed a hundred thousand heathens on a single day on our soil. Until the 18th century, India was one of the richest countries in the world. In the next 100 years she had its worst famines with around 25 million people dead. The British masters derided the precepts of Indian culture and traditions and imposed Western values and concepts. The impact was sinister and lasting.

Even after Independence, the Constitution that came from the Constituent Assembly was not made by 'We the people of India'. The Constitution makers were some of the wisest men and women but it cannot be denied that the leadership was largely foreign educated, Western oriented and nurtured in British concepts and culture or fascinated by British institutions. Neither the ethos and genius of India nor the views of Aurobindo, Gandhi or JP seemed to have influenced them. Seventy-five per cent of the Government of India Act, 1935, read with the Cabinet Mission Plan, 1946, and the Indian Independence Act 1947—all the three documents owed their authorship to the British. Seen thus, the Constitution of independent India was made more by the British than by us.

A slave looks up to his master as a model and an ideal. He is anxious to copy. It was natural that we looked up to the system and the institutions of our rulers as the best. No wonder we adopted not only the English style of dressing, education and language but also the whole of their administrative, legal and political system. Even during the early days of the freedom struggle, one of the Congress demands used to be that the British should concede to their Indian subjects the same institutions and freedoms that they themselves enjoyed back home. The seeds of the colonial model of government in India can be traced back to this demand. Also, it is said that those fighting against their masters were not really fighting against the evil of slavery but they were eager to themselves take the place of their masters and have slaves working under them.

What actually happened on independence of India was that ordinary people in their fields and hamlets did not feel the glow of freedom on their faces or the transfer of power to their hands. The colonial model continued. Even today, the source of many of our problems of lack of good, citizen-friendly, clean, development-oriented, corruption-free governance is in the continuation of this Western colonial model which was designed to divide and rule. A time comes in history when urgent action becomes a categorical imperative. It seems, at last that time has come. We must seize the opportunity and bring about necessary systematic reforms in governance in order to enable us to repossess ourselves and the soul of our ancient nation. It is now or never. The opportunity may not recur and if it is missed, the consequences may be disastrous for our democratic polity. Also, without necessary political reforms to discard the colonial model, neither economic nor judicial, administrative, educational or other reforms are likely to succeed or survive.

The latest Western offensive is in the much bandied about globalisation. There is nothing wrong or new in the concept of the world being one. But, it is to be noted that there is a fundamental difference in the Western and Indian approaches.

While we need development, economic growth is not everything. India cannot afford to sacrifice the noble values of her culture and high principles of her spiritual heritage at the alter of higher GDP and GNP growth. Quality of life and human worth cannot be measured in economic terms. The West is wrong in considering man as a machine, a commodity or merely as a resource to be developed for maximisation of production and profits. The Western concept of human beings as a resource has become fashionable and often got embedded in our management and official discourse today. In fact, human personality—both individual and collective—should be regarded as the ultimate end purpose for whose development all the resources have to be harnessed. For thousands of years, the highest thinking in India has been of the superiority of moral and spiritual values to material wealth and worldly attainments.

Sacrifice of self interest to help and serve others has always commanded respect and love of the people. The highest ideals of life have included *Asteya, Aparigraha, Santosh,* minimisation of wants and simple living. Sustainable consumption is more important than what is being talked of as sustainable development or production.

Those who always rant about India's past greatness cannot afford to forget that there was much in our history for which we may have to hang our heads in shame. For example, a foreign invader came, looted, murdered, ruled and while leaving left his slave to rule over us and we had the slave dynasty ruling over our great land. We still eulogise its brave queen Razia Sultan. But, all the same, we need to give up the perennial tendency to deprecate our culture and traditions. Instead of taking pride in our own achievements and advanced culture, we have been looking Westwards with sad consequences. To the extent that the society has come to consider affluence, power, material success and competitive consumerism as supreme values, it is sick. What is needed is a new beginning. India has a destiny to realise and a vision to give to the West. The world today needs ancient India's core values and her message more than ever before. The anguished world of today needs a vision and light that only India of tomorrow can provide. The soul of India shall once again rise, awakening will dawn, light will shine, national regeneration will follow. Time has come to fulfil Sri Aurobindo's prophesy that 'the sun of India's destiny would rise and fill all India with its light and overflow India and overflow Asia and overflow the world'.

Nations that lose their vision perish. Societies that fail to provide to their succeeding generations their heritage, the quintessence of the accumulated wisdom of centuries and their system of values are relegated to debris. The rubble and the shambles of history and the stories of dead civilisations are a mute testimony to many such fallen stars.

Thousands of years ago, our common ancestors asked themselves a question: Who am I? where did I come from? What is the aim of life and what heights of perfection can I reach? The highest Upanishadic philosophy of *Advait* teaches us that we are not sinners needing redemption; every man is divine and there is the same *Atman* in every being. In reality, one is only *Atman*. Thus conceived, there is no high or low and no scope for disrespecting another person or for any discrimination on grounds of his race, caste, religion, place of birth, colour, creed or the like. Human personality owes its place of pride and honour and spirit of equality and oneness to the same divine—eternal, infinite and immortal—within each one of us. This is the most ancient and the most pristine concept of secularism where each other person is regarded as *tat tvamsavi*. The sphere of 'I' gets so widened that it comes to include within it entire humanity. One comes to see everyone in oneself and oneself in everyone else. The suffering of the other becomes ones own. In the words of Walt Whitman:

> I do not ask the wounded man, how he feels,
> I myself become the wounded man.

The individual comes to feel and realise within himself the microcosm of the whole universe. Once the drop knows that it is water, the drop and the limitless sea become one and the same. The sense of the other, of duality, disappears. *Aham Brahmasmi* or *Shivoham* is not different from the concept of *Analhak* and to realise that there is nothing sectarian or merely religious in the Indian concept of self, one has only to look at the thoughts of Islamic philosophers like Al Gazali, Ibnul Arabi, Al Farabi, Ibne Sina, Jallaluddin Rumi and our own Md Iqbal. Iqbal's *Asrar i Khudi* (Secrets of the Self) and *Javid Nama* echo much of Vedantic thought. Jawaharlal Nehru once told Norman Cousins:

> We are in search of our soul. We are groping and trying for some kind of adjustment—integration, if you like—of our national life, our international as well as individual lives.

Much is made of the great liberal and progressive Western concept of Secularism. There, it is known to have emerged from a conflict between the authorities of the Church and the State. The conflict was sought to be resolved by a separation between the two. In India, a more genuine Secularism was a practice of very long standing going back to Vedic and Upanishadic times. The Rigveda has declared the ultimate reality as:

Ekam sat (or *tat ekam*), *viparah bahudha vadanith*

Truth is one, the wise call it by various names.

All ways to search the truth are equally valid. The *Vedas* exhort us to 'let good thoughts come to us from everywhere'. In the *Bhagawad Gita*, Lord Krishna assures the adherents of all religions that whosoever they may pray to, their prayers reach the same one God. The culture of Hinduism has given India an unrivalled tradition of religious freedom, tolerance and respect for all faiths. It was born of the consciousness that truth could never be the monopoly of any sect or creed and that others may be equally right in their convictions. The ancient ideal that has survived in the consciousness of millions of ordinary Indians has been that of happiness and welfare of all:

Sarve bhavantu sukhinah, sarve santu nirmaya.

or

Sarvesham mangalam bhavatu, sarve bhavantu sukhinah

or

Sabka Saath, Sabka Vikas

Like Secularism, another concept which is paraded as a great Western gift is that of Human Rights. Actually, there is nothing entirely Western in it. The idea can be traced to the most ancient Eastern texts. In the words of an enlightened French scholar:

> India holds the key to the world's future, for India is the only nation that still preserves in the darkness of her Himalayan caves, on the luminous Ghats of Benares, in the hearts of her countless yogis, or even in the minds of her ordinary folk, the key to the planetary evolution, its future and its hope.

Non-Violence and Peace

Role of Education

WE LIVE in turbulent times. Events today move at the speed of light. We have dissected the nuclei of the atom and unleashed its enormous energy. With the fear of the nuclear trigger, all-out war has perhaps ceased to be much of a possible option, the choice being between coexistence in peace and coextinction or MAD (Mutually Assured Destruction) in war. Today the greatest dangers to peace come more from religious fundamentalism, terrorism and subversion—external and internal. They threaten human survival at the level of the individual, the nation and globally.

In the context of the continuous threats of turmoil, terror and proxy wars, we need to heed the voices of sanity and peace more than ever before. It is time that peace movements round the globe are rejuvenated and strengthened. There is nothing nobler than the pursuit of peace.

As far as non-violence is concerned, even though the connotation of this word seems to be negative, it is, in fact, a positive concept. Just as peace is not merely the absence of war, non-violence also is not merely the absence of violence. It is a positive state of harmony and love and of doing good even to evil doers. The concept of non-violence and peace in its widest sense, encompasses truth, justice, love, compassion and equality for all everywhere. For Mahatma Gandhi, non-violence was the supreme value of truth. It is synonymous with love and truth. It exists not only for sadhus but for all the human beings. It is not for the cowardly and the weak, it is the weapon of the strong and the brave. It calls for great strength of character and courage of spirit within.

On an individual level, non-violence means not hurting others by words, thought or action and really feeling hurt in case of injury caused to another, even one's enemy. Non-violence includes justice and is inseparable from compassion. For Gandhi again, non-violence as love and harmony constitutes the law of our species that sustain the universe. Non-violence and peace have been natural to humanity—permanent attributes and innate tendencies of man—all through the story of evolution. If despite war and violence, human beings could have survived at all, it is because fortunately, war and violence have only been exceptions and aberrations in the long history of human civilisation. Non-violence and peace are essential for human evolution, survival, development and progress. Non-violence is the answer to oppression and violence. It rejects recourse to revenge, retaliation and aggression. In another sense, faith in non-violence represents reverence for life. The soldier in Eugene O'Neil felt that every time he fired a shot and killed another in war, he was actually killing himself again and again. Non-violence recognises the oneness of all beings. Violence is an attack on life. It solves nothing. The great conqueror, Napoleon said once:

> What astonishes me most in this world is the inability of force to create anything. In the long run, sword is always beaten by the spirit.

The people who had seen the apostle of peace and non-violence, Mahatma Gandhi walk this earth in flesh and blood and speak to us would like to believe that Gandhi's ideas are part of the heritage of the whole world. Gandhi accepted the inevitability of conflicts in human life. Conflict is normal and natural. The living always have problems and conflicts to face. It is only the dead who are beyond them. Conflict in life is perennial. However, equally perennial is the search for peace and conflict resolution. Man is always in search of peace. In his *Communist Manifesto*, Karl Marx said: History of mankind is the history of mankind's search for peace. We certainly do not want the peace of the grave, not the peace forced on the vanquished by the victor and not the peace of submission by a slave to his master. Path of peace has got to be laid with bricks of justice and respect for human life.

In global affairs today, peace is the avowed objective and the beacon light for working out relationships between sovereign nations on terms of equality and mutual respect. Education in peace is needed to inculcate the faith that all disputes can be resolved through cooperation and peaceful conflict resolution means. Article 51 of the Constitution of India directs the state to endeavour to (a) promote international peace and security, (b) maintain just and honourable relations between nations, (c) foster respect for international law and treaty obligations in the dealings of organised peoples with one another, and (d) encourage settlement of international disputes by arbitration.

We are all different and diverse in many ways and have multiple identities in terms of language, culture, beliefs, values, views, religion etc. But we are all human. We all want to be happy. We all want peace and harmony. The joy of life lies in resolving and transcending conflicts and fighting for peace and tranquility all the time.

Peace is also not the end of conflict or struggle. Peace is not a static end-product. It is an unending struggle of moving from conflict to cooperation. It is a constant, ever continuing dynamic process. In this journey, there is no journey's end. Gandhi who believed in the culture of peace, waged a life-long struggle for peace against injustice. In our times, His Holiness, the XIV Dalai Lama is another example of a person leading a lifelong non-violent struggle for peace and cooperation against injustice. His Holiness has given us what might be called his unique Doctrine of Universal Responsibility which means that every individual is responsible for the well-being of all others in the universe in the context of total interdependence of all humanity. The essence of the concept is that each one of us has a responsibility towards mankind at large. Each one of us has to think for the rest of the universe. The more we care for the happiness of others, the greater our own sense of well-being becomes. As Gandhi said, if you want to change the world, be the change and begin by changing yourself. In order to enable the society to develop, all its members have to assume responsibilities and make their contributions.

All development and progress are dependent on collective effort. Universal responsibility flows from the principles of non-violence and love as the fundamental laws of nature. Humanity is one and this small planet is our only home. To protect this home, each one of us has to discharge his responsibility. This incidentally is also the essence of the modern concept of participatory democracy, of all citizens having a duty or responsibility to be active and vigilant participants in the process of democratic governance. As the world grows smaller, we increasingly need each other more. Humanity has reached a critical juncture. Today's world requires us to accept the oneness of humanity. Whatever happens in one region eventually affects many other areas. Within the context of this new interdependence, even self interest clearly lies in considering the interest of others as well. Without our caring for others, our own existence is in danger. All existence today is coexistence. Living in harmony and peace, following the noble ideals of non-violence and love has become a categorical imperative for all of us. World peace and happiness and welfare of the entire humanity follows spontaneously.

The doctrine of universal responsibility emphasises the global connectedness—not only in terms of markets, technologies and political economies—but more fundamentally as human beings belonging to the same family.

The root cause of many of the present day conflicts is the struggle for sharing the resources on the earth, the desire to dominate over fellow human beings and the insatiable greed, possessiveness and quest for multiplication of wants and competitive consumerism. Causes of many conflicts are traceable to injustice, oppression, exploitation and inequitable distribution of resources.

All of us are the common inheritors of the resources of mother earth. The Hindu prayer speaks of *Sarve Jana Sukhina Santu* (Let all the peoples be happy) and ends with *Om Shanti, Shanti, Shanti* (Let there be peace everywhere). Islam means peace and the muslims greet each other with *Asalam-Walekum* which means let there be *salamati,* well-being or peace all round. Other religions also similarly extol peace over conflict. Gandhian techniques for conflict resolution were based on faith in human nature, unity of mankind, truth and non-violence. His mission was to knit all the peoples of this world together as a family, as parts of one whole. He stood for universal brotherhood, and believed that for every conflict a peaceful solution was possible. In his inimitable style, Gandhi said: 'There is no way to Peace. Peace is the way'.Whether as individuals or as nations, we have to realise that peace is the way—it is the most desirable path to be chosen. Peace based on non-violence and human compassion could make the earth a better place to live. A bomb could be beaten by the baton of peace.

Gandhi said there was enough on earth to meet the needs of everyone but not enough to satisfy the greed of anyone. Tolstoy and Gandhi, both used the Biblical parable of the miracle of five loaves and two fishes which when pooled together and distributed, proved more than enough to feed some five thousand people.

Competitive consumerism, stark materialism and unabashed possessiveness have become the yardsticks of respect in society. Since everything around seems rotten, we tend to withdraw into shells of privacy and make selfishness the greatest virtue. The villain is modern economics of maximisation of profits through multiplication of wants and consumption. In keeping with Indian traditions, Gandhi stood for minimisation of wants. Development economists talk of sustainable development but forget the categorical imperative of ensuring sustainable consumption. Gandhi was against greed economics and stood for true economics of justice. In the context of one-third of humanity suffering from abject poverty, starvation and misery, there was no justification for the very high levels of *per capita* consumption in some countries of the world. We are all children of one God, equally entitled to live a life of human dignity. Human family is one. No country should seek to prosper at the cost of the other. Patriotism based on exploitation of other nations is a sham. Unfortunately, money has become the supreme value. Economic interests of some people may require to keep small wars and regional conflicts going.

So long as there is domination of one class over the other, so long as the poor are exploited by the rich, there will be no justice, and without justice there will be no peace. The International Community has a moral responsibility to end human suffering.

While non-violence does not mean a world without problems or that the need to wage a war in certain situations can be totally discounted, it is important that the individuals and nations all understand the need to take care of each other's interests in order to coexist. One nation's problems can no longer be solved satisfactorily by itself alone; too much depends on the interest, attitude and cooperation of other nations. A universal humanitarian approach to world problems seems to be the only sound basis for world peace. Unfortunately, we are not willing to invest in peace but are prepared to spend colossal amounts of money and other resources in preparing for war avowedly to ensure peace. Today, we know very well that in the event of a nuclear war, there will be no victors because there will be no survivors.

The cliché of interdependence of nations, free market economy and globalization are much bandied about these days, both in academia and in public discourse. Thousands of years earlier, India also had a global vision. The ancients spoke of '*udaar charitanamtu vasudhaiv kutumbakam*' (For the noble-hearted, the whole world is a family). The two concepts of the whole world being one are fundamentally different. In a family, the relationship is that of sharing the joys and sorrows, of caring for each other, of giving to each according to his needs. Present day globalisation, on the other hand, is not based on any feeling of the oneness of mankind or even on nations competing with each other in terms of equality. It is based on greed and the desire to maximise sales, profits and exploitation by giving freedom to market forces—an euphemism for treating the large countries of the developing world as markets for the manufactured goods of the more developed countries. This kind of globalisation can hardly be a recipe for lasting peace or for transcending conflicts into cooperation.

The remedy lies in education. We must begin at the beginning. Qualities of love, compassion, peace and non-violence can be cultivated and sustained only through systematic moral education so that a more humane and peaceful world may emerge. The Preamble to the UNESCO charter said that since war begins in the minds of men, it is in the minds of men that the foundation of peace must be constructed. Minds are trained and conditioned by the education they receive. The aim of true education is to develop human personality to its highest potential and to impart a universal outlook of human unity and brotherhood. Gandhi was primarily a great communicator and educator. He said: 'Education means all-round drawing out of the best in child and man—body, mind and spirit.' Education should lead to character development including moral and ethical. Above all, it should orient us to resolving conflicts through peaceful, non-violent means because no solution arrived at through violence can be lasting particularly when we are in a global interdependent world. Education must foster universal and eternal values. Ethical education is an essential ingredient of education for peace. It should help eliminate violence and fanaticism. The objective of true education is to work for bettering the world around for facilitating the upward ascent of the collectivity of human consciousness. Education is the name of the journey from an individual to the universe. Education awakens the consciousness of the oneness of the family, neighbourhood, society, nation and humanity at large. When in every other man, the individual sees himself, he begins to wish well for everyone as he does for himself. Thus are built the foundations of peace in the minds of men.

It is a pity that that there has been terrible marketisation of education. The idea of human beings as a resource for reaching higher levels of GNP or GDP or, for realising greater production or profitability became so fashionable that the old Ministry of Education at the Centre was renamed as Ministry of Human Resource Development, as if human beings were merely cannon fodder, only a resource like iron ore or coal and not an end in themselves. If the ultimate aim of education is to develop human personality, all the resources must be used for that end. It is a matter of shame that during 70 years, we could not remove illiteracy from India. It seems that our leadership in all parties had a vested interest in keeping us uneducated, poor and backward.

If there is any hope left today, it is in the new generation of the Nachiketas of the *Kathopanishad*, who can surely deliver if major changes are instituted in our educational system from the school onwards. That education can be a very potent force in conditioning the minds and attitudes of the people and changing the course of human history is amply proved by the course of colonialism in India. After travelling round the country, Macaulay recorded:

> I do not think we would ever conquer this country unless we break the backbone of this nation, which is her spiritual and cultural heritage and, therefore, I propose that we replace her old and ancient Education System, her culture, for if the

> Indians think that all that is foreign & English is good & great, they will lose self-esteem, their native culture and they will become what we want —a truly dominated nation.

Rest is well-known. The existing schools and institutions were destroyed. English education was started through Government Schools with Macaulay's curricula and the foundations of British domination were firmly laid. No wonder that it was during the period between the two world wars, that a sort of movement for peace education first took shape. One heard and read a great deal about peace studies, peace economics, and peace research and making them a part of the curriculam. The declared objective was to develop through education abilities to manage the potential conflicts better and ensure peace by transforming attitudes, approaches and mindsets towards war and peace. It was also felt that the history books and other text books extolled the war heroes and there were more stories and narratives about battles, wars and violent events than about achievements in times of peace. This created a mentality of war and violence. It was necessary to condition the minds of teachers and students to accept, celebrate and enjoy difference of opinion and learn to coexist in peace.

The emphasis on peace education as part of studies in International Relations has continued, more particularly at Universities on the American continent except that it has become multi-disciplinary and is more often referred to as Peace Science. Present-day Peace Science scholars and peace economists, particularly after the recent economic meltdown, are finding Gandhian thought more and more relevant for their work. An American Vietnam veteran, it was reported, tore off his US passport and was anxious to be granted asylum in India. He wanted to settle down in India and acquire Indian citizenship because he regarded himself to be a staunch disciple of Mahatma Gandhi, opponent of war and committed to non-violence.

There is a great need to promote peace education on a massive scale universally, beginning with the self and one's own area. We require a world-wide transformation of curriculam in education. In place of teaching to prepare for war, the young have to be taught to resolve all conflicts peacefully and prepare for life. In addition to its traditional role, education must promote an atmosphere for peace and peace development activities. We need to imbibe the necessary values by looking at the common humanitarian heritage of all nations of the world. War can have no glamour or attraction. It is a monstrosity. It's very nature is one of tragedy and suffering. Peace education has to be directed to the need of developing a new world order based on the commonalities of the interests of all humanity and responsibilities of all individuals. Peace is the only way of survival of the human community and an organic and continuing state of peace can come only from duly awakened inner harmony and spirit of cooperation.

Appropriate value education inputs assume the highest importance in transforming animal consciousness to human consciousness and the need to realisation of total interconnectedness of humanity. Philosophy of peace cannot be taught through direct lecturing in classrooms. It has to be imbibed and assimilated gradually by being made an integral part of the much talked about EHV or Education in Human Values. Situations of serious conflict do arise within the nation as also internationally. Peace education is aimed at inculcating an approach of conflict resolution through love and cooperation—the two derivatives of non-violence. The result of such nonviolent resolution of conflicts is a win-win situation for all. Through moral pressure and personal sacrifice, it is enmity that is sought to be destroyed. It is important to include in our educational curricula teachings in the non-violent tools and techniques of preventive political management. Often we are not trained to pay adequate attention to situations of potential conflict at early developing stage. Control becomes difficult when it explodes and becomes dangerous. We need to pay much more attention to situations of conflict if peace has to have a chance. Also, we need to know that individuals can make a difference and create a happier and more peaceful world through the practice of mutual love and non-violence.

It is to be hoped that the new breed of scholars in the field of Peace Studies all over the world, will someday prove the relevance of education for peace by convincing the powers that be that all natural resources of the earth are the common heritage of mankind and have to be shared by all as equitably as possible.

Education in Citizenship Values

Models and Modules

EDUCATION IS a lifelong process. It is an interactive exercise between the teacher and the taught. A good teacher has to be committed to ensure that a student remains always anxious to learn. 'Physician heal thyself' is an old saying. It may also be said that time has come for teachers to realise that they have to first teach themselves. And to be able to do so, teachers need better capacity building, quality improvement in methodologies and techniques and more developed communication, transmission and teaching skills. However, all these have to be founded on some basic objectives of education like human values and societal needs.

An important aspect of teaching the teachers is based on basic constitutional values and fundamental citizenship duties that the nation is passing through challenging times and a period of transition. There is a widespread crisis of character, devaluations of values and deinstitutionalisation of institutions. Money, power and success, whatever be the costs, have become supreme concerns. In their pursuit, we are prepared to make all sorts of compromises with principles and there are no limits to how low we can stoop. We have no regard for any values beyond our own crude self-interests. Horrendous level of corruption in the past decades just gone by, not only in politics but in all professions and walks of life, have made us hang our heads in shame. This state of affairs can be directly attributed to the absence of value education in our classrooms.

During recent years, a great deal has been written and spoken about the need for value education in our curriculum and modules for learning teaching proccesses. Perhaps, we need more models than modules—role models that students can emulate than the modules that they are subjected to. Sometimes it seems that we, the older generation, are guilty because we failed to present before the youth the models of good conduct and of lives lived with adherence to noble values. When we were young students, we had before us excellent role models at home in the form of our parents and elders, at school and college in our teachers and in society at large in our national leaders who were anxious 'to give' their best and not 'to take' the maximum. They were people who practised their principles, performed their duties towards their families, students, society and the nation at large. They placed values above their narrow self-interests and needs of earning wealth and power in order to become what are called success stories in our times. There were teachers who abondoned careers in ICS and the like and decided to give their life to academic pursuits and to educating the coming generations. One professor used to say: 'Learning is a very jealous goddess, she tolerates no rivals'. 'A teacher must live like a hermit and work like a horse'. Even at a ripe old age, we could see him working at his desk fourteen to sixteen hours a day. For the students, the closest role models outside their homes are their teachers. We cannot expect our students to respect any charter of values if they find their teachers disregarding all values in their daily lives.

Only when the teacher himself or herself is value-oriented that he or she will be able to help, inspire and guide the students.

There are no absolutes in the universe of values. All of us, as individuals or as social groups, have to make some compromises and adjustments. What is important is where we draw the line and whether we have a *Lakshman Rekha* that we draw ourselves but which we are determined never to cross whatever be the need or temptations. We have to make conscious choices and prioritise our preferences. It is good to remember Abraham Maslow's *Hierarchy of Needs* where the highest human need is that of Self-Actualisation which is close to our Upanishadic concept of self-realisation or Allama Iqbal's *Asrar-e-Khudi.* An oft-cited couplet of Iqbal reads: *Kar Khudi ko buland itna ki har taqdir se pehle, khuda bande se khud pooche bata teri raza kya hai* [Raise yourself to such heights that before every destiny, God himself asks man to state his wish].

This is hardly attainable without a value system in place. Value education enables a student to learn to prioritise life principles and goals according to their relative value in his perception. Also, these become the building blocks of an individual, social, national and even global character. These days, we hear a lot about the primacy and greater efficacy of Emotional Intelligence or EQ over IQ. Value education falls in the territory of EQ. Maintaining relationships and dealings with other human beings also requires a high degree of EQ without which even the application of IQ would be problematic. Value education is what keeps the humane element alive which is the true edge of a human being over any artificial intelligence. Also, that is what helps develop decision making, character and sensitivity building and spirit of responsibility assuming traits.

In the present day scenario where all the information and much of the needed scholarship and knowledge are only a click away on every child's Laptop, Tablet, I-pad or smart cell phone, the role of the teacher needs to be revisited. It needs to be transformed to developing values of discrimination between right and wrong and to learn the art of appreciating the real purpose of what Swami Vivekananda called 'the man-making and character building education directed towards all-round development of every student's personality to his highest possibilities—physical, intellectual, emotional and spiritual'.

The 1986 New Policy on Education announced by the Government of India had stressed the need for value-based education or education in values. But, by and large, despite all the initiatives by CBSE and NCERT, on the ground, it did not seem to have any effect. Only lip service was paid to value education by leaving it to the teacher of each subject. The main impediments in operationalising any agenda for value education have been two: one, the disconnect between the value orientation sought to be taught in the classroom and the reality outside or the conduct of teachers themselves and second, the most unfortunate suspicion of values being related to religious or moral education and as such opposed to secularism. However, the basic values and citizenship duties enshrined in the Constitution can by no stretch of imagination be dubbed as non-secular. The Constitution that the founding fathers gave us is a secular source and reservoir of all the quintessential values. And, it is these values that need to be absorbed and made an integral part of education. The Preamble speaks of we, the people of India, constituting India into a sovereign socialist secular democratic republic and to secure to all citizens— Justice, social, economic and political; Liberty of thought, expression, belief, faith and worship; Equality of status and of opportunity and Fraternity assuring the dignity of the individual and the unity and integrity of the nation. The values that emerge from the Preamble are:

- of sovereignty vesting in the people,
- people of India being one and indivisible,
- justice, liberty, equality and fraternity,
- finally assuring dignity of the individual and the unity of the nation.

These are all supreme values that deserve to be instilled into the minds and hearts of all students, teachers and the people at large.

In the widest possible terms, citizenship values are certain indispensable or desirable principles or qualities that are integral to a citizren's political behaviour in a democratic polity. This would involve all the rights, responsibilities and duties of citizens *vis a vis* other citizens, society at large and the state. Citizenship under the Constitution makes adherence to citizenship values a categorial imperative for all of us in whatever position. And, the citizenship values are rooted not only in our legal status as citizens but in foundational norms or basic values of citizenship enshrined in the Constitution and permeating all it's provisions. All citizens must value citizenship and it's values. These basic values represent the constants of the Constitution. They have been elaborated in chapters on Fundamental Rights, Directive Principles and Fundamental Duties. Part IVA, Article 51A of the Constitution contains a charter of Fundamental Duties for citizens. It was brought in by an amendment to establish that citizenship must carry with it certain fundamental obligations.

In March, 1998, a former Chief Justice of India, Justice Ranganath Mishra, wrote to the then Chief Justice of India a letter expressing serious concern about the expression of fundamental duties of the citizens. He suggested that as a nation building measure, Fundamental Duties need to be taught in every educational institution and as a part of in-service training everywhere as these cannot be inculcated in our citizens unless these are brought into our minds and living processes through teaching and education. He added that it was the obligation of the state to educate the citizens in the matter of Fundamental Duties. The Government of India agreed and a Committee was set up to operationalise the suggestions to teach Fundamental Duties to the citizens. The Committee was headed by Justice JS Verma, former Chief Justice of India. Dr Karan Singh, Dr LM Singhvi and Dr Subhash C Kashyap were members of the Committee, apart from RS Rajput/AS Sharma as Member Secretary. The committee requested the Citizenship Development Society to prepare a handbook on Operationalisation and Teaching of Fundamental Duties under the

Constitution. The Handbook was appreciated by the Committee and reproduced in full in its report. It contains some useful source material for teacher-training programmes. It is available in the form of a book.[1]

Article 51A of the Constitution lays down in unambiguous language eleven duties expected to be fulfilled by every citizen. In building up good citizens for the future, our educational system and the teachers played a very special role. They must develop tools and techniques to ensure that the behaviour expected of a good citizen gets ingrained into every student's mind and becomes a natural part of his or her personality. Course materials have to be developed and effective curricular and extra-curricular programmes have to be devised to ensure that necessary behaviour modification becomes an esential ingredient of the educational process. A great deal depends on the ingenuity and dedication of teachers. The need was for a nation-wide movement to train and honour teachers for inculcating citizenship duties thereby bringing an impressive transformation of society.

The Justice Verma Committee fully agreed and said that it could bring about impressive transformation in our educational system. The Committee felt that there was need to review education in fundamental citizenship values and to reorient approaches to curriculum for teaching these in schools and teacher training institutions. Citizenship values need to be understoood as a combination of rights and duties. The Human Rights Education Initiative should, therefore, better be reffered to as Human Rights and Fundamental Duties Initiative. Along with the Preamble to the Constitution, the remaining citizenship duties should be printed in all school textbooks, materials and general publications published by the NCERT and Textbook Bureaus of States. A few other suggeations made by the Verma Committee in regard to teaching citizenship values and fundamental duties were:

[1] See *Citizenship Value's under the Constitution: Operationalisation and Teaching, ed.* Subhash C Kashyap, Pub. CDS & Gyan Pub. House, 2013.

- Arranging regular seminars, debates, competitions etc. on different aspects related to Fundamentals Duties,
- Developing an instructional design that fits into the present-day multi-channel learning environment,
- While the debate may continue whether values and duties should be taught as a separate subject or all areas of curriculum should be woven round the concepts of values anad duties. Flexibility to experiment with either approach can be left to curriculum developers,
- Internalising constitutional values and duties of citizens and not merely concentrating on giving information in regard to them,
- Eliminating from school and college textbook gender biases and sex-stereotyping in order to ensure dignity of women,
- Not only making teachers aware of values and duties but also educating them in communicating these to the students and while emphasising on them the need to abide by them,
- Orienting and training teachers of all subjects at all levels to a serious business of education in Fundamental Duties,
- Preparation of teachers through well designed teacher-education programmes to ensure understanding and internalising of Fundamental Duties,
- Preparing a sensitising module based on Fundamental Duties and making it an integral part of all teacher education programmes,
- Incorporating Fundamental Duties in the elementary and secondary pre-service teacher education curriculum especially in terms of attitude and value development, and
- Presentation of Constitutional values inherent in each clause of Article 51A through anecdotal talks at morning assemblies etc. in schools.[2]

---

[2] For details see *Fundamental Duties of Citizens—Report of the Committee set up by Govt. of India to Operationalise the Suggestions to Teach Fundamental Duties to the Citizens of the Country*, GOI, Min. of HRD, New Delhi, 1999, Vol. 1.

The founding fathers were anxious to stress that the most important and overriding values were those of individual dignity and national unity and integrity. So far as citizenship duties are concerned, it can be mentioned specially that the very first duty of every citizen is 'to abide by the Constitution and respect it's ideals and institutions, the National Flag and the National Anthem'. Unfortunately, there is tremendous constitutional illiteracy in our country and it exists even among the educated. If we do not know about our Constitution and are not adequately oriented to its provisions, how can we respect it's ideals and institutions. Therefore, the foremost need is to ensure that every citizen is made conversant with the nation's Constitution and every single child is exposed and oriented to its values, ideals and institutions.[3] Some of these are a repeatition of the values enshrined in the Preamble and in any case all of them are most important and deserve to be taught and learnt most widely throughout the country. Unless this is done by all the teachers imbibing these values in their lives and becoming role models before young students, we shall be failing the trust reposed in us as teachers, and if that happens, democracy and freedom also cannot last long in our country. After all, citizenship values under the Constitution are basically democratic values and it is the responsibility of the citizens themselves to protect them.

The vibrancy of democratic polity is contingent upon the spread and quality of education. The relationship between democracy and education is reciprocal. The job of teachers in a democratic polity is , above all, to make their pupils good citizens. The importance of learning the art of teaching democratic citizenship values, therefore, is unique and cannot be over emphasised. The responsibility of teachers is stupendous and calls for a spirit of service and sacrifice. As the *Upanishads* say: *Tena Tyaktena Bhunjitha.*

---

[3] For further study see Subhash C Kashyap, *Citizens and the Constitution*, Pub. Div., Min. of I & B, GOI, New Delhi, 2nd Ed. 2003.

Higher Education in India

Challenges of the 21st Century

A GREAT deal has been written and spoken about problems of education in India since independence. A large number of commissions and committees have examined the various perspectives and reform options and made their recommendations. These include the Radhakrishnan Commission (1948), the Kothari Commission (1964), the Punnaya Committee (1993), the Birla Ambani Committee (1993), the Swaminathan Committee (1994), the Majumdar Committee (1999) and others. However, as the Swaminathan Commiittee concluded, despite all the commissions and committees and their reports, no serious attempts have been made for implementing any reform proposals in the field of education. Also, for more than 60 years after independence, education had hardly occupied a place of primacy on the national agenda.

India had an ancient tradition of imparting higher education and had an elaborate university system. The great universities of Takshashila and Nalanda were well known seats of learning. Modern higher education in India began with the establishment of Hindu College at Kolkata in 1817. For the first time in 1887, three universities in the Presidencies of Bombay, Calcutta and Madras were established. At the time of independence, there were 19 universities throughout the country. The University Education Commission (1948-49) recommended rapid expansion of higher education on a priority basis. What followed was haphazard expansion of higher education and proliferation of universities.

At present, the institutions of higher education in India fall into four categories—(i) those established by Acts of Parliament or of States Legislatures; (ii) degree awarding institutions established under Acts of Parliament such as IITs; (iii) deemed universities under the provisions of UGC Act; and (iv) diploma awarding institutions, which are neither established by Acts of Parliament nor are deemed universities. The higher education system has witnessed a manifold increase in the number of universities, colleges and enrolment of students since independence. There are close to 800 Universities, 38,000 colleges including women's colleges in the country and about 250 million students.

Today the Indian higher education system is the second largest in the world. Yet, the fact remains that only 6-7% of our population in the relevant age group of 18-23 is getting the benefit of higher education. These figures are dismal and when compared to the figures of over 50% for the countries belonging to the Organisation of Economic Co-operation and Development (OECD) it appears negligible. But though the percentage of the enrolment figures appears shameful, yet in terms of numbers and output it is very large. It is commendable that India has the third largest reservoir of scientific and technical manpower in the world.

Higher education and education in general was a State

responsibility until 1976 and was then brought into the concurrent list. Thus the Union government was assigned considerable powers and responsibilities without disturbing the State governments' freedom on the subject. In the first five-year plan the government plan to allocate for education was 7.8% of the total plan funds of which higher education got the share of 9%. In the successive plans, allocation to education declined. It came down to around 2.7% during the sixth plan and increased to 4.5% in the eighth plan. The share of higher education doubled to 18% in the second plan and reached 25% in the 4th plan. Since then there has been a steady decline. In the 8th plan its share was reduced to 7% of the plan allocation but the ninth plan saw a rise to 12%. The report of the education Commission (1964-66) strongly agreed to devoting 6% of the GNP to education. The Majumdar Committee (MHRD, 1999) reiterated the same. The National Policy on Education 1968 and 1986 also categorically laid down and endorsed that the GNP allocation to education should be at least 6%. The NPE 1992 stated that the 8th plan onward the GNP share will uniformly exceed 6%. The target could not be achieved. However, the situation has been improving. Budget allocation for education was 9.9 per cent in 2017 and 2018 estimates showed an increase of more than 3 per cent with the Finance Minister envisaging revitalising the infra-structure and systems by 2022.

Primary vs Higher Education

There is a strong body of opinionated people in the country who would like the government to accord the highest priority to universal primary education and to put all possible resources and efforts into it. Actually, the 2002 constitutional amendment makes free and compulsory education to be given to children between the ages 6 to 14 a fundamental right. Powerful foreign lobbies are trying for India not to put focus on higher education. It is like the mischievous and motivated suggestion that India should lay emphasis on agriculture and production of raw materials only. While there is every reason to ensure universalisation of primary education, only recently a realisation has dawned that it would be a disaster if skill development and higher education are ignored in the name of primary education. It is not an either/or scenario. Both are necessary and have to be addressed at the same time. With all its shortcomings, it is, after all, because of higher education that Indians can compete with foreigners in all international fora.

Purpose of Higher Education

The first question that we have to grapple with is that of the purpose of higher education. Higher education usually connotes education beyond the school level imparted at universities or other centres of higher learning like the IITs, IIMs and various research institutes.

Ideally, universities and other institutions of higher learning are storehouses of knowledge and creators of those who make knowledge grow. They are expected to represent the best brains and are centres for achieving excellence and for inculcation of higher values leading to the development of the personality of the individual to its fullest potential and to the well -being of the nation. Higher education must play an important role in the transformation of our institutions and values. The function of a university, according to Jawaharlal Nehru, was to train a student in body, mind and spirit. While delivering a convocation address at Allahabad University he said, 'A University stands for humanism, for tolerance, for reason, for progress, for the adventure of ideas, and for the search for the truth. It stands for the onward race towards even higher objectives. If the universities discharge their duties properly then it is well for the nation.'

Higher education does not mean imparting of information or knowledge. It should aim at total development of a person. Education must train the student to be a good citizen and to be able to take decisions and act wisely in life. Wisdom is the ability to discriminate and decide between right and wrong. The objective of higher education is to inculcate such wisdom.

Education in Values

The new education policy announced by the Government of India in 1986 *inter alia* had stressed the need for value-based education or education in values. The policy document said:

> 'In our culturally plural society, education should foster universal and eternal values, oriented towards the unity and integration of our people. Such value education should help eliminate obscurantism, religious fanaticism, violence, superstitions and fatalism.
>
> Apart from this combative role, value education has a profound positive content, based on our heritage, national goals and universal perceptions.'

We need educators who can instill a vision and a faith in the younger generation by their own examples. It is a great misfortune that we are not able to present examples which can provide inspiration to today's youth. Actually, the older generation has done such violence to all the ideals and values and presented such an ugly example before posterity that they must hang their heads in shame. Education in politics, morality and all other fields, has failed to do what it should have done and done all that it should have never done.

The elders—teachers and parents of today—do not realise that we are doing nothing about our own value system and pay no attention to our character and conduct that we place before the youth to emulate. It is said that the student does not learn from what the teacher says but from what he does. True educators are needed for making the world around better, for inculcating higher values for facilitating the upward ascent of the collectivity of human consciousness and for developing integrated human personalities with will and wisdom.

The New Challenges

The challenges of the 21st century are very different. Who is interested today in imbibing higher values? There has been general devaluation of all values in every walk of life. The only values, if any, left are money, power and success. In today's scenario, it is difficult to find those who want to better the world around or to ameliorate the sufferings of fellow human beings or to suffer and sacrifice for a cause or even to bother about matters like character building. Qualities of education and training that ensure the growth of such beings are not in demand. Market forces are at work today and what is asked for is orientation for securing a paid job and training in the methodologies and techniques for getting things done, for fixing deals and forging ahead. It was an astounding experience when a candidate for a job position revealed during the interview that he had done a professional course in how to get things done; in other words, he claimed expertise in giving bribe or in finding the weaknesses of the concerned person and exploiting it.

Experience has taught the new generation that success stories are built not on pursuing 'ideals' but on negotiating profitable 'deals'. Competitive consumerism, hedonism, stark materialism and unabashed possessivism have become the yardsticks of respect in society. We do not even talk of the old ideals of *Aparigraha Asteya* and *santosham* or of limitation or minimisation of wants. Since everything around seems rotten, we tend to withdraw into shells of privatism and make selfishness not only the greatest but the only feasible virtue. The goal is to start making big money quick, achieving status and living well. Character and individuality have lost significance. Worldly success, comfort and vulgar exhibitionism have become the most important concerns. and they require a different kind of education and orientation.

Society is run on reward-punishment principles. If values pay—not necessarily in money—they will be adopted. When politics is not value-based, public life is shorn of all values. If no values are respected in social intercourse, in business or in professions, how can we expect only education to be value-based?

Looked at from another angle, society itself has come to such an impasse because of the failure of the system of higher education. There is a terrible disconnect between societal needs and university education. It is sometimes said that education imparted at the colleges and universities must be relevant to social needs or, in other words, it must be related to the availability of jobs in different disciplines so as to meet real life problems in today's world. But, education for character building and for learning job skills, cannot be separated from each other. Nor can they be viewed separately. They have all to be accepted as essential parts of the educational process. It is natural to expect that education would enable the student to face the ordeals and travails of the life struggle, to meet his needs and sort out his personal problems, to equip him for a vocation of his liking and enable him to earn his livelihood and the basic comforts of life.

There is another dimension to the challenges to higher education in the 21st century. The context of higher education has changed with the aggressive advent of economic liberalisation, market globalisation and technological leap forward into an information age and a knowledge based society.

The world during this short period has seen many changes affecting the institutions, society, polity, market culture, as well as the overall thinking of men. Higher education is not immune to this whole process. The whole concept of higher education as we conceive it today is getting eroded with new conditions that are evolving. Challenges are due to the changed conditions, which demand a fresh look, an understanding of changing conditions and the fulfillment of required needs.

Challenges to higher education come in the form of demands for higher education and provision of quality that will fulfill the needs generated by societal forces. Most reform measures recommended in the arena of higher education revolve around the major proposition of improving efficiency and mobilising resources.

Mobilisation of Resources

The government's inability to fund higher education has led to looking for other avenues. The Swaminathan and the Punnayya Committees looked into the possibilities of resource mobilisation in technical education and the funding of central universities respectively. The recommendations suggest improving efficiency in the functioning of the institutions of higher education to reduce waste and to save resources and mobilse them from sources other than the government. The Swaminathan Committee recommended the revision of the tuition fees and other fees. It suggested hiring the infrastructure and providing consultancy to the government and other agencies to generate resources and also to activate the administration to bring in donations. Both the reports advocate promotion of the distance learning mode of education.

The suggestions also implied subsidies in higher education by diversifying the sources of funding either to the beneficiaries (students) or to their users (employers). Fee structure according to the paying capacity of the student was one of the recommendations that came up to improve resource mobilisation. There seems to be absolutely no justification for continuing with the present ridiculously low fee structure at the universities. Quite often, the fees at private schools are several hundred times more than the universities fees. The need to augment cost recoveries from students, developing a self-generating and self-sustaining fund, supplemented by other entrepreneurial avenues, has come up as the major issue in higher education discourse.

Privatisation and Private Funding

The resource crunch in the area of higher education as well as the opening up of this sector due to the processes of liberalisation, marketisation and technological innovations with a burden as well as a need for quality and job oriented education has opened up the debate of private funding and privatisation of higher education. The Birla Ambani Report (1993) had strongly advocated privatisation of higher education in India. It pleaded for the reduction of government funding for the universities and self-generation of resources and recommended more Private Universities in the field of science, technology and management. This led to a lot of debate and apprehensions in educational circles. There has been a confusion in two different forms of private funding.

Private funding can be simply for profit as we see in most private institutions that currently operate or private funding can be used to create non-profit institutions. Unfortunately, India has seen not much of the latter happening. We have only seen the establishment of private institutions that are mostly capitation fee charging professional institutions, the admissions to which are determined mainly on the basis of the paying capacity of the parents. Also, they naturally neglect those subjects which have less commercial value such as language and literature, music, fine arts, history, philosophy and many other social sciences and humanitarian subjects. Other worries in case of private funding in higher education are those of upholding academic standards, providing access to the economically disadvantaged and ensuring that academics rather than entrepreneurs control educational decisions. Thus, there is a dilemma before policy makers in the field of higher education. A way out perhaps is a mix of State Universities and centres of higher learning and research with private universities and other institutions being allowed to compete. Regulatory and monitoring agencies of the State may be devised to ensure standards in the quality of education. This may be coupled with other measures like making it obligatory for private institutions to admit a certain percentage, say 50 per cent strictly on merit with provision of loans or fellowships to the needy and delinking of jobs with degrees.

Autonomy and Accountability

One of the most fundamental principles is that the universities and other centres of higher learning must enjoy autonomy and be allowed full functional freedom in their academic and research pursuits. In their search after truth, knowledge and excellence, they can brook no interference. Unfortunately, most Indian universities have become highly bureaucratic and the UGC has become a mechanism for interfering in the affairs of universities and depriving them of the freedom allowed to them under the visible statutes. As the Radhakrishnan Commission had stated, the UGC's role is that of a friend of the universities and not that of a policeman or inspector.

State governments also exert pressure in the case of State universities by using their financial powers. It is a sad thought that even a Chancellor who in the case of States is often the Governor, is not able to act independently in the best interests of the university because the purse strings are controlled by the Chief Minister. To mention a personal experience, the Governor of a State made the mistake of appointing me as his nominee on the Executive Council and the Council compounded that mistake by putting me in the search committee for selecting a Vice-Chancellor for the University. The Governor came to Delhi and called me to tell me why a particular person suggested by the Chief Minister had to be appointed. The university was broke and if CM's candidate was not made Vice-Chancellor, no funds would be forthcoming from the State. I quickly resigned from the Search Committee and from the Executive Council and the next Council meeting approved the appointment of the VC. Thus, sometimes, people not qualified to be lecturers are appointed as Vice-Chancellors. Instead of being the crowning honour of an academic career which it once was, university Vice Chancellorship these days is becoming a preserve of retired army officers, police officers, IAS officers and the like. Even the Academic Councils, Senates and Executive Councils of universities get packed by non-academics and political party or mafia gang nominees.

It has to be remembered that autonomy does not mean absence of accountability. Wherever public funds are involved, the institutions concerned howsoever autonomous, have to be accountable to the people through elected representatives in the legislature. Autonomy carries no licence for misuse of funds, financial irregularities or arbitrary use of powers.

In many universities classes are not being held, examinations get repeatedly postponed, copying at examinations is accepted as normal, teachers are not interested in teaching and students not bothered about attending classes. This cannot be allowed to go on under the garb of autonomy and freedom.

Excellence and Expansion

The other serious problem facing the universities is that of marrying the requirements of expansion to meet the increasing numbers anxious to get admitted with the need of maintaining high standards of quality and striving for excellence.

Today, there is a crisis of quality in higher education imparted by universities. Universities are expected to be centres of excellence and experimentation contributing to 'production and transmission of knowledge'. A developing country like India particularly depends for its progress and survival on modern knowledge and technological innovations. The record of Indian universities in this regard has been generally dismal. Precious little has come out of the universities that can be said to be relevant to present-day societal needs or that would impact national developments or policy formulation.

The courses and curricula in many universities are antiquated, colonial and at best of 19th century vintage. And, there is tremendous resistance to all ideas of change, reform and modernisation. There have been no innovations or changes in the course structures and the concept of academic standards is non-existent. The infrastructural conditions of universities and colleges are in shambles. A university degree or course holds no importance in terms of value as far as the job market is concerned nor is it aptly designed for rigorous academic value. We have more PhDs and less research, more teachers but little teaching. Universities have been reduced to examination holding and degree awarding industries. Then there are fake universities. Degrees are on sale. There is a flourishing racket of professional thesis writers. Even honorary degrees may be acquired for a price. Public money is spent in churning out large numbers of unemployables—graduates and PhDs—who can neither take care of their lives nor contribute anything to society. Also, they have no moral backbone. What is worse, the few genuine ones suffer.

Globalisation and the scenario of a stiff competitive process in the emerging international knowledge market makes it imperative for our universities to care for high quality and achieve international standards. That our boys and girls are second to none is amply shown by the IITs and IIMs. Our universities and institutes of higher education will have to evolve programmes that are flexible and cost-effective. At the entrepreneurial level, research in consumer goods and services and other user-sectors must get top priority as free-flow or dumping of mass-produced foreign goods and services may ruin Indian enterprise with far reaching social, political and economic consequences. It would be most advisable and necessary to devise a number of courses that are market-friendly and commercially viable. Need based skills would have to be developed and scope for self-financing vocationalisation must be explored. Universities can be linked to big business houses and should be able to undertake consultancy, laboratory tests etc. for private industries. There are, however two views on whether universities should run variety of vocational courses at different levels or this task may be left to separate vocational institutions, polytechnics etc. In either case, care has to be taken to ensure that fundamental research and study in areas like linguistic, literature, fine arts, philosophy, social sciences and humanities or in pure science does not become a casualty and that universities continue to remain centres of pursuit of excellence in these areas as well.

Quality of education also depends on the quality of teachers and teaching methods. First the teachers have to learn to be lifelong students who are always anxious to learn. A person who is not a good student can never be a good teacher. The irony is that for becoming a school teacher, one needs some training in pedagogy and a degree in teaching or education but for being a university lecturer or Assistant Professor no training is required. Sometimes, research credentials are equated with teaching abilities. But a university teacher has to be a communicator and imparter of knowledge through interaction and discourse. He has the responsibility of shaping the lives of the younger generation and preserving the prestige of the domain of knowledge, ideas and ideals. All of this may require some basic reorientation in teaching processes.

Also, there is a great need for training educational administrators. Not every good teacher can be a good Principal, Proctor, Registrar or Vice-Chancellor without adequate training and orientation.

Role of Emerging Technologies

The most striking development of the 20th century that history will record has presumably been the information revolution characterised by digitalisation of information. It has enabled the building of information highways and superways, e-mail, internet, cyber cafes, multi-media tele-conferencing and the rest. Digitalisation of information has completely transformed the ways of our thinking and living.

Techonological innovations have also transformed the way we look at higher education. Getting information from anywhere over the globe at our very table with a click of a mouse; or classes and presentations through computers are the in-thing today. We have moved beyond think tanks and talk of knowledge workers, information tanks and knowledge pools. We can have virtual classrooms and the libraries that will contain microchips storing all the relevant data. But it is a matter of immediate concern that despite the technological innovations, such as internet having the potential of democratisation, the world is becoming increasingly divided into the information rich and the information poor or the haves and have-nots of the digital age. The advent of globalisation has sharpened this division not just between the societies within nations but also between nations. More so in the developing countries where a bulk of the population still lives below the poverty line with marginal livelihood, the access to such technological innovation is still a distant dream and the divide becoming more determining and damning with times. The present leadership in India is well aware of the problem and is trying to make amends by brining the digital revolution to the common people.

A question is whether the technology of storage, retrieval, processing, communication, defusing and sharing of information will be compatible with the demands of economic and cultural upliftment of the masses, social justice and participation of the thus far deprived sections in the development process. The new digital environment will test the capability of technology to adapt and grow. This would require capital equipment and infrastructure, careful planning and resource pooling. The new challenges demand new opportunities and delivery systems, new attitudes and flexibility and openness to harness the great potential of technology for quality education as well as societal needs.

Politicisation, Criminalisation and Corruption

Finally, the worst scourge for higher education and the ugliest stigma on its face today is that of politics, crime and corruption entering the portals of our universities—the temples of learning and character building. Campuses are plagued by party politics. Higher education has been politicised and has become a part of the patronage or spoils system and of the struggle for power. Universities are replete with teacher politicians and student politicians. Non teaching employees in universities also do not lag behind and have their own trade union leaders and politicians with affiliation with political parties—A, B or C.

It would be unfair to generalise but it is well known that today corruption, communal, criminal and political party pressures influence admissions, appointments and examinations.

Universities are hardly open for 120 days in a year and that also if there are no strikes by teachers, students or employees. A student politicians continue to be on the roll of the university for 10, 15, 20 years or until the party he belongs to manages to give him a break by making him a candidate for some elective office. Under the present circumstances, university hostels become dens of criminals and petty politicians. I recall, we had university unions in our days too but those elected Presidents were also the best students of the university.

It is easy to suggest immediate depoliticisation of university campuses and hostels but one would have to reckon with the very powerful vested interests of teacher and student politicians.

Conclusion

To sum up and conclude, the case for systematic reforms in higher education is unassailable. It has to keep pace with changing societal needs and adjust to the era of new technologies, information revolution and globalisation. Challenges for higher education in the 21st century are formidable and staggering but every challenge is also an opportunity for innovation and development. To put it in bullet points:

- Higher education must be geared to building character, inculcating values and vision and developing human personality to its highest potentials.
- Access to higher education in India is low and must be increased. It must not be neglected on the ground of priority to universalisation of primary education. Both governmental and private resources need to be harnessed.
- Institutions of higher education must raise their resources internally so that their dependence on outside help is reduced.
- State Universities should be supplemented by more private universities and institutions devoted to technical, vocational and market-need-oriented professional education.
- Expansion of higher education must be accompanied by improving its quality to international standards so as to enable us to compete globally. Quality of teachers, curriculum and

infrastructure must improve.

- Autonomy of institutions of higher education is important but accountability is equally important.
- The best use of emerging technologies is crucial in any scheme of educational reforms but it must percolate to the bottom so that the digital divide between haves and have-nots does not lead to new societal tensions.
- Universities must be freed from the clutches of professional politicians, teacher-politicians, student-politicians as also from the curses of communalism, casteism, corruption and criminalisation.

Lastly, educational reforms cannot be taken up successfully in isolation from other reforms—political, economic and administrative—because there is close interlinking between them. For educational reforms to be meaningful the whole societal structure would need to be shaken and revamped. It may appear like a tall order but there are no shortcuts and no alternative to strong will and a determination to change.

References

- Azad JL, *Changing Complexion of Higher Education (A Study of the Impact of Emerging Socio-Economic Configuration)*, *Journal of Higher Education,* Vol. 22, No. 1, Spring 1999.
- Beteille Andre, *Teaching and Research, The Hindu,* 1 November 2001.
- Chauhan CPS, *Higher Education in India: Challenges of Global Trends, University News,* Vol.40, No. 17, April/May29-5,2002, p.4-5.
- Kashyap Subhash C (ed.) *Urgency of Value Education and Primacy of Girl Child—National Agenda for Value Education,* Sterling, New Delhi, 1998.
- Kashyap, Subhash C, *Agenda for Educational Reforms in Kashyap* (ed.), *op. cit.*
- Mehta, Pratap Bhanu, *The Education Leviathan, The Hindu*, 12 June 2001.

- Mehta, Pratap Bhanu, *Private Funding and Higher Education, The Hindu,* 26 December 2001.
- *Ministry of Human Resource Development, Annual Report, 2001-2002,* p. 120.
- Nehru Jawaharlal, *Jawaharlal Nehru's Speeches,* vol. I, September 1946- May 1949, Publication Division, Ministry of Information and Broadcasting Government of India, 1967, p. 329.
- Panagariya Arvind, *Abolish this Monopoly, Economic Times,* 28 March 2001.
- Pathak Avijit, *Droves in Academe, The Pioneer,* 28 March 2001.
- Patil VK (et al), *Education in the Context of the Changing World, University News,* Vol. 40, No. 17, April/May 29-5, 2002, p.4-5
- Reddy DC, *Bridging the Digital Divide: A Challenge for Higher Education, University News,* Vol. 39, No. 42, October 15-21, 2001.
- Theony Condos, *Comparative Education Review,* Vol. 45, No. 2, May 2001, p.287.
- Varghese NV, *Reforming Education Financing, Seminar* 498, October, 2000, pp.22-23.
- Venkateswaran S, *Higher Education in 21st Century- Certain Issues, University News,* Vol. 52, 25 December, 2000, p.21.

Secularism and Hinduism

Recalling the Vision of Swami Vivekananda

SWAMI VIVEKANANDA was among the tallest figures that ever strode this earth. He was born on 12 January 1863. His mother believed he was a gift from Lord Shiva. He was, therefore, first named Vireswar Shiva. After Adi Shankaracharya, he was largely responsible for the great Hindu renaissance and national resurgence towards the closing years of the 19th and the early years of the 20th century. We owe a great deal to him for restoring to Hinduism its pristine glory and respect.* He was a man of vision and played a pioneering role in

* Swami Vivekananda's 150th Birth Anniversary Celebrations were organised in many countries of the world—in the East and the West as well as in the North and the South during 2013-14. As the Honorary Chairman of Swami Vivekananda Saardh Shati Samaroha Samiti and as a lifelong student of Swamiji, the author had the honour and sublime pleasure of participating in some of the events.

reinterpreting Hinduism and establishing its quintessentials for the modern age while carrying his message to corridors of different lands. Perhaps, for the first time after many centuries, those inhabiting the West realised that they also had something to learn from Hinduism or that it contained answers to much that ailed their societies. Among Hindus themselves, all over the globe, Swamiji revived self respect and a feeling of pride in their ancient culture, philosophy and spiritual attainments. Once the true foundations of culture and national unity were seen as closely linked to Hinduism, the people were bound to take pride in their past and great spiritual heritage.

The powerful waves of the movement for independence that followed were also largely influenced by him. Freedom fighters and their leaders swore by his ideas and exhortations. In the words of Netaji Subhash Bose: Swamiji harmonised the East and the West, religion and science, past and present. Deeply immersed in Vedas and Upanishads, in Vedanta and Advait philosophy, Swamiji stood for a discovery of the self by everyone at the individual, social and national levels and also for the collective consciousness of humanity at large. All the knowledge, values and wisdom, he believed, were already within each one of us. We had only to recognise and discover them through education, meditation and yoga sadhana. Once we got to know and realise that we are divine children of immortality with limitless potentialities of reaching perfection, we will not have to keep confessing that we are all essentially sinners needing redemption. Vivekananda said:

> Each soul is potentially divine, the goal is to manifest this divinity within by controlling nature, external and internal. Do this either by work or worship, or psychic control, or philosophy—by one or more or all of these—and be free. This is the whole of religion. Doctrines, or dogmas, or rituals, or books, or temples, or forms, are, but secondary details.

Following the Upanishadic wisdom, Swamiji teaches us that

fundamentally there is the same *Atman* in every being. In reality, each one of us is only *Atman*. Thus conceived, there is no high or low. Every member of society is equally important. Everyone has his own place of pride and honour because behind his individuality is the *Atman*—eternal, infinite and immortal. The human personality owes its creative energy and the spirit of oneness and equality to the *Atman*. Vedanta says;

Aham Brahmasmi; tat tvam asi, meaning I am Brahaman—the supreme being—you are also the same

or

Ekam sat, vipra bahudha vadanti, meaning truth is one, the wise describe it in different ways.

When in every other person, one sees one's own self or the sphere of 'I' gets so widened that it comes to encompass within it the entire humanity, and when all the different paths leading to the supreme are respected, what can be a better example of '*sarva dharma sambhavah*', secularism or equal regard for all religions?

Once we see the divine in every human being, it is impossible to discriminate or not to extend equal respect to all irrespective of the religion, the God or the form of worship they follow. Expressing his own concept of universal religion, Swamiji said: 'I accept all religions that were in the past and worship with all of them I worship God with everyone of them, in whatever form they worship him'.

That is how Swamiji understood Hinduism. His vigorous presentations in the United States and in Europe brought forward the best in Hinduism and made it a lively intellectual and spiritual force to be reckoned with in matters of the welfare of humanity at large.

There were many people in the West who were deeply influenced by Swamiji's life and message. I remember my old landlady, Mrs Keebler in Washington DC, many years back. Once wanting to show me something very special, she brought a photograph of Swami Vivekananda autographed by Swamiji himself in 1897. She said it was given to her by her mother who had met Swamiji and played host to him. Mrs Keebler got very emotional while remembering the stories that her mother had narrated to her about Swamiji's spell and said that of all that she had inherited from her parents, that little photograph was the most precious to her.

Swamiji was convinced that the future of any nation depended on its youth and therefore exhorted the youth to wake up, recognise their divinity and infinite strength to rejuvenate society. Fond of the *Kathopanishad*, Swamiji had full faith in modern day Nachiketas. Swamiji's message was, above all, to be vigorous and strong. He was a devotee of Durga or Kali—the Goddess of power and strength. He could see 'Durga' in 'Bharat Mata' and 'Bharat Mata' in 'Durga'. His overarching message to the youth was to be vigorous and strong. Strength is a sign of life, hope and growth and everything good and worth striving for. Weakness is death and sheer misery. He says:

> Make your nerves strong. What we want is muscles of iron and nerves of steel. We have wept long enough, no more weeping, but stand on your feet and be men. It is man-making religion that we want. It is man-making theories that we want. It is man-making education all round that we want. And here is the test of truth—anything that makes you weak physically, intellectually and spiritually, reject as poison; there is no life in it, it can not be true. Truth is strengthening.

Above all, Swamiji stood for the poor and the downtrodden. He strove for a world where all could live happily and in harmony and no one felt discriminated against or exploited. So long as anyone remained hungry, he said, the first religion was to feed him. Swamiji saw the living God in the bodies of the poor, ill-clad, ill-fed children. For him, the ancient principles of renunciation and God realisation had to be combined with service to God in man. He was the first to propound the concept of *Daridranarayan* later adopted and popularised by Mahatma Gandhi. Swamiji was the first religious leader to equate the voice of the people with the voice of God and the service of the people with the service of God. He advocated greater attention to needs of economic growth, industrial development, agricultural research, scientific studies and eradication of poverty, illiteracy and unemployment.

The concern of Swami Vivekananda for the regeneration of Hinduism made him extend his thoughts to many vital areas. A great deal has been spoken and written about his views on the role of the youth in national resurgence, empowerment of women, upliftment of the masses and removal of poverty, unemployment and illiteracy. In the present climate it is necessary to specially flag one aspect of Swamiji's contribution to our thinking viz. the relevance of Hinduism for the ideal of Secularism.

Swamiji said: 'Not only toleration, for so-called toleration is often blasphemy, and I do not believe in it. I believe in acceptance.'

For Swamiji, Vedanta is the doctrine of oneness. It means faith in all, because you are all. Realisation of essential divinity of all—all are in you and you are in all—is the surest guarantee of secularism. Swamiji sees *Shiva* in every *Jiva*. He says:

> If one religion is true, then all the others must also be true. Thus, the Hindu faith is yours as much as mine...we Hindus do not merely tolerate, we unite ourselves with every religion...there are so many attempts of the human soul to grasp and realise the Infinite. So we gather all these flowers, and bind them together with a cord of love and make them into a wonderful bouquet of worship.

In world history, the Western concepts of nation states and secularism are of relatively recent origin.

Secularism has always been the hallmark of the Hindu ethos. Hinduism is not antithetical to what is called secularism meaning, *dharma sambhava*, ie. respect for all religions, non-discrimination on grounds, of religion and accepting all paths to truth as equally respectable alternatives. Swami Vivekananda emphasises that Hinduism respects alternate ways to the Divine. The most fundamental tenet of Hinduism is *ekam sat vipra bahudha vadanti*—truth is one (scholars describe it differently).

Through the ages, culture has been the greatest integrating force while politics has tended to divide. Rich in diversities of various kind, Hinduism was never an ethnic monolith of people with a commonality of race or language. It has always been multi-ethnic, multi-racial and multi-lingual. The rich plurality of Hindu society was partly due to its openness and tradition of tolerance. The thread of unity among the people was largely due to the culture of Hinduism that permeated the people for thousands of years without any distinction of race, caste or religion. In that sense, Hinduism can be deemed to be the original, eternal or *Sanatana* faith. Hinduism, as distilled by Swamiji, is a universal religion or is meta-religious—life affirming, self-enlarging system of spiritual culture in the alchemy of which all religions can meet in harmony. The concept of genuine secularism, shorn of its political ramifications, can be easily traced back to Vedic times. In his book, *Clash of Civilisations*, Samuel Huntington writes, 'only in Hindu civilisation were religion and politics so distinctly separated'.

Religious tolerance or still better respect for all religions in Swamiji's thoughts becomes a natural and necessary response to pluralism in society. Diversity itself becomes the greatest strength for national unity. Hinduism in the twenty-first century has to be viewed as synonymous with secularism and as a universal value and not as something tied to a particular form of religion. Conversely, the surest way to destroy a country is to make it lose respect for its culture and heritage. If secularism has to exist as a living reality it would have to come to grips with Hinduism. A meaningful dialogue and dialectic between these two strains is necessary if positive secularism, ie. equal respect for all religions (*sarva dharma sambhava*) or non-discrimination on grounds of religion has to become a reality. If positive secularism has to have meaning, it cannot be equated with anti-Hinduism. In other words, in a nation with more than 80 per cent Hindu population, secularism cannot survive if it comes to mean anti-Hinduism.

Today, when our societies are passing through critical times with widespread devaluation of old values and deinstitutionalisation of established institutions, we need to revisit the message and vision of Swami Vivekananda. His ideas have become even more relevant today in the context of every individual and section of society engrossed in the competitive struggle for rights without any regard to our duties towards each other and to society at large in a spirit of selfless detachment.

Swamiji had a very short life of only 39 years on this earth but he will live for eternity in his vision and work and in the minds and hearts of all those around the globe devoted and dedicated to taking on his mission for humanity forward. The youth, in particular, will continue to draw inspiration and encouragement from his thoughts for generations to come. His clarion call will never cease to reverberate:

> Come up, O lions, and shake off the delusion that you are sheep; you are souls immortal, spirits free, blessed and eternal; Ye are not matter, Ye are not bodies; matter is your servant, not you the servant of matter.

It was God's will that the conclusion of the 150th Birthday Celebrations should be followed by a new wave of activities in the direction of regeneration and rejuvenation of our nation.

Biography Writing

The Indian Genre

BIOGRAPHY IS a history of the life, times and work of a person. This simple and concise definition is given by Carlyle. Dryden who first used the word defined it as 'the history of a particular man's life.' For Edmund Gosse, it is 'the faithful portrait of a soul in its adventures through life.' It is usually in written form. There may, however, be other variants like a biographical film or a pictorial biography depicting the story of somebody's life through photographs, pictures or paintings. Also, there may be oral or spoken biographies, computer-based biographical data files on hard disks or floppies. Electronic and other media like audio or video cassettes etc. may be used to recreate the life history of a person and his environs.

Biography, one of the oldest literary forms, is generally in prose. The classic example of a biography from ancient Indian literature is that of Bana Bhatt's *Harshacharitam.* Poetry, however, is not barred.

Valmiki's *Ramayana,* for example, is Rama's life history in verse—a biographical epic. Every biography is not necessarily a piece of literature. It may be a simple historical writing or, not quite often, mere trash so far as literature is concerned. As a general rule, biographies only of the more prominent or outstanding personalities are attempted. When one writes about his own life history, it becomes an autobiography. Biographical writings are a part of history and in fact constitute valuable source material for contemporary historical research.

The traditional approach to the structure of biography has been that of placing the material in regard to a person's life history in a chronological order, beginning with a person's family background and ancestry, the time and environs of birth, moving to childhood, school, college and other higher education, and finally the crisis management, successes and failures, achievements in life, etc. There are, however, alternative styles. For example, to make a biography more interesting and readable, the author(s) may begin with something recent in the subject's life history and then go back and show his entire life through a flashback. Also, sometimes events and developments in the biographee's life may be woven round a few main themes or subject heads, with the biography in that case being divided into subjectwise chapters.

In recent decades, very specialised and sophisticated strategies and methodologies, techniques and tools have been developed. Variety of source materials and ways of getting at them have been successfully identified. Besides the published and unpublished written materials like books, articles, diaries, dissertations, press clippings, periodicals, manuscripts, correspondence files, photos, films, tapes, etc. a good biographer would collect valuable information from visits to places connected with the life of the subject and from interviews with the biographee(if he is still around), his relatives, friends, opponents, colleagues and others concerned. Further, there are the latest psychological techniques for ascertaining facts and counterchecking their veracity.

A worthwhile biography is not a mere chronology of events

or a record of attainments. The whole approach, ideally speaking, is supposed to depict and analyse, on the basis of authentic source material, the evolution or flowering of a person's personality, his reaction to his environs, places and persons, and his contributions to the world.

According to the Western tradition, the earliest biographies are known to have been written only in the 16th century or so. However, the biographies in India have been written right from the earliest periods of recorded history. Often, they have not only been the life story of a person but a treatise on his times, prevailing societal structures, human relationships and cultural environs as well.

The most difficult task facing a biographer, particularly in India, is that of getting reliable data and materials and of testing its authenticity. For long periods, even after their death, documents connected with the life and work of prominent public figures are not made public to study and scrutiny by researches. Meanwhile, very often, papers are subjected to a close examination to separate what can or should be thrown open and what should remain strictly classified or even be destroyed or weeded out, thus leaving for prosperity an already doctored record. Our Official Secrets Act and the archival laws are the most primitive and anti-intellectual.

Then, there is the question of the inbuilt bias of the biographer himself. Normally, in the very process of choosing the subject, the biographer gives away his fascination for the person selected. Unless there is a basic sympathy or felt appreciation for the subject, a writer may not lift his pen to write the individual's biography; but, then, he has to guard against the sympathy becoming blind adulation and appreciation reaching levels of sycophancy. If the person happens to be known to the biographer personally, his task becomes even more difficult despite certain plus points in the situation. In order to produce an authentic biography, it is of utmost importance for the biographer to consciously suppress his personal prejudices, preferences, likes and dislikes. He is supposed to provide an impartial and objective account of the life, times and activities of the biographee and an assessment of his personality and character, of frustrations and triumphs and the life, positive and negative traits of nature and conduct.

The other problem is that of the people's right to full information and unexpurgated facts versus the individual's right to privacy. How much of the private life of a prominent public figure, for instance, should be open to public gaze and scrutiny? To what extent revealing the ugly, naked and unpleasant truths of anybody's personal life under the principle of writer's obligation to truth serves any public purpose? This is an ethical challenge every biographer has to face and answer.

Encyclopaedia Britannica speaks of the several types of biographies. There are thus informative, critical, standard, interpretative, fictionalised and special purpose biographies. Present day biographies in India, however, belong to a special genre. The pure art of biography writing in the Western sense has hardly developed in India. Hero worship and a feudal orientation is in our blood. Our subject is either a perfect or an ideal person, a paragon-of-all-virtues, a hero or not worth writing about at all. With some hon'ble exceptions our biographies are eulogies; every event, place or person connected with the biographee is bestowed with a special halo, most often a balanced assessment is not even attempted. In the words of Johnson, 'Biographers should pass slightly over what produces vulgar greatness, should display the minute details of private life, showing that men excel only by prudence and virtue.'

Some of the biographies are, in fact, commissioned—made to order and handsomely paid for. In this category come the biographies of some top industrialists and businessmen, and sometimes even some politicians. These biographies are all exercises in image building and should be viewed only as PR or ad material directed at personal publicity and promotion of future prospects of some individual or individuals. In the same category can be placed what may be called specialised campaign biographies which are prepared and published for wide circulation and free distribution during election campaigns.

There is also the new category of negative biographies that are motivated by desire of some vested interests to destroy or deflate a reputation for ulterior purposes.

Even the most respectable biographies with a few more honourable exceptions—that are written by established authors or reputed scholars with some credentials—most often smack of a strange flattery and sycophancy directed at pleasing someone or his descendants or followers obviously with ulterior motives or for the purpose of deriving some mundane benefits.

The justification that is sometimes given for one-sided biographies is that of presenting before the people, particularly the upcoming new generations, noble lives of great men and women whose life and work should become a message and whose high ideals should inspire emulation. It is forgotten that the new generations are wiser than we presume. It is left to the child to recognise that the King is naked.

Associated with Parliament right from the first Lok Sabha days of Pt. Nehru, Dr Subhash Kashyap has held some of the highest posts in India and, as an International Civil Servant, abroad. Involved in drafting several constitutions, he was a Member and Chairman Drafting Committee of the National Commission to Review the Working of the Constitution (NCRWC). He has received several prestigious Awards and honours in India and abroad including Padma Bhushan 2015, Doctor of Laws (LL.D.) 2017, and Commander of the Honorary Order of the Academy of San Francisco for services to constitutional studies. At present, Dr Kashyap is Honorary Research Professor at the Centre for Policy Research, Advocate and Consultant and President of Indian National Bar Association (INBA), Asian Confluence, Vidhi Bharti and Rashtriya Jagriti Sansthan (RJS). His works include *Constitutional Law of India* (3 Vols), *Parliamentary Procedure*, *History of Parliament* (6 Vols), *Constitutional History of India* (2 Vols), *Indian Constitution—Conflicts and Controversies*, *Anti-Defection Law and Parliamentary Privileges*, *Parliamentary Wit and Humour*, among the NBT best sellers—*Our Constitution*, *Our Parliament and Our Political System*. Many of his works have been translated into several languages. He is very frequently invited by the academia (universities, institutes etc) and media (print and electronic) in India and abroad.